ALSO BY ANDREW LEVY

The First Emancipator

A Brain Wider Than the Sky

Mark Twain and the Era That Shaped His Masterpiece

HUCK
FINN'S
AMERICA

———

ANDREW LEVY

SIMON & SCHUSTER

NEW YORK   LONDON   TORONTO   SYDNEY   NEW DELHI

Simon & Schuster
1230 Avenue of the Americas
New York, NY 10020

First Simon & Schuster hardcover edition January 2015

SIMON & SCHUSTER and colophon are registered
trademarks of Simon & Schuster, Inc.

For information about special discounts for bulk purchases,
please contact Simon & Schuster Special Sales at
1-866-506-1949 or business@simonandschuster.com

The Simon & Schuster Speakers Bureau can bring authors to your live event.
For more information or to book an event contact the Simon & Schuster Speakers
Bureau at 1-866-248-3049 or visit our website at www.simonspeakers.com.

Interior design: Akasha Archer
Jacket design: Julie Metz
Jacket photography: © Ian Berry/Magnum Photos

Manufactured in the United States of America

10 9 8 7 6 5 4 3 2

Library of Congress Cataloging-in-Publication Data

ISBN 978-1-4391-8696-1
ISBN 978-1-4391-8698-5 (ebook)

To Aedan

Ladies and Gentlemen: I am perfectly astonished—a-s-t-o-n-i-s-h-e-d—ladies and gentlemen—astonished at the way history repeats itself. I find myself situated at this moment exactly and precisely as I was once before, years ago, to a jot, to a tittle—to a very hair. There isn't a shade of difference. It is the most amazing coincidence that ever—but wait. I will tell you the former instance, and then you will see it for yourself.

MARK TWAIN, ADDRESS AT THE ANNUAL "LADIES' DAY,"
PAPYRUS CLUB, BOSTON, FEBRUARY 24, 1881

CONTENTS

HUCK
FINN'S
AMERICA

PREFACE

For anyone who wants to try to unravel the tangled knot that ties modern Americans to their past, Mark Twain's *Adventures of Huckleberry Finn* (1885) remains essential. According to the most recent studies, Twain's novel about a white boy and a runaway slave escaping down the Mississippi River is the most frequently read classic American book in American schools. Few critics' lists of the "greatest American novels" fail to cite it; few reporters describing its influence fail to quote Hemingway's famous claim that "all modern American literature comes from one book by Mark Twain called *Huckleberry Finn.*"

At the same time, it also remains one of the most controversial books in American history, and in many schools has been removed from reading lists or shifted into elective courses. One hundred years after his death, Mark Twain can still put a book on top of the bestseller list—as his *Autobiography* did in October 2010. And *Huck Finn,* 125 years after its publication, can trend high on Twitter, as it did in January 2011 when NewSouth Books announced it would publish a version that excised the racial epithet "nigger," which appears more than 200 times in the original, and replace it with "slave"—an editorial gesture both praised and derided with an intensity rarely reserved for the classics anymore. *Huck Finn* was, and remains, "an amazing, troubling book," as novelist Toni Morrison tells us; an "idol and target," as critic Jonathan Arac writes.

Predictably, our regard for the book is even more two-sided than that summary suggests. For over a century, Twain's oft-beloved novel has been taught both as a serious opportunity to reflect on matters of race and as a lighthearted adventure for children. Authors, historians, teachers, and politicians have sung its praises as a model of interracial empathy, or debated the wisdom and limits of that claim; studio motion pictures, big-budget musicals, cartoons, comic books, and children's editions have all focused on it as a story of boyish escapade, an "adventure" with, at best, modest political ambitions. Since 1987, eight books plus dozens of scholarly articles and chapters have been published on race and *Huckleberry Finn*. But not one book, and only a modest number of chapters and essays during that span, have dealt deeply with Mark Twain's portrayal of children in *Huck Finn*. The vast majority of newspaper editorials, Twitter posts, and public debates about *Huckleberry Finn* have focused upon race. References to childhood and Huck Finn in popular media abound, but he and his friend Tom Sawyer remain, in the public imagination, largely uncomplicated "emblems of freedom, high-spiritedness, and solid comradeship," as James S. Leonard and Thomas A. Tenney have written. Huck is a "charming rascal," one preview for a local production of the musical *Big River* claims. "Make your own kids [*sic*] fishing pole—Huck Finn Style," an "adventure for boys blog" offers: "You may not be as free to roam as Huck, but you can spend a day lazing on the riverbank just like he did."

After years of reading, teaching, and writing about the book, though, I've come to believe that we got this backward—that our understanding of what is comic and what is serious in *Huck Finn* says more about America in the last century than America in the time Twain wrote the book. Contemporary reviews of Twain's novel, dozens of which appeared in American newspapers in the spring of 1885, barely mentioned race at all; they talked about children, and what message the book sent them, with great and varied passion. There is a shimmer to Twain's portrait of white childhood in the antebellum era. But there are also murders, suicidal ideation, child abuse, and a profound satire on standardized education, and the ambivalent ways American parents both protect their children from, and provide them uncritical access to, popular culture. *Huck Finn* is a book about the disconnection between our children's inner lives and our ways of raising and teaching them—a disconnection so intimidating that, naturally, we placed this tribute to children's alienation at the center of public school curricula.

Neither is *Huck Finn* a model of successful interracial politics, nor a book that we should regard, in our rearview mirrors, as essentially retrograde. Here, perhaps, it is more comic than we have considered, or than the national conversation can easily hold: moral satire in powerful ways, but also unnerving burlesque about things few modern Americans find funny. And yet, precisely because it is both these things, it is also truly and disconsolately visionary about how the culture doesn't always go forward but sideways, even backward, on matters of race and freedom.

The best way to read *Huck Finn*, in fact, might be to see that Twain found the borders that divide parents and children as false as the borders that divide black and white—and that he even saw the way those borders overlapped. In turn, he attacked both with the same rough play, a tricksterish mix of comedy and political seriousness that meshed with the stereotypes of the time but fought them, too. And now we are indulging in more rough play—myths of nostalgia and myths of progress, and the instinct to classify, classify, classify—that inspires modern politicians, critics, teachers, filmmakers, and readers to divide the book into two books, one funny and "harmless" and one not. *Huck Finn* can show us more about how we keep the discussion of childhood stalled, and the engine of racial difference humming, than any other book in our canon. To benefit from that insight, however, we would have to admit that it is not a book (flawed or otherwise) about children and adventure, or about racial progress. It is a book about what Junot Díaz calls "dedicated amnesia" on a national scale. It is a plea—as is this book—to *remember*, and a fatalistic comedy about how we don't.

This work is a cultural biography of Twain in his era, one that shows how *Huck Finn* is *the* great book about American forgetfulness, and how our misjudgments of the book's messages about race and children reveal the architecture of our forgetting. I started it twenty years ago with a dim idea that there was something about the child in Huck that was misunderstood and something in the argument about the book's treatment of race that had reached an impasse. I spent months in the late 1990s reading ancient newspapers, tracking Twain as he toured America in 1884 and 1885 alongside Louisiana writer George Washington Cable in a show he called the "Twins of Genius," which was intended to help Twain promote the publication of *Huck*

Finn. I explored the debate about children and schools that raged at the time to see if *Huck Finn* entered into it. And I explored what black readers of the day said about Twain's book, scouring through the frayed remains of black newspapers from the 1880s. Yet what stayed with me was the milieu, not the thesis: the whispers of a lost, dying America, and an America uncannily like our own. A lot had changed. And nothing had.

I spent several more years writing about all this, then—like Twain with *Huck*—dropping it, picking it up, dropping it. When I finally committed to the subject, I also committed to my first, raw impulse. By 2009, very little had been said, in a serious way, about children and *Huck Finn*, though some decisive academic forays had been offered. On race, meanwhile, almost nothing had been left unsaid: in fact, "teaching the debate" had become almost as canonical as the book itself. I was sure this was wrong—not the content of the discussion, nor its passion, but the proportions. In a fine history of American education fittingly named *Huck's Raft*, Steven Mintz describes several of the most persistent myths surrounding American children: "the myth of a carefree childhood"; the myth that "childhood is the same for all children"; the "myth of progress, and its inverse, a myth of decline." *Huck Finn* wasn't just trapped in those myths—it was being used to perpetuate them, when all around me there seemed evidence that it could be something richer. I was raising a boy, Aedan, now twelve, and every week he did something that reminded me of Huck—something sublime and curious, and not easily dismissed as a "boyish escapade." My wife, Siobhán, a social scientist who specializes in youth and politics, introduced me to an international conversation about children and their ability to shape, and not just be shaped by, the culture around them—a conversation from which most modern *Huck Finn* readers, even as they enjoyed their time with "America's child," remained remote.

My university students tuned in Huck on a higher frequency: his loneliness was theirs, and they were hungry to put a name on it. With the least encouragement, they could generate papers about *Huck Finn* and video games, *Huck Finn* and the *Hunger Games*, *Huck Finn* and teenage smoking, *Huck Finn* and social media, *Huck Finn* and

ADHD. Education students trained to teach young adult fiction and eschew classics found, instead, a classic that felt like today's young adult fiction, if only one twisted the lens. They saw how Tom and Huck weren't just two kids with fishin' poles but embodiments of the axiom common in childhood studies that "the young make their own histories"—that they are amazing yarn spinners, cultural salvage artists, controllers of their own narratives.

Likewise, my students admired how attuned Twain seemed to the ideas they had acquired in professional education classes: how Huck illustrated Howard Gardner's theory of "multiple intelligences," for instance—he was smart in several ways, but none that would show up on a standardized test—and how his maturation process matched psychologist Jean Piaget's influential portrait of dynamic and interactive growth during childhood. And more often than not, they gravitated toward the position that Twain took in the debates of his day (and that his book could represent in ours): that young people should not be patronized, because human development rarely occurs in lockstep with the institutions designed to guide it. "In most cases changes take place in us without our being aware of it at the time," Twain wrote in 1901, "and in after life we give the credit of it—if it be of a creditable nature—to mamma, or the school or the pulpit."

Contrarily, my students regarded the conversation about race in *Huck Finn* with wariness. For most readers, the current fight over *Huck Finn* is most recognizably a fight over the "n-word," and whether or not the book ought to appear in secondary school classrooms. What does its presence in the pages of *Huck Finn* signify, we now ask, and have asked since the 1950s: Is the book racist, or a textbook illustration of the antiracist uses of racism? As a compacted method for talking about race in America, the debate about racial slur is still very live. But it is not young, either, and by and large, my students think that what the book says about children, that they should not be patronized, is a broken promise here. They know what's on Twitter— they know what's on the radio. They already know the terms of engagement, already know the debate, the major schools of thought on appropriate uses: "eradicationists" and "regulationists," according to Harvard law professor Randall Kennedy.

Like professionals, we discuss ameliorative and enhancing strategies: teaching *Huck* in tandem with African-American authors;
teaching it on higher levels, in elective classes, only; teaching it using
disclaimers, units on historical context, pop culture, or new techniques like "switching," where students "switch" the race, or gender,
or era of selected characters; teaching the edited version; not teaching
it at all. But even the best ideas still sometimes feel like bandages on
an untreated wound. My students know something is still wrong,
that neither the complex vitality of children's culture nor the existential persistence of racial division is truly being addressed amid the
vortex of mixed signals that surround them. For better or worse, they
don't require a book to speak on behalf of a nation, or to speak with
one voice when it does: they understand that *Huck Finn* hurts some
readers, enthralls others, and challenges many in-between. What
they want is something blunter, the literary equivalent of a truth
commission, that unmixes the signals, tells them how we got here,
and what we might do next.

So I went back to the archives. As I scanned page after page of
old newspapers, this time on a hand-cranked microfiche machine
I bought on eBay, I recognized anew the fresh view that the "Twins
of Genius" provided for understanding Twain's novel. It didn't just
change the book for me—it changed the story of the book, its place
in the culture. And now I paid *conscious* attention to the other news
stories, the points of reference a reader of *Huck* in 1885 might employ: reports of Huck-like boys, weaned on pop culture, committing
murders; a national election that many believed would lead to the
reintroduction of slavery. The world around Twain wasn't the filler;
it was the point. Twain's childhood, and his evolution as a writer
and national figure, came into focus for me: one could see how the
country and the man grew up together and reached a crossroads at
the same time.

I found George Washington Cable, the other Twin of Genius
on that tour, to be a crucial contrast to Twain. His great essay "The
Freedman's Case in Equity," which was published alongside chapters
from *Huck Finn* in the same issue of the same magazine, and which
called for the integration of public places, was both inspiration and
foil to Twain's novel. We have a tendency to see Twain as a "racial

savior," as Michael J. Kiskis has written, or, rebounding from that excess, a *racist*. But the spectrum itself is wrong. It is not Twain but Cable who shows us what commitment on race from a white American of his time looked like. Twain, on the other hand, was *the* great spokesman for the idea that culture trumps politics—the one man in our history who could say (in the voice of Satan, of course) that "against the assault of Laughter nothing can stand" and almost be believed.

Reading reviews of Twain performances in the "Twins of Genius" reminded me that comedy, profane and tricky, was his expertise, and that the minstrel show, a now disowned but once extraordinarily popular type of theater in which "blackness" was performed, was the key influence on *Huck Finn* that would help unlock a larger conversation. Scholars have known about this link between a celebrated American classic and a taboo pop form for decades; in fact, they have used original documents from the 1800s to uncover a wide palette of political emotions in minstrelsy in general, and with that a deeper sense of how old racisms transmit themselves stealthily into new centuries. But this scholarly discussion, dense and ambivalent as it is, has not significantly moved the public discussion. That most readers don't see the connection between *Huck* and minstrelsy is because we equate minstrelsy with blackface stage makeup, which has been discredited, not with the songs, dances, jokes, and cultural strategies that endure. And that other readers, recognizing the connection, generally don't focus on it, is because public discussion of minstrelsy's role in shaping America has been buried alongside the appalling mask that best represented it.

Buster Keaton did minstrelsy; so did Bing Crosby; so did Bugs Bunny. It echoes throughout post–World War II music, through rock, hip-hop (the most popular current use of "minstrelsy" is in condemnations of stereotypes in rap, or among black comedians), jazz, and country, in situation comedies, "buddy" movies, in fashion, in literature. It ties Macklemore and Lewis, Miley Cyrus, and Tyler Perry to performers from 150 years ago, and it ties *Huck Finn* to us in ways we haven't been willing to really acknowledge. Critics denounce the minstrelsy in *Huck Finn*, claiming that a "real," or at least empathetic, portrait of Jim, the African-American man at the heart of the book, disappears beneath a "stereotype mask." Defenders argue, as did Ralph Ellison, that "Jim's dignity . . . and Twain's complexity" rise from behind that mask. But few push through the basic frame of the argument, which implies that Twain did this work unconsciously, or that his courage simply failed, when in fact, for better or worse, these connections were something he wanted his audience to see from the very start. One talks about the minstrel show, and Twain's particular take on it, to see how deep *Huck Finn* can be on race, not how shallow—to see what a complicated parable of the persistence of racism Twain had really built, and what an unconscious parable of the persistence of racism we built, in turn, by celebrating the book according to the terms we have.

There was, in other words, a serious debate about how to raise and educate children in the American 1880s. And Twain was contributing something more than a lighthearted "boy's book" to that debate: he was thinking and speaking about literacy, popular culture, compulsory education, juvenile delinquency, at-risk children, and the different ways we raise boys from girls, and rich from poor. And there was a serious debate about the future of race relations in the American 1880s, too. But Twain was not as much a part of it as we tend to think. He was somewhere nearby, ingenious, outraged, self-interested, vastly more interested in how many Americans *play* with race than in how they rise above it, or render its terms obsolete at the ballot box—an important conversation, but not the one we think we're having.

And lastly, all through the research and composition of this book, and especially as I pored through the old newspapers, I never stopped hearing whispers testifying to an uncanny relationship between our present and our past. For many, it is an unspoken canon that "we," at any given time, are the most tolerant of Americans that ever existed, that the clock on phenomena like racism or child-rearing, for instance, only ticks in one direction. Others construct vast technologies of nostalgia with little authority, and swear that the past was better. Many do neither—but are worn down by the kaleidoscopic subjectivity it takes to tell (and hear) the national story in a way that does justice to everyone who has contributed to it. As Mintz writes, though, few ever really tamper with the notion that we are either progressing or in decline. The people in the past are either worse than us or better. That they might have been like us, and, more to the point, that they may have explored paths forward we have abnegated, had access to sources of wisdom we have lost, and were already frustrated by political debates that still persist to this day, is rarely part of the story we tell ourselves.

At times, during my research, the men and women of the American 1880s struck me as quaint ancestors. More often, however, I was struck by the similarity of their political debates to ours; not identical, certainly, but not less evolved. Historians warn us to respect the otherness of the past, and it is good advice, but maybe once in a while we need to hear that we're stuck. Twain delivered *Huck Finn* to a country where Jim Crow ensured that African-Americans had more difficulty voting, held fewer public offices, and had fewer economic opportunities than they did in the previous decade, and where a racially biased judicial system drove many African-Americans into convict leasing systems that rented out their bodies for pennies a day. A modern reader trying to make sense of *Huck Finn* lives in a country where, as Michelle Alexander writes in *The New Jim Crow*, large percentages of the African-American male population of major cities (three out of four in Washington, DC, over half in Chicago) are either imprisoned—where their labor can be sold for pennies a day—or released from prison, but with restricted voting rights, mobility, and access to economic benefits.

Likewise, Twain offered *Huck Finn* to a country where parents, educators, and politicians worried that children, especially boys, were too exposed to violent media, that they were too susceptible to amoral market forces that made them anarchic and violent themselves. The twenty-first-century reader lives in a country worried about the exact same things, only with fresher media. In fact, the debate over children has changed so little over the last century—across a variety of issues—that Lawrence Kutner and Cheryl K. Olson, in *Grand Theft Childhood*, describe the history of that debate as "déjà vu, all over again and again."

In this light, it matters that we have been misreading *Huck Finn*, because that misreading is both wasted opportunity and metaphor for our larger failure to recognize our close relation to the past. Twain, however, was incredibly alert to such matters: *Huck* is a "prescient book," Ishmael Reed tells us, that "lays down patterns"—our patterns. From childhood, Twain was a "great boy" for reading history—his mother told us that. He was reading it the day he died. "Story up history," he once jotted in his notebook; it was a kind of mission. Sometimes, he thought that he saw progress everywhere, but more often he did not. In his essays, he frequently found ways to argue that the sins and virtues of one era or country reinvent themselves in others. And as he was writing the last chapters of *Huck Finn*, he devised a history game called "Mark Twain's Memory-Builder": "The board represents *any* century," Twain told its players. "Also, it represents *all* centuries. . . . If you choose, you can throw your game open to all history and all centuries." It was exactly the game one might invent if one had concluded that history *was* a game—the same thing over and over.

And *Huck Finn* ends with its narrator right back where he started: "I been there before" are his last words, and he sounds weary when he says them.

We misread *Huck Finn*, on matters of race and children especially, for the same reason we repeat the cultural and political schema of the Gilded Age—because the appealing idea that every generation is better off than the one before conceals our foreboding that we live in a land of echoes.

And yet we read *Huck Finn*, after all these years, because the foreboding speaks to us anyway.

PART
ONE

1

A New Kind of Entertainment

If you want to see how much the United States has changed over the last century, and how little, nothing works quite like reading an old newspaper. The smell and feel of the aging paper alone acts like time travel for the senses. And if you pick the right era—the late nineteenth century, for instance—reading an old newspaper can be like getting very drunk and then watching cable news.

The front page of the *Providence Journal* for October 2, 2013, for instance, displays seven articles and a weather graphic. The front page of the same paper for October 2, 1884, presented seventy-six articles (and fourteen advertisements), almost all of which ran seventy-five words or less. The form was "graphic and telegraphic"— quick, disorderly stories that seemed to respond to some national memory that only required tickling.

A twentieth-first-century reader glancing through these papers can't help but be struck by the vague familiarity of the political news—an amalgam of disputed elections; race politics; sectionalism; immigration, budget, and faith concerns; and international entanglements half a world away.

Unemployment was a pressing concern: mass layoffs and closed factories were front-page news. Some editorial writers contemplated whether or not America's economic vitality was a thing of the past. Others worried about whether or not the government was too big:

some newspapers kept running tallies of the national debt, which hovered around $1.85 billion, on the front page.

Educators and church leaders argued over whether or not Darwin should be taught in the schools. In Pittsburgh, for instance, Dr. Samuel H. Kellogg, a professor of theology, was called before the board of the Western Theological Seminary to defend teaching the "doctrine of evolution": "I believe that the Bible," Kellogg argued, "while attributing the origin of species to God, does not give us any information as to how God originated species."

Overseas, military forces deployed in the Mideast and Africa—some American, some French, some British—were bogged down in local rebellions: the still-famous siege of Gordon in Khartoum by a local Islamic army was front-page news daily, as were riots in the "Arab world." The Mexican border was a site of violence and disorder. Immigration was regarded as out of control: non–English-speaking immigrants were pouring into the country so quickly that, to many, the traditional fabric of the country seemed under threat. Asian students outpaced American students, or seemed to, at the best universities: "the fact that a Chinaman took the first prize in English composition at Yale ought to astonish none," the *Chicago Tribune* complained. "American students can't attend to foot-ball and study at the same time."

Contrarily, that same twenty-first-century reader perusing those same pages might be more startled by what has changed than what has not. The ads were a quaint wonder, for instance. We are programmed to laugh at these signs of distance between the pop culture of the past and the present, and we generally do. Here's that *ProJo* page one again: "WE ASKED YOU LAST WEEK If You Would Buy an Overcoat Carried from Last Season, If You Could Buy It at HALF PRICE." More than six hundred did. "BOYS' CLOTHING!" Jerome Kennedy & Co. shouted at us from the top of the rightmost column, the place in modern newspapers where the lead story can be found. But also: four separate ads for candles, and one for a "REVOLVING FLY TRAP," "a perfect invention for exterminating flies . . . amusing as a toy . . . grown people as well as children delight in watching it."

The entertainment choices, everywhere, were stellar, and incorporated old-fashioned fun (both high- and lowbrow) with perverse curiosity about all those new immigrants and their countries of origin. New Yorkers could see *The Merchant of Venice* or "The Thrilling and Sensational Drama of Outlaw Brothers, Frank and Jesse James," featuring Jesse James's actual horse and actual wife. Chicagoans could see ballet, opera, *Hamlet,* a panorama of the Battle of Gettysburg, or for a dime tour the "Monster Model Museum . . . everything instructive, refined, amusing."

On a Monday in Indianapolis, any man or woman with a few cents could go ice skating or go see Jo-Jo the Dog-Faced Boy, who had been discovered, it was said, in a cave in Russia, his face covered with "silky hair . . . like a skye terrier's." In Cincinnati, one could go to an underwear sale conducted "WITHOUT MERCY" (to their prices, one assumes), or go see "TOMAH the African Horned Man . . . having an actual horn two inches long growing from the center of his forehead."

More than anything, though, what jumps out at the twentieth-century reader is the violence. It jumped out at them back then, too: "The papers, all of a sudden, are being filled with assassinations, and second-degree murders, and prize-fights, and suicides," Mark Twain, as good an emissary as we have from the Gilded Age, wrote, fittingly, in a newspaper. "It is a wonderful state of things. . . . now I have to have my regular suicide before breakfast, like a cocktail, and my side-dish of murder in the first degree for a relish, and my savory assassination to top off while I pick my teeth and smoke . . ."

His sarcasm was not misplaced. Nineteenth-century newspapers portrayed a bloodstained and unstable country; their tone, callous and carnivalesque, makes even modern tabloids look restrained. The nation's infrastructure was a work in progress: ships wrecked, trains collided, mines collapsed. A dynamite factory explosion that could be heard twenty miles away, nine dead, was buried on page eight. Three fatal train disasters in one day was matter-of-fact. Generic, topical headlines like "Politics and Bloodshed" made reporting and editing easier. That one could bring a gun to a political rally was a given; one could even bring a cannon.

And just when you adjust, when your twenty-first-century political sensibility begins to metabolize this diet of little fiascos, you get called up short by a story so violent, so shocking, that you can't believe that it's not common knowledge to us 130 years later, that there's no piece of the national story committed singularly to it. And if you have something familiar nearby, a piece of the national story that has gotten its fair share of attention and then some—like Twain's classic novel *The Adventures of Huckleberry Finn*, which was at this moment in 1884 almost ready to join the carnival—then you also have the opportunity to experience the kind of cultural vertigo that makes history ring new.

Throughout March, the biggest news story in the city of Cincinnati was the trial of William Berner, whom the newspapers, in bold headlines, called "THE BOY MURDERER." Neither defense nor prosecution disputed the facts of his case. On Christmas Eve 1883, Berner and an older "Negro" accomplice named Joe Palmer had killed and robbed their employer, a farmer named Kirk with a reputation for carrying a bankroll of tens and twenties. They had killed him so many ways, in fact, that the prosecutor swore out multiple counts of murder for the one killing: one count for striking Kirk with a hammer; one count for hitting him in the head with a club; one count for looping a noose around his neck and strangling him, "one pulling at each end."

Finally Berner and Palmer "divided the money" they found on Kirk (roughly $240), threw his body in the back of a wagon, and rode to town, where they bought Christmas gifts for their families and sweethearts. They were arrested shortly after.

Palmer would be tried, convicted, and hanged without controversy; but the fate of his partner attracted vastly more interest. The courtroom where William Berner stood trial was filled; boys excited by the drama crowded the outside windows and packed the corridor. Some newspaper sketch artists portrayed a clean-cut, blue-eyed boy, a figure so small that his feet could not reach the floor underneath his chair. Other newspapers, however, reminded their readers that Berner was already seventeen, his arms sinewy and his hands rough from day labor. Although they agreed on virtually nothing else, all the newspapers agreed on the anticipated outcome of the trial: Berner was clearly guilty of murder, and "we should be able to try and hang a murderer in ten days," one editorial writer argued. Few, if any, argued for clemency on account of his age.

When the paid jury returned a verdict of manslaughter, not murder, and a sentence of twenty years in prison, not the gallows, an "indignation meeting" was immediately called for the great downtown Music Hall. More than six thousand people filled the hall the evening of March 28. Observers spoke of a "cosmopolitan audience" where all nationalities, races, and classes were represented, "every man . . . honest and determined; every man . . . ready for the work." "Everybody appeared to be in good humor," wrote one newspaper columnist. As the crowd exited the music hall, they turned in the direction of the Hamilton County jail and attacked it, not knowing that Berner had already been secreted away. Fighting persisted into the night, and the next day, and the day after. Within forty-eight hours, the "magnificent and costly" courthouse was burned to the ground, and police had killed several dozen rioters and wounded hundreds of others.

In the immediate aftermath, as the state militia patrolled downtown Cincinnati, the national press focused on three aspects of the story: first, that the individual responsible for transforming a peaceful protest into a riot was a black man named Gus Gaines, forty, single, a plasterer. Second, that the mob was a righteous one: the *Cincinnati Enquirer* wrote the words "AT LAST" above their front-page coverage of the event. Third, that among the dead and wounded there existed "a very large proportion of uncouth boys." Sandwiched between armed police and their "own natures made morbid by the habit of reading," these teenagers had become "the victims as well as the patrons of the literature of crime." In this way, the story of the riot seemed to match the story of the crime that inspired it: black men, the editorials implied, always seemed to open the gates to civil unrest, just or criminal. And boys, especially white ones, were always ready to rush through.

We don't know if Twain, seven hundred miles to the northeast, absorbed himself in the story of William Berner. It would have been hard to miss: it was prominent news in New York, the talk of London and Paris. But if he had pondered it, he might have found it too close for comfort, as anyone even vaguely familiar with the plot of the novel he was just then finishing might recognize as well.

He, too, was spending that spring focused on an uncouth boy who hated the law, who smoked, swore, robbed—who, even in his own estimation, "might come to be a murderer myself." The boy's best friend was an older black man who had his own reasons to hate the law, too, and who was one step closer to the noose than his young white sidekick at every turn. His other best friend read way too much, was obsessed about violence, ran his own gang, and—like the teenagers of Cincinnati—took a bullet for living out his fantasies too brazenly. It was William Berner's story in a fun-house mirror.

But while the citizens of Cincinnati all reviled Berner, Twain loved his child at all costs. "I shall love him, even if no one else does," he told his wife, Olivia. Later that year, he would take him to the stage with him, put him in print, and bank his own reputation, even his future, on a long shot: that the country would love Huck Finn, too, despite an instinctual hatred for bad boys of his type.

We think we know *Huck Finn*. It is, arguably, the most celebrated book in American history: only the Bible and Shakespeare are clearly more recognized by the average American reader. And since the early twentieth century, America has celebrated *Huck Finn*, and for two separate reasons: in high schools and colleges, it has been taught as a serious reflection of the conscience of the nation on matters of race and freedom. In popular culture, in movies and cartoons and in public libraries, it has long been viewed as a child-friendly classic, a carefree celebration of boyhood.

However, one look at William Berner—and America in 1884 was evidently full of other boys much like him—and one begins to wrestle with new thoughts: Could we have this turned inside out? Could it be that the plot of Twain's book feels so much like Berner's story because both were part of the same national debate, an extremely serious one about children that touched the same hot spots: delinquency, literacy, violence, and popular culture, for instance? And could the persistence of alliances between black men and white boys in both Twain's imagination and the imaginations of Cincinnati's best reporters also tell us that *Huck Finn* might have been talking about race to its white readers in a language they were trained to hear:

not about equality, but about the imaginary role "blackness" already played in the national story?

Could these fractures between how Twain's audience might have understood *Huck* in its own time and how we adapted it for political and cultural uses in ours help explain the anomaly of a book famously and theoretically forward-looking on race but loaded with racial slurs and stereotypes? Could they help explain how a book can be regarded as a simple ode to childhood for over a century despite the presence of thirteen dead bodies (not to mention near-death experiences, assaults, graft, petty crime, and lynch law) in its pages?

What, exactly, was Twain telling us about America's children, and what was he telling us about blacks and whites in America? And what does it say about us that we might have spent a century and more making an interpretive mistake—two interpretive mistakes, twins of each other—of such magnitude?

To answer these questions—and to understand why they matter so—there is only one place and one time to start: the Opera House in New Haven, Connecticut, November 5, 1884. It is about 8:40 in the evening. The footlights are a little too bright. A man with hair the color of dusty brick walks slowly, ever so slowly, toward the center of the stage. During Twain's career, one critic after another said something crucial about him, something lost amid the vast encyclopedia of images and writings he left behind: you read his books and you think you've got it. But to *hear* him speak was like having his books interpreted for you by their best reader. "Every modulation of his voice," a reviewer commented, revealed something "new and unsuspected . . . in writings that may have been read over a dozen times." We need to hear him, too—we need the benefit of his voice. Without it, we have missed so much—about him, about his work, and about our relationship to the century about which he had so much to say.

Most in the audience for the opening night of the "Twins of Genius" tour had come to see Mark Twain. But he was not yet *our* Mark Twain, that familiar icon in the white suit with the shock of white hair. That suit and that hair were still two decades away. But he was getting there: it had been fifteen years since his first national success, *The Innocents Abroad*, and he was a fixture on the American scene, as famous as a president—even more so. Observers said it was worth hearing him speak just so you could tell your grandchildren you had seen him. Others already considered him past his prime.

He was not quite handsome: his cheeks were a little too jowly, and his eyes too shiny, seemingly borrowed from another face altogether. His hair was overpowdered and unkempt: one critic said it stood up like the crest of a cockatoo. His mustache was badly trimmed: one scholar has called it "sardonic." His suit was black—a staid suit, for funerals. There was something in its fit that evoked a clown costume.

He walked slowly. One side of him dragged, limped. Perhaps someone in the audience laughed a little nervously, and Twain looked up suddenly. He seemed startled to discover that an audience was present. This caused more people to laugh. Twain now seemed mortified. A few more people laughed, uncomfortably, hopefully.

The cadence had begun, the subtle, wonderful dance of Mark Twain's tomfoolery, as emptied of wasted gesture as Kabuki. He reached center stage and gathered himself. A few more expectant laughs. He glared out now, squinting into the darkness, no longer seeming mortified but angry. Was it actually possible, he seemed to be asking with that squint, that those people were not there for a serious lecture?

More silence. More scattered laughter. Make them wait. He'd write later, "The pause . . . is a dainty thing, and delicate, and also uncertain and treacherous; for it must be exactly the right length . . ."

Finally he began to speak, in a deliberate monotone. He knew it was "slow"—one critic called his performing style "drowsy"—and liked it that way. Twain had an extraordinary ear, and that gift was nowhere more evident as he tuned his own instrument into this drawling deadpan. It was the base, a perfect contrast: against it his renditions of how other people talk would rise like ghosts.

Laugh at his joke, and he would look down or put his left hand in his pocket. Or maybe he would look sad. Or maybe his left hand would cradle his right arm and his right hand would stroke his chin. Or maybe his mouth would twitch. But he would never laugh with you, and wouldn't smile, either. When he hinted at something bold, you couldn't tell if he was being wise or naïve. There was a distance in his voice—what we today would call "plausible deniability"—that made it all right to laugh at something that might pierce you otherwise.

Those who had never seen Twain onstage before were, in these first moments, often disappointed. But that never lasted. Soon the laughter was coming like a "storm," as one colleague said. And all the discomfort, all the semiotic confusion—it helped make the storm. "Every word, almost," a reviewer wrote, "was a joke." It's all about the pauses, Twain said, over and over. They made meaning where there wasn't any on the written page. And they gave the speaker a chance to watch his audience, to size them up, before he made his next move. One could write a book addressed to a cultural moment, but the moment would change, and the book wouldn't. But the voice, the staging of that voice—that adjusted to the cultural moment, created the transient meanings that made men and women laugh so hard they lost themselves.

And for four months in the winter of 1884–85, that was exactly what Twain wanted. Sometimes he loved public speaking, and sometimes he hated it, but he was exceptional when he wanted to be: Sir Henry Irving, one of the great theater figures of his time, told Twain once that he had missed his true calling when he chose writing over acting. And there was something about *Huck Finn*, and the commercial and artistic risks it represented, that made this one of the times he wanted to show off that side of his genius.

It seems a simple idea to us, who are well used to authors touring to promote new books, musicians touring to promote new recordings: roughly 100 performances in roughly 115 days, as far east as Boston, as far north as Toronto, as far south as Louisville, as far west as St. Louis. Nothing with Twain was ever simple, though. Authors might tour (although the vogue had lapsed a decade before), but not to *support* a book.

Twain, however, wanted this particular book to have support—and he wanted more. Originally, he had planned to travel with a group of five other authors, some Southern, some Northern, some famous for their renditions of children, others for their renditions of blacks and ethnic minorities. They'd call themselves the "Happy

Family"—the same name P. T. Barnum gave his saturnine little zoo where predators and prey shared a single cage. When his plan fell through, Twain settled for one partner, a rising literary star from New Orleans named George Washington Cable who was already drawing comparisons to Hawthorne, Poe, and Balzac, and had a certain reputation as a bold thinker on race relations. Together, they'd be the "Twins of Genius," one "genius," one "versatility."

And together, Twain and Cable, for almost four months, ran what might be regarded as the most singular, most successful book tour ever. At the very least, it brought a huge amount of attention to the imminent publication of *Huck Finn*: we have canonized the book for so long that we forgot the tremendous push it got at the start. But critics at the time knew that something was different. *Huck Finn* was "the best advertised book of the present age," the *Alta California* claimed on March 24, 1885. Mark Twain, the *Boston Globe* opined, "has consented to convert himself into a walking sign."

Even more, Twain and Cable broke open the culture in some fundamental way: it was "the beginning of a new kind of entertainment," the *Washington Post* noted. As his efforts to build a "happy family" implied, he wanted *Huck Finn* to debut surrounded by a cadre of America's most prominent writers speaking like people they weren't, blending region and race and class into a fresh irreverent brew. And even with only one partner, he stayed true to this vision. In lyceums, opera houses, and churches, in front of "cultivated" audiences, "intelligent" audiences, audiences with "long nose[s]," usually lecturers lectured. But reading from *Huck*—speaking like a boy from rural Missouri in a voice, it was said, that sounded exactly like a boy from rural Missouri and Mark Twain at the same time—that was different, and risky, given the country's unease about uncouth boy criminals like William Berner. And Cable, the Southern representative, read from a book in which *Northern* soldiers were reassured that their "cause was just"—that was risky, too, and he would pay for it.

And racial and ethnic mimickry—America has seen this, but not from such respectable, white-faced gentlemen. Cable "did" voices—Irish, Creole. Twain "did" German. And they both "did" African-American. Twain performed as an elderly black slave and scared the crowd with ghost stories from before the Civil War. And Cable sang slave songs he first heard as a child in Place Congo in New Orleans, now known as Congo Square and regarded as one of the birthplaces of modern jazz and blues. Women fainted; men shouted for encores. "Nigger from the ground up," one audience member wrote. It was meant as a compliment.

That this all worked, though—that the "Twins of Genius" tour and the book it promoted were truly "a new kind of entertainment" and rattled the country—is best evidenced by the way Twain and Cable interacted with, and even dominated, the headline political news of the day. For months, the country had been engaged in a heated, scandal-ridden presidential campaign between Grover Cleveland, the Democrat, and James Blaine, the Republican. The election marked a new alliance of Southern Democrats and "Mugwump" Republicans, who broke away from the alliance of black and white Northern voters that had controlled Reconstruction-era politics; if Cleveland won, he would be the first Democrat, and the first candidate with white Southern support, to win the office since before the Civil War.

For days after the election, its result remained in doubt. Akin to the aftermath of the 2000 election, Americans joked that they had two presidents, and waited while a few hundred votes were counted in one or two states to settle the matter. Meanwhile, accusations of black voter suppression made headlines in Republican newspapers. And when Cleveland's victory was assured, those same newspapers argued that the clock on American politics was running backward to the antebellum era. "It is not a twelvemonth, but twenty-four years since the South 'governed the Yankees,'" one New England paper observed, referencing the Confederate victory at Bull Run, "but the wild rejoicings in that section indicate that they think that their day has come again." And African-Americans, in turn, "regard[ed] the advent of that party to national power," the *Philadelphia Inquirer* claimed, "as the signal of their re-enslavement." Newspapers in the South reported "good feeling"; newspapers in the North noted the cruel "jocularity" of some southerners, who were enjoying telling "colored men that they were now worth $1000 apiece."

Twain, of course, didn't control the election, or its result; but he did control his tour schedule, and it was telling that he picked the

day after Election Day to open. Whether or not he had a role in
the national story at this time, he took one upon himself. Relish-
ing the resonance of the November 5 starting date, he called the
book tour a "campaign," even a "raid," as if it represented a shadow
change in administration similar to the one about to take place in
Washington. Twain was also among the most prominent Mugwump
supporters, and he played with that, too. The "Twins of Genius" tour
advertised itself as a new alliance of South and North, like that of
the Mugwumps and Southern Democrats—early publicity described
the team of Twain and Cable as a "literary bridging of the bloody
chasm."

Seen from the early twenty-first century, paging through the old
newspapers, one can't help but be startled at how much Twain's metaphorical representation of the confusion and trauma of the political moment upstaged the political moment itself. The November 27
Washington Post placed its review of the Twain-Cable reading in the
first column of the front page, while coverage of the disputed election
fell three columns to its left. *The New York Times* shoved that election leftward on its front page so that Mark Twain could be the lead
story. And so he was. President Arthur came to see the Twins; so did
Frederick Douglass. When Twain and Cable visited President-elect
Cleveland in his office in Albany, in fact, they clearly, if accidentally,
made the point that the Twins of Genius was the bigger story. In
an incident reported widely, Twain sat on the president-elect's desk
and activated with the seat of his pants the bells that called Cleveland's secretaries. Twain's ass—no mistake about it—was running the
country.

And Twain, under the hot lights, met the backward-looking election narrative on more than equal terms. He loved it when his life
story crashed against newspaper headlines. Let's honor that here. The
New York Times ran its review of Twain and Cable right next to a
feature entitled "Negroes' Foolish Fears," one of many national stories that mocked concerns that slavery would start all over again. The
New York Sun ran a similar alignment, running together on its first
page the headlines "Some of Mark Twain's Fun" and "Scaring Timid
Negroes." But what did the juxtaposition of these headlines signify:
agreement, or counternarrative? Was Twain endorsing the mean and

playful spirit of many white Americans of this era? Or was he offering a different kind of laughter: an antidote?

Was he offering a brilliant preview of the multicultural, polyglot culture of post–World War II America—a privileged white man crashing the gates of that stratified Victorian culture, demanding that all of America's voices would be heard? Or was he offering the newest technology in exploitation, also generations ahead of its time, the first in a long line of taste entrepreneurs to co-opt some unstable amalgam of white youth and African-American cultures and turn it to profit?

Modern readers make our first mistake, then, when we conclude that *Huck Finn* was just a book, let alone a great one. *Huck Finn* was not meant to stand alone, an isolated "classic" palmed by diffident teens between the hours of eight and three. It began its career as a piece of performance art, as part of something bigger, stranger, more wonderful, and more conflicted—spoken as much as written, and even sung as much as spoken. It had a time and a place, and things to say about the brutal national conversations about race and about children of that time and place.

We keep the book around because we know, deep down, that it speaks some ornery truth we can't say in the open. But we need new resources, and new sensibilities, to help us learn to read it again, and to learn to say the things that can't be said. A fresh glance at the "Twins of Genius"—the piece of performance art that brought *Huck* to life for enraptured and confused Victorian audiences—gives us an extraordinary second chance to see a crucial, storm-tossed piece of American culture with new eyes. It shows us something we can't see as clearly when the book must explain itself alone: that a serious statement about race was Twain's hidden agenda, literally. And that a fight about the lives of children was, to its author and his audience, the truer foreground. If we can tell the story of Twain's life as it led to this place, to 1884, accounting for all the different aspects of the *Huck Finn* project as he built it—the written, the verbal, the commercial, the political, the theatrical—we can see more clearly what mattered to him and his audience. We can see more clearly where we tripped up in the years that followed—and how, in many ways, our trip was a design feature, part of the peculiar genius of a man who could turn to profit the most trenchant critique of his audience. And we can even see that critique beneath the sleight of hand that only partially conceals it: that a country that confuses its comedy and its tragedy can convince itself it is moving forward when it is not.

Turn your pencil around, and put that eraser on the very edges of that old dog-eared copy of *Huck* you own, and rub until the place where the border between the book and the world disappears. Focus instead on the newer, older, multimedia *Huck* and the story that follows now: of where it came from, how its author built it, what it meant to say to the world, and what the world did and didn't hear.

2

Shiftless, Lazy, and Dadblasted Tired

As Mark Twain told it—in autobiographical writings, letters, newspaper columns, notebooks, speeches, and partially fiction-alized re-creations, some facts corroborated by other witnesses, some not—his childhood was a riot of sensory, political, and even spiritual data. It was filled with both hilarious and horrible anecdotes, idylls mixed with tragedy and violence. It laid the groundwork for the strategies and sensibility of the author he would become: a brilliant and elusive troublemaker with a guilty conscience. And it provided the raw materials for many of his best novels, including *Huck Finn* and *Tom Sawyer*: from the originals of most of those books' most fa-mous characters, to scenes like the iconic whitewashing of the fence.

But it also provided inspirations that we know much less well. Nostalgia was one of the reasons Mark Twain told and retold the sto-ries of his childhood in the 1840s throughout the 1870s and 1880s, but it is a simplistic explanation for why he went back there. Many middle- and upper-class Victorians, thriving in the late years of the Industrial Revolution, built large blocks of their cultural lives from antimodern materials: "Why, as science has become more cocksure," Andrew Lang wrote in the *Nation*, "have men and women become more and more fond of old follies, and more pleased with the stirring of ancient dread in their veins?" But the smartest ones used the past to say something that was, in fact, quite new. Freud used folklore and mythology to map the unconscious; Darwin jarred millions by claiming that humans had a past more ancient than anyone dreamt; Frazer's ambitious catalog of religious archetypes in *The Golden Bough* was a best seller.

And Twain correctly sensed his own childhood's relevance within the context of a national history that circled as much as it progressed: that the 1840s might be turned to use in the postbellum age with surprisingly little tinkering. As little tinkering as possible, in fact— that was the point. Backward, or forward—wherever his inner ear tuned to an echo that he could track, he followed. And we follow him back there, likewise, not just to create the expected biographical narrative, but to track echoes ourselves that start in small-town Hannibal in the years before the Civil War, and continue to the present day. Echoes of the resilient myths that guide our attitudes toward childhood. And of the way white Americans, torn in their feelings for their African-American slaves, servants, and neighbors, made an enduring and crude ritual out of their ambivalence, a disorderly collage of comedy and song that Twain found more useful, one way or the other, than almost anything he could imagine.

He was born two months premature to John and Jane Clemens, at the tail end of November 1835. He was not really expected to survive, but he did. His birth was so sudden that the landlord's wife had to scare up clothes for him—her daughter's clothes. In the life of someone who liked to dress up like people he wasn't, this was a good place to start.

History remembers Sam Clemens's father as remote, respectable, a justice of the peace, a grocer, and a dreamy, honorable, and ineffective land speculator; his mother was a rock-ribbed Presbyterian with a tart, inheritable wit.

They lived in several houses of varying pedigree in and around Hannibal, moving and shifting with fortune. Sam spent his early days in a one-room all-grades school, the first of three schools he'd eventually attend, all of which he hated. "Shiftless, lazy, and dad-blasted tired," one classmate would later describe him. "No study in him." At his father's deathbed, his mother channeled the pathos of the moment in an attempt to reform him. Tearful Sam agreed to do anything she asked—"except to go to school; I can't do that."

Even at that early age, he couldn't be manipulated into betraying the principles of truancy.

He cut a figure: "fuzzy light curls all over his head," another classmate remembered, "that really ought to have belonged to a girl," and blue-gray eyes that could shine green. And then there was his "long talk," an odd mannerism he also inherited from his mother. He talked v-e-r-y slow, which made half-funny things funny, and funny things very funny: "I used to play with the pause," he said later, "as other children play with a toy."

He loved pranks, too: mediocre at everything but spelling, he was head of the class at "devilment." "There's something in my pocket for you," he told his mother once: it was a live bat. He got beat for tricks like that, with a hickory, he claimed, that he had to provide himself: "They whipped boys, then, for every little thing . . . for fixing pins in the benches for boys to sit down on; for catching flies during morning prayers, and even for throwing rocks at passing strangers, in recess, when the motive was in no wise dishonorable . . ."

Tragedy struck early, and he experienced religious vision without comfort. He saw two siblings die: Margaret in 1839, Benjamin in 1842. His mother made him touch Benjamin's chilled face, to experience the seriousness of death. He probably didn't need the lesson: the night before she died of yellow fever, he had sleepwalked into Margaret's room and clutched her sheets, a sign, it was believed, that he knew what was coming.

He spent his Sundays in a church where the preachers were very clear about hell and the odds of a wayward child going there. He wept to his mother that he had "ceased to be a Christian," but his "trained Presbyterian conscience," as he later called it, swallowed guilt like air. There was no death in his family or among his friends he did not blame himself for: "I took all the tragedies to myself; and tallied them off in turn as they happened, saying to myself in each case, with a sigh, 'Another one gone—and on my account.'" Later there would be no economic or social injustice in which he regarded his hands as clean.

In the meantime, he went to revival meetings, though he always returned unconverted. He found Satan interesting enough to want to write a biography of him—at age seven.

His free afternoons he spent with the respectable kids, sometimes joined by a semi-couth boy named Tom Blankenship, "ignorant, unwashed, insufficiently fed," but with "as good a heart as ever any boy had." There were dogs and cats everywhere in Hannibal, and a fake meow from under your window meant Tom wanted you to come out to play. The other kids envied Blankenship because he had total liberty. His father was one of the town drunks. His sisters, one of whom was his twin, were assumed by many to be prostitutes. He didn't have to go to school and didn't have to go to church. He could fish all day and live in the open air, and kept company with a young slave named "Black John."

The requisite pleasures of nature and the life of a small child in a small town imprinted themselves upon Sam. He memorized, unconsciously, the sound of every voice. He memorized a deep catalog of nature's effects. He loved to read, as long as he wasn't being forced. He scripted his play, and the play of his friends, upon the rules of adventure as written in Dumas and Cervantes, Cooper and Scott. He saved the best roles for himself.

He also had a death wish. When measles swept the town, he snuck out one night and crawled into bed with the afflicted Will Bowen, his best friend. His parents were horrified, but the boy was enchanted with the proximity to mortality this action produced. "I have never enjoyed anything in my life any more than I enjoyed dying that time," he wrote decades later.

He loved the water, and by his recollection almost drowned eight or nine times: either number made him seem catlike, a comparison he never minded much. Another time he dove off a riverboat to retrieve a lost hat, but swam so far downstream the town suspected he was dead, and began firing cannons over the water to coax his body to the surface. "People born to be hanged are safe in water," his mother told him.

He was a sleepwalker. He tried, at nine, to sneak off on a riverboat. At fourteen, he got caught dancing naked by two anonymous girls as he rehearsed for his part as "bear" in a playlet to be performed at one of his older sister's parties. In a bedroom he thought unoccupied except for himself and a slave named Sandy, he did "handsprings" and got down on all fours and "snarled," while they hid behind a screen, themselves only partially dressed, until Sandy told a joke that flushed out the laughter that gave them away. Sam was mortified for weeks, possibly decades: "I had never guessed those girls out," he wrote near the end of his life, "nor wanting to, either."

He loved smoking, role-playing, arguing, and getting people to defend what they, in other circumstances, would decry, or to do willingly what they would otherwise refuse. Tom Sawyer's whitewashed fence had its basis: once Sam Clemens actually did take out contracts to whitewash all the fences in the neighborhood, then "cat-meowed" his friends outside and persuaded them that whitewashing all those fences at night would destroy the flowers that grew near them, and cause a wonderful panic in the morning. He bossed them all night long, until their hands blistered and their eyes stung from lime, and the job was done. It wasn't quite what Tom Sawyer would do, on the written page, thirty-five years later, but it was close.

And along the way, Sam Clemens got a remarkable education on black culture and race relations in the years before the Civil War: in fact, he was a keen autodidact on the subject. During the summers of his early childhood, for instance, Sam stayed at his uncle John's farm. His evenings there he spent in the company of his uncle's slaves, including one he called "Uncle Dan'l," a tall man in his forties named Daniel Quarles who was a prodigious storyteller. Twain would never forget these evenings: as he later described it, Quarles would travel with him, "spiritually," for decades.

Every evening, the children, black and white, gathered around the kitchen hearth to hear Quarles tell stories, including one about a cunning rabbit outwitting a hungry, vicious fox in a briar patch. The prey beat the predator almost every time. It was an interesting story for a slave to tell over and over to his master's children.

For the last story of the night, Quarles always told a ghost story about a woman with a golden arm. There was wailing, "rising & falling cadences of the wind, so easily mimicked with one's mouth," and "impressive pauses & eloquent silences." The story ended with a start that never failed to make Sam and the other children jump.

And after the story, the white children went up to a cool room with soft beds and a window that left Sam and his siblings engulfed in moonlight. The slave children crossed the orchard and disappeared into their quarters.

"We were comrades," he said later, speaking about those black children with whom he played, "and yet not comrades."

He watched as his father gave a slave named Lewis "a lashing now & then" for being clumsy. He watched as his father beat a slave named Jenny for grabbing a whip out of Sam's mother's hands. It was "the custom of the time," he observed later. He watched as his father sold slaves: Jenny for her transgression, Charley to pay off a debt. Jenny had saved Sam once, pulling him out of a creek before drowning, but that act of heroism didn't save her.

Like everyone in Hannibal, Sam closely followed the trial of three abolitionists who had been captured trying to free five slaves. Sam's father was the foreman of the jury, which received "considerable applause" when they sentenced the abolitionists to twelve years' hard labor.

He watched (concealed and alone, he'd emphasize later) as a slave he called "Negro Jerry" mounted the woodpile at his master's house and delivered a parody of a political speech or a sermon— interrupting himself periodically to make a sound with his mouth uncannily like sawing wood so that his master would think he was working. "I believed he was the greatest orator in the United States," Twain wrote.

And entwined with his education on race relations, both part and apart from it, came a startling education on violence and the fragility of American civilization. A man named Sam Smarr, for instance, was gunned down on a Hannibal street in 1845, when Sam Clemens was nine. Twain never made clear if he saw the murder itself, but he certainly saw what came after: some "thoughtful idiot," as tradition mandated, placed a massive Bible on the bosom of the man struggling through his dying breaths. "An anvil would have been in better taste there . . . less open to sarcastic criticism," he observed years later.

There was a town drunk, in and out of the local jail. Sam took pity on him and gave him matches so he could smoke. The man lit his pipe, and his jail cell, too, and burned to death in ten minutes. A "hundred nights" of dreams, Twain said, followed "in which I saw his appealing face as I had seen it in the pathetic reality, pressed against the window-bars, with the red hell glowing behind him."

Among his father's duties as justice of the peace was coroner's work. Sam snuck into his father's office one evening and found a corpse in the darkness. A "white human hand . . . in the moonlight" created an image from that startled moment that Twain carried for decades.

He apparently watched his father's autopsy through a keyhole.

When one of the less popular boys accepted a taunt to dive into a "muddy creek" and stay underwater "longest," it was Sam who drew the straw that made it his job to dive and catch hold of the lifeless wrist that confirmed the worst.

There was another local boy who had to be locked and chained in the yard, and refused to wear clothes; when he became convinced that his left hand was sinful, he broke free, grabbed a hatchet, and cut it off. "Religious mania," Twain noted.

He saw a slaveholder throw a piece of burning iron ore into the face of a slave, punishment for "doing something awkwardly." "It bounded from the man's skull," he wrote later. "He was dead in an hour."

He watched a knife fight in which a "young Californian emigrant" took a bowie knife in the chest. "I saw the red life gush from his breast," he remembered.

There were the murderous Hyde brothers, who tried to kill their "harmless old uncle." One held him down and the other tried to kill him with a faulty pistol. "I happened along just then, of course," Twain recalled.

While playing on a river island, his gang was terrified as the remains of an assassinated slave named Neriam Todd rose out of the water. Weeks before, Todd had run off and made it to the island. Bence, Tom Blankenship's older brother, found him and, disdaining the reward, fed him for a few weeks, until bounty hunters heard a rumor and sailed to the island. Todd drowned trying to flee. The bounty hunters mutilated his body and left him to drift in the river. He ran aground where children could find him, and they did.

•   •   •

On one particular evening, though, there was no violence. Newspaper clippings suggest it was a night sometime in April 1847, when Sam was eleven—one month after his father had died. In his memories, Twain himself would place it a year or two earlier. It was one of the idylls, one of the rare times where all the tragic and mirthful aspects of his hyperbolic childhood would find expression, even resolution. It would hit him like a thunderbolt, a "glad and stunning surprise." It "made life a pleasure," he'd say, fifty-nine years later—a fulfillment, as well as counterpoint, to the evenings spent with Daniel Quarles. And it would travel with him as far and for as long as did those storytelling evenings hearing about the woman with the golden arm.

That was the night the minstrel show came to Hannibal.

The "full minstrel show"—a true theatrical production, two hours or so long, featuring ensemble, musical program, and comic skits—was a fairly new national sensation, having just debuted in 1843 in New York, with ads promising the "oddities, peculiarities, eccentricities, and comicalities of that Sable Genus of Humanity." But it carried with it a long and complicated prehistory. In America, playing with race was a well-established tradition, with many contradictory political uses, from droll to subversive to exploitative and deadly: from the slaves who donned their masters' clothing and talked "white" in the Carolinas in the years before the Revolution, to the Revolutionaries themselves, those Boston Tea Partiers dressed up as Native Americans, to the urban "Callithumpians," gangs who sooted their faces, banged on pots, and invaded the homes of adulterers or old men who married young women. Belsnickel, a proto-Santa, visited children with "face of black": carrying candy in one hand and a whip in the others, he scared them out of their minds. White rioters in Philadelphia, one decade before the minstrel show reached Hannibal, practiced "blackface-on-Black violence," blacking up to attack African-American churches and Christmas celebrants.

Around 1830, a young man named Thomas Dartmouth Rice, from Five Points in New York, introduced onto American stages a song and dance called "Jump Jim Crow," creating a sensation that

hadn't yet subsided by the time the minstrels came to Hannibal—
that, truthfully, still hasn't subsided. All the loose energies that co-
hered around the idea of a "face of black" became utterly racialized in
song, in dance, in humor. A lexicon of characters, dances, theatrical
forms, and songs emerged, with borrowings, thefts, amalgams, sometimes mocking blacks viciously, sometimes paying them homage. At
first, minstrelsy was elastic, dangerous: in mixed race crowds in New
York dives and elsewhere, it signaled an alliance of the low that might
rock the nation.

Black charisma was "invented" or, at least, named. Jim Crow—
the figure himself, not yet the name for the national apartheid that
governed race relations from the 1870s to the 1960s—was played
by a young white man in makeup and costume who lamented the
"misfortune" of whites who would "spend every dollar" to become
"gentlemen ob colour." And liberation was contemplated from behind Jim Crow's mask: "I am for freedom," he sang in the 1830s,
and "De white is called my broder." The amalgams themselves were
indecipherable tributes to the richness and confusion of the American cultural marketplace: the character of Jim Crow was of African
origin, but the melody was distinctly Irish. The dance came from everywhere and nowhere: in different accounts, Louisville, Pittsburgh,
New York, Baltimore, and elsewhere. The song was performed in
parody by anti-Catholic crowds on their way to burn down con-
vents, and it was performed for American diplomats by musicians in
foreign countries who earnestly believed it was our national anthem.
The lyricist of one early minstrel hit, as listed on the sheet music, was
Santa Claus.

By the mid-1840s, minstrelsy was a theatrical institution: troupes
formed, plays were scripted. The politics rapidly grew more uni-
laterally racist but still maintained a certain anarchy and surprise,
depending on the troupe, the song, the audience, the decade, the
line you quote, the line you don't, and a thousand other cues lost to
time. Operas, respectable theater, and other genres of European and
high art were sucked into this mad vortex, nationalized, effectively,
by being blacked up. The racism was American, as was the promise of
liberation; the homage to the culture and labor of the disenfranchised
was American, as was its appropriation. For many white Americans,

it was a solvent of political difference: it had empathy, it had hate, and it didn't ask you which you felt or to what degree. Minstrels would perform in the White House for Abe Lincoln. Walt Whitman loved it. Commodore Matthew Perry, looking for something "American" with which to entertain his Japanese hosts after they showed him Kabuki, blacked up some of his sailors and put on a minstrel act. Admiring progressive thinkers like Margaret Fuller saw "Jump Jim Crow" as evidence that "all symptoms of invention" in American culture were "confined to the African race."

Meanwhile black leaders like Frederick Douglass uttered criticisms that would take decades, if not a century, for most Americans to hear, calling minstrels "the filthy scum of white society, who have stolen from us a complexion denied to them by nature, in which to make money, and pander to the corrupt taste of their fellow white citizens."

All young Sam Clemens knew, however, was that the churchgoing men and women of Hannibal weren't going, and that whiff of scandal was good enough for him.

If this minstrel show was like others from the time, there was no curtain, as though the show was continuous with everyday life. The minstrels emerged from stage side, instruments in hand, and greeted the audience like old friends.

Burnt cork was cheap, a how-to guide assures us: you could buy enough for a troupe of eight for dimes, and it washed off easily. Champagne corks, if you could find them, were best. There were two "end men," who sat at either end of the stage: Tambo and Bones, maybe Banjo and Bones. They spoke in the deepest dialect and did the most clowning. In the middle sat the "interlocutor," or middleman, who spoke something like formal English and usually wore some combination of clothing and makeup that made him seem "white." It was a parody of "high and citified society," Twain would write later, and it fooled many of the "innocent villagers."

Banjo and Bones were hard to settle: "Gentlemen, be seated," the interlocutor would often tell them, to a kind of fanfare of horns and drums. They mock-argued onstage, supposedly "happy" imitations of the way blacks actually argued. "A delightful jangle of assertion and contradiction," Twain wrote later, that rose to "impressive threats." They told toneless pun after toneless pun, jumped hard on bad punch lines: "What plant is most fatal to mice?" "The *cat-nip*."

They told Why-did-the-chicken-cross-the-road jokes; they invented them, in fact. They dressed in drag: a pair of comically big feet poking out from underneath frilly petticoats signaled the uproarious reveal. They muddied Shakespeare: "Take any other shape but that," would say Macbeth, fearful of Banquo's ghost, to which "Anthony" would respond, "I neber took a sheep in my life." They performed stump speeches, mock orations that butchered the official political speech of the day:

"When in de course ob human events . . ."

And then, amazingly, began to offer a glimpse of black political preference:

"it becomes actually and really necessary for de colored portion ob dis community fur to go in and look out for demselves—"

before abruptly stopping, a dream deferred:

"Ain't I right, eh?"

There was often a frightening physicality to the evening, something like the spectral air of zombie and horror that often hangs over contemporary pop performances, or the creep many grown men and women feel when they see a clown in full makeup. (The modern clown's makeup, like the white gloves on Mickey Mouse, Sonic the Hedgehog, and Mario, is a minstrel show leftover.) The blacking up wasn't casual, and evolved over time: the earliest minstrels, it appears, applied makeup lightly, looking much like themselves with skin modulated to a darker but not uniform hue. As minstrelsy acquired a more markedly racist character, however, the performers would use cork or grease or shoe polish so that everyone looked hauntingly alike, and so the whites of their eyes picked up the footlights and glittered eerily. Soon they painted their mouths and lips white, too, sometimes broad and red, so that the very idea of "mouth" took on a furtive, desperate life of its own.

They wore motley, baggy clothing covered in colorful patches, a kind of emblematic slave garment. It was a parody of what couldn't be parodied, as Twain noted: buttons, for instance, each as big as a "blacking box." And within those oversized, colorful rags, legs and arms struck overlong, antiestablishment postures. The minstrels couldn't keep still but, even when sitting, moved and moved, the kind of endless, jerking motion that we would recognize today in the restless dances of teenagers.

They played extraordinary instruments of low origin: bones and tambourine (of course), fiddle and banjo. The bones were real sawed-off horse ribs that contributed to what one minstrel proudly called a "horrible noise." The tambourine was not a modern tambourine but a bigger Irish drum that gave each song a bottom and still jangled. Fiddle, banjo, nothing well tuned: the band scratched and wheezed and rang, craftily underplaying.

Perhaps they danced, and if they danced, they might have danced "Jump Jim Crow," the dance that Rice had made into a national sensation. "I wheel about / I turn about / I do just so," the minstrel sang as he spun on the axis of one foot placed behind himself. We call this the "wheel step" now: Michael Jackson did it, as did M. C. Hammer, and Mick Jagger, and countless other modern performers.

Probably, some early minstrels had worked at their imitations of black culture. They were troupers, rehearsed seriously. They announced their "authenticity" like researchers. They did not regard black America as monolithic. Songs and dances had regional sources, and dialects varied. Some came from places where blacks and whites lived together; some didn't. Songs were transcribed from their black sources, fashioned, adapted, blended as the minstrels wanted. Or they were transcribed from their Irish sources, their Central European sources, their roots in symphonic music, and then Americanized with dialects, black characters: the song "When the Niggars in Virginia," an 1854 playbill tells us, is sung to the tune of "When the fair land of Poland."

Sometimes, rebellion bled through: T. D. Rice penned and produced a version of *Othello* with a happy ending in which Desdemona lives and enters into a biracial marriage with the Moor prince, and their child, one cheek black, one white, parades before the audience at the close. More often, though, minstrels invited their audiences to regard slavery as entertainment and being a second-class citizen as sly, cracked fun. At this point in time, the minstrel shows really didn't have much use for nostalgic representations of slavery. They didn't yet have their rural black figure set in stone, although they were working on it. But they had the free black, often called "Zip Coon," or even "Cool White," and he was plenty: raunchy, citified, too bold sometimes but careful, too, his words coded with strategies for speaking your mind in a way invisible to your masters or your bosses.

They sang songs that remain with us, that we love to have our children sing in their third-grade music classes, the dialects dropped, a few suave deletions burying the nineteenth century. "Jingle Bells" began life as "The Darkey Sleighing Party," "Turkey in the Straw" as "Zip Coon," "Camptown Races" as a Yoruba lullaby transformed, very possibly, into a song about prostitution. Stephen Foster himself tried to scrub the dialect and slurs from songs like "Oh! Susanna," although it would take subsequent generations to cut out the surreal and violent second verse, in which "five hundred Nigga" are electrocuted for no particular reason.

Sometimes, they sang about sex:

My Susy looms it bery tall
Wid udder like a cow
She'd give nine quarts easy
But white gals don't know how.

Sometimes, they sang about drinking like it was sex, and not always heterosexual sex:

I kiss him two three time
And den I suck him dry
Dat jug, he's none but mine.

Usually the minstrels sang about how good their masters were to them:

Old Massa to us darkies am good
Tra la la, tra la la
For he gibs us our clothes
and he gibs us our food . . .

But sometimes they sang about putting their masters six feet under:

My ole massa dead and gone,
A dose of poison help him on
De debul say he funeral song.

They sang about the unconditional pleasures of entertaining white audiences:

We live on excitement, we're bound to hab our fun,
Dars nofin' old dat pleases 'cept de risin' ob de sun,
So we'll kick up a rumpus and gib our tongues a run,
For we'll gib de white folks a concert.

And sometimes they sang about how whites should go away:

An I caution all white dandies,
Not to come in my way,
For if dey insult me,
Dey'll in de gutter lay.

And sometimes they sang in code:

A Bull frog dress'd sogers close,
Went in de field to shoot some crows;
De crows smell powder and fly away,
De Bull frog mighty mad dat day.

When the time came to replay his childhood in fiction, Twain would include the minstrel show as a high point: in *Tom Sawyer*, Tom and his friends are so caught up in the "sensation" that they black up themselves and put on a show. And when the time came to reflect on the show in his own voice, he usually spoke with un-disguised affection: it was the "show which to me had no peer, and whose peer has not yet arrived." But what did he see, really see, that evening? And what stayed with him?

He probably knew the codes, if those minstrels offered them. If he had been paying attention when Daniel Quarles told stories about rabbits outwitting foxes, he recognized that those stories about prey animals outsmarting predators were full of messages for black and white children about the politics playing out right in front of them.

He probably knew the songs, but he had never seen them per-formed like that. And he had probably never seen the dancing, ei-ther. He liked black men and women more than most white men and women he knew—his solitary infatuation with "Negro Jerry," the greatest orator in the United States, certainly pointed in this direction—and saw this as a public acknowledgment that their cul-ture mattered, as Margaret Fuller did. But he liked slavery, too—at least at this time—and minstrelsy's accents and cues of white racial superiority would have fallen on sympathetic ears tuned to hear them.

He could see that there was a big difference between the applause and fortune these minstrels received and the jail sentence that aboli-tionists received—that there was a safe way to identify with blacks, and a dangerous way.

And he could see, too, that white boys could speak through black voices, could say what was on their minds through a kind of veil. He would forever associate blacks with freedom, and with youth. He also saw that blacks could be used—just not as slaves, not for the sweat of their brows. He saw that you could play with race: you could pro-duce blackness. And you could make money making blackness.

He thought the minstrels were "accurate," too—that the black-ness they made matched something real and recognizable. That would make a big difference to the Twain-to-come that believed in the pitch-perfect imitation. But he told correspondents in later years that "the so-called 'negro minstrels' simply mis-represent." That this line of thinking contradicted the previous line of thinking was some-thing he didn't see—or did, but loved both authenticity and imita-tion too much to choose.

He also decided that most people didn't understand all these things. He knew those were white men masquerading; he even knew the "interlocutor" was playing a "white person." But the audience didn't seem to know. The "innocent villagers" thought it was the "real thing," he emphasized. Or they noticed and Twain buried the fact that they noticed. And that, too, would make a big difference in the Twain-to-come, the part of him that believed that most Americans were so committed to their illusions that no amount of reality could persuade them otherwise.

More likely, though, he didn't learn any one thing. His childhood had boiled with so many impulses, so many imprints, so many ideologies. He didn't need to hear one message: he needed more than that. And the minstrels didn't have one message (unlike those luckless abolitionists); that was why they succeeded. They taught him that there were crazy, selfish artists who didn't tell you what to think, who revered and bent and stole without conditions, who pressed their advantages and kept moving, and raised more questions than they could answer. They were never caught naked by any audience. They always wore some kind of a mask.

And he learned he'd want to be someone like that.

3

Strange Animals, to Change Their Clothes So Often

Young Sam Clemens grew up straight and tall, or really not so straight or so tall, but wickedly crooked. He topped out at five foot eight or eight and a half, around 160 pounds, and even offstage walked with a roll you can still see on YouTube, and which was easily mistaken for a drunken stagger. His voice filled out to that drawl so slow—"the syllables came about every half minute," one observer joked—that it, too, could be mistaken for many things it wasn't. He recorded it once, sometime early in the twentieth century, but the original wax was not saved, nor, apparently, were any copies.

We know Twain's basic story: it is stored in countless documentaries, photographs, schoolbooks. We certainly sanction some of his countercultural wildness: the enduring popularity of his elliptical, sacred-cow–busting bank of quotations (many falsely ascribed to him) are reflective of this. But just as the rough edges of his childhood are sanded down in our recollection, so, too, are the rough edges of the man that childhood produced. His story is better told, for instance, if we acknowledge that there were times in his life, especially his young adulthood, when he did or said something we'd identify as uncategorically racist. It is only against that background that the transformation he subsequently made, where he became one of his nation's most progressive voices on such matters, appears as remarkable as it truly was. And, in turn, it is only against the background of that remarkable transformation that the resiliency of many of those youthful attitudes becomes as perplexing and resonant as it deserves to be.

The story of Mark Twain's adulthood—the story that leads us to the point where he sits down with pen and paper to write the opening pages of *Huck Finn*—is a remarkable story about remaking oneself. But it is also a story about salvaging the tricky past, about saving the dirty bathwater with the baby. The boy who liked slavery and loathed its enemies would not recognize himself in the man who wrote *Huck Finn*. But the boy who eavesdropped on slaves as they talked and sang, who saw abolitionists jailed and minstrels cheered, who feared exposure but not death, most certainly would.

Even a legend can be underestimated. It simply does not seem possible that Sam Clemens could have been this adventurous, this restless, and have done so many things so young, even as he retained that nugget of provincialism that provided such opportunities to self-lampoon. He ran away from Hannibal (without saying good-bye to his *mother*) at seventeen, lived in or visited New York, Philadelphia, Washington, St. Louis, and Cincinnati, worked as typesetter and paid militiaman, all before he famously talked his way onto Horace Bixby's steamboat and became a "cub-pilot" at twenty-one, then memorized "twelve or thirteen hundred miles" of the Mississippi curve by curve over two years to earn his pilot's license.

He joined, and deserted, the Confederate army in 1861, after three weeks as "lieutenant" in a band of volunteer rangers. They had faced their first skirmish, or so they thought, and shot an unarmed civilian. That was enough. He headed west and tried to make a fortune as a speculator, miner, and timberman. Then he got his first true writing job, on the Virginia City, Nevada, newspaper the *Territorial Enterprise*, in 1862, and adopted the pseudonym and performing name "Mark Twain" the following year.

Having moved to California to stay one step ahead of a duel challenge back in Virginia City, he became a star writer for the San Francisco papers before the end of the Civil War. Dodging a fraudulent bond in 1865, a few weeks holed up at a spot called Jackass Hill in the Sierra Nevadas yielded the material for his first national success,

"The Celebrated Jumping Frog of Calaveras County." He lived for months on the Sandwich Islands in the middle of the Pacific, traveled through Nicaragua, and got hired as secretary to a U.S. senator. A trip through Europe to Palestine sponsored by a Barbary Coast newspaper inspired *The Innocents Abroad*, the book that made him a star in 1869.

In public, he played a violator of social norms, and made sure it was hard to tell if he was only playing. Until he married, and even sometimes afterward, he dressed to affront. He'd show up in editorial offices, in congressional rooms, in travel offices, in a "battered old slouch hat," a coat covered in dust or a "seedy suit," a "frazzled" old cigar "protrud[ing] from the corner of his mouth," or his breath coated, as if for the occasion, in whiskey. He was scary on bad days, merely disarming on good. He was known as a "deadbeat" and an "alcoholic," and spent more nights in jail for being disorderly than Johnny Cash ever did: "I enjoyed the thing considerably," he said of one overnight stay in New York in 1867, "for an hour or so."

But he could write, and he already possessed a keen and complex intellectual vision. His eye and ear were as clear as glass, and his desire to transcribe what he saw around him was almost primal: he'd write fifty thousand letters, three thousand newspaper pieces, and thirty books before he was through. He loved to lie and smoke, loved fake names, loved exaggerated portraits of violence. He was cagey, at best, about sex. He hated the church, but believed in the supernatural. He had a dream about his brother Henry's coffin, and then his brother died a short time after, blown up on a steamboat Twain would have been steering if he hadn't beaten up the captain days before.

He loved language, everything from the pregnant pauses to the barbaric yawps. He admired and imitated the steamboat captain who read Shakespeare during downtime. And he equally admired the steamboat captain for his prodigious "feats of fancy blasphemy" that were "calculated to fill the hearer with awe & admiration." In truth, he could swear quite admirably himself: "profanity," he told his brother, "is more necessary than is immunity from colds." In his twenties and thirties, he would drop swearwords into his journals, abbreviated demurely: "sht," for instance. Later in life, he would turn over his manuscripts to his wife Olivia, or his good friend the editor

and author William Dean Howells, and together they'd cut unpleasant words like "hell" and "reeking."

At the same time, Hannibal, to which he would only return a
handful of times in his life, remained in his "great deep," as he called
it. And the lessons of that childhood, its violence and joys and that
one evening of dazzling minstrelsy, all remained there, too. Walking
the multiracial streets of New York in 1853 when he was seventeen,
the minstrel show fit his contempt and shock like a glove: "I reckon
I had better black my face," he sneered to his mother, "for in these
Eastern States niggers are considerably better than white people." He
called the abolitionists he came across "infernal" and hated the whole
melting pot of "Mulattoes, quadroons, Chinese, and some the Lord
no doubt originally intended to be white, but the dirt on whose faces
leaves one uncertain as to that fact. . . ." "This mass of human vermin," he added, "would raise the ire of the most patient person that
ever lived."

He'd take all this back, eventually, but that takes us ahead of our
story, which is about how, exactly, he found repentance on these matters. Why, first of all, would someone who thought like this even
want to run away from Hannibal to New York—then as now a diversity center—at seventeen? What part of his childhood inspired that
move? A decade and a half later, in 1867, he'd set foot in Tangier,
Morocco (and what, exactly, was he doing *there*?), and exclaim, "We
have found it"—"the spot we have been longing for all the time."
And what did "we" find there? A completely "foreign" place, "foreign
inside and outside and all around." And what made it "foreign"? "No
white men visible."

Never mind that, within a day, he tired of Tangier, which became
"a weary prison": it was fun to be "the other" for a while, but (like
prison) only a while. It was still an extraordinary journey from the
open racism of his childhood to this place. And that "we" concealed
the fact that Twain was very much an "I" here, very much one of the
handful of white American men who wandered this far to escape his
whiteness.

In part, Twain's inspiration was men like Daniel Quarles and the
intense empathy he felt for them. But the slippery politics of dis-
guise and covert empathy of the early minstrels, commingled with

that fantastic guilt of his, may have guided him even more. Over and over, the idea of costume and race appealed to him. He fell in love with New Orleans and the Mardi Gras, the parade of "men, women and children in fine, fancy, splendid, ugly, coarse, ridiculous, grotesque, laughable costumes . . . giants, Indians, nigger minstrels, monks, priests, clowns,—birds, beasts—everything," and insisted that America's true heart lay in that carnival: "I think that I may say that an American has not seen the United States until he has seen Mardi-Gras. . . ." In a cemetery in the French Quarter, he toyed with a chameleon: "strange animals," he told one correspondent, "to change their clothes so often! I found a dingy looking one, drove him on a black rag, and he turned black as ink. . . ." That chameleon was as much minstrel as reptile.

As he matured, fled west, took up residence in the wild boom-towns of Nevada and California, he grew more playful, became a kind of politician-performer-journalist—a conservative ripple on the surface, a ripple of subversion underneath, perfectly balanced (to him, if not to us) when he was on, awkward when he was not. Here he learned to master his natural deadpan, partly from humorists like Artemus Ward, but also from minstrels like Billy Birch. Newspapers linked him explicitly to the minstrel show, as a marker of his well-known contempt for "respectable" culture: "as a general thing he prefers negro minstrelsy to Italian opera," the *Dramatic Chronicle* of San Francisco observed.

He wrote travel letters from New York, where in seedy Manhattan bars he was the Western "innocent" spectating nineteenth-century variations of lap dancing and male exhibitionism—men twirling "Highland" style in nothing but "short coat and short stockings." Back west, he took a liking to "*genuine* music," "glory-beaming banjo," from Tommy Bree, Charley Rhoades, and the African-American Sam Pride. He also became a fan of the San Francisco Minstrels, who specialized in political satire drawn from current headlines, and unpredictably empathetic race play. While other minstrel troupes after the Civil War represented free blacks lamenting the loss of the plantation, providing wish fulfillment for many white audience members, the San Francisco Minstrels—their geographic name placing them, as it might today, on the unpredictable left of the political spectrum—asked "Mister Ku-klux" to "let me be," and urged audiences to "let the poor have the bread they earn."

This more complicated approach to race, entertainment, and politics began appearing in Twain's own writings. He had used racial slurs in his teenage years with unconscious contempt. Now, rarely but pointedly, he began to use them as masks from behind which he tweaked his own audience's humorless racisms. And as far as Twain was concerned, they hurt no one; he'd have to imagine a black audience to fathom that possibility. In the *Territorial Enterprise* in June 1865, for instance, he published a false article about "a young white woman" who had been living "with a strapping young nigger for six months" without knowing it was wrong. "Her lack of awareness that there was anything 'unbecoming,'" Fred Kaplan asks us, "indirectly raised the question, Was there?"

In July, Twain published "Mark Twain on the Colored Man," a brief report about a Fourth of July parade where both whites and blacks marched: "the day was dusty and no man could tell where the white folks left off and the niggers began." It was "a fine stroke," Twain observed, before himself turning on the kinds of readers who might have been lulled by his complacently racist vocabulary, "in the face of the fact that they have got to sing with them in heaven or scorch with them in hell some day in the most familiar and sociable way, on a footing of most perfect equality."

It was no coincidence that these essays appeared in the two months after the Civil War ended, as the Thirteenth Amendment to the Constitution, banning slavery, was being enacted. Twain, like many, was caught up in an extraordinary moment. But generally, during this time, he had no agenda, and little calculation. He insulted the elites; he insulted free blacks, making truly disturbing jokes about body odor and, in private, roasting flesh. To him, bad words were good; popular or polite ideas were bad. The in-between was a complicated place where he might parody an important civil rights landmark one month and be moved to the deepest outrage by a racist street assault on the next. His response to the Emancipation Proclamation, for instance, was a fictitious report claiming the local Virginia City chapter of the Sanitary Fund (the early Red Cross) was sending its donations to a Miscegenation Society back east—a subtext-laden and suggestive

joke that infuriated the matrons who governed the fund, and hastened his flight to San Francisco.

In San Francisco, however, he nearly surrendered his job as correspondent for the *Morning Call* because their editors would not publish an outraged piece he wrote after the stoning of a Chinese laborer.
The article would make their readers angry, the editor told Twain.
That was, of course, exactly what Twain intended. He did back off,
cursing himself as he did, but not forgetting, and publishing the
piece later at a somewhat safer remove from the San Francisco police
he described as "either asleep or dead," and the reporters "gone mad
with admiration of the energy, the virtue, the high effectiveness, and
the dare-devil intrepidity of that very police."

It was a fierce and foreboding piece, saying what Twain couldn't
yet say about American slavery and its aftermath, but would eventually say about racism wherever he saw it. The real outrage, Twain
noted with high-pitched sarcasm, was the "disgraceful persecution"
and arrest of the boy who threw the stones. Newspapers published
countless reports having for "a dazzling central incident a Chinaman
guilty of a shilling's worth of crime." The state held that the "Chinaman had no rights that any man was bound to respect." And "nobody befriended them, nobody spared them suffering when it was
convenient to inflict it." Why, then, arrest the child who, walking
down the street, had concluded, "Ah, there goes a Chinaman! God
will not love me if I do not stone him"? It wasn't the isolated act of
racism that should be punished, Twain told his readers in his best
upside-down voice; it was the structure underlying the isolated act.
And that he did so while defending the perspective of a child, however sardonically—that, too, pointed at things to come.

Like many Americans, the Civil War had changed Twain; its cul-
mination, and the Reconstruction, the national transformation
that followed, would change him even more. At the tail end of the
Civil War and in its aftermath, the Republican-led federal government instituted a variety of measures designed to "reconstruct" the
governments of the Southern states. Constitutional amendments
outlawed slavery, guaranteed citizenship rights and due process re-

gardless of color, and strengthened the right to vote. The Freedmen's
Bureau was organized to support freed slaves, and the idea of land
redistribution—"forty acres and a mule"—received political consideration. Federal armies and officials spread throughout the South and
conducted biracial elections that created biracial governments. A civil
rights act, passed in 1875, guaranteed equal access to public accom-
modations, including schools, train cars, parks, and theaters.

Spectating from the edges of the continent at first, Twain quickly
moved as the politics moved. In two or three years he shifted
from using racial slurs (except in quotation marks) to "colored" to
"Negro"—with capitalization, the most progressive locution of the
era—both in public and private. In the *Buffalo Express* in 1869,
he wrote an editorial response to the story of a lynched black man
cleared, after death, of the crime that inspired his lynching. Twain
called it "Only A Nigger" and air-quoted the racial slur throughout,
parodying the voice of complacent racism from a distance and with a
calm he had previously found inaccessible: "Only 'a nigger' killed by
mistake—that is all . . . What are the lives of a few 'niggers' in comparison with the preservation of the impetuous instincts of a proud
and fiery race?"

Meantime, his travel, which had spanned over half the globe, was
clearly providing valuable lessons in cultural difference that coincided
with a national trend in travel writing. In *The Innocents Abroad*, he
described a scene in Italy in 1867 where his guide was "a cultivated
negro, the offspring of a South Carolina slave." Noting that "Negroes
are deemed as good as white people, in Venice," Twain observed that
"this man feels no desire to go back to his native land." "His judgment," Twain added, with a flatness denoting the absence of irony,
"is correct."

Similarly, middle- and upper-class Victorians loved anthropology
and folklore—by century's end, most major universities would have
departments for one or both, the Smithsonian would be flush with
new collections, and *National Geographic* would be a middle-class
icon—and Twain brought its rhetoric into his domain. In his lectures
on the Sandwich Islands from 1867, for instance, he parodied the
study of "primitive" cultures then entering vogue: "the white people," he titled one section, "and their peculiarities." Later, he'd lecture

on "Our Fellow Savages of the Sandwich Islands"—another one of his favorite comic inversions, one that would become a staple in his repertoire for decades.

Before long, he made these challenges to nationalism and racial pride the cornerstone of his career. In a series of wildly successful lectures in 1868 and 1869 titled "The American Vandal Abroad," Twain openly told his audiences that travel "rubs out a multitude of . . . old unworthy bias and prejudices." It was a remarkable turn, not at all funny, and yet immensely profitable. He was packing in thousands many evenings: "You never saw a bigoted, opinionated, stubborn, narrow-minded, self-conceited, *almighty mean man* in your life," he called out at the end of his lecture, "but he had stuck in one place ever since he was born."

By the early 1870s, as Twain entered his mid-thirties, he looked back on the provincial racism of his youth with embarrassment. He now wrote to an old friend that, at nineteen or twenty, he had been nothing but "ignorance, intolerance, egotism, self-assertion, opaque perception, dense and pitiful chuckle-headedness—and an almost pathetic unconsciousness of it all." And now he pointed forward with an all-encompassing desire to keep remaking himself. There were many complicated reasons that Twain courted and then married Olivia Langdon of Elmira, New York, in 1870: she was rich, beautiful, and coolly smart in a way that balanced his wildness. But she was also the daughter and granddaughter of abolitionists, that political class of men and women Twain had been told, as a child, to regard as infernal.

It would not be surprising that Twain would marry into a prominent Northern family whose house had been a stop on the Underground Railroad, a family who routinely—and against the unwritten rules of even their liberal town—hosted prominent African-Americans like Frederick Douglass in their home. Having been raised in a slave state, and having made his name in the West, these were the family and the friends Twain now wanted, men and women from the progressive North, abolitionists or friends of abolitionists, blacks as well as whites. When he and Olivia moved to the Nook Farm section of Hartford in 1874, their new home shared a property line with Harriet Beecher Stowe, author of *Uncle Tom's Cabin*, and yet another symbol of how far Twain had traveled from the slave state of his childhood. He now lived in what he called "the freest corner of the country," and was pleased about it.

As the 1870s progressed, and Twain published and lectured widely, and established himself as a national figure, he became, too, a symbol of regional outreach and transformation: a "Yankee" with a difference, what William Dean Howells called the preeminent "de-southernized Southerner" of his time. And yet, the more he adapted to this new way of living, the more the past came back to him like an aggrieved ghost. A letter in 1870 to his boyhood friend Will Bowen, with whom he had tried to share measles thirty years before, described an extraordinary day where "I have rained reminiscences for four & twenty hours . . . the old life has swept before me like a panorama; the old days have trooped by in their old glory, again; the old faces have looked out of the mists of the past." Twain wrote this exactly four days after taking marriage vows to Olivia Langdon, as if all it had taken was a dapple of connubial bliss with a respectable woman from the North to awaken that gorgeous, dangerous childhood—or as if that gorgeous, dangerous childhood had awoken itself at the point where its owner seemed poised to leave it behind for good.

Daniel Quarles also reappeared, briefly, as "Uncle Dan'l" in Twain's coauthored (with Charles Dudley Warner) 1873 novel *The Gilded Age*. So, too, did Twain's early connection to black voices: voyeurism, empathy, appropriation. In Elmira, he hid in bushes and eavesdropped on African-American servants. At dinner parties, he sang "Swing Low, Sweet Chariot," "Go Down, Moses," and other spirituals from his youth, and danced something akin to Jim Crow. On tour in Paris, Illinois, on New Year's Eve, 1871, he spent a morning at a village church service, and it worked like a time machine: "It was as if twenty-five years had fallen away from me like a garment & I was a lad of eleven again . . ." And—just before or just after, probably, in the same little town—he had a conversation at his hotel with a ten-year-old African-American child, and the talk stayed with him so deeply that he crafted it into a piece he called "Sociable Jimmy," published three years later in the *New York Times*.

At this point, Twain, like many others, had turned against the minstrel shows, or at least the notion that they accurately represented African-Americans: hearing the Fisk Jubilee Singers perform slave spirituals in the early 1870s, he wrote that "white people cannot imitate—and never can." But white people could transcribe: these were the decades when German and English ethnographers began cataloging the old dialects of Europe before they disappeared into that continent's nascent nation-states, when John Wesley Powell recorded Native American language while on geological surveys, and itinerant folklorists scoured the South for remnants of slave song, vocabulary, dance, and story. And "Sociable Jimmy" showed just what Twain took from the minstrel show, and what he owed to these newer efforts to "accurately" represent the experience of marginalized others. The piece was almost entirely dialogue, almost entirely in the voice of the child. Twain spoke in standard English, like the "interlocutor": "Did you have a pleasant Christmas, Jimmy?" And "Jimmy" spoke in dialect, like a minstrel show's end man: "No, sah— not zackly. . . ." Unlike conventional end men, however, Jimmy was not telling jokes. Mostly, he just talked: "Dat's Kit, Sah. She ain't only nine year ole. But she's de mos' lady-like one in de whole bilin'."

And Twain insisted on authenticity, the words and the way he wrote them, the chain of apostrophes and misspellings meant to duplicate the servant's voice: "I took down what he had to say, just as he said it—without altering a word or adding one." Likewise, he posed "Jimmy" in an "equal" position as he talked, "both his legs" hung "over one of the arms" of a "big arm-chair . . . comfortable and conversational." And lastly, he treated "artless, social, and exhaustless" conversation as "a revelation," not a comedy. If the white minstrels ever bonded with blacks, they never acknowledged the value of the bond to themselves. That was the point. But Twain spiritualized it, wished for it: "I think I could swing my legs over the arms of a chair," he told Olivia, "& that boy's spirit would descend upon me & into me."

That same month, he also published "A True Story, Repeated Word for Word As I Heard It," a conversation with a family servant, Mary Ann Cord, whom Twain in the piece called "Aunt Rachel." Like "Sociable Jimmy," "A True Story," as its title suggested, insisted on authenticity: Twain, again, portrays himself as the conductor through which a black voice gets broadcast, an artless intermediary.

And, like "Sociable Jimmy," the essay was almost completely made of dialogue between Twain (in standard English) and a servant (in dialect), with the servant doing most of the talking. Framing brilliantly, as always, Twain places "Aunt Rachel" "sitting respectfully below our level, on the steps" of his front porch. Laughing—"peal after peal of laughter"—at the jokes of "Misto C," he asks her how she could have "lived sixty years and never had any trouble." And then she sobers him for two thousand–plus words, describing how she lost seven children to slave traders, and how one found his way back to her for a still-heartbreaking reunion. "I hain't had no trouble," she tells "Misto C" in the last sentence. "An' no *joy!*"

He struggled on this piece: "I amend dialect stuff," he told Howells, "by talking & talking & *talking* it till it sounds right—& I had difficulty with this negro talk . . ." Howells, then editor of the *Atlantic*, loved it—his magazine, like the *Century* or the *Nation*, was running plenty of dialect and folklore pieces alongside their fiction and Civil War memoirs—and made sure Twain got paid twice the going rate for it. And "A True Story" was such a success that Howells beseeched Twain for another one like it: another piece like the "colored one," he said. That Twain's first appearance in an elite Northern magazine occurred as he harvested the words and voice of a black servant might come to us as a surprise. That Twain might make a lot of money selling what he regarded as a faithful version of a black voice, and a black story—he had learned that lesson a long time ago. That the black voice might upbraid "Misto C"—that Mary Ann Cord might tell him what he *didn't* know—that was new. Racial mimickry, one way or the other, had reinforced the idea that whites *knew* blacks. Twain seemed to be creating a kind of mimickry in which he acknowledged they didn't.

By the early 1880s, he definitely knew what he wanted to say, and he said it in private moments, in terms that few even approach today: "Whenever a colored man commits an unright action," he told Karl and Hattie Gerhardt in a private letter, "upon his head is the guilt of only about one tenth of it, and upon your heads and mine and the rest of the white race lies fairly and justly the other nine tenths of the guilt." He told Howells that he would do his "part of the reparation due from every white to every black man," and this thinking governed many of his philanthropies during this decade. In 1881, he defended Frederick Douglass, a "personal friend," from termination as marshal of the District of Columbia: "I . . . so admire his brave, long crusade for the liberties and elevation of his race," he told James A. Garfield, before gently reminding the president-elect that he had endorsed him during the past campaign.

In 1882, Twain endowed $2,500 to Lincoln University, in Pennsylvania, to pay the tuition of black students. By the end of the decade, he would pay tuition for other students—including Warner T. McGuinn, one of the first black students at Yale Law. Twain also began making uncompensated appearances at "African church[es]" and in front of "dusky audiences," often for charity. In response to the avalanche of semiliterate appearance requests that now inundated him, he acknowledged losing his temper, "except when they come from colored (& therefore ignorant) people." "Consider everybody colored till he is proved white," his wife counseled.

In other venues, though—larger ones, more public ones, and homogenously white ones—his public face deflected both the anger and the complicity he felt about the larger history of racial inequality and violence. There was no question his national appeal would shrivel if many Americans knew what he said and wrote in private. But there was a deeper motivation: his fear of exposing himself went back to his childhood, but so, too, did his pleasure in creating a turbulent mirth out of the blood tide of history. He could get away with murder if he wanted, and sometimes he did. On December 22, 1881, for instance, he delivered a speech on "Plymouth Rock and the Pilgrims" to the New England Society, the kinds of men who could trace their ancestry to the *Mayflower*. He surveyed them peaceably, then wondered aloud: "Where are my ancestors? Whom shall I celebrate? Where shall I find the raw material?"

Then he told those sons of Puritans who *his* ancestors were: "My first American ancestor, gentlemen, was an Indian—an early Indian. Your ancestors skinned him alive, and I am an orphan. Not one drop of my blood flows in that Indian's veins today . . . They skinned him! I do not object to that, if they needed his fur; but alive, gentlemen—

alive! They skinned him alive—and before company! That is what rankles. Think of how he must have felt; for he was a sensitive person and easily embarrassed."

Then Quakers, whipped and exiled. Then Roger Williams, exiled, too, by the Puritans to what is now Rhode Island. Then the Salem witches. Then: "The first slave brought into New England out of Africa by your progenitors was an ancestor of mine—for I am of a mixed breed, an infinitely shaded and exquisite Mongrel."

And if this cut too close, he drifted into a stupendous temperance parody, calling upon the New England Society to disband itself: "I see water, I see milk, I see the wild and deadly lemonade. . . . Next we shall see tea, then chocolate, then coffee—hotel coffee. . . . You are on the broad road which leads to dissipation . . ." Look at the way those lines about his "early Indian" ancestor drift into anarchy and burlesque, ever funnier, ever safer for that audience of Brahmins. Or the way the temperance parody softens the earlier blows. You could never tell when the knife with which he was taunting you was going to stop scratching the skin and actually poke through to muscle and bone—but you knew it would, and that he was ready to retract at the first sign of a real frown. He was one with the men and women who had their labor and their land taken to help build America. And he was one with the men and women who had done the taking. It was no postmodern confusion: it was the game he intended. It's not ambivalence if you can get away with it, and he could.

4

An Appeal in Behalf of Extending the Suffrage to Boys

If Twain's feelings about race had undergone a revolution between 1852, when he first left Hannibal, and the 1870s, when he experienced international celebrity, so, too, did his feelings about children. In that same letter he wrote his mother sneering at the multiracial "mass of human vermin" he found on the streets of New York, for instance, he called the homeless boys and girls of Manhattan "brats" and "trundle-bed trash—children, I mean."

Not an auspicious start for an author whose most famous character would be the semi-orphaned and homeless son of the town drunk. In fact, during the vital middle period of his career, children would become his great subject, dwarfing all others. From 1876 onward, he published book after book featuring child protagonists, usually boys, including some of the most famous in the nation's history: *Tom Sawyer*, *The Prince and the Pauper*, *Huck Finn*, and even the *Personal Recollections of Joan of Arc*. These publications coincided with the growth of the first modern market for juvenile fiction, inspired by "boys' books" such as Thomas Bailey Aldrich's *The Story of a Bad Boy* and Robert Louis Stevenson's *Treasure Island*, and "girls' books" such as Louisa May Alcott's *Little Women* and Johanna Spyri's *Heidi*. But Twain's efforts were not exclusively directed at turning a profit. He believed there were "heaps of money" to be made writing for children. As he would write later in life, though, he didn't want to become primarily a writer of books for or about children. He wanted to be an intermediary between the worlds of children and adults—an "ambassador of the children," as he said late in life. In this in-between—unsure of whether he was writing for parents or their children; unsure, truthfully, whose side he was on—he did much of his most memorable work.

And that work, contrary to the innocuous glow of nostalgia with which we tend to remember it, was often rough-edged and testy. It was more controversial, in its time, than his work on race relations. But what makes it most interesting, in retrospect, was how much it *paralleled* his work on race relations: how much it blended stereotypes with the search for something "authentic" and truly empathic. "An age category such as childhood," Colin Heywood tells us in *A History of Childhood* in 2001, "can hardly be explored without reference to other forms of social differentiation." Twain, a century and more earlier, seemed to know this intuitively. On race, travel was the engine for Twain's growth; on children, it would be parenthood. On the lecture circuit, in his novels, he would rehearse one or the other matter; the genius of *Huck Finn* would be putting them together in the same place. But first, he'd need to figure out what he wanted to say about children, and he had another boy in mind for that task.

From 1853, when he wrote that letter to his mother from New York, until he sat down to start writing *Tom Sawyer*, it took Twain twenty years for his heart to mature on the subject of children—decades during which American attitudes toward children also evolved rapidly. When we look back at children from the mid- and late nineteenth century, we tend to see a handful of images, a limited range of experience—the ones we salvage from books like *Huck* and *Tom* as well as *Little Women* or, a generation later, *Little House on the Prairie*. These images—and the way we remember them—tend to tilt rural, white, and wholesome, as if, as many modern Americans seem to think, the country was more homogenous back then, that families were more stable, that the churches were reliably full.

But the experience of childhood was as different across the social spectrum as it is today—more so, perhaps. One in six children didn't live to the age of five. One in six labored. In fields in the South, black

children harvested the same crops their slave grandparents did, for little or no compensation. In New York, immigrant children—Twain's
"trundle-bed trash," many of them—didn't know their birthdays.
In mining towns out west, many preteens were already experienced
smokers, swearers, and gamblers, and teachers sometimes felt obliged
to wear firearms in the classroom to maintain order. In cities, meanwhile, and small towns everywhere, a new middle class grew, and
with it several new generations of children who were expected to go
to school, to play in their free time, to get toys, and to do better than
their parents.

Things were changing, however. The idea that children shared a
common culture, or should, was in ascendance: by 1870, seven hundred doctors nationwide had specialties in children, and the number
was increasing. Public playgrounds, hitherto nonexistent, were starting to be built. Nascent social scientists began what would be called
the "child study" movement. In 1904, Clark University psychologist
G. Stanley Hall would publish *Adolescence* and credential the idea of
a teen age—a middle place between childhood and adulthood waiting to be discovered, and in turn examined.

Above all, reformers nationwide—teachers, politicians, religious
leaders of a largely progressive bent—regarded the growth of public
schooling as the essential revolution in the life of children. American schools in the late nineteenth century—the good ones, the ones
that spent upwards of twenty or thirty dollars per student per year
and insisted on college degrees for their teachers—were regimented
institutions. Desks were bolted down, and sometimes parceled out
forty or forty-eight to a room. Students rose in place when called
on to offer one-word or one-sentence responses to teachers' queries
or to recite what they had memorized. Compulsory attendance laws
were a vogue of education reform in the post–Civil War era: by
1890, twenty-seven states would have them. Kindergartens, an idea
imported from Germany, sprouted everywhere. So did high schools.
Readers like *Sheldon's Modern School Third Reader* revolutionized literacy, but loaded down eight-year-olds with lessons about hard work
and contented poverty—perfect lessons, it would seem, to inculcate
those new immigrants and the otherwise marginalized children being
brought into the system. When asked what he does when there is no

food, the boy hero of "A Contented Boy" tells a stranger that "I do as well as I can without. I work on, and never think of it."

In editorials that might ring familiarly to modern ears, American journalists wondered if schools were too "high pressure," if "marking and examination systems" stigmatized low-performing children, if districts with better tax bases provided better education than poorer districts. They thought that the "nineteenth-century" might be making kids soft, docile. Teachers were encouraged to schedule three-minute exercise sessions, to give students opportunities to think for themselves, and to experience nature. They brought strawberry plants into class so students could see where fruit came from. They offered "observational lessons" where students were escorted outside and made to watch insects. Teachers walked their students through intense memorization exercises on the one hand, and then picked up their professional journals with the other and read that "the learner educates himself by his personal experience." Editorial writers encouraged them to keep their students busy—"a young man who is busy has not time for tobacco"—but told them as well to "teach them to look and listen to the voices of nature."

For teachers of all political stripes, truancy was the bane of the age: "Truancy is an evil of great magnitude," wrote May L. Clifford of the State Normal School of Plymouth, New Hampshire, "a passion with some boys." Likewise, tobacco among children was widely regarded as "a real social scourge," its appeal most profound to "the boy" who "desire[s] . . . to appear a man." Worst of all, though, were the dime store novels—early detective, Western, or pirate books that Anthony Comstock in *Traps for the Young* called "literary poison" and "leprous influences." They were everywhere in the 1870s and 1880s: cheap, easy to buy, easy to throw out (paper covers) or return. Publishers like Beadle and Adams helpfully sized theirs to fit inside school textbooks. They were easy to read, too: "The dialogue is short, sharp, and continuous," William Graham Sumner wrote in "What Our Boys Are Reading" in *Scribner's* in 1878, "broken by a minimum of description." And they were "intensely stupid," Sumner emphasized.

At minimum, observers believed, the vogue of teen literacy and dime novels was creating a culture of imbecility: "It now and then happens that a youth of seventeen becomes almost an intellectual idiot or an effeminate weakling," Noah Porter, Yale's president, wrote, "by living exclusively upon the enfeebling wash or the poisoned stimulants that are sold so readily under the title of tales and novels." At most, it was promising a wave of youth violence: fourteen-year-old Jesse Pomeroy, accused in 1874 of murdering two other children, told an interviewer that he had read sixty of the "blood and thunder" stories, about "killing and scalping injuns and so forth," and said they "excited" him to bloodshed.

By 1883 and 1884, the debate was fully joined. In Cincinnati, William Berner's trial and the tragic riot that followed seemed to prove that teenage boys were attracted to violence like moths to light. In Milwaukee, a journalist named George W. Peck published a comic novel, *Peck's Bad Boy and His Pa*, and it sold in the hundreds of thousands. The tone was coarse, urban, raucous, with lots of dialect, play swearing ("Helen Damnation"), pranks, drinking, and graphic beatings. The "'Bad Boy' is not a 'myth,'" Peck wrote, and the nation agreed. Across the country, states passed laws banning or restricting the distribution of violent or salacious publications. Newspaper editorials railed against what they called "the bad boy of America," a distinctly American creation, a kid who could not be civilized even though he was growing up in the middle of a civilization. His "language is slang and profanity," they wrote, "his amusement is violence." "While other nations are giving their attention to the decline of imperialism and the decay of commerce and loyalty," they wrote, "America is called upon to protect itself against the fell swoop of its children."

Newspapers dutifully reported stories of children committing crimes or dying young or killing each other, often with the inspiration of a dime novel or two. One boy playing hockey might brain another with his stick, watch as the second boy died, and be taken into custody. In a Boston newspaper, you could read about a twelve-year-old boy named James Kelly and a fourteen-year-old companion named O'Connor who were arrested for firing two rifles randomly along the Boston and Albany Road, their stated ambition to "shoot anything we could hit." In New York, you might read about three teenagers arrested holding "four gold-mounted revolvers, a number of actresses' photographs, and several dime novels." In Cincinnati, you could read about the "Jesse James Gang . . . organized according to the heroic juvenile literature," and "having good quarters in the second story of an unoccupied stable," committing burglaries "for a considerable time."

To a modern reader, the number of these stories is simply numbing. And when children weren't shooting, or stealing, or clubbing one another, there were other hazards—ones where the carelessness of adults was to blame. Children, it seemed, were both criminals *and* victims. A brick might fall on a ten-year-old boy's head without explanation and be reported in one paragraph on page 3. Girls walking home from school or from work were assaulted with frequency: "INSULTING LITTLE GIRLS" ran the typical headline. Large-scale tragedies were uncovered: 1,200 children died every year in Philadelphia alone, Dr. J. Cheston Morris told the Social Science Association, from drinking milk sold in improperly cleaned and treated jars.

And individual fatalities were reported with lamentable, gruesome calm: when critics attacked Twain for exposing children to violent subject matter in *Huck Finn*—and they would—he'd point at these kinds of articles and wonder what *they* had been reading. In Providence, a mother turned away from her four-year-old girl to close some window blinds, and the child "ran into a table on which a kerosene lamp sat, knocking the lamp onto herself and immolating her clothing." Her "cries," the *Journal* observed, "were 'pitiful to hear' until she died" later that evening. In Boston, "Deios Mars, 18 months old . . . intently watch[ed] his grandmother" clean "a pair of gloves with naphtha, which was in an ordinary-sized teacup." When she "had occasion to go across the room . . . the little boy . . . took hold of the cup and drank" the solvent: "In less than five minutes he was seized with spasms, and in ten minutes he was dead."

Partly in response to this perceived chaos among American children, the United States Senate in the early 1880s took up and then argued over the "Blair Education Bill," which would have allocated the then unheard-of sum of $105 million to extend the system of "good" public schools across the country. Proponents of the bill argued, as Horace Mann had in the 1840s, the "*absolute* right of every human being that comes into the world to an education," and hoped that more schools and tight truancy laws would stanch the perceived rise of delinquency and violence. Opponents countered that all the reading and writing would only serve to promote, as the *Nation* argued, "the special needs of the ignorant, the weak, the lazy, and the incompetent . . ."

It is an amazing, underexamined moment in American cultural history. American parents contemplated, and debated, the possibility that their children should be raised not by themselves but by the media and the schools. "Who Should Have Charge of the Education of Our Children?" editorial writers asked. There were class issues, and there were race issues, and there were religious issues: people were arguing about whether or not poor immigrants, blacks, and even Catholics should receive schooling. And they were arguing over the children of a growing industrial middle class, regarding those newly entitled kids with a mix of deference and resentment. The *Boston Globe*, for instance, ran a poem entitled "The Mechanical Boy": "Every indulgence is claimed as a right / By the lively Mechanical Boy. / But urge him to labor, though ever so slight, / That instant he's stupid and coy . . ." But what emerged politically was a language that discussed *all* children, and how to raise *all* of them—and whether that job should be farmed out. The Blair Education Bill, in fact, was rejected or tabled no less than ten times in the 1880s as its opponents argued "the principle, which is urged as a universal one, that the parent has the right to do what he thinks best with his child" and its supporters countered that "the parent has no monopoly of responsibility or privilege in the education of the child."

Against this backdrop, Twain's own attitudes on children changed quickly, maturing and synchronizing to the national discussion. Looking back, a modern reader can trace one line that shows a rising national panic about bad boys reaching its peak in the mid-1880s, and a second line showing Twain himself reaching a creative peak on the same issue culminating with the release of *Huck Finn* in 1885. At first, no more than a decade removed from his own boyhood, his earliest portraits of children were merciless. In the *New York Sunday Mercury* in early 1864, for instance, he published "Those Blasted Children," describing a group of "noisy and inevitable children" disrupting his midday "reveries," "soldiers—infantry . . . not more

than thirty or forty of them" making noise in the hall, arguing—
in dialect—over lunch ("Gimme ever so little o' that, will you?"),
over toys ("You wouldn't lemme play with that dead rat"), over who
was black and who wasn't: "Sandy Baker, I know what makes your
pa's hair kink so . . ." Their "talk," which takes over his column, is
"amusing," Twain notes, but "not instructive." "It is a living wonder
to me," Twain writes, "that I haven't scalped some of those children
before now."

He also offered medical advice. For the child with measles: saffron
tea, and "something to make the patient sleep—say a table-spoonful
of arsenic." For the child with fits: "soak it"—the child—"in a barrel of rain-water over night . . . if this does not put an end to its
troubles, soak it a week." For the infant that stammers: "remove the
under-jaw." For cramps: "take your offspring . . . and immerse it in
a commodious soup-tureen . . . [P]lace it over a slow fire, and add
reasonable quantities of pepper, mustard, horse-radish, saltpetre,
strychnine . . ."

By the mid-1860s, however—about the time his views on race
began to shift—his approach to children also began a subtle change.
His stories about kids still endorsed the idea that a child's natural
state was a kind of criminality. On that measure, the popularity of
the dime novels and the reports of teenage misconduct left him oddly
in the mainstream. From another perspective, though, he had made a
fundamental switch, one that would hint at revolutionary directions.
Making fun of children was good. But making fun of preacherly stories about "good" boys and girls—the ones that filled the Sheldon
readers and Sunday-school sermons nationwide—was better.

In the San Francisco magazine the *Youth's Companion* in June in
1865, he offered two short pieces, "Advice for Good Little Boys" and
"Advice for Good Little Girls." To the boys, he advised: "You ought
never to take anything that don't belong to you—if you can't carry
it off," and "You should never do anything wicked and then lay it
on your brother, when it is just as convenient to lay it on another
boy." To the girls, he advised: "If at any time you find it necessary to
correct your brother, do not correct him with mud . . . it is better to
scald him a little . . ."

That same year, he offered "The Christmas Fireside" in the *Califor-*

nian entitled, "The Story of the Bad Little Boy That Bore a Charmed Life," about a boy named "Jim" whose life inverted every cliché of the "Sunday books":

> But the strangest thing that ever happened to Jim was the time he went boating on Sunday and didn't get drowned, and that other time that he got caught out in the storm when he was fishing on Sunday, and didn't get struck by lightning. Why, you might look, and look, and look through the Sunday-school books, from now till next Christmas, and you would never come across anything like this. Oh, no—you would find that all the bad boys who go boating on Sunday invariably get drowned, and all the bad boys who get caught out in storms, when they are fishing on Sunday, infallibly get struck by lightning. Boats with bad boys in them always upset on Sunday, and it always storms when bad boys go fishing on the Sabbath. How this Jim ever escaped is a mystery to me.

The story ends as "Jim" grows up, "married, and raised a large family, and brained them all with an axe one night, and got wealthy by all manner of cheating and rascality, and now he is the infernalest wickedest scoundrel in his native village, and is universally respected, and belongs to the Legislature."

Five years later, in the *Buffalo Express*, he published a companion piece, "The Story of the Good Little Boy Who Did Not Prosper," about "Jacob Blivens," who "always obeyed his parents, no matter how absurd and unreasonable their demands were," who "would not play hookey, even when his sober judgment told him it was the most profitable thing he could do," and who "was so honest that he was simply ridiculous." The story ends as he is blown to bits in an "old iron foundry" by a surreal combination of leftover nitroglycerin and an authority figure's misplaced spank: "they had to hold five inquests on him to find out whether he was dead or not, and how it occurred. You never saw a boy scattered so."

This inversion mattered to him, and he played with it over and over, and the underlying point was always the same: children should not be expected to live up to standards set by adults, and he was perfectly willing to be the adult who, with a smirk, stood up as their counsel. He wrote about George Washington's boyhood, and turned that founding father's most celebrated virtue into a drollery: "As a boy he gave no promise of the greatness he was one day to achieve. He was ignorant of the commonest accomplishments of youth. He could not even lie . . ."

He wrote about Ben Franklin, and systematically tore up Poor Richard's most famous aphorisms about hard work and steady habits: "His maxims were full of animosity toward boys," Twain wrote in July 1870. " 'Early to bed and early to rise / Make a man healthy and wealthy and wise' . . . As if it were any object to a boy to be healthy and wealthy and wise on such terms."

He even wrote about the Son of God, claiming to find an apocryphal New Testament in a New York library that showed a boy Jesus bringing toys to life, being mistaken for a "sorcerer," and so filled with "resentments" that he kills boy after boy who displeases him, resurrecting some and not others. "His society was pleasant," Twain notes of the boy Jesus, "but attended by serious drawbacks." Most pointedly, given Twain's own struggles in school, boy Jesus kills the schoolmaster who tries to whip him for failing to "tell his letters."

Twain understood this material was not the kind of writing about children that made "heaps of money." The *Atlantic*, which had fallen over itself to publish "A True Story" around this time, rejected out of hand Twain's efforts on children: it wouldn't "leave" them with "a single Presbyterian, Baptist, Unitarian, Episcopalian, Methodist, or Millerite *paying* subscriber," Howells told him.

Seen from that perspective, in fact, Twain could only recognize what we have long forgotten: that he was more radical talking about children than talking about African-Americans. And for the time being, that suited him. As Twain married and assimilated to domestic life in the 1870s, his portraits of children grew denser, richer, more personal, and showed every sign of artistic commitment—but they still maintained this initial subversive spark, and always would.

The turning point, perhaps, was reading Thomas Aldrich's best-selling *Bad Boy* in late 1869, though Twain, in what looks like a competitive pique, claimed privately to disdain it. "This is the story of a bad boy," Aldrich's memoirish novel began, "Well, not such a very bad, but a pretty bad boy; and I ought to know, for I am, or rather I was, that boy myself." "No one else seems to have thought of telling the story of a boy's life, with so great desire to show what a boy's life is, and so little purpose of teaching what it should be," Howells gushed in the *Atlantic* in early 1870 as the book raced through eleven editions, and converted respectable readers to the notion that they could swallow a moderately bad boy as long as the language was clean and he seemed likely to turn out right. It is easy to see how Twain might have kicked himself that he didn't think of it first, and write that book, and without the stilted and halting "oughts" and "rathers."

Or it may have been Twain's writing *The Gilded Age*, a book so pessimistic about the politics of its time that it might understandably drive its author back to his "golden" childhood. Or it may have been that second day of marriage to Olivia Langdon, when the ghosts of his childhood in Hannibal came flooding back: those "old faces," revivified, would become Tom, and Huck, and dozens of others. Or perhaps it was the marriage itself, and the assumption of adult duties it implied. Twain always liked acting "boyishly"—as much, to draw the parallel closer, as he liked acting like he was of another color—and savored the touch of creativity embedded in adolescent rebellion. This idea resonated more fully for him once he accepted the responsibilities of husband and father, however. There was always a "gang" he wanted to revive, even if the other "boys" were reasonably starched grown men like Howells or Aldrich. Even Olivia, whom he called "Livy," forswore any such self-evident nickname for her husband, and instead called him "Youth."

The falling-into-childhood came naturally to him, and only grew stronger as he grew older: "All acquired and meaningless conventions were laid aside," one New York schoolteacher, watching Twain talk to a twelve-year-old, observed, "we said what we meant, and spontaneity took the place of calculation." At the same time, what finally catalyzed all this—what fully transformed the author of those uneven essays into an "ambassador" for children—was something remarkably uncomplicated: he and Olivia became parents. Five days after Langdon Clemens was born in November 1870, as underweight and sickly as his father had been thirty-five years before, Twain was sending out letters to relatives, narrated by the baby: "They all say I look very old & venerable—& I am aware, myself, that I never smile. Life seems a serious thing . . ."

As biographers note, Twain seemed detached from this child during his eighteen-month life, on the road much of the time, stoic in letters. Yet, it is clear that Langdon's birth unlocked something expressive. It was at this time that Twain made his connection with Sociable Jimmy, the boy whose spirit, he wished, would descend into his; he turned eleven again in that church in Paris, Illinois, and "Sociable Jimmy," in fact, would be the first time he tried in public a child's voice. Sometime just before or after Langdon was born, Twain tried an *unmediated* boy's voice for the first time in an extended piece, in a fragment scholars now call the "Boy's Manuscript": "I don't take any pleasure, nights, now, but carrying on with the boys out in the street . . ." And as he prepared his next lecture tour, he fell upon an idea so politically raucous that he ached to try it in public, although he never did: it would be called "An Appeal in Behalf of Extending the Suffrage to Boys," and it would "lift up a voice for the poor little male juvenile."

And when Langdon died of diphtheria—a death for which, as always, Twain blamed himself—the father mourned little in public. Within weeks, however, Twain began to write *The Adventures of Tom Sawyer*, and didn't stop writing about children for two decades. This fixation with childhood was about Langdon, in part. But it was also about Susy, Clara, and Jean, the three daughters Olivia bore in the six years that followed. Twain wrote about children like he was trying to revive something that was lost, but also like a father with living kin as his models, his playmates, even his editors—an extraordinary perspective that gave him twice as many reasons to want to bring fictive children to life with as much vivacity and empathy as possible.

Tom Sawyer begins with Aunt Polly looking all over for Tom using her "state pair," her formal spectacles, the ones she "seldom or never looked *through* . . . for so small a thing as a boy." Refocus our state pair, Twain seems to be telling us, and look at children freshly: it is a brilliant, subtle invocation.

As Twain composed the book, over three years, he found a place to put the ghosts of his childhood. Hannibal became "St. Petersburg," another way, of course, of saying "Heaven," and many of its citizens became minor characters. Tom himself was a "composite": bits of Twain (truthfully, many bits), as well as Will Bowen and other respectable, troublemaking children. Twain's mother became Aunt Polly, Tom's caregiver. Tom Blankenship, Twain's favorite disreputable playmate, became Tom's sidekick, Huck Finn. Sandy, the slave who took part in Sam Clemens's embarrassing "playing bear" episode, became a young slave named Jim. Laura Hawkins, the childhood playmate who thought young Sam had hair like a girl, became Becky Thatcher, the judge's daughter.

Events and locales from Hannibal, too, recur. The river, the island, the hills, the cave. Like Sam Clemens, Tom nearly dies from measles, is mistakenly thought drowned in the river, gives matches to an imprisoned town drunk (who, unlike his real life counterpart, is not immolated). He has a good brother to play alter ego to his mischievous one: Sam had Henry, and Tom has Sid. ("Henry was a very much finer and better boy than ever Sid was," Twain would note later.) Tom gets doused by buckets of cold water by well-meaning Aunt Polly, just as Jane Clemens, a hydropath, did to his creator. He hates school, loves role-play. He is surrounded by cats, the cats familiars to the boys and girls, who like Twain's childhood peers "meow" to lure each other outdoors.

By borrowing realistic characters and events from his own childhood, tinted by the warmth of memory, Twain gave flesh and bone to the cartoonish parodies of Sunday-school books he had written in the 1860s. But he added things, too—for all the attention understandably paid to Twain's autobiographical impulses in fiction, the revolution in *Tom Sawyer* lay in what he made up. Tom was a boy who didn't obey the rules of the readers and Sunday-school books, or even more respected children's novels—but he didn't kill his family with an ax, either, like Twain's "charmed" bad boy from a decade before. Instead, he did both good and bad, was punished and escaped punishment, and by novel's end found a fortune in gold in that old cave—a fairly savage revision of the Sunday-school stories of the time, which had inundated American homes with images of heroic boys who found respectability through hard work and deference. Other books, like Aldrich's, had "bad boys," but the bad boys reformed. Twain appeared to be flirting with the idea that reform was the villain.

There is not much plot to *Tom Sawyer*: Tom gets in and out of trouble with Aunt Polly, Tom courts Becky Thatcher, Tom's "harum-scarum" gets him in and out of trouble with the whole town, from the teachers and judges to "Injun Joe," the book's lamentable villain. He takes "lashings," and "flaying[s]," sometimes "merciless[ly]," or at least "vigorous[ly]." He gets several "whipping[s]," has his head "cracked . . . soundly," while his friends get "knocked . . . sprawling." He receives numerous guarantees that he will be "skinned alive," or something like it. And he gets celebrated as a hero, or fussed over when a grateful town who thought him dead finds out he is not, or rich when he wasn't: "their past history was raked up," Twain notes, after Tom, with Huck Finn by his side, find the treasure and get yanked up the ladder of class, "and discovered to bear marks of conspicuous originality."

School is horrible: all "captivity and fetters." The lessons are all repetition; the teacher, Mr. Dobbins, dull and violent, is responsible for the book's worst beating. But play is horrible in a different, pleasurable way: Tom and his friends pretend to be robbers, pirates, Indians, Robin Hood; they play destroyers and subverters of their civilization. Tom always takes the lead, and uses some fairly ludicrous source materials for scholarly authority: Ned Buntline's *Black Avenger of the Spanish Main*, Joseph Cundall's *Robin Hood and His Merry Foresters*. Their play is joyous, engrossing. But when it isn't, Tom and his friends think profoundly lonesome thoughts. They even think of suicide, although no one inside or outside the book takes them seriously: "Ah, if he could only die *temporarily*," Tom wonders. Of course, that is exactly what he spends one-third of the book doing—thought drowned, thought dying of measles, thought lost in a cave.

Along the way, Tom ceaselessly engages in psychological warfare with his caregivers—a fight they start, but he is all too eager to keep going. He is only defused by their love—and then, only briefly, as that love always implies sanction for the harum-scarum that follows. Aunt Polly knows he is messing with her, but he clearly interests her more than brother Sid, who wouldn't disobey a rule on a dare and happily rats out those who do. *Tom Sawyer*, in fact, is one of the great works about parental ambivalence, of the mixed messages parents send children. Mothers call their children "poor" and "abused" on one page, recall the last beating on the next, give out "cuffs and kisses" in the same day, according to their "varying moods."

But it is also one of the great books about how children steal the agenda-setting power from parents. It's not war, but it's close. Tom knows the etiquette, can read the signs in a grown-up face: "He said to himself, 'Now it's coming!' And the next instant he was sprawling on the floor." Knowing the etiquette, he times the beatings, and controls their effects. He takes a beating for something his good brother did, so he can make Aunt Polly feel guilty. He takes a beating at school in the hope that Becky Thatcher will admire him for it. "What's a licking," he wonders coolly at one point. Reacting against being called "Thomas," he says, "that's the name they lick me by."

By book's end, Twain's portrait of this psychological warfare is sublime. Many of the things adults do to help children also look and feel like abuse, scarcely less so than the beatings: Aunt Polly performs dentistry by tying a rope to one of Tom's teeth and shoving a hot coal in his face, causing him to jump back with molar-wrenching alacrity. But many of the things the kids do seem genuinely dangerous or cruel as well, and oddly reflective of the parents in that way. Pages after Aunt Polly sticks that coal in Tom's face, Joe Harper, we learn, has stuck a lit firecracker under his mother's nose; shortly after Aunt Polly refuses to apologize for wrongly whipping Tom ("discipline forbade that"), Tom withholds evidence that he loves Aunt Polly to maintain his advantage.

Polly knows something is off, calling herself an "old fool" on the second page of the book. But she is less worried that he can outsmart her—"how is a body to know what's coming," she asks herself—than that she is raising a heartless monster. "He warn't *bad*, so to say," she insists, over and over, the "so to say" speaking insecure volumes. And Tom knows this, knows she's hard and soft at the same time, and uses it against her, which makes him neither monster nor not—and which leaves us, and her, looking into the soul of a child and seeing only mystery, our child-rearing practices, whatever they are, utterly without mandate.

Twain was proud of what he was doing, but a little unsure, too, about who he was addressing, and to what end. It was, in fact, a fluid time for children's literature. Despite the gendering implied by nomenclature like "boys' books," girls read what was meant for boys, and vice versa. Likewise, age distinctions meant little: reviewers routinely spoke of books that were "nominally intended for the little ones," but actually "cater[ed] to the grown-up folks." Howells urged Twain to take Tom Sawyer to adulthood, believing the book was so good that it would be a shame otherwise. "You wont [*sic*] have such another chance," he told Twain in July 1875, "don't waste it on a *boy*."

But Twain, who usually took Howells's advice, ignored him here: "I have finished the story & didn't take the chap beyond childhood . . ." For emphasis, Twain even added a short conclusion, in which he told the reader that this "being strictly a history of a *boy*, it must stop here; the story could not go much further without becoming the history of a *man*." Italics and all, it was a brilliant conclusion that matched the introduction, when Aunt Polly tried to see Tom through her "state pair." We shouldn't be interested in children for their value as potential adults, Twain told his readers. We can be interested in them for themselves.

Twain, however, was more ambivalent about the issue of audience. Having decided to end it while Tom was still a child, Twain insisted, "It is *not* a boy's book, at all . . . It is only written for adults." Howells, reading the complete manuscript, dissented: "I think you ought to treat it explicitly as a boy's story," he told Twain. "Mrs. Clemens" agreed with Howells, so Twain consented that "the book should issue as a book for boys, pure & simple." But the distinction made no formal sense: there are parts of *Tom Sawyer* that are directly addressed to adults, which raises the curious question of what, exactly, children were supposed to do when they were reading those passages. When the book was published, reviewers weren't sure what it was, either: they had no category for a book that blurred generic boundaries so aggressively. The *New York Times*, for instance, saw what Twain was trying to do, and complimented him for not writing the kind of preachy book in which "a child was supposed to be a vessel which was to be constantly filled up." But had Twain written a dime-store novel instead? the *Times* pondered. "Without advocating the utter suppression of that wild disposition which is natural in many a fine lad," they added, "we think our American boys require no extra promptings."

Likely, Twain pondered, too. Who, really, was the audience, and who was the subject? And if he wasn't writing a sermon, and he wasn't writing exploitative trash—underestimating children in one mode, underestimating them even more in the other—then what was he doing? Wonderfully, though, he was committed to this confusion, wherever that might lead.

5

Boy No. 2

In the summer of 1876, before *Tom Sawyer* was even published in America, Twain began work on "Boy No. 2," as Howells called him, while relaxing on a farm belonging to in-laws in Elmira. There is not much about slavery in *Tom Sawyer*, and what is there, arguably, is far more disturbingly idyllic than the portrait of childhood so often celebrated for its nostalgic glow. St. Petersburg is the kind of town where a slave gets beaten, discreetly, off-screen, to be kept *from* doing work—as Aunt Polly does to young Jim to prevent him from whitewashing the famous fence in Tom's stead. And Jim is little more than show: when we meet him, he is singing "Buffalo Gals," a minstrel standard, and seems to have little to do. Tom's a good whistler; he learned this from "a negro." That's the extent of their service to him.

This stupefied calm is disturbed, at least from a political standpoint, when a little white boy in outsized men's clothing shows up carrying, fittingly, a dead cat. It is when Huck Finn shows up in the book that racial epithets do, too. And so, too, does a more complicated conversation about race. Huck uses racial slurs unconsciously, but he also respects African-Americans in a way Tom does not: they almost immediately begin arguing about a cure for warts, with Huck citing his source as a "nigger," and Tom disrespecting both Huck and his source. Later in the book, Huck tells Tom that a slave named "Uncle Jake" lets him sleep in his master's hayloft, and gives him extra food when he is hungry; in exchange, Huck "tote[s] water for Uncle Jake whenever he wants me to," and "eat[s] *with* him." Uncle Jake likes him, Huck explains, "becuz I don't ever act as if I was above him."

In St. Petersburg, only Huck knows privation ("A body's got to do things when he's awful hungry," he tells Tom), only Huck is servant to a slave, and only Huck is perceptive enough to recognize that the slave would value a show (and show it is, as Huck makes clear) of equality. By book's end, one can see that Twain is starting to discover that Huck is interesting—maybe more interesting than Tom—and is giving him more onstage time, and more interesting things to say ("I ain't everybody, and I can't *stand* it") in a distinctive dialect that jumped off the page.

Tom is at war with grown-ups, but he savors the war: it is a codependency among people more alike than different. But Huck likes neither the war nor the peace, and does not share the codependency. He is somewhere where race and youth intersect in a more potent way, and where even a benign adult gesture like trying to fix a kid's hair is a profane invasion: "They comb me all to thunder," he says, and a century later one can feel the bite of the teeth of that comb on his unkempt forehead. Without Huck, *Tom Sawyer* is cute and sneakily deep about the matter of how we raise our children. With him, the issue of the rift between children and adults—and its surprising resemblance to the racial divide—is available for existential examination.

Tom needs grown-ups. But Huck does not.

Twain's main regret about *Tom*, Twain told Howells, was that it wasn't written in the first person. He would fix that. Embarking on *Huck Finn*, he used the first person, as he had with Langdon, but this boy didn't sound like formal and "old" like Langdon. He sounded, as Shelley Fisher Fishkin argued in *Was Huck Black?*, much more like Sociable Jimmy:

> *You don't know about me, without you have read a book by the name of "The Adventures of Tom Sawyer," but that ain't no matter. That book was made by Mr. Mark Twain, and he told the truth, mainly. There was things which he stretched, but mainly he told the truth . . .*

Is reading dynamic? one wonders as these words dance past. Is there enough time between each word? Does the imagination suspend its judgment until the period, or is a sentence a chain of the smaller sentences composed as you read, one new word in each instant changing and shaping the meaning of the sentence?

It is if you read like you listen, and you write like you talk, and you talk very slowly with lots of pauses. Here is the real start of *Huck Finn*, as it emerged from several drafts—

You.
You don't.
You don't know.
You don't know about.
You don't know about me.

—an invitation (how many books start with "you," which is to say, how many books start with us?), followed by a series of challenges, telling us first that we don't act, that we don't know, and that, finally, we've never seen this kid before. The thinly buried contempt of an early teenager for his teachers, his parents, for his society. Huck knows he better keep it buried. So does Twain. But it's there, some inner rage, a real, authentic, undiluted flash of a child's torment and a child's pleasure. Something that started a long time ago, back in the old white town, in the days before the war.

The first person made the difference. If *Tom Sawyer* had been dappled with old Hannibal, *Huck Finn* was a different matter. Twain's memories were reconstructed into new, electric plotlines that pricked at childhood traumas. As Twain wrote those opening chapters, he continued to pour not only Tom Blankenship into Huck, but also himself and other children, too. Tom Sawyer remained the same polyglot as before, but looked more bullying and egotistical from Huck's point of view. Jim, a child in *Tom Sawyer*, was a man now, and moved into the foreground. Mary Ann Newcomb, one of Twain's childhood teachers and a Clemens boarder, became Miss Watson, Jim's master and Huck's tormentor-educator. Jimmy Finn, Hannibal's most celebrated town drunk (until he died in a tanning vat), was poured straight into Pap Finn, Huck's father. At novel's start, he is believed dead, but is resurrected to try to grift the boy's share of the loot he and Tom Sawyer found in the cave at the end of the last novel, to kidnap Huck and force the boy to fake his own death and flee.

And Huck, like Tom Blankenship's older brother, would find an escaped slave on an island and decide to help him. In real life, Neriam Todd was caught and murdered, his mutilated body left to terrify Sam Clemens and his friends. When Twain reached the parallel passage in the novel, though, Huck goes ashore dressed as a girl and discovers the bounty party before they can sail to the island and find the escaped slave. No bounty hunters would kill Jim. Instead, he and Huck sail away down the Mississippi, and Twain rewrites a traumatic event from his childhood with a happier—if not exactly happy—outcome.

What follows—as Twain wrote in that lovely, flat script of his, in the glistening hills of New York State, in the summer of 1876, in a little octagonal study filled with cats, its windows gleefully thrown open in inclement weather—was fantasy projection and subterranean memoir. Huck and Jim sail down the river, then accidentally sail past Cairo, Illinois, the left turn to the Ohio River and to liberty. A steamboat runs over their raft, Jim disappears, Huck is taken in by a "Southern" family named Grangerford, while Jim is sent offstage to hide in a swamp. Along the way, Huck adjusts, as his creator did, to the idea that he might shift to the side of the abolitionists. At first, Huck plays practical jokes on Jim—a snake in his sleeping bag, for instance—and Jim is simply a passive and uninformed victim, or seems to be. When Huck insists that an accident that happened to the raft was a dream, however, and compels Jim to "interpret" the dream, Jim upbraids him the way Aunt Rachel upbraided Misto C, with a flash of anger not suited to any stereotype of docility, or even a strategic reading of how a slave might handle an unreliable and playfully malign white presence: "Trash is what people is dat puts dirt on de head er dey fren's en makes 'em ashamed," he tells Huck. And when Huck responds, "It was fifteen minutes before I could work myself up to go and humble myself to a nigger—but I done it, and I warn't ever sorry for it afterwards," one hears a twisted and rusticated echo of Twain's comment in private correspondence that "nine tenths" of racial "guilt" lies "fairly and justly . . . on the white race."

On race, in fact, Twain seemed to be drawing upon all his resources to bring something to life: some vision of an attractive
cross-racial world, something that could happen, or something that
was already happening, but was denied by law and custom. "A True
Story" and "Sociable Jimmy" offered themselves as careful transcrip-
tions carrying messages across the color line; the Plymouth Rock
speech was a slick assault on that same line. But this was a dream
by comparison, with the logic of one. Twain built Jim from a mix
of black men he knew, from Daniel Quarles and later free black servants like John T. Lewis, who once saved members of Twain's family
on a runaway horse carriage, and George Griffin, Twain's butler in
Hartford. And he built him from the simple-minded yet loyal black
men who starred in so many minstrel shows and Victorian fictions
about the antebellum South: Jim sees ghosts and panics, tells an elaborate corkscrewing story about his bank account, but also calls Huck
"honey" and stays loyally by his (and, eventually, Tom Sawyer's) side.

Twain lifted plot points from slave narratives, the well-known
first-person accounts of servitude and escape written by free blacks—
an interesting recognition of authentic African-American voices
as well as the abolitionist cause. He also seemed to show a subtle
empathy for, and knowledge of, the language of slaves. In the second chapter, for instance, Jim brags to other slaves that he has been
"rode . . . all over the world" by witches, until his "back was all over
saddle-boils." But the reader who knows the ropes—and who, one
wonders, would that reader have been in 1885?—might have recognized a signal coming from behind this superstitious façade. Claiming to be ridden by witches until his back was "saddle-boils" was a
loaded thing for a man owned by Miss Watson and about to escape
to say; given that some slaveholders masqueraded as witches and
ghosts to terrify their slaves, and their slaves knew it, Jim might have
been using a code to tell the others that he was being beaten to his
limit. Jim likewise tells his audience that the witches then rode him
to "New Orleans": as the southernmost point on the Mississippi,
and a major slave market, New Orleans was a slave's code for hell.
Jim vows that he "knowed all kinds of signs," all sorts of veiled ways
the world and its residents communicate covert meanings to each
other—but Twain seems to know them, too.

In fact, he left signs like these all over the place, all pointing toward a secret history of American culture: there is mixing to which you'd never admit, he said to his imaginary audience over and over in a subtle low voice. Raftsmen, clogging up a whole chapter with some remarkable partying, "patted Juba," and have a "break-down," dancing what they could only have learned from minstrel shows, or directly from African-Americans. There was, too, intelligence in places you didn't expect. Jim and Huck talk about the wisdom of blacks they meet, and what a good job they do concealing it from whites—a topic they *both* like:

> "Dat Jack's a good nigger, en pooty smart."
> "Yes, he is. He ain't ever told me you was here; told me to come, and he'd show me a lot of water-moccasins. If anything happens, he ain't mixed up in it. He can say he never seen us together, and it'll be the truth."

And everywhere, there were signs of Twain's vision that popular culture contains the roots of wisdom, growth, and dangerous ideology. Best, perhaps, is that scene where Huck dresses up like a girl—on Jim's suggestion—to go into town and get information incognito. It leads, like all males cross-dressing in the nineteenth century, to the hilarious reveal. The woman Huck encounters, Judith Loftus, finds three ways Huck does a bad job playing a girl: he throws too well, can't thread a needle, and claps his legs together to catch a rock thrown at his lap, something someone used to wearing skirts would never do.

But Twain plays this broad comedy for something more than laughs. Huck races back to Jim, and tells him that "They're after us!" even though they are only after Jim. It is an unconscious bit of empathy that tells what Huck really learned from the reveal: if gender was nothing more than performance, then maybe race was nothing more than performance, too, and maybe, then, Huck—or anybody— could use the word "us" a lot more than we've been trained to do.

On childhood, meanwhile, Twain poked and teased at contemporary political debates. It might have been hard for a Victorian reader to see through a scene like the one with Mrs. Loftus and Huck's skirt and recognize what an extraordinary example it represents of the dynamic ways that children learn. But that same Victorian reader wouldn't have needed more than five minutes to recognize that Huck was one of those contemporary "bad boys" against which countless editorial screeds were being composed. To make him a hero would guarantee a mixed reception at best: "Who on earth except Mark Twain," the *New York Sun* would ask nine years later, when the book was published, "would ever cotton to a youth like Huckleberry Finn?"

But the particulars were even more extraordinary. In these early pages, Twain wrote *Huck* as if it were a finely tuned commentary on education reform during the era. He was writing in a political environment where proponents of reform insisted that "courses of study must have for their centre the child," and critics sarcastically responded that "any child who could analyse the system intelligently would conclude that the children are the most important persons in this world." In such a climate, writing about children *as* children alone meant taking sides with the reformers. For many, children remained appendages of their parents' will; for others, the story of a child still only mattered as a prelude to the adult he or she would become. But Twain, whatever other messages he might send, had cleanly crossed both those lines and was focused on the child as an autonomous figure in American culture, both fulfilling and repudiating stereotypes.

Huck wasn't just a bad boy. He was a specific type, the child "never sent to school or church" who compulsory attendance laws and school finance schemes like the Blair Education Bill were supposed to repatriate into society. Huck spends the early chapters being made to learn to read and write and cipher and moralize: we see him receiving lessons on Moses, heaven and hell, spelling homework, and graduating from someone who can only make a "mark" into someone who can "read, and write just a little."

Then there was this new, distilled Tom Sawyer, who shows up in Chapter Two to offer to tie Jim to a tree "for fun" and induct Huck into a gang he governs using rules he's gleaned from "pirate books, and robber books." If Huck was one type—the boy outside the system, being forced inside by well-meaning reformers—then Tom is pared down here to another type: the boy on whom literacy was wasted, who read too many dime novels, the "ambitious, unscrupulous adventurer," as Father Isaac Hecker complained, who "is the legitimate product of" a common school "education."

For the most part, education progressives, had they been reading over Twain's shoulder, would have witnessed their own wisdom repeated back to them. In Tom, they would have seen the kind of boy, they insisted, who would be turned away from "trash" by systemic reading instruction in early primary school. In Pap Finn, they could have recognized a parody of the position, held by many opponents of education reform, that parents governed their children absolutely: "Here's the law a-standing ready to take a man's son away from him—a man's own son . . ." he slurs, during a long tirade directed against the spread of government. And they would have seen Huck's rejection of Miss Watson's tedious version of heaven on the third page of the book—"then she told me all about the bad place, and I said I wished I was there"—as a mirthful endorsement of their views that moral instruction should be, as "the Teachers of Maine" insisted, "fresh and breezy."

Similarly, they could have recognized the scenes where Huck gets beaten as affirmation of their anti–corporal punishment beliefs, which were so fierce that they couldn't even advocate detention or teachers raising their voices. "Be not impatient because the child does not love his lessons," they counseled. "It is cruel as well as stupid to attempt to scold a child into learning a lesson . . ." As teachers read how Huck lived comfortably within nature, how he feuded with Tom Sawyer about the value of lived experience over book-fed fantasies—"I reckoned he believed in the A-rabs and the elephants," Huck says about the Sunday-school picnic Tom's gang disrupts, "but as for me I think different. It had all the marks of a Sunday school"—they could have consulted their own professional journals and told themselves: "*We* could teach that boy."

Except, of course, they couldn't. He skipped school, and they were devoutly anti-truant: boys who fit Huck's irredeemable profile should be sent, they believed, to "work farms." And he smoked, and defended the practice. And he wasn't confused on the matter of God. Twain fills the first two chapters with a remarkable list of superstitions (some of slave origin, some not) in which Huck believes wholeheartedly. In fact, Twain's childhood affection for truancy and youthful nonconformity revives wonderfully here, bringing life to a scathing, child's-point-of-view critique of Victorian schools, both strict *and* progressive. Homework, to the child, was an assault: Miss Watson "took a set at me now, with a spelling-book. She worked me middling hard for about an hour, and then the widow made her ease up . . ." And truancy was a good thing, with a worth one weighed dispassionately against its demerits: "Whenever I got uncommon tired I played hookey," Huck tells us, "and the hiding I got next day done me good and cheered me up." Pap may have been a parody of the prideful parent, but Huck, to a point, agrees with him: "It warn't long after that till I was used to being where I was," he confides from the cabin where Pap keeps him locked, "and liked it, all but the cow-hide part . . ."

As for Tom, we assume that his gang is funny because they're harmless, because their ambition to "kill," "rob," and "ransom" ends with them charging headfirst into a Sunday-school picnic and scattering a "primer-class." Given contemporary newspaper headlines about teenagers forming actual gangs and committing actual murders, however, these scenes were far from benign. Imagine if, today, an author published a book in which a group of suburban children, based on images they gleaned from video games, formed a gang and pretended to deal drugs. It would be a joke with a jag.

Huck, too, was built around similar popular images of the troubled youth of his day. Twain softened his edges, giving him that radiant, gentle voice, making him the victim of abusive adults and their institutions—but the boy and his sidekick Tom weren't meant to be angels. What Twain wrote in 1876—those opening fifteen or sixteen chapters—was deliriously unstable, taking rapidly evolving national images of children as victims and criminals and superimposing one over the other. At the very least, Twain was endorsing the child-centered approach of education reformers—while mocking the faulty logic that insisted that every child go through a systematic education and still learn from direct and personal experience of the world. Twain's hero was a master truant, and addicted to tobacco. But he'd never need to be told what a strawberry plant looked like. He was a criminal and a liar, but he was careful with a gun. And he'd never have his vision blurred by the influence of dime store novels, since he couldn't read.

Twenty-five years later, Twain would say this more clearly, articulating his belief about the unpredictability of how children learn, and the fixed narratives created by adult institutions. "Books, home, the school and the pulpit may and must do the *directing*," he wrote, "but the countless unconscious and unintentional trainers do the real work." In the 1870s, though, Twain was pushing buttons wildly, the way he tended to do: what children should do with their literacy, if they had any; whether they should be cosseted in regimented schools or liberated to risk their own deaths. *Huck Finn* was a bomb thrown straight into a national debate that has never exactly receded, only transformed to recognize new technologies.

It must have been fun. But it must also have felt like too much trouble, and it is little surprise that Twain set aside the manuscript later that summer of 1876, telling Howells that he "like[d] it only tolerably well" and thought he might "burn the MS when it is done." It was the kind of manuscript, perhaps, one kept to oneself. But the itch remained, the creative energies still flowed, and there was one more story to tell. It is no coincidence that the years Twain did most of his writing on children overlapped with the period he and Olivia raised their three daughters from infancy to teenagerhood. On August 8, 1876—roughly when he stopped writing the first piece of *Huck Finn*—he also started a journal called *A Record of the Small Foolishnesses of Susie and "Bay" Clemens (Infants)*, about his own children. And he stopped it in 1885—the same year *Huck Finn* was published—and that was no coincidence either.

Looking back, it is striking how rarely we talk about how much writing *Huck Finn* and raising his own children mingled in Twain's imagination. This omission is even more striking given that he actually had two children roughly Tom and Huck's ages when the book was published. But because his real children were girls, and his fictive ones were boys—emblematic boys, at that—we rarely consider how much Susy and Clara, the older daughters, are embodied in Tom and Huck. The Clemens family, however, happily played around with that possibility. Jean, the youngest, at two and a half started call-ing Susy "Guck," or something like it, weirdly close to "Huck," and called Clara "Ben"—not Tom, but not far off. One has to wonder how often she heard those two boy's names to attach them, approx-imately, to her sisters. The family, however, was not displeased when she did: they started calling Clara, at least, by the boy's name her younger sister gave her.

In fact, reading *Huck Finn* in tandem with *A Record of the Small Foolishnesses*—something almost no one ever does—the reader sees the links free and clear. And those links, in turn, tell us something valuable about how to read *Huck Finn*. It was a book written by a man looking backward to his own childhood. But it was also a book written in a present day about a present day, and not just the pres-ent day defined by political debates and "graphic and telegraphic" reports in the media. It was a book written by a parent, doing what most parents do: observing the child-rearing practices of friends and relatives, keeping pained tallies of things done wrong and things done right, and concluding that his family, while imperfect, was run better than most. *Huck Finn*, read through this lens, radiates the joy, the pride—the ambivalence—of parenting, and even allows us the chance to contemplate how the act of parenting can influence, and be influenced by, a larger vision of history.

In Twain's telling—mostly in *A Record* but scattered across other, unpublished writings as well—his real children are much more like his fictional ones than even he can admit or recognize. Susy, the old-est, is blond, serious browed, a "magazine" of moods and emotions, so much her father's little female double he misses it by a mile. She starts life given to "tempests," and at age three they start "flogging" her regularly, Twain writes—daily, then less, until within a year she regulates her moods, and they stop. By the time she is eight, she advises on her punishments, and always chooses the most effective one. If she strikes her sister on the day before a hayride she longs to attend, she grounds herself, explaining that "if I don't get to ride on the hay wagon, I can remember *easily*." In Twain's eyes, Susy is a straight shooter, incorruptible, like her mother. "Poor child!" he says, respecting and lamenting her "Spartan fidelity to the bitter task."

Next was Clara, two years younger, dark-haired: if Susy was "reflective, dreamy," Clara was "enterprising, business-like." Or so her father says. He seems to lie to himself here, too, and miss another double. Susy, Huck-like, is a "persuadable follower of reckless inventors of [adventures]." But Clara, Tom-like, is the inventor. She's the one who gets them stuck in a self-locking bin where they almost suffocate. She's the death-defying one who gets pulled back from a hotel lobby abyss, or saved from drowning, or pulled out of a fire.

Third was Jean, and even Twain admits that his notebooks leave only a fuzzy vision of what she was like at this time. He could put no frame around her: she wouldn't allow it. When he went to whip her—for not saying "please"—she howled with such ferocity and refusal to acquiesce that he gave up the switch. Months later, he was chasing a loose mouse in the nursery, and Jean warned the rodent to "better go way . . . papa come, take you in bath woom + spak you + make you say pease." For years after, Twain would regard her as "masterful," a little girl who could switch back and forth between German and English for effect (English for "light skirmishing," German for "'business'") and win any argument. "I ought to have spanked her," he said, describing one afternoon where she disobeyed him, "but I didn't. I fraternized with the enemy."

They were raised in Hartford, summers in Elmira, taken all over Europe—raised in Paris, in Germany, at a time when such European cosmopolitanism was even rarer than now. Raised everywhere but Hannibal, in fact, and slept everywhere except the hogshead barrel Huck favors. On their own, they played with dolls, conducted roleplay with maximum theatricality, learned bits and pieces of many languages. As Huck learned slave folklore from Jim, they acquired antebellum "superstitions" from Mary Ann Cord, Twain's patroness in "A True Story," and one of many servants working wherever the Clemenses resided. They doted on small animals, played macabre games: Susy would make Clara lie on the rug, and then tell her, "I'm an angel . . . + you are a little dead girl."

When Papa was working or playing billiards, he'd stay in his study from ten till five, often skipping lunch, and he'd join them for dinner and read them what he wrote. One meal a day: that's what he wanted, or said he wanted. Coffee and four boiled eggs covered with ridiculous amounts of salt and pepper; that's what Clara re-

membered. When he wasn't working, he'd take them ice-skating out
behind the house, staying out past dark. Or he'd turn the library into
a Kiplingesque jungle, complete with Kiplingesque colonial subtext:
the girls would be the hunters, he would be the elephant on whose
back they rode, and George Griffin, the African-American butler,
would be the hunted tiger or lion.

Despite Twain's religious skepticism during his own boyhood,
they were brought up to love Jesus. But, like Papa, they became skep-
tics and rebels early, too. Susy would stare off, indulging in "long
stillnesses" that her parents assumed were spent fashioning imaginary adventures for her dolls, and then ask, "Mamma, what does the
world go on, for?" By nine she acknowledged—in Paris—that she
"don't pray as much as" she "used to," and warned her mother that
"you would not approve of the way I pray now." The parents made
them read books in German, kept English books away from them,
and were then startled when the older kids, at six and eight respec-
tively, stole a book of English poetry and taught themselves to read
in that language in ten or twelve days—"without help or instruction
from any body," Twain underlined twice.

Twain loved this; loved that they learned to read without being
forced; loved that they could and would teach themselves by grabbing at what was forbidden. Otherwise, he and Livy insisted on complete disclosure and honesty: "the absolute truth, unembroidered +
ungilded." And the children returned the favor. The house was full of
stories, mostly his, and Susy and Clara chastised him when his heroes
lied—"He wasn't ever a heedless boy," they scolded him—and even
when his bad guys lied, "My villains must not lie," he noted. Susy
also scolded her parents when they were rude to her in public—"You
didn't speak to me *right*, mama"—and Mama conceded: "Her mother
had to confess that she hadn't spoken to her 'right.'" Clara, by six,
started to "lean toward an almost hypercritical exactness." But she
still trailed her older sister, at eight already inheriting her father's
"discriminating habit of language." Asked if Jean is "crying hard," in
the nursery, she'd say, "Well, no—it's a weary, lonesome cry."

He took down their "dialect" with the same precision and enthusiasm that he reserved for the African-American spoken word.
"Bay got boofu' hair," Susy said about newborn Clara, and Twain

noted the phrase and the time, *one hour and four minutes* after Clara's birth—a social scientist's precision, from a man acting more like a social scientist with every passing year, and an astonishing thing for a father to be finding memorable sixty-four minutes after his second daughter was born. But they got him back. Before she was even three, Susy learned to mimic his long talk: "When my dolly's hat fell," she told the nurse, "papa said 'I-f i-t f-a-l-l-s o-f-f a-g-a-i-n, I—l-l p-i-c-k i-t u-p.'"

"Considering that she had probably never heard my drawling manner of speech imitated," her father noted, well past half-proud, "this wasn't bad—nor reverent, either."

Reading *A Record of the Small Foolishnesses*, one feels Twain's pride over and over: there is something special, in his regard, about Susy. And despite the class and gender divides, there is simply no way Huck becomes Huck without her. Years later, he'd admit that much of what he said about her in *A Record* was a lie: "The Record is incomplete," he'd say, plangently understating. It turned out that she did lie—she lied a lot—and it turned out that they tried "whipping" for only a couple of weeks, and it failed—and that she stopped lying only after they stopped trying to punish her for it. *A Record*, it turned out, was kind of a fiction of a well-regulated family, and he owned up to it. But in his own recollection, he didn't lie about how tart and funny she was, and how much she had his number: "Mamma loves morals," she said, at eleven, "Papa loves cats."

Susy was the little "philosopher" with "a proclivity for large words" that gave Twain the courage to give Huck a philosopher's heart and a meaningful vocabulary, two things that Tom—a master strategist but no deep thinker or poet—never had. She was the bad speller whose bad spelling Twain adored, calling it "innocent" and "free," the perfect parallel to Huck's indifferent relationship with standard English. Susy's hyperarticulation and Huck's homespun clarity were mirror images, but both spoke to the possibilities of wisdom and mature aesthetics in the preteen's management of the English language. And the darkness so young, the colossal sensitivity to the stillnesses—the complex politics of the child both cowed by and enabled to defiance by being beaten and brought in line—spoke to the hidden depths that both real and fictive children could plumb. Susy says, "I hardly ever pray, now; when I want anything, I just leave it to Him"; Huck says, "I'd noticed that Providence always did put the right words in my mouth, if I left it alone." And Huck, like Susy, knows the difference between a sad sound and a truly lonesome one; knows her words, the sentiment behind them, practices her exactness: "I heard the dim hum of a spinning wheel wailing," he tells us late in the book, "then I knowed for certain I wished I was dead—for that *is* the lonesomest sound in the world."

Amid these messages, the ones he transcribed and the ones he didn't, Twain developed the intense, passionate ambivalence toward children and toward parenting that would make his great books speak to different generations at the same time. Twain looked at himself and especially at Livy, and looked at the adults he was casting in *Tom* and in *Huck*, and he saw opposites. No one forced his kids to *learn*, or shut them up in a school, or coerced them to religious faith. And unlike the mothers in his books, Livy's consistency shone out to him: "They have never known what it was to owe allegiance to, and be the shuttle-cock of, a capricious fool in petticoats, who is all sugar one moment + all aqua-fortis the next . . ."

But the hickory, or its psychological equivalent, was never far. Striking his children, or approving it, was something Twain couldn't stomach. In *Huck Finn*, Jim delivers an emotional monologue expressing remorse for angrily hitting his daughter, Elizabeth, not knowing that she was ignoring him because she had gone deaf from scarlet fever: "De Lord God Amighty fogive po' ole Jim," he tells Huck, "kaze he never gwyne to fogive hisself." But this was Twain talking, too, Twain also not forgiving himself: he wrote this scene shortly after Jean disputed his right to strike her, and he made sure the key passage stuck—"This expression shall not be changed," he wrote in the margin.

Likewise, Twain may have been proud of the way his children took their punishment as their own responsibility. But he was too much the anarchist to celebrate this kind of "inward colonization," either, as Richard H. Brodhead labels such keenly manipulative parenting practices during the era. His children were still sad, not at all playful innocents waiting to be molded, no matter how much he might later pretend. And they had vocabularies of words and ideas of uncommon breadth and depth. Calling him "Youth," Livy acknowledged his boyishness—but this boyishness had as much to do with historical vision and a vision of child-rearing as it had to do with nostalgia and immaturity.

As historians note, many Victorians believed, as a "commonplace," that there was a "link between the childhood of the individual and the childhood of the race"—that children thought and behaved like the citizens of 'primitive' cultures, and after a period of appropriate wildness matured into citizens of "civilized" ones. "If the earlier stages of growth relatively represent what man has in common with animals, . . ." G. Stanley Hall, speaking for many experts in his time, observed in *Adolescence*, "[the] last stages . . . make him most distinctively human." This belief—known later as the theory of recapitulation—probably circulated around Twain's mind as he teamed his dream child, Huck, with the "primitive" Jim, likely making it easier for his readers to accept the biracial alliance: in the Victorian imagination, white boys and men of color, despite their age differences, were similarly "evolved." But it also must have circulated around his feelings about children and history. How can you be the adult when you don't really believe that history and human development goes all one way? And how can you believe that history and human development goes all one way when your children say and do such smart and powerful things?

Twain could outmaneuver a roomful of Brahmins. They were adults, and he knew how to handle that race. But children were different. In the spring of 1885, while *Huck Finn* was still new, still just getting its first reviews, he read an article from the *Christian Union* about a disobedient child refusing to be moved by the threat of corporal punishment. And he wrote back that the story made his "body's blood boil." Left to his own devices, he implied, he'd be as "ludicrous an ass" as the father in the story. But he had Livy. In his home, he said, the whippings were rare but, when necessary, conducted "on purely business principles," after which the child was "loved back into happy-heartedness and a joyful spirit" by a gracious mother. It was the only time he wrote about Livy in public, he noted, and another strong signal that writing *Huck Finn* and raising his own children—that the idea itself of raising children—overlapped in his thoughts.

If one compares what he wrote at the time, and what he wrote later, about corporal punishment at his house, it is impossible to tell if he is lying or not, whether his motive was paying tribute to Livy, or teasing her, or weighing his own worthiness as a father, or making sure readers knew that his family was better run than the ones he wrote about. The idea of it all going public frightened him somewhat: as he had with the early draft of *Huck*, he talked about putting this letter, too, "in the stove." But the children were delighted that he didn't, and that, ultimately, might have been his real motive. Susy, then writing her father's biography in her own big script—as if the fact that he had just finished writing about a child meant it was now time for a child to write about him—spent pages delighting conspiratorially in her mother's embarrassment. "C. and I had great fun," she noted, teasing first the mother, then the father.

In this family, where both discipline and rebellion were honored, there was no shortage of ways to show love and defiance at the same time. And that its patriarch, instructed by all involved to never create a hero who lied, instead spent years creating the most empathetic liar in American literary history, shows us one more way. He wrote *Huck Finn* because he loved having children. But he wrote it the way he wrote it to get their goat. He saw a world rife with generational conflict, and fought for both sides—expecting, naturally, that his children would, too.

PART
TWO

6

The Trouble Begins

Whatever *Huck Finn* meant to Twain in 1876—however his forty years of rich and contradictory life experience found expression in the pages of its early chapters—it would take him close to another decade to finish it, to take that narrative fragment and its rendition of race relations, childhood, and American culture and turn it into something whole. Some sensibility was emerging—an antipathy for the way that both racial and generational divisions denied the human instinct for empathy—but it was hard to hold, both more and less dangerous than he wanted it to be. From 1876 to 1883, the manuscript of *Huck* was closer to the fire than the writing desk. But Twain continued to write and publish actively, especially about children. From 1878 to 1881, for instance, he composed and brought to publication another children's "classic," *The Prince and the Pauper*, the only one of his books written purely for the juvenile market: a "yarn for youth," he told Howells.

Like *Tom Sawyer* and the half-finished *Huck Finn*, Twain's story of Tom Canty, the ragged London youth who trades places with the young Prince Edward, had a couple of boy teenagers as its leads. And like Huck and Tom Sawyer, they came from two different classes. Unlike Huck and Tom, though, they talked liked this: "Fathers be alike, mayhap. Mine hath not a doll's temper."

The Prince and the Pauper was designed to be genteel, to be serialized in a respectable children's magazine of the day (the *St. Nicho-*

las Magazine for Boys and Girls), and to delight Twain's wife and his daughters, to whom it was dedicated. Its plot was safe—it was a bit of a rip-off, even—of Charlotte M. Yonge's *Prince and the Page*, in which a prince and his servant trade places—a book Twain knew his children loved. As Twain composed it, he read fresh drafts aloud to a group of neighborhood teens he called "the Young Girls Club," six chapters at a time. He asked all his friends—the Parkers, the Warners, the Twichells, the Howellses—to read it aloud to their own families and report back. He encouraged Susy and Clara to act as "honest little critics," to provide their earnest opinions as he read to them in their Hartford living room, the two of them "perched" on the arms of the chair in which he sat.

Despite all these careful crowdsourcing efforts, though, it didn't sell well. Twain would remember that. But it would never be banned, either, and it would in fact delight his own children: Susy described it as his "best" book, and alongside Clara and their neighborhood friends she happily took on the role of the prince in the sedately gender-bending family theatrical productions they performed for their Hartford neighbors.

And if *Prince* didn't look and feel like *Huck* or *Tom*, it still shared the same gene pool of ideas about children. The same headline-worthy debates that gave spark to the still-unfinished *Huck* and best-selling *Tom*—the ones about standardized education, about the children with and the children without, about abuse, about reading—bled into the stilted Olde English of *The Prince and the Pauper* as well.

As in *Huck*, there is an abusive father who beats his child—who beats Prince Edward, even, when given the chance. There's even an abusive grandmother: "When he came home empty handed at night, he knew his father would curse him and thrash him first, and that when he was done the awful grandmother would do it all over again and improve on it . . ." There are casually abusive adults everywhere, harrowing scenes of domestic violence, mobs chanting for blood, hermits who (like Huck's father) plan the murder of a child to propitiate a hallucinatory vision.

And as in *Huck*, there is a child who regards study and sitting still as institutional abuse: "In what have I offended, that the good God should take me away from the fields and the free air and the

sunshine . . . ?" Tom Canty wonders, as his ascension to faux royalty requires him, like so many middle-class Victorian children, to be
shuttered indoors doing "dull work."

And then there is the child who, like Tom Sawyer, like those
dime-novel devotees, gets lost in books so thoroughly that he loses
his grasp on reality. Before Tom Canty gets switched with Prince
Edward, he is branded by his family in Pudding Lane as a "foolish"
reader, convinced by the volumes borrowed from a local priest that
he is a royal. But he doesn't suffer for it. Rather, Tom Canty's reading-
infused delusions, like Tom Sawyer's, make him more audacious:
"His dreamings and readings worked certain changes in him, by and
by," Twain tells us. And, like Tom Sawyer, they gain him followers:
"Tom's influence among these young people began to grow . . . a sort
of wondering awe." And eventually, they lead him to fall upward into
royalty in the kind of romantic accident that a kid like Tom Sawyer
believed could really happen, or could be dreamt into happening.

"Foolish" reading, then, led to upward mobility. And a revolution
of sorts. It didn't matter whether it was Tom Canty, or Edward, the
poor boy, or the rich one, who wears the crown. By novel's end, both
are celebrated for their mercy and wisdom. And while Twain carefully aligns this wisdom to the idea of innocence—Edward even vowing to treat children with special mercy for precisely this quality—his
plot rewards the addled nerve of Tom Canty in inhabiting the role of
king even when he knows he's not, and the self-assurance of Edward
in retrieving his royal crown.

Overall, it was a tastefully rebellious book: even today, a reader
has to bear down to see its anger and rough edges, buried as they are
beneath Twain's proper prose. Writing *The Prince and the Pauper* took
Twain away from writing *Huck Finn*—but as the many resemblances
between the two books implies, it didn't take him very far, and may
even have recharged him somewhat. He had ended the 1876 fragment with Huck asking about a feud between the Grangerfords, the
Southern family that has taken him in, and the Shepherdsons, a rival
clan. Sometime in 1880, Twain again picked up the *Huck* manuscript
and answered Huck's query, adding a violent shooting scene in which
Huck witnesses the death of the boy to whom he asked the question.
A boy his own age, with a name—Buck—too close for comfort. And

then Twain took Huck and Jim deeper south into some barren little river towns in Arkansas.

In one small town, its moral impoverishment rendered with despairing detail, Huck sees another murder, a man gunned down in the street. Twain brought back the memorable death of Sam Smarr from his childhood for this one, and even brought back the heavy Bible sunk onto Sam Smarr's chest.

The townsmen gather for the lynching of the murderer. There is some indecision: in his good, purple ink, Twain writes that Colonel Sherburn, the murderer, gets away. Then in pencil, underneath, he scrawls: *No, let them lynch him.*

Then Twain stopped again. Maybe he ran out of inspiration. As the 1880s dawned, however, he wasn't acting like a man running out of things to say, but, rather, like an artist making an adaptation or two and gearing up for something big. Before he'd finish *Huck Finn*, there'd be other books to write, more trips to take. But what inspired the completion of *Huck Finn*, finally, was the same thing that had inspired Twain decades before: Daniel Quarles and the minstrel show. The real voice and the fake. It would take a trip down the Mississippi to rediscover the sound and the story, and a friend from New Orleans to help him ring all the right bells. But once the old voices revived, he'd recognize that *Huck Finn*, that old manuscript, was the perfect vehicle for updating them for a new era and new uses. What he'd write now wouldn't exactly match what he wrote before: the country had changed, and he was changing, too. But it would add to it, taking that hopeful and presumably linear story he was telling about racial empathy and growing up and turning it inside out to see what lay within. As radiant as the early chapters of *Huck* were, what he would do now—how he would end *Huck*, how he would shape it into an innovative theatrical event for Victorian audiences—would be what made his novel the bright bit of chaos that Americans still fight about.

That Twain thought much about race during the 1870s and 1880s was no great surprise; nor was the fact that what he thought and wrote possessed a keynote of humor of an often sinister kind. In these regards, he is very much an emissary from the past, recovering for us the way many Americans thought at the time, the degree of fixation they brought to bear on the subject, and the nervousness and ill will that shaped and scarred that fixation.

Amid news reports about disasters and tainted elections, and anecdotes about the craftiness of Asian immigrants and the sentimental ragings of the Irish (or the mysteries of the Jew, or the imperturbability of the German), and even among the many, many stories detailing the violence and victimization of children, there remained an ascendant issue in American culture: race. Within a few short years of its hopeful inception, "Reconstruction" began to fall apart. The Freedmen's Bureau was shuttered in 1872, and "Forty Acres and a Mule" or any program like it never happened: it became "the nation's most famous broken promise," as Stacey Margolis has written. Accusations of corruption against northern officials and their southern supporters proliferated, and paramilitaries of resistance—like the Ku Klux Klan and the Knights of the White Camellia—organized to suppress the African-American vote.

In 1877, federal armies were completely withdrawn—Republican Rutherford B. Hayes, whom Twain had endorsed the same summer he started *Huck*, implemented this as part of a compromise to seal his deeply disputed victory in the 1876 election—and Southern governments became homogenously white again. New laws and governments compelled many African-Americans into unemployment, vagrancy, imprisonment, and the forced labor system known as "convict-lease." In 1883, the Supreme Court overturned the Civil Rights Act of 1875, implicitly allowing localities everywhere to bar blacks from public spaces. By 1884, the new national narrative was "reunion" between white Northerners and Southerners— that "bloody chasm" bridged—the legal framework for the major Jim Crow segregation laws of the 1890s and 1900s was shifting into place, and the president-elect, for the first time since the antebellum era, was a Democrat elected with white Southern support.

Seen from some angles, African-Americans were experiencing freedom and economic success. Grover Cleveland, justifying the faith of Mugwumps like Twain, appointed more African-Americans to federal posts than his predecessors. The African-American press

produced vastly more newspapers than today. And many more prosperous African-Americans experienced what Joel Williamson calls
"tokens" of acceptance into the mainstream: a seat in a first-class train
car or a restaurant. But measured statistically and not anecdotally,
most African-Americans faced extraordinary hardship. Prisons—
mostly work camps—were formed at a "boom" pace that Michelle
Alexander has likened to our modern prison expansion. And black
men filled them in the tens of thousands—many convicted for small
property thefts, the kind one might commit fending off starvation.
Two decades after the Civil War ended, 90 percent of all convicts
in the South were African-American, and they died as much as ten
times faster at work camps than did free men and women: "One
dies," a Louisiana government man noted casually, "we get another."
Outside of prison, economic repression, illiteracy, and violence left
most free blacks in a serf-like state within an industrializing society,
with mortality rates double or triple those of whites in cities like Atlanta, Charleston, and Richmond.

Such political changes required and accommodated hard, divisive
cultural work. Southern politicians spoke of an African-American
"predestination" for "cheap labor," and increasingly portrayed blacks,
especially black men, as innately violent. Physicians and Victorian-
era academics assisted, creating a "scientific" portrait of "an inferior
race." And editorial writers spoke of regression: they argued that
African-Americans liberated from bondage were actually reverting to
a pre-slavery primal state. In retrospect, there is no way to adequately
describe the intensity with which Southern and Midwestern newspapers during this period built a negative image of blacks and blackness
for their readers. Because it left a photographic and symbolic residue,
the minstrel show is readily and reasonably derided in contemporary
conversations about the history of racism in America; but surviving
manuscripts of minstrel shows from this time period show racism no
more, and often less, corrosive than that found in some of the era's
more respected media.

Nor were the newspapers' efforts monotonal: they produced a
rich, varied, narrative racism marked alternately by smug wit and
an air of impending panic. There were rhetorical nuances, regional
variances. Racial slurs would only appear in Northern newspapers,

and then, as Twain had done in the *Buffalo Express*, exclusively as an ironic indictment of racism. An account of a lynching might be titled "Only a 'Nigger' Anyhow"; a critique of British imperialism might note that the English "stigmatize all dark-skinned races" by calling them "'nigger.'" But the Southern papers were adepts at shifting between the terms "colored," "negro," "darky," and occasionally "coon" and even "nager" to mark movements between "serious" reportage and derisive anecdotes—standard comedy pieces about "Uncle Primus," elderly women talking to the devil at camp meetings, or the resilient appeal of "voodooism."

Twain would engage with all this, of course—was already engaging with it—in *Huck*: Jim's superstitions about witches, at least on the surface, depressingly played along with stereotype; Huck's frequent use of racial slurs would have been read one way by Northern readers inured to their ironic employment, and another, less comfortable way by Southerners who acted like they were past all that. But no one was past anything, and even Twain, possibly the premier political comedian of the time, had no easy response to such an avalanche of ill feeling. There were reports of violence everywhere, on every front page, inevitably with black protagonists, arranged almost theatrically. Robberies, knife fights, gunplay, riots, insurrections, and lynchings, often two or three articles per issue, supplemented by editorials, letters to the editor. The blacks of Nashville, if one believed the *Daily American*, were unceasing and inveterate thieves. "As thieves the negroes are most expert," the paper announced, in a special report on "Chicken and Cane-Stealing in the West Indies." The black men of New Orleans seemed to engage in two or three fights every week over the affections of some "light mulatress." Black men dropped dead for no reason ("A Negro Falls Dead," announced the *Atlanta Constitution* on May 17, 1885), or turned up dead for no reason ("He had evidently been dead for two or three days . . . one side of his face was eaten off by the hogs"), or fled after gutting "open the breadbasket of another."

Over and over, newspapers described black crime and announced blacks apprehended: "A Fight Among Negro Gamblers"; "Negro Burglar Arrested"; "Waylaid by Negroes." Often, the reports featured a tone of smug triumph or comedy. "Tempting Bait," a headline in a Nashville paper announced, "Four Negroes Arrested in the Act of Stealing Meat." In other instances, white journalists exhibited weariness about the repetition of the details of the frame story they told over and over. "A Row in Negrodom," the *New Orleans Picayune* announced on its first page, "The Inevitable Knife to the Rescue."

Throughout the heartland, deep into the South, and in Northern Democratic organs such as the *Philadelphia Inquirer* or the *New York Herald*, newspaper editors sustained a two-headed narrative about the relations of blacks to whites, and blacks to each other. On the one hand, they asserted that the black population was lawless and well armed. On the other, they comforted their readers with the half-conscious idea that whatever threat was constituted by black arms and black anger was almost completely feckless.

In part, this meant keeping the threat of inversion lively. "White slaves," headlines blared, were being made everywhere. Others were being "Africanize[d]." And freed slaves declared not just equality but domination: "Boss," one "ruffian negro" was quoted as saying at an Election Day riot, "you wah my master yesterday, but I'se youah's today." And in part, this meant publishing reports that reassured white readers that a plainly inequitable system of justice and punishment maintained antebellum strictures: "Nine convicts were whipped at Newcastle this morning . . . [A] negro received twenty lashes and stood one hour in the pillory. The others received ten lashes each."

Southern editors isolated neutral euphemisms to report lynchings, but couldn't resist conveying the sense that they found them entertaining. The *Raleigh News & Observer* on December 25, 1884, in an article entitled, "Lynched, No Doubt," describes the lynching of "the negro burglars, Charles Smith and Thomas Davis," and comments that "the affair creates a sensation. The whole story of the detection of these men, their conviction and their fate is of deep interest." Within this "story" the behavior of the lynched man was a crucial point, as though much hinged on how he fulfilled his role in the drama. The *Baltimore Sun* on December 29 punctuated its interview with a lynching witness by noting that "it was his opinion, as well as others, that Briscoe died game."

In other ways, the frame story that portrayed black Americans as both threatening and unthreatening was simply unsustainable, and bore no small resemblance to the ludicrous plots of the dime novels. Throughout the crime reporting of the day, armed black men, who often reportedly outnumbered their prey, couldn't seem to complete an act of violence. On January 7, according to the *Atlanta Journal,* a white butcher named Dock Guerin was assaulted by two "large ne-gro[es]" bearing knives. One "large negro" attempted to stab Guerin but missed, while the other's attempt to stab him merely cut "a long slit in his coat." At this point, the two attackers paused long enough to allow Guerin time to bend down, lift a large rock, and drop it onto the head of "the larger of the negroes." "Officer Norman," the *Journal* assured, a final note of confidence making clear who controlled the narrative, "is working up the matter today."

And if local stories reiterated the idea that black individuals were incapable of generating any kind of potent adversarial force, other news articles reinforced that larger numbers of blacks working in concert were equally ineffectual. Reports describing a riot in Yazoo City pitted twelve hundred black men, "all of whom, as is usual in such cases, went armed," against twenty-five white men, "only nine of whom are known to have been armed." Outnumbered almost fifty to one, the white men "stood their ground valiantly, and though not half of them were armed they presented a steady front and even once repulsed the negroes." "Pistol shots flew around like hail," the *New Orleans Picayune* reported. Subsequently, an investigating party of "citizens" arrived at the riot site and "were fired into by a body of negroes in ambush," who completely missed them as well. The total death toll inflicted by twelve hundred armed black men and women, in this case, was three, all murdered "with demoniacal ferocity" by hand. A later report lowered this number to one.

Despite the apparent incompetence of the African-American population, journalists repeatedly invoked the image of a looming race war. At the same time, reporting that raised the specter of revolution almost always deflated the prospect. Follow-up reports on the Yazoo City riot described angry blacks threatening to "descend upon [the town] in their fury and demolish the inhabitants," then "holding meetings preparatory to going on a regular war footing," but finally "all scared to death." On January 3, 1885, the *Atlanta Journal* reprinted a report concerning a "War Between the Races" in Unionville, Georgia, that left five black men dead and no arrests made. In each of these events, newspapers printed that "it is believed that the negroes fired the first shot." In each case, they seem to have been unable to hit anything white.

Many Northern and Republican newspapers, of course, disputed this version of the nation's racial politics. They railed against the outcome of the 1884 election, focusing upon the corruption of Southern white culture: shortly after the election, the *Boston Morning Journal* shared Republican candidate James G. Blaine's astonishment at the "level of lawlessness prevailing in South Carolina and Mississippi." The *Providence Journal* reported "Defiance to Federal Authority in Louisiana," where "Violence and Murder" were "Urged to Defeat a Free Vote." Two months later, the *Detroit Free Press* was still angry enough to proclaim succinctly that "crooks run us."

Like other Republican organs, black-run newspapers in particular detested Grover Cleveland's election: the *Washington Bee* argued that "the hundred and fifty three electoral votes from the South were obtained through theft and assassination." Unlike white Republican newspapers, however, black-run newspapers understood their defensive position left them few opportunities to change minds among a white readership they simply couldn't reach. "All over the Union," the *New York Globe* wrote in a vociferous editorial on November 8, "there are papers devoted to the vile purpose of traducing the black man; of attempting to show that he is incapable of entering into and becoming a part of the people of this country; of showing that he is thriftless and mendacious and is religiously a hypocrite or a Voodooist."

For black audiences, however, and for whatever fragment of the white audience strayed in their direction, black journalists produced a positive self-image of the present and future of the African-American community. Like many black newspapers, the *New York Freeman* featured sketches of the lives of "successful" black individuals. In Boston, the *Hub* covered the opening of the opera season on the front page. In tiny Nicodemus, Kansas, the symbolic center of the "Exo-duster" movement, the *Western Cyclone* celebrated the mercantile potential of "the first colony of colored people ever settled on government land" with a fervor that bordered on the spiritual:

"Our town is like the embryo seedling, just unfolding into the broad sunlight, waiting only for a start. That force which is to send it forth into notice is now at work . . ."

But black journalists fought a persistent tide. Not only were they outnumbered, but there was a relentlessness as well in the creative options employed by white writers and editors, in the advantages that majority demographics offered, and perhaps most importantly in the confidence that the color line provided to those on its good side. One party was allowed to "play" with racial disharmony, and one was obliged to wear a straight face. Throughout serious newspapers in the South and Midwest, in fact, reporters described scenes of racial discord with mirth in their voices. In its coverage of the Yazoo City riots, the *New Orleans Picayune* employed the headline "Lively Times in Mississippi." Reporting on the Election Day riots in Cincinnati, the *St. Louis Post-Dispatch* utilized the phrase "All went to fooling."

For black Americans, however, the election of 1884 was a cruel joke, a lumbering narrative, badly told from the start, with gaps and false places, but that nevertheless achieved closure at the hundreds of balloting places where the Klan and other paramilitaries turned away the black vote. All the individual stories about unsuccessful black criminals, all those inept black insurrections, reinforced the election story that celebrated the pleasures of denying black political agency. In an editorial on November 18, the *New York Sun* spoke for many of its readers: "At the south . . . the whites have now had their way, and will be less disposed to regard [blacks] with suspicion . . . [T]he whites are no longer irritated against the blacks as successful political enemies. . . . [I]t is an era of good feeling in the South." The *Providence Journal* concurred, less happily: "The election in South Carolina was quite unanimous. The negroes were evidently not anxious to feel 'the prowess of the whites in their bones,' in the form of cold lead, and promoted harmony by staying in the woods until after dark . . ."

There is no question that Twain was paying attention. And there was no question he was angry. It is not surprising that the first section of *Huck* sat in his desk as efforts to scuttle Reconstruction gained momentum; that private promises like those made to Warner T.

McGuinn were proffered as national promises were retracted. At the same time, the political changes taking place in the early post-Reconstruction era, and the emerging national narratives on race that shifted into place during this time, tested and inspired him. The historical moment was so rich, so confused, so self-evidently going in the wrong direction, but Twain's range of resources to respond to such situations was always surprisingly massive. He could swim in and out of the cultural mainstream with remarkable ease, launch himself into bohemian or bourgeois subcultures when needed, hide in his own domestic circle if he had to—even, in his own mind if not elsewhere, efface himself of his race and class, or take refuge in the past. And as he turned back to *Huck Finn*—a slow turning at this point, taking about three years—he would use almost all of these strategies. He would use the newspapers, he would use the minstrel show, he would use the folklorists, seeing through the limits of each, but also seeing what they had in common, for good or ill. He would use them all.

In turning to the techniques being practiced in the newly professionalizing fields of folklore studies and dialectology, for instance—most prominent in "Sociable Jimmy" and "A True Story," but present in much of his work at this time—Twain was clearly rehearsing a fact-based alternative to the riot of mistruths and exaggerations offered by the newspapers and the politicians. At the very least, he was joining up with the men and women he believed were fighting for a truthful accounting: in 1888, right between *Huck Finn* and *A Connecticut Yankee in King Arthur's Court*, he became one of the founding members of the high-profile American Folklore Society.

Through this prism, a modern reader can see remnants of Twain's literally academic interest in folklore throughout *Huck Finn*: these remnants almost disrupt it as a novel. It begins with an "explanatory" note listing the kinds of dialect he employs ("the Missouri negro dialect; the extremest form of the backwoods South-Western dialect," etc.), and claiming Twain's bona fides as a serious researcher: "The shadings have not been done in a haphazard fashion, or by guesswork." Its plot winds around key points where a folkloric artifact or belief acts as a flashpoint: Huck's certainty that killing a spider is a bad omen, the cross carved into the sole of Pap's boot to ward off the devil, and Jim, of course, and the witches.

At the same time, characteristically, Twain did not commit to these new ways of thinking: having helped found the American Folklore Society, he shortly after resigned his membership. Hearing him mock the study of primitive cultures in his Sandwich Island lectures back in 1867, in fact, one senses his skepticism about the endeavor from the start. In part, the academics simply weren't entertaining enough: ultimately, Twain may have turned to "authenticity" not because it was the opposite of "imitation" but because both endeavors spoke the same emotional language. If his affinity for the minstrel show bonded him to white America's first nineteenth-century attempt, however crude, to "understand" African-Americans, his fascination with the anthropology movement—and *its* fascination with "popular" or "primitive" subcultures, including that of Southern blacks— linked him to the second such large-scale movement. Guided by whatever strategy gave him the most artistic license, the most opportunities for voyeurship, empathy, and appropriation, he could conceivably find uses in both academic anthropology and the minstrel show—a contradiction to others, but not to him.

As his jibes at the study of "primitive" cultures imply, though, he may have seen the limitations of science as an alternative to lore—or he may have simply understood the zeitgeist better than most. Pursuits of professional accuracy regarding the study of the "folk" played out alongside the same immense excitement and insecurity about the newly freed black population, and the influx of immigrants from across both oceans, that filled newspaper columns: the freak shows that claimed giants and half humans walked the earth were only degrees separate from the medicine textbooks that described persons of color as possessing different anatomies than those of Caucasians. And like the newspapers, the anthropologists also focused on children: works like Alexander F. Chamberlain's *The Child and Childhood in Folk-Thought* also occupied the rapidly growing ethnography bookshelf of the era, neatly paralleling the work of early child psychologists linking "primitive" cultures to adolescence, and the work of their colleagues in medicine linking contemporary members of "colored" races to their "savage" peers on other continents and in the fog of the extended Darwinian past.

High or low, professional or amateur, all eyes were turned toward the same blurry map of America's insiders and outsiders. In the newspapers, children and African-Americans shared something, and that thing they shared was dangerous to the body politic. In the world of the amateur and professional anthropologists, children and African-Americans also shared something—and it was access to ancient and simple truths that only required a civilized and mature white person to interpret. Twain could play these Victorian games, and he would—but it was not in his nature to play the civilized white person, or the adult, for very long before he strained to play someone or something else.

As *Huck Finn* evolved in his imagination, then, in the early years of the 1880s, Twain found himself a cultural tourist, an avid note-taker and eavesdropper, keeping company with men and women who shared his interest in the stories, songs, and language of marginalized others. And it would be as a tourist, and in the company of such friends, that a response to the pernicious twin narratives of his era—the reversal of political advances for blacks and the reframing of American children as the "enemy"—would take shape. In response to Howells's request for another "colored one," an essay like "A True Story," Twain in 1875 had offered a series of essays titled "Old Times on the Mississippi." Howells agreed, and the essays were published to enthusiastic reviews. Twain then proposed a trip down the Mississippi, something he and Howells and the "boys" could do—collect some new notes, and make a book of it. They didn't go, but as he settled deeper into Hartford and his respectable and generally happy marriage, he kept thinking about a trip home. In April 1882, with a small entourage (sans Howells) in tow, he finally took a train from New York to St. Louis, and from there booked a riverboat passage.

Sounding disarmingly East Coast to modern ears, Twain wrote, like an explorer, that he was entering "the region of full goatees": "the goatee extends over a wide extent of country; and is accompanied by an iron-clad belief in Adam and the biblical history of creation, which has not suffered from the assaults of the scientists . . ." But the place he was exploring was, oddly, his own past: the region of full goatees released the old, raw material. He thought of his childhood in Missouri, and with a tangle of emotion in his voice: "The things about me and before me made me feel like a boy again," he wrote in *Life on the Mississippi*, the book this trip inspired. "I had simply been dreaming an unusually long dream."

Twain saw black men and women everywhere, as if he hadn't seen them in years. His eyes sought them out—his ears were antennae. He found "colored folk" occupying the old house in which he grew up in Hannibal: they were "of no more value than I am," he noted. He observed them dressed well and gaily ("upholstered" was the verb he chose) during a flood in Helena, Arkansas, effacing the few white residents even outdoors, and providing "a glaring and hilarious contrast to the mournful mud and the pensive puddles."

Like a folklorist, he transcribed into his notes sentences he overheard, left himself instructions tuning and dropping consonants to align the written word with the sounds he heard in his head: "Note the absence of 'R' from the southern dialect. They also eliminate the final 'g' in -ing." Other times, he transcribed entire songs, like "Mary's Gone Wid de Coon": "Oh, dar's heaps of trouble on the old man's mind," it began, "Come darkies weep wid me."

He recorded whole dialogues, such as an exchange between two laundresses on the riverboat south of Baton Rouge while he lay in bed one afternoon. The first commented that a particular shirt belonged to "Mark Twain"; the second asked, "Who is Mark Twain?" and the first said "I dun'no." Then they reflected on "how this entire steamboat is in debt to them." Then one said: "That's a mighty beautiful plantation," and the other reminded her that "many a poor nigger has been killed there, jest for nuffin." When the first said she'd like to have a moment back in slave times, just to be reminded what it was like, the second said, "*I* don't want 'em back again for a minute." Then the first sang "all sorts of strange plantation melodies which nobody but one of her race would ever be able to learn."

Given that this transcription was no doubt selective, it seemed to suggest volumes about what it meant to be Mark Twain at this moment in time: a hunger to determine how little he knew about these men and women who fascinated him, and what he owed them. Meanwhile, they washed his clothes and he lay in bed.

He made notes to himself to purchase books about black language and culture. He wrote fellow writers to compare notes on a specific slave ghost story, the one about the woman and her golden arm that had stayed with him since childhood. It wasn't quite scholarly precision he sought, but it was close. He seemed to be trying to save something, or retrieve something, like a museum curator practicing on a live subject.

And as he sailed down the river to New Orleans in the spring of 1882, he sailed, too, toward the two white men in America he thought most shared this interest in "authentic" re-creations of African-American and other marginalized cultures—and the countercultural politics implicit in such re-creations. The first was Joel Chandler Harris, the journalist who had transcribed the stories aging slaves had told him about a cunning rabbit from a "brer" patch and published them in 1880 as *Uncle Remus: His Songs and His Sayings,* a runaway success.

The book, by contemporary standards, was a riot of contradictory racial politics. It began with a quasi-scholarly introduction that lamented the "intolerable misrepresentations of the minstrel stage," and insisted that the stories should be read as politically as possible: "It needs no scientific investigation," Harris wrote of Remus, "to show why he selects as his hero the weakest and most harmless of all animals . . ." Harris didn't want his reader to miss the point when the crawfishes overthrew the elephants or when, at book's end, Brer Fox gets killed, Miss Fox marries Brer Rabbit, and "some say" that rabbits and foxes lived together in peace ever after. At the same time, Harris also made it clear that Remus "has nothing but pleasant memories of the discipline of slavery." Faced with the prospect of Union invasion of his master's plantation, Remus recalls in one tale, he grabbed a rifle and shot off a blue soldier's arm.

Parents everywhere read aloud the Brer Patch stories to their children, and did so in the "dialect" Harris provided. Twain thought Harris the "only master" of "Negro dialect . . . the country has produced," and loved the stories themselves so much that he started addressing business letters to entities such as "Brer Osgood" and "Brer Whitmo'." In person, however, Harris—who took an overnight train from Atlanta to meet Twain—was a profound disappointment. Mr. Harris "ought to be able to read the negro dialect better than anybody else," Twain reasoned. But Harris refused to read to the children who had "flocked eagerly . . . to get a glimpse of the illustrious sage and oracle of the nation's nurseries," and "grieved" when they discovered (and shouted out) that "he's white!" It was, needless to say, awkward. "We had to read about Brer Rabbit ourselves," Twain noted, dejectedly.

Twain had better luck, however, with the other author: George Washington Cable, whom he regarded as "the only master in the writing of French dialects"—the forms of Anglicized French sometimes mixed with African or Caribbean influences practiced in and around New Orleans. Unlike Harris, Cable loved to read aloud, and not just in Creole. He did a "nicely-shaded German dialect," and Italian and Irish accents, and was proficient at several "dramatic strokes of gesture and attitude" with which he could simulate "the charm and the grace of the women he wished us to know."

He was also, by every account, an astonishing singer: his own family called him "Minstrel Boy." "Did you ever hear George Cable sing?" one Southern writer asked another. "I shall never forget it." His best material—the songs everyone wanted to hear—were the songs that he and historian Lafcadio Hearn had started gathering in 1878 from older blacks and Creoles in the poorer parishes.

Cable was a match—maybe more than a match—for an omnivorous devourer of culture and politics like Twain. And in the early 1880s he may have been creating more headlines, and startling more people, than even Twain himself. Born in a large house on Annunciation Square in 1845, Cable spent hours of his childhood watching slaves working on the wharves of New Orleans, and was fascinated by the songs and dances he heard and saw on the streets and at open-air markets—the Bamboula, Counjaille, Calinda. But he was no Southern dandy. His father made (and lost) a fortune catering the riverboats, but his mother was of rock-ribbed Methodist stock from

Indiana, and taught him religion. Twain himself, observing the un-yielding ways in which Cable kept the Sabbath and forswore liquor and foul language, wrote that "the apostles were mere policemen to Cable."

Cable grew up lively, nervous, and proud, confessing that his "black sheep"—his cardinal sin—was ambition. He joined the Con-federate army three days before he was of age, got wounded twice, and cut a remarkable figure: five foot five, weighing around one hun-dred pounds, he showed up for duty on an anemic, dandruffy horse he had scavenged. "Great Heavens! Abe Lincoln told the truth," one plantation owner muttered as Cable rode up, "We *are* robbing the cradle."

He prayed in public—not as easy to do in the Confederate army as a modern reader might suppose—and carried math and Latin books for the long lulls between skirmishes. He told fellow soldiers that he thought secession was wrong—also difficult to do in the Confederate army. Yet, when a Union general became his superior after Appomat-tox, Cable reported for duty in his gray rebel uniform and politely vowed to the officer that if he couldn't wear the uniform he would choose to wear no clothes at all.

After the war, he served as a "surveyor's boy," contracted malaria working on the Red River, found a new job clerking back in New Orleans. He married, like Twain, a respectable Northern woman and raised a large family, mostly daughters. But that black sheep was al-ways creeping around. He started writing a column for the *Pica-yune* as "Drop Shot," and spent evenings in the city archives studying the secret history of New Orleans. Stumbling across the "old Black code"—the early nineteenth-century laws that mandated torture and dismemberment as punishments for unruly slaves—he experienced an anger so intense that he felt compelled to write his first stories, seemingly "romantic" portraits of antebellum Louisiana that also cuttingly satirized its Creole residents for racial hypocrisy.

The stories were often grim—the editors of the *Atlantic* rejected one in 1875 "on account of the unmitigatedly distressful effect" it produced—but they created a sensation. By 1880 he had published one collection of short stories (*Old Creole Days*) and one novel (*The Grandissimes: A Story of Creole Life*), and his reputation was well established even while he was still clerking. In his writing, he hit notes no one else was even trying for: at a time when even progressive whites were equivocating on slavery's "discipline," he focused *The Grandissimes* around the story of Bras Coupé, an African prince kidnapped, enslaved, and graphically slaughtered, an outcome so clearly and unaffectedly tragic that it still leaps off the page.

In person, Cable was quick, hospitable, and physically striking, "a little man with a black beard" and a mustache he coiled and oiled so that it extended, like a wire, two inches away from his face on either side. He took stairs two at a time, his daughter noted, favored crimson neckties and a gray felt hat. People loved his principles: "O, Mr. Cable," a New England socialite once purred, "come to Connecticut & teach us how to reform!" But what made him "the fashion of the moment" were his voices: "Your broken French is capital," one New York editor told him. "It is something more than dialect—it is drama."

When Twain arrived in 1882, Cable was already being compared, favorably, to the greatest writers of the day. And by 1884 Cable's star would grow even hotter. His Creole voices had charmed the country almost as much as Harris's Uncle Remus. Howells and his wife spent an entire weekend talking in Cable's broken French, addicted: "We speak nothing else now but that dialect," Howells told him. At his house in the Garden District, Cable hosted celebrities suddenly attracted to New Orleans, who regarded Cable as its laureate. He hosted not just Twain but Artemus Ward, Edward King, and even Oscar Wilde, who visited in June of 1882, a mass of long hair and velvet that caught everyone off guard, hopeful that Cable could guide him to a voodoo dance.

In New York, where Cable was spending more time, he dined with Matthew Arnold and Andrew Carnegie, and walked the Brooklyn Bridge. He frequented salons with actors and performers. At one party in October 1882, he traded African-American songs with the great opera singer Clara Louise Kellogg, he singing "Rock Me, Julie, Rock Me," she "The Yalla Gal" and playing the banjo until "the clock struck twelve."

In Baltimore in March 1883, his own vocal performances held rapt an audience at Johns Hopkins for seven lectures: "The author's exact reproduction of the various dialects with which he has made us familiar," wrote the university's president, Daniel Coit Gilman, "were delightful."

"It's touchingly gratifying," Cable noted, "to hear them laugh & applaud where nothing funny is intended."

In New England, they adored him. Yale gave him an "honorary Master of Arts," acknowledging his "success" in "embalming in literature a unique phase of American social life which is rapidly passing away." In Hartford, they flattered him so much that it maddened Howells, who told him that "those Hartford people made me furious with their praises of you. I hate to see people foolish about a man, even if he *is* a great artist and every way charming." For readings in Boston, Oliver Wendell Holmes, Howells, and others wrote Cable free advertising. John Greenleaf Whittier visited him in his hotel, and intoned—conveniently, in front of a reporter—that "I've read every line thee ever wrote, and I knew thee would be a great writer as soon as I saw thy first productions."

Critics continued to fawn upon his writing, describing him as "the ablest writer the South has had since Poe," ranked as "a novelist with Howells and James." But the reviews of his performances, which played to jammed houses, were even more unreal. The *Boston Evening Transcript* praised the songs for their "curiously mingled medley of French troubadour grace and wild African fervor," and called the stories "the most unique case of indigenous literary genius America has yet produced." "If we insisted on a comparison," they concluded, "we should be obliged to go back to the actors of the Shakespearian era."

Twain, too, couldn't get enough of him. He admired Cable's facility for "creating worshipers on all hands" through a combination of genuine moral virtues—"moral honesty, limpid innocence, and utterly blemishless piety"—and clear thinking. "He is a marvelous talker on a deep subject," Twain told Howells, doubting that he knew anyone who "could unwind a thought more smoothly or orderly." He admired what Cable represented: someone who was making a new model for Southern literature, politically progressive, free from nostalgia for the plantation.

In letters, Twain, a decade older, addressed Cable as "My Dear

Nephew"; Cable called Twain "My Dear Uncle." For Cable, Twain was a large-hearted, even saintly man who would be perfect if he controlled the language that he used: "God bless you!" he told Twain, "May something,—*anything* that isn't affliction or distress—cure you of swearing & so make you *perfectly* lovely!" Twain didn't mind that Cable's churchiness softened him a bit: "Only give me room to swear," he told him. But he was bemused, too, by Cable's two-sidedness, the strange mix of "blemishless piety" and his love of a good bohemian party that ran all night. Describing one "large time"—"Aldrich and myself . . . properly fortified," Twain wrote—Cable used the word "orgy." "And no doubt it was," Twain added dryly, "viewed from his standpoint."

As the friendship grew, Twain recruited Cable for something big. They talked about a lecture tour in the spring months of 1882. Twain wanted something he could call a "circus," or "menagerie." He wanted Harris, and Cable, and Howells, and Thomas Bailey Aldrich up on-stage, "each read[ing] two minutes or so and pos[ing] as 'the happy family' between times." The plan refashioned the minstrel troupes of Twain's youth, without the burnt cork. Just as the minstrel show featured two comic 'end men' in blackface sandwiching a respectable 'middleman' or two in whiteface, Twain's "happy family" would have juxtaposed "Uncle Remus" and Twain himself—or versatile Cable, doing his voices and his songs—against the more serious Northern Howells and Aldrich.

Howells and Aldrich, however, weren't interested: they both had plans to go to Europe. Twain lamented that "Uncle Remus" (he didn't even seem to know Harris's real name anymore) had "vanished southward again," and would never "conquer his diffidence" enough to test "his voice in some empty Boston hall." But Cable was more than game, telling his daughters that "Mark Twain writes that he has a big idea and I must make no engagement until I see him."

Twain then spent most of summer, fall, and winter in 1882 and 1883 writing *Life on the Mississippi*, laboring at the end, churning out 9,500 words one January day in order to meet a self-imposed production deadline. By spring he called himself "an utterly free person," enjoying "the absence of the chains of slavery," and turned to Cable and his lecture tour again. Twain decided that he wanted

Cable to "try" his "lecture-wings" and his voice in a larger hall. He organized a petition to Cable from the citizens of Hartford, requesting that he perform there—which he did in April 1883, his "Creole dialect," according to the *Courant* reviewer, leaving the audience "almost breathless."

By June, Twain returned to Elmira for the summer, set himself in that little octagonal study the Cranes built atop a sharp hill, and broke out the old manuscript of *Huck Finn*. The trip down the river in 1882 to New Orleans had been cathartic. But so, too, had the friendship he made there. The words came bursting now, and not from obligation: "I haven't piled up MS so in years," he told Howells, "it's like old times . . . got health & spirits to *waste* . . ." He'd write 3,000 words some days, 4,000 words others, lie in bed and "read & smoke" for a couple of days, and then start up again.

He consulted notes that he had compiled over the previous few years, epigrammatic lines to himself about plot threads and scenes he would include, and many he didn't. The book could go darker, he had thought to himself, and it could be a more serious meditation on race and slavery; or it could be a total farce. He considered a scene where a free black was lynched: but he'd not write that scene. He considered some kind of "negro sermon," one line telling us what it might have been about: "See dat sinner how he run." He thought maybe Huck could "teach . . . Jim to read & write." But there'd be no sermon, no teaching, either. He also thought he'd bring in some "mesmeric foolishness"—hypnotism, another con game. He asked himself: Couldn't Huck "escape from somewhere" on an elephant? And he told himself *no*—elephants on the Mississippi were too much.

Just the right amount of tragedy. Just the right amount of politics. Just the right amount of farce.

He added some more chapters, mostly featuring a couple of confidence men calling themselves a King and a Duke: they'd commandeer Huck and Jim's raft, and float from village to village grifting, until one village catches them mid-fraud, and tars and feathers them. Before their unfortunate ending, though, lots and lots of the low stuff. Twain made it fit.

The King and the Duke brought with them a hilariously fractured version of Hamlet's "To be or not to be" soliloquy, leaking *Macbeth* and *King Lear* around the edges—classic minstrel stuff, but completely appropriate in a book whose boy protagonist also pondered suicide, and was taking a long time to make up his mind to do the right thing.

They also brought with them an act called "The Burning Shame," which Twain had loved for decades, the lowest of low culture, where the performer appeared naked, sometimes painted, and with a lit candle protruding from an intimate place. For an author so tightly controlled onstage, whose boy-hero instinctively chose to lie to any audience he faced rather than expose himself, this was a resonant moment. Huck stops short of telling us exactly what he sees onstage, though. And Twain calls it the "Royal Nonesuch" to cover his tracks. He had not forgotten that he was writing a book at least partly for children.

And when he hit "dull place[s]" in his "head," Twain played with time, literally: he worked on an outdoor version of "Mark Twain's Memory-Builder," his history game, knocking pegs into the driveway, measuring years in feet, and testing his daughters. They could stand on the porch and see the Norman Conquest at the base of the driveway, Victoria's reign up near his study. If possible, he was dawdling and racing at the same time, as if playing with time sped things up. But it always took him in circles instead. "*Never* dream of a recent thing," he jotted in his notebook, and he didn't: "America in 1985," he wrote shortly after, "the age of darkness back again."

He worked on a Scheherazade parody, one where boy and girl babies are swapped, and even worked a riff about the *Arabian Nights* into *Huck* for good measure: Huck, mixing his royals, nations, and centuries like the history game mandates, conflates the *Nights'* King Shahryar for Henry the Eighth. Twain even took some time and concocted a plan for a perpetual calendar—yet another invention befitting a man who believed history went round and round.

In seven or eight weeks, he had added 70,000 words to the 50,000 words he had written years before. And this time, rather than wanting to burn the manuscript, he was defiantly pleased: "*I* shall *like* it, whether anybody else does or not," he told Howells. He talked like it was done, that there wasn't "anything left to do, now, but revise." But he wasn't *totally* happy. For six months and more, into 1884, he continued to edit, proof, worry. Over one thousand edits total are still visible in the original manuscript, testing Huck's voice, testing Jim's, testing his own.

He had a gift for contrast, for recognizing the resemblances he was putting into play, the ambiguities he was introducing, and editing to taste. He weighed the phrases he used to describe Huck's abuse at the hands of Miss Watson and Widow Douglas with great care, toning down their rhetorical violence one or two notches: "made me hump myself" became "worked me middling hard"; "tackled" became "took a set at me"; "bully ragging" became "bothering over."

On the other hand, Pap became more dangerous: instead of giving Huck a "lick," he gave him the "raw hide."

He added racial tension in bits and pieces: a sign in a printer's shop advertising "stallions" in the first draft became an ad for "horses + runaway niggers" in the last, reminding us about Jim and where he stood in the scheme of American things.

Out went the chapter with the raftsmen patting juba, out went a misplaced anecdote about Jim and a medical school cadaver, a piece lost to the public until the *New Yorker* retrieved and published it in 1995. In went some new, vivid scenes. There was the *Walter Scott* incident, plugged into a chapter one-fourth of the way into the book. If Twain had written the early chapters of the book during a time when the bad-boy crisis was forming, this scene was clearly written when it was booming. As Jim and Huck float down the river, they find a sinking steamboat that Huck insists they board. There they discover two thieves threatening to abandon a captive partner. Huck, through accident more than design, steals their loot and takes their skiff. As he and Jim float away from the wreck, Huck feels compassion for the criminals, saying, "There ain't no telling but I might come to be a murderer myself." A few pages later, the wreck comes "sliding along down," not "much chance for anybody being alive in her"—and he is guilty, at least, of manslaughter.

"Child with rusty unloaded gun always kills," Twain jotted in the upper margin on manuscript page 365, a convoluted rule of narrative, or of life, but one that captured the drift of his thinking nicely.

Twain also added a comic interlude: an argument between Huck and the slave Jim about whether or not Solomon was a wise man, and a second, overlapping comic argument about why humans speak different languages. It was unmistakably minstrel banter. He dropped these into the book right after Huck called himself an almost-murderer, and right before Huck and Jim missed the essential left turn for the Ohio River. "So I quit," Twain wrote, Huck's last words in the second argument and, fittingly, the last words Twain wrote in the entire book. On the original manuscript, those three words stretch into the margin, making it hard to tell who, exactly, was quitting, and why.

Huck Finn, as scholars have since noted, now took on the three-part structure of a theatrical minstrel show: comic dialogues at the start, extended mock speeches and skits in the middle, and an extended closing parody that burlesqued plantation life. Everything but song. But the form was technical, academic—a ghost for his readers, perhaps, to feel but never name. As well, Twain accepted illustrations commissioned from E. W. Kemble that unquestionably made Jim look like a slack-jawed and bug-eyed stereotype. These are infuriating to look at, and have been for decades. Oppositely, Twain composed that "explanatory" note on dialects where he used the word "negro," distinguishing himself from Huck on that matter.

Disappointed by the slow sales of both *The Prince and the Pauper* and *Life on the Mississippi*, Twain decided he'd publish *Huck* himself, setting up his nephew-in-law, Charles L. Webster, as the namesake for a publishing company where he called the shots. By February 1884, as the manuscript went to the typesetters, as Charles Webster and Company opened its New York office, Twain met Cable again. On the day of the thirteenth, they holed up in Twain's drawing room. Twain smoked a pipe. Cable paced "back & forth," and Twain "up & down." They talked about some "earnest" subject. Then they discussed a "literary scheme." Within weeks, Twain made up his mind: the "circus," the "menagerie," whatever he called it, would be the vehicle with which he launched this new book, and his new publishing company. And Cable was his partner-in-crime. By late spring, Twain's representatives were making their contract offers for a fall tour to Cable alone. They offered Cable $350 a week, but he held out for $450. They argued over expenses. Twain offered "food" (despite Cable's oddly prodigious appetite), "lodging, & transportation," but declined to pay "all." "If he should become unmanageable & go to thrashing people," Twain wrote, "I should not want to have to pay his daily police court expenses. And it will be just like him to do that."

By fall, Cable was taking elocution lessons and trying his voice in empty halls. For readings, he selected some of the older stories, like "Posson Jone," thick with black and Creole dialects, and his newest novel, *Dr. Sevier*, filled with more dialects and stirring Civil War escape scenes. A scene he called "Mary's Night Ride," featuring a mother and her baby riding across battle lines on horseback, would become a tear-inducing set piece. "Cover the child," he would cry out, and the mothers in the audience would wipe their eyes without reserve.

As Cable rehearsed, Twain ran his new manuscript by Howells, Olivia, and other editors. He considered and rejected various sales strategies, supervised the book's illustrations (Huck was a "trifle more Irishy than necessary," which makes one wonder how Irish Twain wanted him to be, how much racial and ethnic difference he was prepared to sell), and micromanaged his nephew at the publishing company to the point of torment. He worked on *Huck* until he was sick of it, calling the process "infernal."

By October, he was refreshed, filling his journals with program ideas for the tour. In 1881, he had gotten Harris to confirm the authenticity of his version of "The Woman with the Golden Arm," and praised the response, noting that it was "nearer the true field-hand standard than that achieved by my Florida, Mo. negroes." He even encouraged Harris to publish it, which he did, in the August 1883 issue of the *Century*. Assured of its authenticity and audience appeal, Twain now decided that his variation of the ghost story would be his nightly finale. "Of course I *tell* it in the negro dialect," he told Harris. "That is necessary."

Let's linger here a moment. Twain, in his *Autobiography*, wrote that he had first heard this story from his "Old Uncle Dan'l, a slave of my uncle's aged 60," who "used to tell us children yarns every night by the kitchen fire." "De Woman Wid De Golden Arm," according to Twain, was "the last yarn demanded, every night," and its performance left a deep impression on the adult author: "under the spell of his impressive delivery we always fell a [*sic*] prey to that climax at the end when the rigid black shape in the twilight sprang at us with a shout."

Twain wanted evenings with the Twins of Genius to end this same way, only he would be the rigid black shape in the twilight.

"Once 'pon a time dey wuz a monsus mean man," he would begin, as he tells us in "How to Tell a Story." The monstrous mean man's wife died and was buried with her golden arm—"all solid gold, fum de shoulder down." The man, greedy and obsessed, digs up his wife's grave—at midnight, in a storm, in the snow, by the light of one lantern—and takes the arm.

On the way home, he hears a voice, beautifully mixed with the wind—Twain takes a "considerable pause," pretends to be startled, and then strikes "a listening attitude"—asking, "W-h-o—g-o-t—m-y—g-o-l-d-e-n—*arm*?"

And Twain shivers.

Then the man's lantern goes out, and the sleet lashes his face, and "soon he hear de voice agin, en"—Twain pauses again—"it 'us comin' *after* him! Bzzz—zzz—zzz—W-h-o—g-o-t—m-y—g-o-l-d-e-n *arm*?"

"You must wail it out very plaintively and accusingly," Twain noted.

The man crosses the pasture, hears it again—Twain repeats the voice, with wind sounds. The man enters his house, climbs into bed, hears it again. Then the man hears steps coming up the stairs, hears the latch turn.

Pause. Then the man feels a presence by the side of the bed. Bending over him.

Pause. Then the man feels "someth'n *c-o-l-d,* right down 'most agin his head!"

Pause. Then the voice says, right next to his ear, "W-h-o—g-o-t—m-y—g-o-l-d-e-n *arm*?"

Twain would then pause again, and select, from the audience, someone he called "the farthest-gone auditor," and stare. And when the pause "reached exactly the right length," he would jump, stamp his feet, his hands turned into claws, and yell, "*You've* got it!"

It was that last pause that made the difference, if you wanted to scare that "auditor," which he did: "you *must* get the pause right," Twain insisted later, "and you will find it the most troublesome and aggravating and uncertain thing you ever undertook."

There were other pieces, too. "The Tragical Tale of the Fishwife," a parody of the mixed genders of the German language. "A Trying Situation," in which a young woman at a hotel in Lucerne remembers him, and he pretends to remember her, with comic results. "The Celebrated Jumping Frog of Calavaras County," the story that made him famous. "A Desperate Encounter with an Interviewer": Twain hated interviews the way he hated autographs and newspapers. "Ah, you are cruel," he told one reporter pre-performance, with a crafted look of "utter sadness," "to attempt to interview a man just at the moment when he needs to feel good."

He considered doing *Huck* for the entire reading, but thought twice. He asked Cable to help him select the best "negro passages" from the book. He had his favorites: those comic arguments between Huck and Jim about the wisdom of Solomon, and why humans speak different languages.

In the first draft of the program, Twain titled this section using Huck's exasperated, ironic penultimate line from the chapter in which they appear: "Can't Learn a Nigger to Argue." Cable talked him out of it. The problem was context. "In the text, whether on the printed page or in the reader's utterances the phrase is absolutely without a hint of grossness," Cable told him, "but alone on a published programme, it invites discreditable conjectures of what the context may be." And the potentially offended audience was not African-Americans but women of a certain class: "I think we should avoid any risk of appearing— even to the most thin-skinned and supersensative [*sic*] and hypercritical matrons and misses—the faintest bit gross."

Twain assented, and instead called these pieces "King Sollermun" and "How Come a Frenchman Doan' Talk Like a Man?" And Cable endorsed them. " 'King Sollermun,' " he assured Twain, "is enough by itself to immortalize its author."

Twain also loved the conclusion of the book, a lengthy burlesque where Huck Finn and Tom Sawyer "free" Jim from slavery using ideas culled from romantic novels like *The Count of Monte Cristo* and *The Man in the Iron Mask*. He'd put it on the program, too, but not at first: one trusted friend from Elmira, Clara Spaulding, had "dashed & destroyed" it, telling him it was atrocious.

They'd charge as much as a dollar to see the show in the cities, as little as twenty-five cents in the towns. They'd run ads in the newspaper alongside those for the freaks, the circuses, the light opera and the Shakespeare, the lectures at the Y on the decline of American spiritual life. Twain would keep most of the money—but he'd also assume most of the risk.

By Cable's insistence, they'd not appear on Sundays. They wouldn't even travel on Sundays.

"The Trouble Begins at Eight," the ads promised.

But the trouble had already begun.

Cable, despite the adulation, was making enemies, too. For starters, he really wasn't the Apostle-dimming saint many made him out to be. He ate too much when others paid, lied a little too frequently, enjoyed rubbing elbows with celebrities a little too much, and tended to exaggerate the esteem in which others held him. He played innocent, for instance, about the unintended laughter in Baltimore, when he did his Louisiana voices for an academic audience at Johns Hopkins. For years, the Creoles in New Orleans thought he was holding them up to national ridicule. When one reviewer argued that his "broken French" was not, in fact, an accurate portrait of how real Creoles talked, Cable wrote back that "I am a creole myself, living today in sight of the house where I was born." It was a lie: like Twain, he may have liked wearing a mask more than he cared to admit.

Cable's real problem, though, was that he was, in many respects, exactly as moral as advertised. He was horrified by the history of slavery. And he was persuaded that everyone in the South would see things the way he saw them, only about ten years after he saw them. At first, he took calculated risks with Southern public opinion. In 1875, for instance, after mobs stormed a mixed-race high school and evicted the students they regarded as colored, Cable wrote an angry letter to the *New Orleans Bulletin* wondering what harm would come to black or white children if they studied together. He signed the letter "A Southern White Man"—anonymous, but anthemic.

As Cable grew in celebrity, he spoke more boldly, if generally, for Southern reform. At commencement ceremonies at Washington and Lee, Emory, and the University of Mississippi, he reflected on the "Southern mind," and the "Southern instinct," with increasing causticity. Are we "not cunning enough to snuff out the stupid wickedness of exalting and abusing our fellow humans class by class and race by race," he asked eight hundred students at Oxford, gathered to hear him speak on "Literature in the Southern States" not long after Twain first recruited him for a tour of some kind.

In private, meanwhile, he gathered evidence that the convict-lease system had substituted "negro tenantry for negro slaves," and that the number of blacks sentenced into it far exceeded the numbers for white criminals guilty of the same crimes. "The plantation idea," he believed, had survived the Civil War, and would shape the next century in the South as surely as it had the past one.

By 1883, the same year that the Supreme Court overturned the Civil Rights Act of 1875, he was dissatisfied with pulling punches, and his success seemed to taunt him. In Alabama in September, on his way to deliver a critical speech on convict-lease to the National Conference of Charities and Correction, he witnessed a young black woman and her small child on a train, "neatly and tastefully dressed in cool, fresh muslins," "still and quiet," forced to share a car "packed . . . full" with chained convicts while seats remained open throughout the rest of the train. Later, he would write that it moved him as much as the moment in the New Orleans archives when he discovered the old black codes that sentenced rebellious slaves to torture and mutilation. At almost the same time that audiences in New England gave him adoring receptions he described as "simply ovations," he began to see extraordinary responsibilities attached to his fame. To a friend, Roswell Smith, he said, "It has come at last"— success "like a flood," that is; "we prayed to the Lord for this & He has given it to us." And then he wondered: "The thing to watch now is to see that success makes a better man of me—not a worse one."

To be a "better man," Cable decided, meant an end to equivocation: "Behind all the fierce conservatism," he would write, years later, in a short essay called *My Politics*, "there was a progressive though silent South needing to be urged to speak and act." In February 1884—right when he and Twain discussed some "deep," anonymous "subject" in Hartford—he published "The Convict Lease System in the Southern States" in the *Century*, and eviscerated the Southern prison and judicial system. It was a brilliant piece of muckraking research, tallying with statistical precision a malignant system that imprisoned indigent Americans for small crimes, and then worked them to death under the terms of privatizing contracts serving unethical employers and state governments. "This system," he wrote in terms that might echo today, "springs primarily from the idea that possession of a convict's person is an opportunity for the State to make money."

Then, on June 18, he addressed the historical society at the University of Alabama, told them about the woman on the train from the previous September, and touched what was then the third rail of American politics: he called for blacks and whites to share public spaces. "The east and north and west of our great and prosperous and happy country, and the rest of the civilized world," he told those no-doubt-startled students in Tuscaloosa, "are standing and waiting to see what we will write upon the white page of to-day's and to-morrow's history."

The Alabama newspapers turned on him quickly. The New Orleans papers, not having heard the speech, defended their laureate, calling their Tuscaloosa colleagues "bumpkins." Cable himself was only emboldened: "Somebody must speak first," he reasoned. "If you were a little 100 pound man with a wife and four children," he told another correspondent, "do you think you'd worry? You couldn't afford to; you'd *have* to keep cool." He agreed to publish the Alabama speech, in article form, in the *Century* sometime during the winter of 1884–85. It would be called "The Freedman's Case in Equity." It would be his national coming-out as a proponent of integration. Everyone, nationwide, would know where he stood.

Then, in September 1884, he published *Dr. Sevier*, the new novel from which he would be reading heavily during the "Twins of Genius" tour. At the end of the book—and so, at the end of its serial run, too—the narrator addresses a group of Northern soldiers, characters in the book, and tells them that "your cause is just." This was fairly surprising, even to Northern readers. Southern newspapers that had loved the earlier installments of the novel now began to doubt. The *Louisville Commercial* observed that Cable was now playing to "the coterie of saints who stand around the throne of culture in Cambridge." In New Orleans, the *Times-Democrat* prepared to "attack the work viciously, on account of its anti-Southern tone," but two of Cable's friends talked Page Baker, the newspaper's editor, out of it. "He is hopelessly down upon you," one warned Cable.

In other words, as J. B. Pond, Twain's road manager, was placing the ads for the "Twins of Genius," Cable was setting in motion his own ambitious and dangerous narrative, one that threatened to swamp even Twain's celebrity. The timing was quite remarkable. Cable gave his speech in Alabama just before he signed with Twain for the "Twins of Genius." *Dr. Sevier* was published after he was signed, but before the tour began. And "The Freedman's Case in Equity" would be circulating nationwide during the tour—almost exactly halfway through, in fact—and it would share space in that issue of the *Century* with some of the first published chapters of *Huck Finn*.

It is unclear what Twain or Pond thought. A twenty-first-century media handler hired to promote the "Twins of Genius" would probably have tried to talk Cable out of this. That May, just before he gave the speech in Tuscaloosa, Cable rented a house in Simsbury, Connecticut, and prepared to move his family north from New Orleans—for a year, maybe longer. "The South makes me sick," he wrote, and he seemed to mean it two different ways. The South did make him physically ill: the scarlet fever visited Louisiana every summer. At the same time, it was a convenient time to be planning a getaway, if he needed one. And he would.

Meanwhile, Twain was working on his own dangerous narrative. It is so easy to accept the inauthenticity of the "Mark Twain" construction: we accept it every time we say his name, knowing, as most do, that he was born and never stopped being Samuel L. Clemens. He knew it was easy to accept, too: "I feel as though I were a sort of fraud; I seem to be playing a part, and please consider I am playing a part for want of something better, and this is not unfamiliar to me; I have often done this before." He didn't say this in his private journal. He said this to an audience at a charity bazaar at the Waldorf Hotel in New York, which meant that they knew it, too, and didn't care, and neither do we.

And so, it is also easy to assume that he played confidently this game of Victorian political roulette as part of the general confidence with which "Mark Twain" conquered, and still conquers, audiences. When it came to children, he probably knew that he was inviting controversy, that Huck and Tom assailed stereotypes of youth in which many Americans were heavily invested. But when it came to the history of black and white in America, he had a deep case of vertigo.

He knew what the Southern newspapers, politicians, and church leaders were doing, and he loathed it. But he made common cause with them in some crucial ways. When he endorsed Grover Cleveland for president, for instance—the last major public initiative he made prior to *Huck Finn*—he did so because, in part, he was enamored with the idea of being a Mugwump, a true independent whose vote defied party allegiance. And he truly believed that Cleveland was less corrupt than Blaine.

At the same time, he couldn't avoid knowing that he was aligning himself with the political party most interested in unmaking the promise of Reconstruction, and that most benefited from the suppression of black voters. And he still couldn't quite shake the idea that black culture, if not black individuals, worked for him and people like him: that only Cable and Harris could be "masters" of dialects millions of people of color spoke daily, for instance. Or that the ghosts of his childhood *labored* for him in his imagination, and with no desire to be free: "He has served me well, these many, many years," he wrote about Daniel Quarles in his *Autobiography*, decades, in fact, after his real uncle John had freed the man. "I have not seen him for more than half a century, and yet spiritually I have had his welcome company a good part of that time," he added, "he has endured it all with the patience and friendliness and loyalty which were his birthright."

Imitating *carefully* the voices of black men and women, telling their stories, then selling that material for twenty-five cents to one buck per ticket, and then making overwhelmingly white ticketholders jump out of respect or fear—this mix satisfied his genuine love of black culture, his eye for the main chance, and his sense of justice all at once. And sharing the stage, as he did so, with the Southern white man known above all others for his support of integration would satisfy his inchoate hope that a new progressive political coalition was possible, one that might replace the one that was falling apart.

Twain knew this concoction was not middle ground. It would please some audiences but not others. That trip southward for *Life on the Mississippi* had reminded him that, like Cable, he was sick of Southern politics and its reactionary conservatism, its fixation with "obsolete forms" and "dead language." In the first draft of that book, he had written that "slavery" was "gone, and permanently"—but in the final draft, he cut that out. He didn't book any lecture halls south of the Mason-Dixon Line, with one or two gentle exceptions just over the Ohio. He didn't send any subscription agents down there, either, or very many review copies of *Huck* to Southern papers.

If Twain wasn't looking southward to sell books, however, he was still looking to his Southern roots for what he would put in them. The setting of *Huck Finn* was the 1840s, the same time Daniel Quarles told prepubescent Sam Clemens about the woman with the golden arm. The sections of *Huckleberry Finn* composed after the trip south in 1882 are those sections that most closely mimic the minstrel shows of Twain's youth. They were the very first, the very ones, that he couldn't wait to perform. And Cable's songs, the ones that entranced Twain and so many others, originated from the streets and squares of New Orleans in the 1840s—just before the local government, fearing insurrection, shut down the open-air markets and the mixed free black and slave celebrations that took place at them.

An older audience member watching the "Twins of Genius" might have concluded that Twain thought that America had left behind something very important around 1845. And that audience member would be right. In *Autobiography* chapters published in 1906, Twain told his audience that "the real negro show," the minstrel show he loved as a child, was "stone dead for thirty years." On the surface,

Twain's comment seems counterintuitive. In 1906, minstrel shows were a staple of the American entertainment industry: *Billboard* magazine even ran a weekly "Minstrelsy" section. But the minstrel show in 1906 or 1884 was not the same as the minstrel show in 1845. With increasingly rare exceptions, most established blackface showmen now told their audience exactly what those third-grade readers told their children about hard work: "Always Be Ready When Your Chance Comes;" "Pull Hard Against the Stream." The figure of Old Darky, comfortable with his massa but longing for his lost family, became set in stone, and Stephen Foster ballads like "Old Folks at Home" became ritual.

The black minstrel troupes got the South, got to play "the true Southern darkey[s]," as ads promised; they could pack in five thousand at a time. In Ghana and Cape Town, Jamaica and Trinidad, local performers blacked up (and whited up and redded up) and created a global form with politics more slippery than anything T. D. Rice ever imagined. Back home, though, the white minstrels went the other way: they grew hard and guileless. They mocked the women's movement, the Indians, the Japanese: a production of the *Black Mikado* ran for hundreds of performances in 1885 and 1886. They took no side in the Civil War, or rather, were actively angry at any abolitionist or radical Southerner who made them fight. The minstrels played Irishmen in blackface, Asians in blackface. They called Jews the "children of the get-dough" in blackface. And, incredibly, they longed for the old days in blackface. "One hundred years ago every man cut his coat according to his cloth," Tambo now complained. "Every man was estimated at his real value, shoddy was not known, nobody had struck 'ile,' and true merit and honest worth were the only grounds for promotion."

By the early 1900s, even this seemed quaint: minstrelsy became, by and large, the soundtrack to lynching and racialized voter disenfranchisement laws. D. W. Griffith's portrayal of "sexually predatory blacks" in the early film *Birth of a Nation* remains one of the most enduring and grotesque markers for modern viewers of minstrelsy's politics. The makeup was intentionally bad; white actors in blackface played slavering would-be rapists in the foregrounds of shots where real African-Americans labored in the backgrounds. The politics were not shocking; only the new medium's ease with the hateful potential of the old form.

Audiences continued to pack the theaters. The minstrels themselves claimed progress: "In the march of time," one pamphleteer claimed, "there has been a marked improvement both in the negro and the character of the entertainment designed to portray his peculiarities." But Twain wasn't remotely alone in believing, as some contemporary historians have argued, that what might have begun as "a way of registering cross-racial charisma and union" had instead undoubtedly become "a way of registering racial separation and disdain." And he wanted to turn back the clock.

In other words, Twain wasn't having an argument with 1880s America about whether or not there should be a minstrel show. That was an argument that others would have, generations later, after World War II. Twain was having an argument about the ways that whites would portray blacks— not whether or not whites would portray blacks.

Not the fact that race could be fun. But the kind of fun that could be had.

Twain and Cable genuinely loved black culture for its vitality, and they genuinely appreciated how stultifying America would be without it. They empathized with the political position of blacks. But what they *loved* was deeper: they loved their own childhoods (as we all do), the primal memories of their cultural awakenings (as we all do), the shadowy African-American mentors who both presided and served, and the inconsistency of that duality, too. What Twain wanted—and Cable assisted—was to re-create the first moment many whites saw something positive, something they wanted to emulate, in blacks, and to revive the complicated subversion of that moment. And he did so just as the Jim Crow curtain was lowering, separating blacks from whites, cutting off the possibility that white Americans might experience racial others without mediation. He did so as American newspapers ran virulently anti-black articles daily, as they blurred American journalism itself into the worst kind of minstrelsy. He did so as African-Americans worried, with substantial justification, that the Civil War hadn't solved anything.

But looking backward to fight looking backward was a two-sided business. Twain and Cable loathed "the plantation idea," and were disturbed by its resilience. But what these men were also doing was salvaging something that only slavery had really made possible during their lifetimes: "safe," unmediated social exchanges between blacks and whites. And they were making plenty of money, too. Their answer, both just and opportunistic, seems inevitable in retrospect. What startles many readers now is that Twain loved minstrel shows, and that he used racial slurs. This was true 130 years ago, too. But what would have startled (and thrilled, and maddened) his Victorian audience was the sight of respectable men in respectable venues performing blackness—*without* the burnt cork on their faces.

And we're so used to that kind of thing that we've forgotten where it came from. Looking backward ourselves, we can see shards of the twentieth century to come in the "Twins of Genius." It was as if Twain and Cable were anthropologists, record moguls, performers, and marketers all in one, holistically merging the strategies—both visionary and exploitative—that have guided the exchange between white and black cultures for a century and more. Verlaine called Rimbaud a "white negro"; Picasso painted African masks onto *Les Demoiselles d'Avignon*; Flo Ziegfeld brought Ethel Williams down from Harlem to Broadway to teach his performers how to ball the jack, and then sent her back uptown. Norman Mailer argued that the American "hipster" of the 1950s "had absorbed the existential synapses of the Negro, and for practical purposes"—whatever these were—"could be considered a white Negro." Elvis Presley's vocal style evolved from genuine affinity for black singers he witnessed at clubs and churches he crossed the color line to hear. And Sam Phillips discovered him, it is said, looking for a white man who could sing like a black one.

More modernly, one can see in Twain's thinking a strange white Victorian version of the contemporary debate over "socially conscious" hip-hop—between music, lyrics, and narrative that portrays "the realities of African-American urbanity," as Carl Hancock Rux writes, or "gangsta obsessions replete with murder, money, sex, alcohol and drug consumption." And one can see traces of the modern "coolhunter" (to use the term Malcolm Gladwell brought to public recognition), marketing consultants who, like Cable gathering slave songs and stories, or Twain traveling down south, tour black, Latino, and transitional neighborhoods to uncover new trends in fashion, music, and language, and deliver them to their corporate employers.

Finally, though, one can see a broader debate about what forms of empathy strike at racism, and what forms sustain it—a debate that continues to this day among sociologists, politicians, and marketers alike. Twain thought that Cable was his "twin." He believed that Cable was equally infatuated with the music, language, and culture of blacks and other disenfranchised American communities, and for roughly the same reasons. Twain didn't register, though, what it might mean that Cable sang like a minstrel but wrote like an abolitionist, and that he was going to offer the American public a straight line to racial integration— with no codes, no winks, and no hedging. Twain was going to test the black voice behind a white face. Cable would do roughly the same thing—while also calling for the removal of political boundaries between black and white. It didn't look like a big difference. But it was.

7

Twins

The Twin of Genius, Mark Twain. The opening remarks, as transcribed by a *Toronto Globe* reviewer with a good memory or a fast pen. The script, from *Huckleberry Finn* . . .

Twain (as himself): Ladies and Gentlemen: you find me appointed to read something entitled 'King Sollermun,' if it may strictly be called reading where you don't use any book, but it is from a book, an unpublished story of mine called 'THE ADVENTURES OF HUCKLEBERRY FINN.' It is a sort of continuation, or sequel, if you please, of a former story of mine, 'Tom Sawyer.' Huck Finn is an outcast, an uneducated, ragged boy, son of the town drunkard in a Mississippi River village, and he is running away from the brutalities of his father, and with him is a negro man, Jim, who is fleeing from slavery . . . They can't venture to travel in the day time, so they bide during the day and travel at night, and they entertain each other with conversations sometimes useful and sometimes otherwise. The story is written from the mouth of Huck Finn. . . .

Twain (as Huck, addressing the audience): I read considerable to Jim about kings, and dukes, and earls and such, and how gaudy they dressed and how much style they put on, and called each other your majesty, and your grace, and your lordship, and so on, 'stead of mister; and Jim's eyes bugged out, and he was interested. . . .

Twain (as Jim): I didn' know dey was so many un um. I hain't hearn 'bout none un um, skasely, but ole King Sollermun, onless you counts dem kings dat's in a pack er k'yards. How much do a king git?

Huck: Get? . . . why, they get a thousand dollars a month if they want it; they can have just as much as they want; everything belongs to them.

Jim: *Ain'* dat gay? En what dey got to do, Huck?

Huck: *They* don't do nothing! Why, how you talk! They just set around.

Jim: No—is dat so?

Huck: Of course it is. They just set around. Except, maybe, when there's a war; then they go to the war. But other times they just lazy around . . . [W]hen things is dull, they fuss with the parlyment; and if everybody don't go just so, he whacks their heads off. But mostly they hang round the harem.

Jim: Roun' de which?

Huck: Harem.

Jim: What's de harem?

Huck: The place where he keeps his wives. Don't you know about the harem? Solomon had one; he had about a million wives.

Jim: Why, yes, dat's so; I—I'd done forgot it. A harem's a bo'd'n house, I reck'n. Mos' likely dey has rackety times in de nussery. En I reck'n de wives quarrels considable; en dat 'crease de racket. Yit dey say Sollermun de wises' man dat ever live'. I doan' take no stock in dat. Bekase why: would a wise man want to live in de mids' er sich a blimblammin' all de time? No—'deed he wouldn't. A wise man 'ud take en buil' a biler-factry; en den he could shet *down* de biler-factry when he want to res'.

Huck: Well, but he *was* the wisest man, anyway; because the widow she told me so, her own self.

Jim: I doan k'yer what de widder say, he *warn't* no wise man nuther. He had some er de dad-fetchedes' ways I ever see. Does you know 'bout dat chile dat he 'uz gwyne to chop in two?

Huck: Yes; the widow told me all about it.

Jim: *Well*, den! Warn' dat de beatenes' notion in de worl'? You jis' take en look at it a minute. Dah's de stump, dah—dat's one er de women; heah's you—dat's de yuther one; I's Sollermun; en dish-yer dollar bill's de chile. Bofe un you claims it. What does I do? Does I shin aroun' mongs' de neighbors en fine out which un you de bill *do* b'long to, en han' it over to de right one, all safe en soun', de way dat anybody dat had any gumption would? No— I take en whack de bill in *two*, en give half un it to you, en de yuther half to de yuther woman. Dat's de way Sollermun was gwyne to do wid de chile. Now I want to ast you: what's de use er dat half a bill?—can't buy noth'n wid it. En what use is a half a chile? I wouldn' give a dern for a million un um.

Huck: But hang it, Jim, you've clean missed the point—blame it, you've missed it a thousand mile.

Jim: Who? Me? Go 'long. Doan' talk to *me* 'bout yo' pints. I reck'n I knows sense when I sees it; en dey ain' no sense in sich doin's as dat. De 'spute warn't 'bout a half a chile, de 'spute was 'bout a whole chile; en de man dat think he kin settle a 'spute 'bout a whole chile wid a half a chile doan' know enough to come in out'n de rain. Doan' talk to me 'bout Sollermun, Huck, I knows him by de back.

Huck: But I tell you you don't get the point.

Jim: Blame de pint! I reck'n I knows what I knows. En mine you, de *real* pint is down furder—it's down deeper. It lays in de way Sollermun was raised. You take a man dat's got on'y one or two chillen: is dat man gwyne to be waseful o' chillen? No, he ain't; he can't 'ford it. *He* know how to value 'em. But you take a man dat's got 'bout five million chillen runnin' roun' de house, en it's diffunt. *He* as soon chop a chile in two as a cat. Dey's plenty mo'. A chile er two, mo' er less, warn't no consekens to Sollermun, dad fetch him!

Huck (addressing the audience): I never see such a nigger. If he got a notion in his head once, there warn't no getting it out again. He was the most down on Solomon of any nigger I ever see. So I went to talking about other kings, and let Solomon slide. I told about Louis Sixteenth that got his head cut off in France long time ago; and about his little boy the dolphin, that would a been a king, but they took and shut him up in jail, and some say he died there.

Jim: Po' little chap.

Huck: But some says he got out and got away, and come to America.

Jim: Dat's good! But he'll be pooty lonesome—dey ain' no kings here, is dey, Huck?

Huck: No.

Jim: Den he cain't git no situation. What he gwyne to do?

Huck: Well, I don't know. Some of them gets on the police, and some of them learns people how to talk French.

Jim: Why, Huck, doan' de French people talk de same way we does?

Huck: *No*, Jim; you couldn't understand a word they said—not a single word.

Jim: Well, now, I be ding-busted! How do dat come?

Huck: *I* don't know; but it's so. I got some of their jabber out of a book. Spose a man was to come to you and say *Polly-voo-franzy*—what would you think?

Jim: I wouldn' think nuff'n; I'd take en bust him over de head. Dat is, ef he warn't white. I wouldn't 'low no nigger to call me dat.

Huck: Shucks, it ain't calling you anything. It's only saying, do you know how to talk French.

Jim: Well, den, why couldn't he *say* it?

Huck: Why, he *is* a-saying it. That's a Frenchman's *way* of saying it.

Jim: Well, it's a blame' ridicklous way, en I doan' want to hear no mo' 'bout it. Dey ain' no sense in it.

Huck: Looky here, Jim, does a cat talk like we do?

Jim: No, a cat don't.

Huck: Well, does a cow?

Jim: No, a cow don't, nuther.

Huck: Does a cat talk like a cow, or a cow talk like a cat?

Jim: No, dey don't.

Huck: It's natural and right for 'em to talk different from each other, ain't it?

Jim: 'Course.

Huck: And ain't it natural and right for a cat and a cow to talk different from *us*?

Jim: Why, mos' sholy it is.

Huck: Well, then, why ain't it natural and right for a *Frenchman* to talk different from us?—you answer me that.

Jim: Is a cat a man, Huck?

Huck: No.

Jim: Well, den, dey ain't no sense in a cat talkin' like a man. Is a cow a man?—er is a cow a cat?

Huck: No, she ain't either of them.

Jim: Well, den, she ain' got no business to talk like either one er the yuther of 'em. Is a Frenchman a man?

Huck: Yes.

Jim: *Well*, den! Dad blame it, why doan he *talk* like a man?—you answer me *dat*!

Huck (addressing the audience): I see it warn't no use wasting words—you can't learn a nigger to argue. So I quit.

"The story of King Sollermun, printed," one newspaper wrote, was "by no means easy reading." Delivered live by Twain, though, the paper added, "it set the audience in a perfect storm of boisterous merriment." Oh, to be a twenty-first-century fly on the wall of one of those lyceums or churches, to hear where the pauses and revisions went, to hear where the laughter waxed and waned. That would settle everything. Imagine reading a transcript of a performance by Steven Colbert, Chris Rock, or Sarah Silverman in a hundred years' time: How much would be lost? But Twain leaves few footprints: he memorized as much as he could, and revised on the fly, watching his audience for clues (something else those pauses were good for). Looking backward, we can hear the familiar accents of American banter comedy: Groucho and Chico Marx, Abbott and Costello, George Costanza and Jerry Seinfeld, but heavily racialized across the fault lines we associate with minstrelsy.

On the surface, Twain seemed to stick to the stereotypes. For certain, Jim's "dialect" defined him—made him exotic, a little harder to hear and to take seriously. And he certainly seems to flounder when it comes to understanding a parable about wisdom and fairness so simple that any Sunday-school student could tell you what it meant. When Huck swears at him at the end in frustration, one can easily imagine that some among that cultivated audience agreed with him.

If one was writing racist indoctrination text, however, one could do much better than this. First, there was Huck himself—Huckleberry Finn. In 1884, audiences had never heard that weird name before, or they remembered it, dimly, as belonging to a supporting character in *Tom Sawyer*, a book from eight years earlier. His first name meant he was a rube. His last name wasn't just Irish, it was stage Irish at a time when being Irish in America meant you were weren't really white: you belonged to a "dark race" still lampooned in the minstrel shows of the day, and that had more than its share of the prison population, too.

And Huck had a "dialect" as well; Twain would have been perspicacious about this. He came from the region of the full goatees. That audience in New England would have surely noticed this. And that audience had more than a little experience with the ironic inversion of a racial slur. They were used to it in distancing quotation marks, not in Huck's unironic-to-himself voice—so Twain was challenging them (as he challenges us). Maybe Twain didn't read those lines. That would have mollified the "matrons." But probably he did. Cable told him he could if he made the context clear, and he had: he had described Jim as a "negro man" in his introduction, as he did in the explanatory note at the start of *Huck*. And he had made sure his audience knew the story was told in Huck's voice, not his. And the placement was so perfect, right at the nub. That Huck uses a racial epithet when he loses—that he uses it with force as he gives up—

there were certainly audience members who would have understood that the joke was on the boy, not the man.

In other words, King Sollermun wasn't exactly a dialogue between white and black, reason and ignorance. What, for instance, does Jim mean when he says that he knows Solomon by the back, when he surely has never met a biblical patriarch? Or that the problem lay with how Solomon was raised? Why, when looking for an analogy for a child, does he pick a dollar bill?

In truth, Jim has met men and women who don't value one child because they "have" so many that they can always lose one without feeling. He knows *them* by the back. And he is familiar, too, with ways of thinking where children turn into money very quickly. There is a reason he is so down on Solomon, and there is a reason he can only insist that he has a point to make, but can't say *exactly* what it is. He can't name names. Which is, in turn, the reason "you" can't teach him to argue—the same reason he can say he'll hit a Frenchman, then pauses and says "unless he was white, of course."

You can bet that Twain paused there. "You can't learn a nigger to argue" because you'll beat him, sell him deeper South, or kill him if he wins. You can only teach him to say what he really thinks through analogies that corkscrew on the edge of intelligibility, but that you can "get"—barely.

And why *can't* a Frenchman talk like a man, anyway? Huck's argument rests on the assumption that one can blur the line between men and women and animals. Jim's argument rests on the assumption that there is a line that divides men and women from animals.

Which argument dovetails with arguments for slavery? And which for freedom? Who is the American voice here?

This was the minstrel show Twain wanted to recover: the one where the stereotype and the comedy leaked sedition. Maybe it existed only in his imagination, ultimately. One could say Twain found a way for the slave's authentic political consciousness to speak through the stereotype. But that wasn't what he was fighting for. He was fighting for the right to speak through Jim himself, using the same strategies he regarded as a deep part of the nineteenth-century African-American experience, and for the same rough motive: because he was afraid of what a white audience would do to him if he told them what he thought out loud. He could get twice the laughs that way, too—the people laughing at Jim, and the people laughing at the people laughing at Jim. It was strangely profitable, and Twain was great at it. All he needed to do was never say exactly what he meant, or say the exact opposite as soon as that audience he watched so closely began to reach for the tar and feathers.

The "Twins of Genius"—and *Huck Finn*, featuring Jim and Huck and their arguments about biblical history and linguistic diversity—debuted with a splash, giving Americans an alternative to their usual entertainments, including those provided by the disputed federal election. They started in New England: New Haven, Springfield, Providence, Melrose, Lowell, Boston, Hartford. In Springfield, on a clear, cool Friday night three days after the election, you could go see Twain and Cable at Gilmore's Opera House, or you could attend "THE GRAND OPENING OF THE SPRINGFIELD ROLLER RINK" for the 1884–85 season. But the big news in town was a spontaneous parade-riot being managed, loosely, by the Democratic Party in celebration of Grover Cleveland's expected win. There were "cannon, rockets, blue-lights, torches, music, marching and cheers." A wagon carrying fireworks blew up, but that was all right, because it made a "brilliant display" anyway, according to the *Springfield Republican*.

A parade started around seven—"lanterns, brooms and transparencies" that read MUGWUMPS TO THE FRONT—and marched right past Gilmore's just after eight, as Cable was warming up his songs from Place Congo in front of his own big crowd. The "superabundant" celebratory singing outside unnerved him, though, so he stopped. He tried a shorter selection later, and the audience loved it so much that they felt "defrauded" that they couldn't hear an encore.

The *Republican* fawned on him: "He presented himself first and impressed every one as a romantic figure, a sort of knightly ideal, with his broad and overhanging forehead, his brilliant eyes . . ." But they had heard him before, and seemed to think he was trying too hard: his readings were "done with far greater elocutionary effect than when he first read it here . . . which hurt the artistic quality."

Twain didn't have that problem. He was overdressed, and his hair was a mess. He told the audience that the programs, which were printed "at great cost," were useless, since he didn't plan to present a single reading listed there.

Instead, he did "A Trying Situation," and "The Tragical Tale of the Fishwife." The first one made him look like a stage idiot. The second one was grounded in Twain's astonishment at the mixing of genders among German nouns: "A tree is male," he'd explain dryly, "its buds are female, its leaves are neuter; horses are sexless, dogs are male, cats are female . . . a person's mouth, neck, bosom, elbows, fingers, nails, feet, and body, are of the male sex, and his head is male or neuter according to the word selected to signify it, and *not* according to the sex of the individual who wears it . . ."

But this was just warming up. Anarchic grammar was an opportunity for other kinds of anarchy, the kinds that unraveled ideologies, and that's where Twain's imagination inevitably turned: "In Germany," Twain would explain, "a man may *think* he is a man, but when he comes to look into the matter closely, he is bound to have his doubts; he finds that in sober truth he is a most ridiculous mixture; and if he ends by trying to comfort himself with the thought that he can at least depend on a third of this mess as being manly and masculine, the humiliating second thought will quickly remind him that in this respect he is no better off than any woman or cow in the land."

He also did "King Sollermun," and "wound up with telling a ghost story after the manner of an old negro." According to the *Republican*, "He positively convulsed his hearers with the deliberate fashion of his speech and the peculiar ways in which he indicated their proper emotions by the inflections of his voice."

In Providence, you could see Twain ("world famous wit") and Cable ("exquisite humor and pathos") at Blackstone Hall for seventy-five cents or a dollar, two shows on Saturday, at 2:00 and 8:00. Twain and Cable didn't quite pack the house, but they did well. Cable dazzled with his dramatic readings from *Dr. Sevier*: "It must certainly be regarded as a mark of talent little short of genius," the *Providence Journal* claimed, "that a man of Mr. Cable's pursuits can so completely obliterate himself by conveying in rapid turns the whispers or hoarse commands of the spy, the husky croak of the negro guide, the terrified cry of the infant awakened by the shots of the sentries, and the agonizing wail of the mother riding for life . . ."

When he tried to sing, though—"a Creole love song to *ma belle p'tit' fille*, without accompaniment"—he "fell flat," and stopped singing after one verse to tell the audience so. "The second verse was much better appreciated," the *Journal* observed.

In Boston, you could go see Twain and Cable as part of the Old Bay State and Roberts Lyceum Union Course. Or you could go to Faneuil Hall and join the "REJOICING" over Grover Cleveland's likely victory, a "great meeting" featuring "young speakers" and a band playing "The Star-Spangled Banner," "America," "Columbia," and "Hail to the Chief."

Twain and Cable filled the Lyceum, and then some: "extra seats" were brought out. Twain told the audience that it was eight years since he had last stood on the stage there, and then added, "I don't see that you have changed much. At that time we were all in a state of doubt and anxiety as to whether or not we had a President, but now all that is fixed splendidly—for a week past we have had two—so that everyone must feel satisfied."

The show was big. Two impromptu shows for Saturday were booked for Chickering Hall, and also brought out good crowds on short notice. After the reading, Howells, who had attended, was effusive: "You *are* a great artist, and you do this public thing so wonderfully well that I don't see how you could ever bear to give it up. I thought the bits from *Huck Finn* told the best—at least I enjoyed them the most."

There was no doubt that this was a hometown crowd: "The humor is notably Yankee," the *Globe* observed. And reviewers warmed up to the Twins' different performance styles. Twain was deadpan: "Mr. Clemens reads, or rather recites, his bits of fun with his usual slow, cool, almost unvarying tone, moving about the stage scarcely any, and using few gestures." And Cable was antic: "Mr. Cable is now here, now there, now standing, now sitting, and all the time his quick, flexible, light voice is pouring out sentence after sentence of Creole dialect." Twain was "purely American:" already a national icon, no matter what he did. And Cable was an emissary for otherness, his readings "treating of a race which though resident upon American soil are yet but little understood or even known . . ."

The contrast seemed to work somehow: they were familiar and strange all at once, mainstream and yet not. And this wasn't just hometown crowds, either. If anything, the New England response was reserved compared to what came next: New York, Philadelphia, Washington, Baltimore. Headlines grew larger, as did the crowds: 2,200 in Boston, 3,000 in Philadelphia. Their pace turned frenetic: the Brooklyn Academy of Music, Saturday night, their eighth show in six days, Cable still nervous, backing and bowing off the stage after his first reading, knocking over (and catching) the bust of Shakespeare pedestaled on the stage as he went onstage for his encore. "The Bard of Avon trembled," the *Brooklyn Daily Eagle* reported, as did the young women who had planted themselves stageside for Twain, and lost "all control of themselves" as he entered, "clapping their hands until their faces glowed."

Then done by ten, back to Manhattan across the Brooklyn Bridge, Cable in time for his Sabbath, Twain in time for "two great chops, 3 eggs, fried potatoes, & a bottle of ale" ("I . . . am growing fat," he warned Livy), then up at six. Cable to church. For Twain, a social call on U. S. Grant with Lew Wallace, author of the best-selling *Ben-Hur*, and fun at the ex-president's expense. "Don't look so cowed, General," he told Grant, "you have written a book, too, and when it is published you can hold up your head & let on to be a person of consequence yourself."

(Twain acquired that book, Grant's *Memoirs*, for his new publishing company, and it made a lot more money than did *Huck*—than did the whole tour, in fact.)

They attracted other politicians: in fact, they seemed to attract only the most important politicians. President Chester Arthur waited patiently backstage in Washington, in the company of one "Miss Frelinghuysen," the daughter of his secretary of state. So did Frederick Douglass, "a runaway slave!" as Cable called him, astonished that he was waiting for them as well.

In Albany, then, Twain sat on president-elect Cleveland's desk ("as the cats used to do at the farm," he wrote back home) and generated that national story when Cleveland's entire office leaped to attention to answer the bells rung by the seat of his pants.

That was three presidents of the United States, all humbled by Twain in the space of one month. It is hard to imagine any modern cultural figure managing that.

As the election settled, the last canvasses taken, the news changed. Front pages occupied themselves reporting on the cholera in Paris (thirty-one deaths reported in one day), the panic among Southern blacks, the decline of Northern industry. "MILLS SHUTTING DOWN," one headline read, "INDUSTRIAL DEPRESSION IN NEW ENGLAND" read another. "Eighteen hundred men" were "thrown out of employment" in the North Chicago mills. The Pittsburgh, Cincinnati and St. Louis Railway laid off seven hundred workers.

And as the stories changed, Twain and Cable only seemed to become more relevant, playing like jesters with national headlines. Sometimes it looked like coincidence, and sometimes it looked like they were working at it. As Twain performed his slave stories, bringing back to life what had disappeared fifty years before, newspaper articles four columns to the left of his reviews claimed that fears of re-enslavement were sweeping through the South.

On the evening that Twain and Cable were making young women blush in Brooklyn, James Blaine stood on his front porch in Augusta, Maine, and lamented the election results that placed him second for the presidency. "There cannot be political inequality among the citizens of a free republic," he warned. Two days later, advertisements read that Twain "will clasp hands across the bloody chasm" between North and South with George Washington Cable.

After newspapers reported that French, German, Portuguese, and American emissaries had met in Paris at the Congo Conference and debated which colonial powers would control the rivers of that massive African territory, Cable revised the introduction to his songs, telling his audience that they had first been sung not in New Orleans but on the banks of the Congo River 150 years before.

They both had their doubts: in different ways, both seemed to feel that they were selling out. Twain, on the way back to some hotel, told Cable that "I am demeaning myself. I am allowing myself to be a mere buffoon. It's ghastly. I can't endure it any longer." And Cable, talking about the singing, told his wife, Louise: "I always shrink from this, though it's always encored."

But they both loved those encores, and the applause that preceded them. By late November and early December, they turned west and north. In Ithaca, the young men from Cornell cheered and cheered. In Toronto, the reviews ran for thousands of words, and the applause—"British applause," Cable called it—was deafening.

Ultimately, it is hard to say who was weirder, more thrilling. But if there was any danger in what they were doing, it was not yet visible. Instead, they were just dangerous enough. Twain was Twain: skipping meals for days, smoking with the windows open on frigid train rides, taking interviews in bed in midday. His neo-mythic form almost seemed to creak and bend as newspaper writers tried to rise to the occasion of describing him. They referred to his "Mephistophelian complexion," his hair like "bleached brick-dust," his walk like "the motion of a tall boy on short stilts," his arms "unmanageable."

His jokes were similarly unmanageable, joyously irreverent, utterly disarming: it is hard to imagine how any listener concerned about "bad boys" could mount resistance to his crowd-greeting request that "no children in arms admitted, if the arms are loaded." And his ability to sustain contradictions, to be all things, reached almost troubling heights: riding a train westward, Twain derided a "small country boy" for saying "nigger" in public within "easy hearing distance" of "a negro woman." She had "more brains & breeding than 7 generations of that boy's family," Twain complained to Livy. Then that evening he went up onstage in Springfield, Illinois, and performed excerpts from *Huck Finn*, during which he very probably employed the same word, recited from the point of view of a small country boy.

And then there was Cable, too, slight enough to look like a woman ("If he were a woman," one reviewer wrote, he "would be what the society editors describe as a petite brunette"), serious enough to look like a preacher, dark enough, some claimed, to look almost "colored." His performance of black and women's and immigrant voices must have been a startling event. In Toronto, women cried copiously all over the hall as Cable recited scenes from *Dr. Sevier*. But men thrilled to other parts of the performance. "The singing," H. C. Bunner wrote to Walter Learned in a private correspondence, "that caught everybody . . . the *go*, and the lilt, and the solid, keen enjoyment he took in it! And the strong, pulsing wild melodies! . . . The huge house woke up as if you had turned a dynamo on it."

On four separate occasions in the first two months of the tour, performances were stopped so that audience members who had fainted could be carried out.

Despite his occasional doubts, Twain was happy with the way the tour was going. Cable was "doing well," he told Livy. The box office was strong. And he loved the laughter he inspired. "Booming," Cable would call it, "A steady crescendo, ending in a double climax." Reports tell us Twain was singing in the carriages, even instructing the driver to take the long route to the hotel or the train so he and Cable could serenade their road manager.

But Twain was restless, too. As they rolled toward Christmas, they also rolled toward something epochal: the American release of *The Adventures of Huckleberry Finn*, scheduled for early in the new year. And he had concerns. He didn't want to release the book until he had 40,000 copies guaranteed sold, and he wasn't near that. Miscommunications between him and Charles Webster had delayed the release of review copies, too. Even worse, bookstores started undercutting the subscription price. And still worse, door-to-door salesmen hawking the book noticed that the sample pages included one in which some anonymous wag had etched a "glaring indecency" onto the crotch of a male character. The salesmen and their pages were withdrawn, a reward was offered (no takers), and the engravings were redone. But none of this promoted a sense of complacency in the author.

He wanted a lawsuit against the bookstores. Livy told him to cool it, warning him that anger wasn't going to solve anything: "How I wish that you were less ready to fight," she wrote. And there were increasing signs that Cable was wearing on him: "I thought Cable would be a novelty," he told Pond. But he responded to his anxiety and boredom with a burst of creative pride instead. During the tour's Christmas break, he decided to retool. He decided to defy Clara Spaulding's "impassability" about the part of the book she had "dashed & destroyed" to him. It was long, and it was coarse—grainier stuff than King Sollermun, even. But he was devoted to it. Right when the first cloth editions were ready to go, he tried it out, in Pittsburgh, on December 29: the end of *Huck*, where "Tom & Huck stock Jim's cabin with reptiles, & then set him free."

If that plot summary sounds like nonsense, that's because it is. In the book, Jim is captured, and Huck, in a powerful soliloquy, vows to "*go* to hell" to free him. But when he arrives at the farm where Jim is held prisoner, he comes across Tom Sawyer, his friend from hundreds of miles up the river.

Huck wants to free Jim and go: he's unguarded, chained to the leg of a bed light enough to lift, inside a cabin with a hole in its wall. But Tom agrees to help only if they free him the proper way, the literary way, which involves making Jim's imprisonment more like a "real" imprisonment. He wants to bring rats, bugs, and snakes into the cabin, forces the construction of a hole under the cabin, makes Jim (by law, illiterate) write a diary of his imprisonment, and tortures him in various other ways.

Jim says that he never realized how hard it was to be a prisoner, and that, "if he ever got out . . . he wouldn't ever be a prisoner again, not for a salary."

Tom says he's having so much fun, he wants to "leave" Jim to the children he'll have someday so they can have fun freeing him, too. He figures this could be "strung out" to take as much as eighty years.

Tom wants to call the incident the "invasion," but gets the word wrong and calls it the "evasion."

But they do free Jim, and amid a hail of bullets inspired by the warning note Tom had sent to the farmer, trying to raise the degree of difficulty a notch higher, Tom is wounded. Jim goes to find a doctor, which leads to his recapture. It turns out that Jim was already free, though, which Tom knew all along: Miss Watson—the witch covering Jim's back with saddle-boils—had died and freed him in her will.

Jim says nothing, but Huck does. What was Tom's idea, taking "all that trouble and bother . . . to set a nigger free that was already free before?" Huck asks Tom.

"Adventures plumb to the mouth of the river"—New Orleans,

the last place a slave would want to go—"and then tell him about his being free," Tom answers.

"Signs is *signs*," Jim promises, reminding the reader to look deeper, as he does.

And Tom gives Jim "forty dollars for being prisoner for us so patient."

It was parody after parody, code after code. Some audience members might have recognized homage and criticism of Victorian minstrel shows, with their sentimental devotion to life on the old plantations. Others would have recognized parody of the adventure novels that so many children were reading uncritically. And the more discerning might have recognized a parcel of hints pointing toward a satire of the failure of Reconstruction. Those references to freeing a black man who was already free. Those "eighty" years Tom wanted to spend freeing Jim—so like the eighty years between the American Revolution and the Emancipation Proclamation. And there was something in that "forty dollars" Tom pays to Jim for his slavery (the third time in the book Jim is bought or sold for that sum): an echo of the forty years in wandering spent by the biblical Israelites after escaping slavery in Egypt, and the forty acres and a mule promised and then not delivered to freed slaves after the War.

The revisions are the tell. Twain played with those forties until publication, adding them in, taking them out, all over the manuscript. By the time he was done, the number appears eighteen times in the book. He took out references to "carpet-bags," the suitcases that were by 1884 linked to political corruption, when they were near Huck, and added them when they were near the King and the Duke, the two con men who take over the middle section of the book.

He even added a passage where dogs are "turn[ed] loose" on Jim. Twain, in fact, added dogs and their violence liberally in late drafts: more vigilant barking, and metaphors suggesting aggression (Tom and Huck's hands "look like they had been chawed by a dog" from digging Jim free). These dogs would remind many readers of the dogs patrolling work camps, as they had patrolled plantation borders before the war: the image of the dog was so joined to the image of the runaway that many theatrical productions with slavery and prison themes used live dogs onstage. It was as if Cable's cause—prison reform—was Twain's own, but on the sly. When combined with the familiar jargon of convict-lease with which he laced the evasion sequence—words like "shackles," "guards," "prisoner"—those dogs in pursuit didn't quite give away the politics. But they made it a little harder to laugh without the ghost of those politics shaping the laugh.

Overlapping this covert, if even conscious, political parable on race, though, was the vastly less covert political parable on children. Maybe that Victorian audience member caught the satire of the decline of Reconstruction, and maybe he didn't; and maybe it was there, and maybe not. But that audience member was supposed to roar at the portrait of the war between children and grown-ups—which ends, in the book's last action, with the neighborhood actually firing their rifles at the boys and imagining themselves fighting for their survival against what they *think* the boys represent.

Tom bullies Jim, and he bullies Huck, but he unequivocally triumphs over the farm family hosting him, especially the mother. When he first sees Aunt Sally, he kisses her full on the lips, and when she is outraged, he says, "They all said kiss her; and said, she'll like it." He's calling her a woman with a reputation, a very complicated and high-concept torment from someone twelve or thirteen. He invades her orderly realm, lets loose snakes that disarm her every bit as much as they torment Jim, hides her silverware in the manner most likely to produce befuddlement, steals sheets and clothing off the line, gets her so wound up that "you could touch her on the back of her neck with a feather and she would jump right out of her stockings."

This is nothing compared to the terrified neighborhood anticipating an "evasion" of abolitionists, but it's fine small work, and Tom is proud of it. She "dusts" him with the "hickry," but is doing even worse against him than Aunt Polly did. The boys get their usual threats of violent retribution: "Well, you *do* need skinning, there ain't no mistake about it," Sally says. But that skinning's not coming, and if it is, this is Huck Finn we're talking about, who knows the rawhide, so it's going to be "one of them lickings . . . that don't amount to shucks."

Poor Aunt Sally can't keep up with the joke until the punch line's told, but at least she gets to be the one to say it: "So it was *you*, you little rapscallions, that's been making all this trouble," she says, and there it is—the key line in *Huck Finn* no one ever talks about. And all the grown-ups know it, too: they sit around saying things like "boys was a pretty harum-scarum lot," or "boys will be boys," aphorisms that admit their defeat. And truthfully Huck, a boy, but often a pacifist in the war between children and adults, knows it, too: he swore to go to hell for Jim, but can't stand up to Tom Sawyer. Everything starts in Tom's head: everyone is working for him or made by him. Planning the "evasion," Tom insists Huck play a servant girl, and when Huck agrees, he doesn't say, "I'll play the servant girl," or "I'll be the servant girl"—he says, "I'm the servant girl." Image equals thing. And when he asks who'll play Jim's mother, Tom says, "I'm his mother." And Huck, of course, ever empathetic, tells Tom he can't steal the slave girl's dress, because she likely owns only one—and Tom, ever bullying, tells him to do it anyway. It all drives Huck nuts, eventually; there's an amazing scene where he has to hide some butter under his hat, and it starts to melt, and Aunt Sally thinks his brain is melting. It is—and his creator's is, too.

What boys, especially white boys, do—and what men, especially white men in their boyish modes, do—is the heart of the trouble. But Twain loves the trouble at least as much as he hates it, and is not defeated by the contradiction. Far from it: "Well, mamma, dear, the child is born," Twain wrote home to Livy after the first performance of the "evasion." He had been performing from *Huck* for almost two months. But it was this moment—the imminent release of the book, the public performance of this particular section—that fully triggered his creative pride.

And yet the reviews were bad that night. The *Pittsburg Dispatch* wrote that the "occasion was supposed to be a humorous one" but was instead an "advertising hippodrome" that was "almost a crime," so "barbarous" that the audience "expected every moment to see Mr. Clemens come out clad in a blanket with face painted and hair bedecked with feathers."

That was the wrong race for the moment: it was, in fact, such a confused critical comment that, looking back, one only sees more evidence that Twain had scrambled the minds of his audience. But Twain barely noticed the criticism, and did notice the applause. He told Livy "it went a-booming," and that the "evasion" (or the "Escape," or "Huck Finn and Tom Sawyer's Brilliant Achievement," as he sometimes called it) was "the biggest card I've got in my whole repertoire." If *Huck Finn* was performance art, this scene was the keenest, roughest joke of all, the place where his fiction and America's reality met most nervously. A scene where two white boys *play* with a free black man as if he is still a slave, and in so doing tear up a perfectly respectable household—one only needed to glance at those headlines, at those "jocular young boys" throughout the South, and at those reports of criminal teens everywhere, to see how that story fit the national mood.

Twain even split the piece in two, and had Cable come out and sing a Creole song as an intermission: in form, it became a near-perfect fusion of bad-boy literature and the minstrel show, with, most remarkably, a prison reform satire stirred in. And all the political valences were where they needed to be: as Tom tore up the plantation, so, too, did he tear up the plantation idea. But to produce what? A place where Jim works as hard as ever, but to *entertain* a new master, as a "prisoner" with a salary? Or a place where Jim gets his reparation, his forty of something, and gets to walk offstage on his own terms? Did the teenager's troublemaking energy cause a revolution? Or did it simply install a new boss ready to spin the old terms to his advantage?

It is no surprise that Twain ended his book with this material, performing it like a centerpiece: it pushed a lot of buttons, and pushed them as hard or as soft as he wanted them pushed. It must have felt like a masterpiece. But would it sell the book? You can bet Twain was wondering. Plenty of great works of literature have been born in obscurity. But when the author is one of the most famous men of his time, when he has ginned up a great publicity engine to sell the book, when he is raising hell and getting front page headlines for it, and then when he starts to perform his "biggest card," one might expect something otherwise.

One might expect even more headlines, controversy, and heated exchanges all over the land.

And there were.

Just not for Twain, or for *Huck*. The most famous book in American history would start its career in the American race debate as a second fiddle.

8

The Freedman's Case

Looking back from the twenty-first century, "The Freedman's Case in Equity" hardly seems like a controversial document.

Cable's essay, marching up and down ten double-columned pages in the January 1885 issue of the *Century*, is dispassionate, even legalistic. It is studded with Victorianisms such as "thus" and "nay," and Cable's convoluted syntax produces sentences within which it is sometimes difficult to tell who is the object of racism and who is its proponent. Moreover, some of Cable's ideas hardly seem progressive. He describes antebellum slavery with some warmth, speaking of the "often really tender and benevolent sentiment of dependence and protection" that constituted the core of "the patriarchal tie" between "master and slave."

And still, Cable's arguments possess an almost prophetic sensibility, or at least a demonstrable yearning to belong to a more rational future. Throughout the essay, Cable positions himself in a later century as a member of a society for whom the racial problems of his generation are viewed from a distant and disapproving perspective: "One of the marvels of future history will be that it was counted a small matter, by a majority of our nation, for six millions of people within it, made by its own decree a component part of it, to be subjected to a system of oppression so rank that nothing could make it seem small . . ."

And from that perspective in "future history," Cable blows up the bridges to his present. Mocking the notion that race problems would diminish as " 'the feelings engendered by the war' " dissipated, he claims instead that such feelings are "older" and urges his readers against believing that the passing of time will solve anything on its own.

In response to objections that integrated classrooms promoted dangerous disorder, Cable writes that "I have seen the two races sitting in the same public high-school and grammar-school classes . . . without one particle of detriment that any one ever pretended to discover . . ."

Discussing the notion that the races should be separated in public venues such as "steamer landing, railway platform, theater, concert-hall, art display, public library, public school, court-house, church, everything," Cable argues that if "there are good and just reasons for their isolation, by all means let them be proven and known; but it is simply tyrannous to assume them without proof."

Observing that the idea of social equality had become "the huge bugbear," Cable invokes a vision of "all Shantytown pouring its hordes of unwashed imps into the company and companionship of our sunny-headed darlings." He then cuts that vision in two with the exclamation "what utter nonsense," and another skeptical plunge into futurity: "We may reach the moon some day, not social equality . . ."

On their own, these arguments might not have inspired national controversy. Cable, however, had been making them in public for two years. He had been in the headlines for two months with the "Twins," and the *Century* was one of the leading magazines in America. For many observers—Mark Twain among the most famous—the election of Grover Cleveland also represented a crucial symbolic passage. The *Century* understood this, too, writing that "every well-wisher of his country will sincerely hope that not only the new Administration, but its allies of the South, will realize the greatness of the opportunity now offered to them."

And the fact that Cable was a white, Southern, male critic of Southern white men gave his words a "peculiar timeliness." "Mr. Cable has an especial right to be heard by Southern men in regard to the freedmen," the *Century* added, "for he is not only a Southerner by birth, but one who took part against the North in the great conflict of arms." Coming from a Northerner, Cable's criticisms of Southern politics would be neither novel nor unexpected. As a Confederate veteran born and raised within the slaveholding aristocracy, however, Cable testified to the possibility of the voluntary dissolution of the American race divide by its most vociferous defenders: "I am the son and grandson of slave-holders," he writes; "these were their faults; posterity will discover ours . . ."

It was visionary, and meant to get attention. And it did. Within days of its publication, by the end of the first week in January 1885, "Freedman" was "the most often talked about issue in the country today," according to one reporter. The response from the South was swift. The *Chicago Tribune,* surveying the damage a few weeks later, wrote that Cable had been "literally belabored with invective and abuse, disowned as a Southerner, the merit of his novels decried . . ."

Having committed thousands of pages arguing for a color line, and thousands of articles dedicated to "traducing the Negro" to justify it, Southern newspapers turned on Cable like he was a traitor. Some Southern newspapers didn't just run one editorial attacking the essay: they ran anthologies. On February 2, the *Times-Democrat* of New Orleans ran no less than nine. Its editors committed themselves to the destruction of Cable's literary reputation, discrediting in particular the realism of his novels, the aspect of his fiction that would best enhance his authority as an accurate reporter of Southern culture: "His whole stock of knowledge as to the French language and the negro patois would not overload the back of a mouse . . . [S]uch Creoles as Mr. Cable has described are creations of his own imagination."

The most frequent criticism of Cable's essay was that it was not "fair." "Nothing has ever yet been said or written characterized by more unfairness, more transparent bitterness toward Southern people," the *Shreveport Times* wrote, "than this article from the pen of Mr. Geo. W. Cable." Many journalists insisted that Cable's motives were financial. The *Cincinnati Enquirer* wrote that "Cable has been trading upon the tender sympathy of Northern people for the 'down-trodden Negro.' " The *Nashville Daily American* argued that the essay was merely "the business advertisement of the man Cable."

Others called for Cable's exile. "We suggest that he should remove himself and his goods, chattels, and effects North," the *Oxford Eagle* wrote, "carrying with him a good mess of crow." And virtually every Southern newspaper insisted that Cable was a dangerous man whose words, as the *Shreveport Times* predicted, would "probably eventuate in strife and bloodshed."

Northern newspapers responded with their own editorials, interviews, and front-page features. The *Chicago Daily News* hailed Cable for his "Northern progressiveness." The *Chicago Tribune* showed Cable in his hotel room opening the day's letters, all of them, the author claimed, in support of his position. Suddenly, black opinion mattered. The *Wisconsin State Journal* printed a letter from Arthur B. Lee, an ex-slave: "Sir, if you are not inundated with grateful letters from colored people, it is not because of any lack of a keen sense of appreciation, but alas!, so few of us <u>can</u> let you know how we feel toward you."

The *Selma Times*, contrarily, printed a letter from "Jack Brown (colored)" in which the correspondent swore that "I shall *always* go to the Southern white man for friendship . . . it is just such men as Mr. Cable that has brought on all the trouble between the white and colored people of the South, not from pure motives, but to fill their pockets with gold or public aggrandizement . . ." "The above article bears every imprint of honesty and truthfulness," the Selma paper added, supporting this claim by dubiously asserting that "we cannot conceive of a white man's putting himself so thoroughly into the place of the negro, mentally, as to have executed such a thing as a forgery."

When black respondents to Cable's essay appeared without white intermediaries, they celebrated Cable. The *Cleveland Gazette* called the article "the sensation of the hour." The *New York Freeman* ran editorials supporting Cable for four months. Unlike white Southern editors, black journalists dwelled upon Cable's backstory, which they interpreted as evidence of his essential fairness. The *Freeman* wrote that "Mr. Cable is by birth and education a Southern man. His knowledge of colored people therefore must be admitted by all candid men." "Mr. Cable," the *Hub* wrote, "is a Southern man, an ex-officer in the Confederate army . . . He has reported what he has seen, and has set down naught in malice against his section."

Repeatedly, black journalists lamented, as did Arthur B. Lee, that a low literacy rate prevented a wider distribution of Cable's article: "That magnificent fair paper of Mr. Cable," the *Freeman* argued, "ought to be read by every colored man, woman, and child in the land, and the millions that cannot read it should have it read to them." Some newspapers hoped, as did the *Cleveland Gazette*, that Cable's article "implied a larger pool of Southern whites who also sought an end to the color line."

In general, however, black journalists seemed prepared to accept that Cable was one-of-a-kind. The *Southwestern Christian Advocate*, a Philadelphia-based religious race paper, wrote that "the Negro has one earnest advocate and defender in the person of George W. Cable," and called him an "instrument in the hands of God . . ." Even the *Gazette*, while arguing that Cable's article provided evidence that the "better class" of Southern whites sympathized with black men and women, nevertheless concluded that "for today, the South has but one solitary Cable . . . [E]very good and great cause has its pioneers."

Unsurprisingly, this new story turned the "Twins of Genius" tour inside out. If Twain had thought he was making a public stand on race—and there really isn't any evidence that he thought he did—then he would surely have been startled by what was happening to his "twin." But if he thought he was trying to sell copies of *Huck Finn*—and there is evidence that he thought about that a lot—then he might have been startled in a different way. Reporters who previously would have been knocking on Twain's hotel room door now knocked on Cable's; reviews that would have focused on the onstage events now focused offstage as well. Three black men from Kansas City told Cable that "in our hearts you rank with the great philanthropists who made humanity their business when American liberty was mocked by the clank of bondsmen's chains." In Chicago, an elderly white couple with abolitionist roots visited Cable and tried to thank him for his essay: the husband burst into tears first, and then the wife.

In Louisville, the *Daily Evening Bulletin* brought a group of blacks to Cable to thank him for the essay. "You would not have got off with dry eyes had you been there," Cable wrote to his wife Louise. He attended services at an African-American church, and was invited to speak at both black and white high schools, where even more people were turned away than at the "Twins" appearance.

The tour rolled on. There were big houses in Chicago. Twain was so delighted with the response to the "Evasion" that he unpacked a grandiose military metaphor to describe the "long roll of artillery-laughter all down the line, interspersed with Congreve rockets & bomb shell explosions, from the first word to the last."

In Ottawa, a fight broke out on the floor of the Canadian parliament when the speaker refused to adjourn so the members could go to the show.

But something had changed. Twain, relegated to second fiddle, seethed. We can note that two months on the road had begun to weary him. But what cannot be denied is that his mood turned bad just about the time that "Freedman" was released, and stayed bad until the two men parted ways in Washington in late February.

Cable noticed it, telling Louise that Twain was "heavy as lead—all unstrung" off and on through the month of January. But he scarcely realized how much he was the reason, as Twain poured out one private letter after another mocking Cable for being cheap, for being stiff-necked, for running on too long, for being "one of the most spoiled men, by success in life, you ever saw."

It started with laundry, on January 2, almost the very day the *Century* came out. Cable, Twain complained, had been dumping mysteriously huge loads of it on hotel staff on the tour's dime. In St. Louis, Twain punched out a window shutter in frustration at being awoken to catch an early train. In Cincinnati, he got into a fight with Cable—a staged fight, anyway, for the benefit of reporters. It still seemed like a sign that all was not well. "I think that in four three minute rounds with soft gloves I could knock him out," Cable said afterward, for attribution. "He's not much on science."

By January 17—a week after Southern papers had begun to unload their own form of artillery on Cable—Twain was redesigning the program. Cable had been taking over half of the stage time, Twain believed, so he trimmed Cable's half of the program and compelled him to go onstage "at the very stroke of the hour" and speak

"15 minutes to an *assembling* house, telling them not to be concerned about *him* . . ." "The good effect is beyond estimation," Twain added, "only half the house hears C.'s first piece—so there isn't too much of C any more—whereas heretofore there has been a thundering sight too much of him."

Given that Cable had stumbled through early performances when disrupted, and that Twain himself loathed an "assembling house," this seemed particularly pointed.

By February, the relationship worsened. Twain complained about Cable's strict observance of the Sabbath: "I would throttle a baby that had it." He called Cable "idiotic," a "paltry child." He fumed as Cable's religion seemed to create "insulting & insolent ways with servants." One Saturday, he observed a difficult conversation between Cable and a hotel bellhop. At a party in Indianapolis on February 8, a Saturday night near midnight, Twain sat in a private smoking room listening to an "elaborate anecdote," when Cable appeared and interrupted the speaker to stagily whisper to Twain, "I will take the carriage, & send it back for you from the hotel."

Twain shot back, not whispering, "You will do nothing of the kind—simply *wait.*"

"That was really it," he told Livy later. Over one hundred years later, one can still feel the breakup radiating off the dusty pages. In all likelihood, Twain was right: that Cable had let success go to his head, that the servants disliked him, that he was otherwise unbearable. And in all likelihood, Cable lacked "novelty," and never changed his program unless he was told to, and that might well have been excruciating if you had to stand next to him and listen to the same program one hundred or more times in four months: "Cover the C H I L D," Twain told Livy wearily, of Cable's tear-inducing set piece, "5 times in Chicago . . . 3 times in a little place like Indianapolis."

At the same time, there's no evidence that Cable ran his performances longer than did Twain, or that audiences were tired of him. Clearly, a measure of jealousy also fueled Twain's anger—if not jealousy, then betrayal over the fact that the Cable he had expected, companionable and genteelly radical, had taken control of the narrative. They were supposed to be selling books, mostly Twain's; they were supposed to be a "raid." Likewise, Twain need only glance at the Nashville or New Orleans papers to understand how easily the same tide of invective that engulfed Cable might threaten him, too. Twain, who was consistently mocked for his pursuit of the main chance, might have reasonably concluded that this was a profitable moment to "untwin" himself. Twain had said that Cable might become "unmanageable," and that he wouldn't bail him out if he did. It had sounded like a joke when he made it, and now it looked like an oddly prescient one.

But Twain's malaise ran even deeper. As Twain was standing onstage delivering a set piece he sometimes called "the evasion," Cable's essay was creating a firestorm for calling Jim Crow "a system of vicious evasions." Cable said out loud, without equivocation, what Twain felt, down to the vocabulary. He put a name on Twain's fun. And Twain may have been stunned to see what America would do to a man like that. But he seemed more stunned by the idea of what kind of man that was: there was something about Cable's way forward, some disconnection between feeling and politics, the personal and public, and race and class—especially race and class—that he disliked with extra vigor. Cable, despite his political courage, could still refer to whites as "a superb race of masters." Twain had complicated feelings about race, but *that* wasn't something he'd ever say; he thought most white people were ridiculous, and measured the pomposity of others with a jeweler's precision. "Apart from [Cable's] colossal self-conceit . . . he is all great & fine: but *with* them as ballast, he averages as other men & floats upon an even keel with the rest," Twain wrote.

They really weren't twins after all, it turned out; not really allies in the ways that might count. As the friendship frayed, so did the partnership and all it implied. In an interview given to the *St. Louis Post-Dispatch*, Twain told a story about how their train narrowly averted a wreck on the bridge crossing the Mississippi. As the train crossed the river, he felt "a sense of crumbling—something crumbling underneath us, where stability was of the highest importance." He then says, in deadpan, that he "wanted to get out and see what was the matter so I could intelligently supply the required relief."

And then he concludes, leaving the story open-ended, that "I fully expected the bridge to break down—I have always done so when I crossed it."

Even if this were merely a story about Twain and the Mississippi River, offered to a newspaper as *Huck Finn* was released, a reader might be attentive. Given the images of "bridges" over metaphorical chasms that surrounded the "Twins of Genius" tour, the partnership of Twain and Cable, and North and South, and black and white, one might easily sense Twain's despondency, and a joking recrimination about his own inability to "supply the required relief."

The Twins of Genius had not bridged anything. The self-recrimination and guilt blossomed. "America in 1985," Twain jotted in his notebook, looking into the future one more time, "Negro supremacy—the whites under foot."

The tour ended on February 28 in Washington. The crowds never got smaller, the box office never faltered. The afterstory is predictable. By the middle of 1885, the invective hardened around Cable, shoving him across the color line. The 1885 volume of the *Southern Historical Society Papers* described Cable as a "predestined slave"; the introduction to the article claimed that "not a few of us have been heartily disgusted with the cringing, crawling, dirt-eating spirit shown by Mr. Cable . . ." In July of 1885, the *Washington Post* lent a column to Richard Brightman of the *New Orleans Times-Democrat*, who composed an extraordinary excoriation of Cable. Brightman called Cable "a pitiful, malevolent little creature" and "universally despised . . . by those who know him best."

Especially exercised at Northerners who treated Cable as "ostracized" and a "martyr," "friendless, forlorn, hated by those for whom he risked his life," Brightman rewrote Cable's past. He claimed Cable was not a Confederate veteran: "He was never a soldier. He never had a musket in his hand." And he denied Cable ever enjoyed popularity and friendship in the South prior to the "Freedman": "He has lost no friends, for he never had any to lose."

Perhaps most personally hurtful for Cable, however, were a series of anonymous "insider" reports on the "Twins of Genius" tour published in the *Boston Herald* in May 1885, which portrayed Cable as obsessively parsimonious and socially rigid—a profile remarkably

similar to the one that Mark Twain was composing in his private letters. Cable considered the possibility that Twain had been the source,
and panicked. He dashed off an anxious telegram to Twain saying
that "all intimations that you . . . are not my Beloved [Friend] are
false and if you can say the same of me do so as privately or publicly
as you like." One day later, he sent a letter to Twain saying, hopefully,
"I do not believe that you have said ought against me that was not
intended as a friend's fair criticism among friends."

Twain's response to the two messages gave Cable little comfort.
"My dear boy," he told Cable, "I do assure you that this thing did
not distress me." And he declined to provide the public repudiation
Cable clearly wanted: "To take notice of it in print is a thing which
would never have occurred to me."

Maybe it *was* me, Twain seemed to say, and maybe not; but either
way you are not my problem anymore. The friendship languished: a
handful of exchanges over two decades, a reading, a letter, a dinner,
an occasional flash of fire from Twain. "Yes *sir!*" he told Cable in
1895," I liked you in spite of your religion; & I always said to myself
that a man that could be good & kindly with that kind of a load on
him was entitled to homage." And then Twain paused, and added, in
past tense: "& I *paid* it."

When Cable returned to New Orleans after the "Twins" tour, he
found that many of his friends were avoiding him; that the wives of
his friends were sponsoring lectures denouncing him; that his house
loan had been revoked; that the city had increased his property taxes
by an exorbitant amount. Even after relocating, however—first to
that safe haven in Simsbury, Connecticut, and finally to Northampton, Massachusetts—he kept trying to perform the pioneering role
he had cast for himself in "Freedman." He toured the South in 1887,
receiving modestly positive receptions everywhere except New Orleans. He published essay after essay on the color line.

He helped found the Open Letter Club—a biracial political salon
for professional men—in Nashville in 1888, but the club closed in
1890 after a controversy engendered by Cable's refusal to apologize
to the white Nashville community for having dinner at the home of
a black lawyer. "I tell you, this soothing and pacifying and conciliat-
ing these people intoxicated with prejudice and political bigotry, is

helping neither them nor any worthy interest," he told one friend, after editorials in the *Nashville Daily American* had destroyed his reputation there.

He even went to Selma, forced the *Times* to try to locate the individual known as "Jack Brown (colored)," and to subsequently admit that no such individual existed, thereby excising from the printed record the only example of a negative black response to "The Freedman's Case in Equity."

He wasn't remotely broken, only subdued, and regarded his sin with detached pride: "I am glad my record is made," he wrote. And there were plenty of men and women who still revered him for it. Andrew Carnegie, whom he had met back in the early 1880s, kept him afloat when the advances ran dry, and even left him five thousand dollars a year in his will. New Orleans forgave him, eventually, though it took thirty years before he could fill a room there. He did brilliant service, founding what would become the "People's College" of Northampton, a chain of "home culture clubs" that spread college-level education to the disenfranchised citizens of that idealistic Massachusetts town. He led Bible study groups in Boston that thronged the Opera House, taught classes at Yale Divinity. He even churned out a potboiler best seller, *The Cavalier*, in 1901.

As a literary star, though, he was done by the second week of January 1885. There'd be no more comparisons to Dickens, to Flaubert. His career as an "artist and serious writer," Edmund Wilson would write later, had fallen victim to "strangulation." And Twain was just catching a new updraft, just beginning the phase of his career where sports matches at Madison Square Garden would have to stop when he entered so that the crowd could cheer *him*. But the second week of January 1885 had stayed with him, too. Addressing an audience gathered in his honor at Delmonico's in New York in 1905, he spoke hypothetically of "a sterilized Christian," and then corrected himself and said "*the* sterilized Christian, for there's only one": the man who, more than any other, exemplified to Twain rigorous adherence to a moral code to the exclusion of all other pleasures and purposes. He never even mentioned the man's name, though he did add, "Dear sir, I wish you wouldn't look at me like that." Everyone knew who he meant.

Numerous biographers remind us that Twain managed his anger badly, and Twain himself acknowledged as much: "sharp tongue & uncertain temper," he called it. In this case, though, Twain's anger had some method. Cable "is a *great* man," Twain conceded to Livy that February, "& I believe that if he continues his fight for the negro (& he will), his greatness will come to be recognized." Angry at laundry, at dull Sundays, Twain never missed that about his "twin." But he was wrong about what would happen next if Cable kept up "his fight." That Cable got pilloried showed Twain that many white provinces of the country were in no mood for movement on social equality. That Cable was recognized and praised by African-Americans, however, showed Twain that his own approach—to sing and celebrate racial empathy, but never vote a straight ticket—inspired no real change. Twain would have other times to reproach himself: in the "procession" of "cowards" that was "the human race," he'd say, he was "carrying a banner." By calling Cable "a sterilized Christian," he reproached his own image in the mirror, too: the man who said the right thing loud and clear, but whose sense of audience was so defiant and obtuse that it didn't matter. "Is anybody brave," he wrote in June of 1882, shortly after he met Cable in New Orleans, "when he has no *audience*?" He and his Louisiana "twin" had found two different ways to answer that question *no*.

9

Huckleberry Capone

As the "Twins of Genius" wound down, as Twain grew angrier with Cable and more morose about his own prospects, on February 18, 1885, *The Adventures of Huckleberry Finn* was released in the United States. If the book sparked any debate about race relations in America, it wasn't being discussed in the newspapers. Virtually no surviving review of the book, and there are dozens, talks about the novel as if it were bringing anything new to the story of black and white in America. And those few references thought what Twain said on the subject was *funny*. "Most amusing," wrote the *Hartford Courant*, "is the struggle Huck has with his conscience in regard to slavery."

In the Southern newspapers, *Huck* was almost invisible. "Possibly Mark Twain's later novels are coarse and dime-novelish," wrote the *Augusta Chronicle & Constitutionalist* in March 1885. "We do not know. We have not read them."

In the black newspapers, Twain *was* invisible, and his book seemingly ignored—no small trick, given that his "twin" was featured on every front page and celebrated for his sacrifice and vision. No black newspaper seems to have even reviewed the "Twins of Genius" tour. Review articles in black newspapers describing the contents of the January *Century* focused on Howells's excerpts from *The Rise of Silas Lapham*, Cable's "Freedman," and the inevitable Civil War memoirs, and provided only perfunctory references to Twain's excerpts from *Huck Finn*.

If Jim and Huck did anything worthy of discussion, Twain had hidden it well. Or behind something. Maybe another generation would find it. Maybe not.

On the matter of children, however, the newspapers were ready to talk—though they did not agree. In the early reviews, there were many kind ones, celebrating, as millions would later, the book's innocent portrait of youth. The *Hartford Times* wrote that the book would "hugely please the boys, and also interest people of more mature years." And Charles A. Dana, writing in the *New York Sun*, noted "no end of stirring incident, river lore, human nature, philology, and fun." But there were also waves of vituperation, arguing that the book was dark and manipulative, a too-violent book about a too-bad boy. On February 26, shortly after the book was released, *Life* excoriated it with stunning mockery. Huck's description of his father's "delirium tremens" was sarcastically recommended to "amuse the children on long, rainy afternoons," and his "description of how Huck killed a pig, smeared its blood on an axe and mixed in a little of his own hair, and then ran off, setting up a job on the old man and the community, and leading them to believe him murdered . . . can be repeated by any smart boy for the amusement of his fond parents."

On March 2, the *New York World*, one of Joseph Pulitzer's newspapers, destroyed Twain and *Huck* with unusual ferocity. Twain had written "cheap and pernicious stuff," and Huck was a "wretchedly low, vulgar, sneaking and lying Southern country boy." The book was too violent, by far, for children. At best, it contained "a number of situations more or less unpleasant," at worst "two or three unusually atrocious murders in cold blood, thrown in by way of incidental diversion." The *San Francisco Evening Bulletin*, on March 14, described Huck's influence on children as "not altogether desirable, nor is it one that most parents who want a future of promise for their young folks would select without some hesitation."

By March 17, the book began its long career of being removed from library bookshelves. One member of the library committee of Concord, Massachusetts, called it "the veriest trash." Another called it "trash of the veriest sort." The book featured "a very low grade of morality" and "bad grammar," and was only being saved from "severe criticism" by the reputation of the author. Newspapers in New England piled on. The *Springfield Daily Republican*, on March 17, said that it was "time that this influential pseudonym should cease to carry into homes and libraries unworthy productions." *Huck Finn*, as well as *Tom Sawyer*, the *Republican* wrote, "are no better in tone than the dime novels which flood the blood-and-thunder reading population. . . . [T]heir perusal cannot be anything less than harmful."

Twain seethed, even though he had long prepared himself for the possibility that few would love this child and the story he told. He couldn't believe the *New York World*, for instance, which minced no words and titled its lacerating review "Mark Twain's Bad Boy." Was it really possible that a newspaper as sensational as the *World* was accusing *him* of placing violence in front of impressionable eyes? He sat down with a copy of the paper and prepared an article in *Huck*'s defense. For eight pages in his notebook, he made a list of lurid stories from one day's edition: "Shot his business Rival," "Died with murder in his heart. (m. & suicide.)," etc. Then he noted the *World*'s daily subscription rate: 143,508. Then he rounded this figure down to "100,000 daily" and cited *more* lurid stories from the newspaper, as well as their column length: "'A Savage fight with hard gloves in New Jersey.'—⅓ col." "'Hacked himself to death'—½ col.—with the gory & slaughterous details." Then he calculated that, at "5 cols a in 1 issue. 10,000 words," the *New York World* weekly "spread[s] a full Huck before 1,000,000 families.—4,000,000 a month, they say . . . while 100,000 have read H F & forgotten him." As a "*Moral*," he concludes: "If you want to rear a family just right for sweet & pure society here & Paradise hereafter, banish Huck Finn from the home circle & introduce the N. Y. World in his place."

He never published the piece, however: "As long as I am still," he noted on the next page of his notebook, "I am an ornament . . . & a satisfaction to the eye; but when I speak—well . . ." Howells and Olivia convinced him instead that he was already winning. In response to the *Springfield Republican*, he circulated letters threatening to unveil the paper's editors as the real-life prototypes for Tom and

Huck. In response to the Concord library committee, in private he called them "idiots." But he also noted that the ban was a "rattling tiptop puff . . . that will sell 25,000 copies for sure." And newspapers across the country agreed with him. The *Sacramento Daily Record-Union*, on March 26, claimed that "if the Concord people are not in league with Mark Twain to advertise the book, they should have kept the proceedings profoundly secret." The *Concord Freeman* noted that sales of the book in Concord increased that week. Having learned his lesson, Twain himself rooted for more bans. If libraries didn't stock his book, he reasoned, more people would have to purchase their own copies.

Within two months, the national story about *Huck Finn* was that Mark Twain had gotten away with murder again. For many, he had written a dime novel, had given it his brand, and was raking it in. *Packard's Short-Hand Reporter and Amanuensis* observed that *Huck* was "just the kind of book that young people are reaching for, and Mark knows it." Of the banning in Concord, Twain published a short letter in the *Boston Daily Advertiser* dryly thanking the library for its "generous action." The *Springfield Republican* reiterated its original criticism, writing that "Mr. Clemens has found that vulgarity pays . . . [H]e ought to be ashamed of *Huckleberry Finn*, but he boastfully declares that he is not . . ." As other newspapers rose to defend him—"There is a large class of people who are impervious to a joke," the *San Francisco Chronicle* noted—Twain counted his sales and smiled to himself. "No other book of mine has sold so many copies within two months after issue," he told his sister. "It seems to me," he told Charles Webster, "that whatever I touch turns to gold."

As spring turned to summer, however, sales slowed. Seen from this moment—midsummer 1885—one might have concluded that *Huck Finn* was a book that sold on Twain's reputation but had no staying power. The British weren't buying it: Twain reasoned it was the dialects, which were hard for a non-American audience to follow. But Twain's real problem was local. For all the controversy that Twain had written trash for boys, the truth was that it wasn't trashy enough. While some reviewers argued that the book was immoral, librarians recommended it for classes in "Practical Morality." It wasn't that the book "should perhaps be left unread by growing boys," as one reviewer wrote. It was that boys wouldn't want to read it. "When a boy under 16 reads a book he wants adventure and plenty of it," the *San Francisco Chronicle* observed. "He doesn't want any moral thrown in or even implied; the elaborate jokes worked out with so much art, which are Mark Twain's specialty, are wasted upon him."

In the long run, though, none of this really mattered. *Huck Finn* sold slowly but persistently, moving through its first edition in six years, buoyed, like Twain's other books, by the outsized celebrity of its creator. Between 1885 and 1895, it was one of the top ten best-selling books (five of the others were also children's books). Twain proudly saved the letters he got from children who shared his "indignation" about the bad reviews and the Concord banning, "so that I might re-read them now and then and apply them as a salve to my soreness."

He tried four sequels: *Huck Finn and Tom Sawyer among the Indians*; *Tom Sawyer Abroad*; *Tom Sawyer, Detective*; and *Tom Sawyer's Conspiracy*. The first was dead in the water after nine chapters, but Twain brought *Abroad* and *Detective* to publication, eager to cash in on Jules Verne and Arthur Conan Doyle. The sequels tend to start petulantly, as if Huck is genuinely aggravated that he's been dragged out of repose by Tom and his oversized ego: "Do you reckon Tom Sawyer was satisfied after all them adventures?" begins *Tom Sawyer Abroad*. Lacking *Huck*'s linguistic juice, they compensate, partially at least, with surrealism. There are minstrel-style breakdowns on balloons over Africa, Tom playing lawyer, a Muslim invasion of Missouri, Jim stuck on the top of the Sphinx, strange reruns: the Duke and the King, nicely recovered from their tar and feathering in the original *Huck*, show up at the end of *Tom Sawyer's Conspiracy*, only to be caught for the murder that the town all too happily pins on Jim.

Better, perhaps, were the *Huck*s he didn't undertake but left unborn in his notebooks: the "WINTER book," in which Tom would fight on behalf of the Levins, fictionalized versions of Jewish twins by that name who had settled in Hannibal when Twain was a child. In his notes, Twain arranged anti-Semitism from German residents, a kidnapping, a daring rescue. He also played—several times, a little compulsively—with a book idea where Tom would blacken up Huck as a slave and sell him into slavery, or blacken up himself and "escape," then unblacken, turn slave catcher, and hunt himself. And he considered teaming up Huck with an all-star lineup of children's characters—Hans Brinker, the boy from the *Uncle Remus* tales, Mary and her little lamb, George Washington, and others—for a story that would begin with Mowgli picking up everyone on his elephant, and end with everyone climbing trees in a meadow.

Once he finished *Huck Finn*, though, Huck and Tom became ghosts from a creative standpoint: they haunted him, but he had no control over them anymore. Children continued to appear in his books, however, and with new edges that Huck and Tom couldn't own. And Twain's message was getting clearer: children had a kind of power, both destructive and constructive, and were often in conflict against the institutions designed, for good or ill, to guide them into adulthood. No longer were his boys and girls the leaders of comical parodies of rebellions. They were actual warriors, in generational conflicts, and he was on their side. Published right after *Huck Finn*, for instance, in 1889, *A Connecticut Yankee in King Arthur's Court* described a remarkable alliance between one iconoclastically Twain-like adult and a coolly lethal army of teenagers. Hank Morgan, the "Yankee" time-transported to medieval England, constructs a system of "hidden schools" to free medieval English children of superstition and monarchy, and employs them as correspondents and paperboys for the newspapers he has also founded. Challenged by the Church, Morgan recruits fifty-two boys, all between the ages of fourteen and seventeen, who then help him eviscerate an army of thirty thousand knights, a merciless slaughter that still startles readers: "That swelling bulk was dead men! Our camp was enclosed with a solid wall of the dead . . ." If Twain had been subtle before, he wasn't here. The new schools, the soulless but sensible child soldiery decimating a corrupt status quo—those were Twain's schools, and Twain's rebellion.

In 1896, he published the *Personal Recollections of Joan of Arc*, a history disguised as memoir. Thinking of Susy, he portrayed Joan as an adorable child, "this little creature," "this child with the good face, the sweet face, the beautiful face . . ." "Outcast cats"—Twain's familiar stand-in for homeless children—gravitated to her, and she advocated for the Huck Finns of medieval France with the kind of innocent wisdom that Victorian children in books used to debate their teachers and parents: "Poor little creatures!" Joan told her childhood priest, responding to a lesson about who was damned and who was not. "What can a person's heart be made of that can pity a Christian's child and yet can't pity a devil's child, that a thousand times more *needs* it!"

But most importantly, Joan was a soldier, a military leader, as well. To Twain, she represented the most extraordinary example in human history of a child *actually* acquiring adult authority, the kind of revolution Tom Sawyer was always dreaming up. "Consider this unique and imposing distinction," the epigram tells us, the first thing one sees as one cracks open the book: "Since the writing of human history began, Joan of Arc is the only person, of either sex, who has ever held supreme command of the military forces of a nation *at the age of seventeen.*"

And there was more. From 1897 to 1908, Twain repeatedly tried to tell the story of a "Young Satan," or "Little Satan, Jr.," a truth-telling troublemaker who, like his Jesus from 1867, brought toys to life as a resurrection designed to awe children in particular. It was like Twain had never forgotten the impulse he felt, at seven, to write Satan's biography. These fragments, known collectively as the *Mysterious Stranger* manuscripts, are tangled up with fragments intended to bring back Tom and Huck: little Satan takes Tom and Huck to a witches' Sabbath; little Satan takes Tom and Huck down to hell on a Sunday afternoon and shows them unbaptized babies roasting. Twain moved his little Satan around, testing Austria in the fifteenth century, Austria in the eighteenth century, and the Hannibal of his youth, but he always remained a boy, "forlorn looking," lonely and seeking company. And when he found it, he was Tom Sawyer with supernatural powers: "Come, we'll be boys together and comrades!" he tells the human kids he meets, who have little choice. "Is it agreed?"

This little Satan talked in a way that confused the line between youth and adulthood as much as Twain's other books did: "*Is* he such a boy . . . ?" one adult from Hannibal wonders. "He looks it, and all that . . ." Twain's young Satan played with time like Twain's history game, "visit[ing] other centuries to ease [his] heart," and turning time backward and forward in such a manner that "the previously killed were getting killed again, the previously wounded were getting hit again in the same place and complaining about it . . ." And he remembered everything, including every stultifying detail of the average awful schoolday in Hannibal in the 1840s: "Becky Thatcher! *Yes, sir, please.* Make the curtsy over again, and do it better. *Yes, sir.* Lower, still! *Yes, sir.*" "The boy had forgotten not a word, nor a tone, nor a look, nor a gesture . . ." the narrator adds. As the incongruities mount—Alabama fried chicken in medieval Europe, for instance— one begins feel that Little Satan is Twain late in life: an imagination floating freely across centuries and continents, yet still moored to the events that provided pleasure and pain when that same imagination belonged to a child. You didn't bore young Sam Clemens for one second—not one second—that he wouldn't remember. And you didn't tell him not to write Satan's biography: he'd remember that, too, and get you back someday. For every teacher, parent, or preacher who hopes that the children in their care will forget the bad and remember the good, Twain offers a counter-testimony so terrifying that it took the devil's own voice to say it.

In his personal life, Twain managed the wild anarchies writing in private liberated him to do. But the vision remained. He developed an infatuation with fourteen-year-old Helen Keller, which she reciprocated, marveling at his gifts of communication: "I could get almost every word," she said, by placing her fingers on his throat as he talked. "He had the power of modulating [his voice] so as to suggest the most delicate shades of meaning . . ." He adopted causes that showed how much he believed children could learn for themselves, and only needed the right, empathetic ambassadors from the adult world to guide them forward. He raised money for the Children's Educational Theatre, an arts school populated mostly by working-class Jewish children in New York, where they learned through theatrical performances they themselves created. "This is the only school in which can be taught the highest and most difficult lessons—morals," Twain said, insisting, as always, that parents and teachers should loosen the reins. "Here the children who come in thousands live through each part."

And along the way, flowing all around and inside those darkening and unfinished portraits of his favorite fictive children, and the causes, he suffered immense personal loss. First was Susy, the brilliant, imitative oldest, who died at age twenty-four. Susy had graduated the school of Clemens and gone to Bryn Mawr, but returned after one year. It is not clear why she left so early, but her father hadn't helped. He had visited during the spring semester and offered to perform. She pleaded with him not to do "The Woman with the Golden Arm"; it is not hard to guess why a first-year at Bryn Mawr would want her famous visiting father to steer clear of his lowest, most nostalgic material, especially a piece that had scared her as a child. But he did anyway, unable and unwilling to stop himself, leaving her tearful with embarrassment and betrayal. She left shortly after, also ambiguously but fiercely attached to a classmate—"If I could only look in on you! We would sleep together tonight"—whom she "lost" to distance or social convention by 1894.

As the family toured Europe in August of 1896, she stayed behind in Hartford, where she contracted spinal meningitis and died almost alone, pacing the floor in a fever and crafting extraordinary hallucinatory letters, imagining herself in correspondence with a dead French opera singer from the early part of the century: "Now go and *hold* this song. Nothing but indecision Go on Go on Yes does she bow her too white head? She must she must she must Yes my black Princess."

Twain never forgave the college ("Bryn Mawr began it. It was there that her health was undermined"), warned of a long "midnight," and wished that four more coffins could be prepared, for himself, Olivia, and their two living daughters: "I wish there were five of the coffins, side by side," he told Livy, "out of my heart of hearts I wish it." He was prophetic to warn, and to measure for extra coffins.

Eight years later, in June 1904, Olivia died, her heart failing in a villa in Italy, her last request to her husband that he sing some of the old spiritual songs. "Our life is wrecked," he told his friend Henry Huttleston Rogers, the industrialist and financier; "we have no plans for the future; she always made the plans." "I come upon memories of little intimate happenings of long ago that drop like stars into the silence," he told Helen Keller. "One day everything breaks and crumbles. It did the day Livy died."

And five years after, on December 24, 1909, Jean, the youngest, drowned in her bathtub, of a seizure almost certainly related to epilepsy, leaving only Twain and Clara surviving. "Nothing she said or thought or did is little now," Twain wrote shortly afterward. ". . . I have had this experience before; but it would still be incredible if I had had it a thousand times." It was the loss from which Twain, whose heart faltered and then stopped four months later, never recovered.

Twain tried surrogate families, replacement children of unsettling pedigree. In the wake of Livy's death, he began a "collection," roughly one dozen schoolgirls he called "Angelfish," to whom he wrote sentimental letters and entertained until he was near death. He thought of them as "grandchildren," compensating for the ones he expected to never have or never see. He taught them to shoot pool, gave them writing advice, addressed them with courtly deference ("It was very sweet of you, dear, to let me shake hands with you, that day"). And he used a disturbingly fetishistic language to describe them—"I collect pets," he wrote in one autobiographical dictation, "young girls—girls from ten to sixteen years old"—reflected on their state of pre-sexual innocence in cloying ways, and affected adolescent hurt if they didn't pay enough attention to him.

In early 1910, grieving Jean's sudden death, his own health failing, he paid deep attention to sixteen-year-old Helen Allen while a guest of her parents in Bermuda. He filled some of his last notebook pages with a "portrait" of her psyche, blaming her parents for her outbursts—"No parent has a right to insult a child. No parent can do it & not damage the child"—and threatening to "carve up" her boyfriend, whom, Twain seems convinced, had designs on her virginity. As Twain's heart and brain faltered, as he left Bermuda for his last voyage home, Twain's relationship with children—his writerly relationship, at least—seems to end with a warning to Helen, crossed out and probably never sent, to "be cautious, watchful, wary." A warning, Twain to a child, to beware the adult world, one way or the other, a sentimental and frightening heads-up—extraordinary, unclassifiable advice from the extraordinary, unclassifiable man-child Twain had remained until the very end.

And through these years, into a new century, *Huck Finn*'s reputation continued to grow, and with it more bannings and restrictions. Twain embraced the book as zealously as he did Helen Keller, as the

Angelfish, as the Children's Educational Theatre—as another surrogate child. Complaints about *Huck*'s morality gave Twain the opening he needed to parody the morality of the source of the complaint, whether it was a newspaper or a church. "The truth is," he wrote in a letter in 1907, "that when a library expels a book of mine and leaves an unexpurgated Bible lying around where unprotected youth and age can get hold of it, the deep unconscious irony of it delights me and doesn't anger me." And complaints about Huck himself activated a protectiveness in Twain: "This is Huck Finn, a child of mine of shady reputation," Twain wrote in a presentation copy of the novel. "Be good to him for his parent's sake."

For Twain, Huck was a battered child. "That abused child of mine," he called him, to Joel Chandler Harris, also declaring, "*I* can't help believing in him . . ." "The child of neglect and acquainted with cold, hunger, privation, humiliation . . ." he called Huck in 1895 on his world tour. Over and over, Twain's diction melted the distinction between Huck and a real child. Centuries in the future, he joked, historians, looking through a cracked glass at Tom and Huck and Clara, Jean, and Susy, would observe that he had "more than one family," more than one set of children. It made sense—more than sense, given everything else he was going through, everyone he had lost, collected, or protected, or failed to protect. Deride Huck, Twain told ministers, librarians, parents, and newspaper editors, and the conversation isn't merely academic. We aren't just talking about a *character*. We're talking about a child. One who can't die. Or grow up.

As the twentieth century progressed, however, most of the complexity and the heat left this debate. "The child of neglect," as Twain called Huck in 1895, disappeared, and so did the "bad boy" designed to tweak Victorian audiences. It took almost no time for Huck to be transformed into a "good" influence on American children, and only a few decades for a book that celebrated truancy and regarded organized education as child abuse to become the most-often-assigned novel in the nation's schools. In Twain's obituary, William Howard Taft claimed that Twain "never wrote a line that a father could not read to his daughter," a line that only someone who had not read very much Mark Twain could possibly say. In 1912, two years later, Harper & Brothers released its "National Edition" of his works, which it marketed as "go-to-bed books" for children. "You can dip into" them "lazily," Harper assured its young readers, "even sleepily, and enjoy the sweet whimsicality of a kindred soul." In 1917, ragtime audiences danced to a song called "Huckleberry Finn": "If I were Huckleberry Finn," the lyrics rhapsodized, "I'd be a kid again." By 1918, a daily comic strip named "Tom Sawyer and Huck Finn" ran in newspapers nationwide, and for almost thirty years locked an image of Tom and Huck as "riverfront scamps" (in Michael Patrick Hearn's words) into the imaginations of millions of American children.

By the 1930s, the idea that *Huckleberry Finn*—that much of Twain's work—was a celebration of boyhood and adventure during a "primitive" time in our nation's history was well established. Twain may not have quite believed in the theory of recapitulation when it came to child rearing, but the theory of recapitulation believed in him: for readers, critics and publishers, Twain's, Huck's, and Tom's childhoods quickly came to represent a lost time when America was a child among nations. "When Mark Twain was young, the West was new," Reuben P. Halleck of Yale wrote in his *History of American Literature* in 1911. "He is the historian of an epoch that will never return." Franklin Roosevelt, dedicating the Mark Twain Memorial Bridge in Hannibal in 1936, told a gathered crowd that "this peaceful valley is known around the world as the cradle of the chronicles of buoyant boyhood."

In this manner, Huck became iconic, like a flag. On the covers of a half century and more of child-friendly, often abridged editions, his image was so familiar to Americans that publishers barely needed more than his silhouette. On the cover and title page of the 1954 Doubleday Junior Deluxe Edition, for instance, he's a sparse ink drawing: the straw hat reduced to its brim, the unkempt hair more straw than the hat, big toothless smile and pupils pointing straight left for maximum slyness, twenty-three or twenty-four freckles, the raft, the companion (Tom Sawyer on the cover, Jim inside), and the corncob pipe, of course (before cigarette ads for children were outlawed, Huck was a Marlboro Man for the preteen set). Open the book, and on the inset pages you see a pantheon of icons of children's literature: the dragon, the crown, the witch (with the broom), a pirate's chest, an ice skate, a gun, an elephant, a black horse, and this boy in overalls, hands on hips, and barefoot, naturally.

In movies, he was played by an all-star team of boy actors, from Jackie Cooper and underrated Mickey Rooney to Elijah Wood: "The Beloved Rascal of . . . Mark Twain's Cavalcade of Boyhood Adventure!" the trailers for the 1939 version promised. "Thrill Upon Thrill After Thrill! Runaway Slaves! Midnight Murder! Steamboat Race! Cheating the Mob! Vagabond Days and Nights of Mystery . . . with the All-American Boy . . . in the Great American Story!" "A story so wondrously deep in our hearts," assured the well-tailored emcee of the 1950s era *Climax!* theater version of *Huck* (brought to you by the Chrysler Corporation). "Don't send the youngsters to bed this once . . . They'll have fun watching, and . . . you'll have fun watching them watching . . ."

Some of the filmmakers tried to respond to the subtleties of the book. Mickey Rooney's and Elijah Wood's Hucks both argue "King Sollermun," and concede—without using racial slurs—that Jim wins the argument. And Patrick Day's Huck is "all over welts," the rare moment any director gave us a visual cue that Huck was abused. Otherwise, though, one wishes there was some sort of congressional action against the use of "I do declare," "tarnation," "land o' Goshen" and banjo to denote folksiness. And watching those movies, leafing through those old editions, one can't help but wonder how much commercial pressure American filmmakers (as well as publishers) feel to transform our complicated past into a soporific for modern kids.

If there is confusion, some of the fault is Twain's. *Huck Finn* is a mess, a hodgepodge. Parts of the book are "fun," and parts are traumatic, and parts are "real," and parts are implausible, and parts are written for children, and parts for adults, and the ghosts of all this playfulness persist: a study at Penn State in 1983 found that, even after "weeks of serious study," approximately one-third of all students missed the "satire" and still saw *Huck Finn* as an "adventure story." Much of the confusion lies not in the book, though, but in our own stalled and confused perceptions of our children. Twain recognized an inclination among American parents, educators, and politicians to regard their children as either too uncontrollable or completely innocent, with no middle ground. He practiced it himself, at least at the ends of his career: exploding boys at the start and Angelfish at the end. But in between he had something, and *Huck Finn*, written in part to scramble that dichotomy, has instead fallen prey to its persistence.

Condemning the newest media because it markets violence to children is one of the oldest tropes in American politics, as old as the marketing itself: the dime novels, Sunday comics, motion pictures, comics, and television, all received punishing reviews in this regard, and were often the subject of government investigation and intervention. Thirty years after Anthony Comstock warned that dime novels "make foul-mouthed bullies, cheats, vagabonds, thieves, desperadoes, and libertines," parents were warned that Sunday comic supplements were "an influence for repulsive and depraving vulgarity . . . a national crime against children." And thirty years after that, filmmakers, scored by widespread claims that "the road to delinquency is heavily dotted with movie addicts," agreed to "Special Regulations on Crime in Motion Pictures" that disallowed any violent content that might "incite demoralizing imitation on the part of youth." And twenty years after that, comic books were called "short courses in murder, mayhem, robbery, rape . . . and virtually every other form of crime," and were subjected to Senate investigation, ritual burnings, and bannings. Before modern-day legislators could ever warn that we were witnessing the most violent children America had ever seen, previous generations of public figures had already condemned the mix of the newest pop culture and youth, had already editorialized, had already seen over and over, as J. Edgar Hoover told the *Los Angeles Times* seven decades ago, "a new 'lost generation,' more hopelessly lost than any that has gone before."

Older media, of course, almost always looks quaint and safe by comparison. In part, this is the result of active censoring of Victorian children's culture throughout the mid-twentieth century. Disney took *Grimm's Fairy Tales* and excised the nineteenth-century edges, so that our nation's kids wouldn't see the blood gushing from the evil stepsisters' feet as they mutilated themselves to fit Prince Charming's Glass Slipper; Bugs Bunny, still tricky, has leisure time his ancestor Brer Rabbit never did. In part, the strangeness of a new technology makes the stories it tells seem more threatening, and makes old forms seem comforting: because we have come to see reading as an unalloyed good, we forget that reading was the Xbox of the Victorian age, and dime novels their equivalent of violent video games. Finally, however, we regard *Huck Finn*, and works like it, as "fun" for children because we haven't shaken those same difficulties that Twain's first reviewers had in classifying his book—in part because writing for children and writing for adults have been regarded as two different things for a century and more. Even when, as in this case, we have been literally talking about the same book.

What's most interesting, perhaps, is that it didn't have to be this way. As children's literature historian Beverly Lyon Clark has observed, many of the most respectable writers of the 1870s and 1880s wrote for both children and adults, and many of the most respectable journals, including those in which Twain appeared, published serious reviews of books for children. Books like Lewis Carroll's *Alice's Adventures in Wonderland*, published in 1865, shattered stereotypes of what a children's book was. By the turn of the twentieth century, however, the world of children and the world of adults had become segregated—the inevitable holistic result of all those child study books, new medical specialties, public schools, and dozens of other changes that professionalized the act of parenting. And among those changes, "children's literature" became a marketing category, "children's sections" began appearing in public libraries, and literary authors like E. B. White were warned that writing children's literature (in his case, *Stuart Little*) was career suicide.

This transformation took place, literally, as Twain prepared and published *Huck Finn*, and explains, in large part, why reviewers in 1885 couldn't seem to create any kind of consensus about whether or not the book was right for children. In 1885, as *Huck* was previewed for American audiences in the *Century*, Horace Scudder in the *Atlantic* was telling that same audience that childhood was an innocent place in which children moved "joyously," the "sanctity" of which must be guarded. By 1904, leading social scientists like G. Stanley Hall were talking about "youth" in terms of "morbid" thoughts and "overassertion of individuality," and arguing that children had to pass through a period of "savagery" before they became good adults. Both of these formulae fit *Huck Finn* like a glove. But they still treated children like a different order if not, as Twain's friend and *Gilded Age* coauthor Charles Dudley Warner put it, a different race, possessing, at least temporarily, the same "instincts and impulses of the African."

Twain entered this debate as he usually did: on all sides. He savored the "innocence" of childhood but insisted on commerce between the world of children and the world of adults. He was troubled by the violence to which children were exposed, but he was downright angered by the sanctimony with which parents, politicians, and teachers responded. He believed there was a shared space where children and adults could laugh and cry at the same things. He knew that many children *like* aestheticized, pretend forms of violence: "Shall invent a violent *game* to go with it," he told his brother Orion of his history game that summer in 1883 when he was also finishing *Huck*. He knew, too, that many American children were victims of real violence, and he defined real violence to include what he regarded as psychological abuse in the classroom and church. Twain did not write a book to be used in schools, then or now, whether or not we choose to do so. Like the truancy and antisocial behavior it celebrates, *Huck Finn* was designed to lie outside the system. Twain, remember, *forbade* reading by his own children until they savored it like forbidden fruit, and delighted when his own books were banned. That was the kind of father, and author, he was.

And yet, these qualities are also what make *Huck* fully relevant to our modern times. More serious criticism of youth literature has been written in the last two decades than in the five preceding, galvanized by what is widely regarded as a newfound sophistication in the genre. And for the first time since the mid-Victorian period, respectable "adult" authors—like Isabel Allende, Joyce Carol Oates, Michael Chabon, Carl Hiaasen, and many others—have begun writing for youth markets. It was Twain's innovation to anticipate how twentieth-century American childhood might be constructed, and marketed—what we recognize as a familiar amalgam of "adult" and "adolescent" tastes. That Twain wrote a book that participated in a pop genre (in his case, dime-store adventure) but added moral and emotional complexity might have confused readers in his time. That Twain sought to write in an "authentic" child's voice might have received only glancing praise. That Twain described children

as active agents and victims at the same time might have seemed
contradictory. That Twain intuitively understood that "children are
quite . . . capable of entering into the adult view of themselves," as
British young-adult author Aidan Chambers has written, might have
produced those moments in *Tom Sawyer* when he directly addresses
parents and seems to leave children behind. But today, such choices
would be recognizable as the essential formulae of young adult
fiction—as, in fact, the essential formulae for most art regarded by
children and teenagers as especially powerful or authentic.

Take your eyes away from the teacher's editions and the lesson
plans, and you can see what hides in plain sight: *Huck Finn* is everywhere, its palette of emotions and politics reproduced across a wide
range of teen and preteen books, movies, television shows, games,
and even music. The celebrations of truancy and creative lying (*Ferris
Bueller's Day Off*). The natural, unaffected first-person description
of school as a kind of incomprehensible minimum-security prison
(*Diary of a Wimpy Kid*). The passages of Gothic loneliness reproduced across sumptuous genre-specific backdrops—"adventure" in
Huck's day, vampires or postapocalyptic rubble in ours. The voyeuris-
tic fixation with violence: "I rushed and got a good place at the window," Huck says, in order to watch a shot man's death throes. All the
absent parents, especially the disappeared mothers—where is Huck's,
and what might her story be?—straight Disney, cliché enough to inspire parodies like M. T. Anderson's *Zombie Mommy*. The alienated,
heroic semi-orphans or orphans those broken families create: our
friends Katniss Everdeen from *The Hunger Games* and Harry Potter.
The independent children raising themselves; the pastiche of neglect,
unlikely wealth, and a couple of criminals to provide a cartoon version of danger (*Home Alone*)—in fact, the entire genre of children
raising themselves, the buffoonish or absent mentors employed daily
on Nickelodeon and the Disney Channel. The children forming into
mock (or slightly less mock) military units and confronting (mock-
ingly or not) vicious, adversarial, or inept adults: *Spy Kids* (the kids
become two armies, one good, one bad). *Home Alone* again: "He's
only a kid, Harry," says one inept thief to another. "We can take
him." Or *Harry Potter* again: "Did you actually believe," one sinister
wizard sneers at the epic's gentle, orphaned boy hero, then leading

his own "army" of students into battle, "that *children* stood a chance against us?"

Freed from its role selling the American past as a confection, and American childhood as a joyride, *Huck Finn* could also emerge more fully as a book with something to say politically about, and to, children. What happens when one truly breaks the seal that treats *Huck Finn* like a children's book about children, and a grown-up's book about race and politics? A wide-ranging discussion of *Huck Finn* and children creates a raft of new uses for the novel—and a new appreciation for the contours of Twain's moral vision.

Take a look at the bookshelf currently available to parents, teachers, and psychologists looking for advice on how to care for children. There are books that tell you how to get your denatured kid back into the outdoors: *Last Child in the Woods, Smart by Nature, The Geography of Childhood*. There are books that portray a "boy crisis" for a country spooked by anomic paroxysms of violence among youth, like James Garbarino's *Lost Boys*. There are books that portray an education system divided between haves and have-nots, between at-risk and privileged children, like Jonathan Kozol's *Savage Inequalities*. Or an education system burdened by too much standardized testing: Diane Ravitch's *The Death and Life of the Great American School System*. There are books concerned with a new listlessness in boys, like Leonard Sax's *Boys Adrift*. There are books that invite us to listen to children better: William Pollack's *Real Boys*, Kindlon and Thompson's *Raising Cain*. There are books—lots of books—that invite us to reintroduce "danger" into the lives of our children: *The Dangerous Book for Boys* (card game, pocket edition, magic set, chemistry set); *The Boys' Book of Survival; For Boys Only: The Biggest, Baddest Book Ever; The Outdoor Book for Adventurous Boys*. And for every *Raising Cain*, there is a *Reviving Ophelia*; for every *Boys Adrift*, a *Girls on the Edge*; for every dangerous book for boys, a "daring" one for girls.

That these books send mixed messages en masse is plain. That they contradict themselves individually, less so. Yet, as Ann Hulbert notes in *Raising America*, child development experts in this country have prospered precisely to the extent they convey ambivalent messages—because most American parents, on the continuum between discipline and permissiveness, between child-centeredness and parental authoritarianism, between looking forward and going backward, are deeply torn. The "dangerous" books really aren't that dangerous. With their Victorian fonts, cloth covers, and advice on how to tan a skin or build a tree house, they actually represent bait-and-switch attempts to get children outdoors with tools in their hands like they "used to." As William Pollack writes, an antique "boy code" from the last century still obtains when it comes to raising our male progeny. Boys will be boys, we say: Let them loose, and they will grow up to be responsible citizens. On the other side, boys are the troublemakers, the gang leaders, the disrupters: Medicate them, we say, or throw them in jail. If they're young men of color, throw them in jail somewhat faster. That essential formula has not changed since Victorian times, and does not appear about to change.

That *Huck Finn* talks back to this national conversation should be obvious to anyone who has even read the first page. All across that child development bookshelf, one sees its shadow everywhere, literally: As Kenneth B. Kidd of the University of Florida notes, Huck is cited frequently in these books, a ghostly icon. Nonetheless, the degree to which Huck Finn meshes with this contemporary conversation is still astonishing. In its own time, *Huck Finn* was a critique of American schools, and it can still be. It was written at a time when educators and politicians argued about how "student-centered" school should be, and they still do. A book about a child incredibly attuned to the outdoors, who travels down hundreds of miles of dangerous river in a raft, speaks loudly to those re-naturing and re-dangering books. In a country where one in four children in certain states live in poverty, a book about a child who knows "cold, privation," and whose best friend (Tom Sawyer) is "respectable," animates our conversations about school systems divided by race, by class. Huck's stunned responses to the violence around him might show us how we normalize violence for our children's perusal, and how they respond to it. And his vicarious interest (and Tom's more committed interest) in violence might help us understand better how to respond to those millions of American children with access to a catalog of FPS (first-person shooter) video games and unaffected enthusiasm about the pixilated slaughters they instigate. Watching Huck struggle with teachers, mentors, abusive parents, and schoolwork, tuning them out, creating his own survival mechanisms—whether modern child development books are talking to us about disaffected middle-class children or at-risk children, it's hard not to feel Huck looking over our shoulder, and Twain looking over his.

Even this list understates the case, however. To understand the relevance of Huck Finn to the current discussion about how we raise our children means truly facing the resiliency of the myths that guide that raising. A century and more ago, teachers also tried to make sure their students connected with nature. Newspaper writers fretted about standardized testing regimes. Politicians made hay by campaigning against violent media and its impact on children. To take one example, it is certainly possible that children are getting progressively less exposure to nature with every passing generation: recent studies show that, since 1970, the distance that the average modern child is allowed to travel without adult supervision has shrunk to one-ninth its previous size. But we also cannot forget that millions more American children once labored long hours trapped in factories, or were otherwise oppressed in ways that have since been outlawed.

Middle-aged Mark Twain made a pastoral of his childhood, and he could: children in rural Missouri in 1845 attended less structured schools than they did in Hartford or Elmira in 1885. But contemporary children also attend far less structured schools than did their ancestors in Hartford or Elmira in 1885. We deified Twain's nostalgic sensibility without also deifying the parts of his vision that were anti-nostalgic, that loathed how people *don't* change. Maybe childhood recedes with every generation—children are indoors more, are exposed to more violent media—or maybe we have grown inured to the myth that it does. The image is hard to separate from the thing, and even attempts to do so are echoes of previous attempts. William Pollack, for instance, reminds us that our "real" children don't match the stereotypes in which we envelope them, and it is bracing when he says it. But it is advice Twain followed a century ago—and even he was copying others when he did so.

Because we have grown used to the myths, we struggle to see the intense relevance that *Huck Finn* bears to the actual lives of our students. Exhibit one, perhaps the best example of this disconnection between the book-as-taught and the book-as-lived: ADD/ADHD.

According to researchers at Northwestern, in America in 2010, 10.4 million children were treated for these disorders—an increase of 66 percent in one decade. It takes very few conversations with a group of college or secondary school students to recognize how "medication" matters to them—as a source of healing for some and of resentment for others, but as an important part of their lives and the lives of their friends, in either case. Those same students, when asked, recognize Huck (and Tom Sawyer) as exactly the kinds of kids who, in our America, would be prescribed Ritalin: they are inattentive in class, easily excited, fidgety, and, to put it mildly, disruptive. In a word, Twain's word, they need to be "sivilize[d]."

Social scientists have noticed this as well. David Nylund's 2000 book on working with children with ADD/ADHD is titled *Treating Huckleberry Finn*. A 1993 article entitled "Mark Twain Meets DSM-III-R" observes that Tom and Huck, if alive today, would be diagnosed with conduct disorder (CD), and treated accordingly. *Slate* ran a story titled "The ADHD-ventures of Tom Sawyer," and the *Washington Post* ran one in a similar vein. One could make a credible case that, aside from race, no aspect of Twain's classic books about children has received as much attention in the past two decades. And yet, the conversation rarely makes the crossing from the world of medicine, where children's body chemistries are diagnosed and treated, to the world of the humanities, where children's hearts and minds are supposed to be offered the chance for expression.

Students have no problem building this bridge, however, if allowed. In classroom situations, they instantly note that the restlessness we officially celebrate in Huck and Tom is medicated when *they* do it ("Would [Ritalin] . . . have inhibited [Huck's] reckless but courageous decision to help Jim?" Nylund pointedly asks). They recognize, too, that the efforts of parents, teachers, and other authority figures to "civilize" them through pills and therapy is directly analogous to what authority figures try to do to Huck. They are not surprised to discover that ADD/ADHD, as much as Huck, is American—that diagnoses of the disorder are made several times more often here than in other developed countries. They are ambivalent about the medication as well as the diagnosis, but they recognize that Twain is talking about something important to them and deeply in the grain of the culture: the persistence of certain attitudes toward children, and the persistence (adjusting for available technologies) of certain solutions. The persistence of stereotypes about them. And the persistence of *classification* as the catch-all cure.

We just need to remember to tell all sides of the story at once—and that the beauty of Twain, and not the trap, is the way he smudged the messages. In canonizing *Huck Finn* the way we do, we instead canonize a raft of ways to think and argue and worry about children that make neither them nor us freer. It is not too late to recognize that we have been trying to shake free the "real" child from the stereotypes of childhood for so long that the effort itself has become a stereotype of what the thinking parent or teacher is supposed to do. *Huck Finn* is not a signal from the past to litigate these battles. It is a call to rise above them. Even in 1885, Twain was playing with the instruments that guided how Americans classified their children. The other boy books, and most of the advice books, made it clear that if you let your boy run wild, you increased the chance that he would grow up to be a productive member of society. Even Peck's Bad Boy, its author promised us, was going to "[buckle] on his harness" someday and be a success. But Huck probably won't; it is hard to tell where he *is* going, but his rebellion doesn't appear to taking him to a job in a bank or a courthouse.

So where is he going, then, if not to a bank or to a judgeship? Our modern conversation about children provides us with no shortage of conjectures. Sometimes Huck is the nineteenth-century analogue of the modern middle-class child, fidgeting in class, scolded by teachers and foster parents to "sit still." And sometimes he is the analogue of the criminal-in-waiting, the at-risk child on the edge, his biography piling up the markers contemporary sociologists use to identify the childhoods that create violent adults: a family with a criminal legacy, a history of abuse, gang membership, access to firearms. Other times, from other angles, Huck provides what several scholars have described as "a remarkably accurate portrait" of an abused child, a child of an alcoholic, of the one in seven that, studies show, ponders suicide, will answer yes if you ask him if he is "so lonesome" that he wishes he were dead.

At the same time, it is as hard to imagine Huck Finn as a murderer, or dead by suicide, as it is to picture him as a banker. He can exemplify a diagnosis, put a face on it—but he transcended diagnosis, and that is what many modern youth like most about him. Twain, faced with the two outcomes the "child study" movement of his day predicted for all American boys—respectability or jail—refused to choose. We can admire the way that Twain provides an avenue from the past to the present, the way his intuitive map of what makes Huck a dangerous and endangered child matches so well what modern academics find. But what matters more is that Twain cuts to the heart of the dilemma: the way that, when it comes to children, we have drawn an ambivalent map where the victim is also the terror. On that delicate turn, where a human being goes from requiring our utmost sympathy to our utmost discipline, does Twain's principled indifference to classifying children rest. To regard Huck as an "innocent" on a lark is to miss this entirely. Huck is not America's child—he is America's children. He is scared, and he is scary. He is the part of every child that threatens to undo what we make if we raise him well, or if we don't. And he is bits and pieces of different races, different genders, different generations, and all sorts of intriguing in-betweens. There's only one thing to do with a kid that frightening and complicated, our Victorian ancestors believed, and that's stick him in school and uncomplicate him—and that's exactly where we have sent *Huck*, and a big part of the reason why.

In the years after he published *Huck Finn*, Twain continued to think about race like a man with a conscience playing tricks on itself. He still loved minstrelsy, perhaps as much as ever: his journals in the 1890s sometimes fill with "darky" song lyrics from earlier decades. In 1906 he reminisced about minstrels like the San Francisco Minstrels—"the real nigger show—the genuine nigger show," he called them, using stage terminology of the day with troubling retrograde intensity. And hours after finding that bad investments had bankrupted him in December 1894, he soothed himself by putting on blackface (as Uncle Remus) in his own house: "It drove my troubles out of my mind," he wrote afterward.

Meantime, in his books, he fixated on racial inversions in ways that suggested sorrow, discernment, and an almost surreal vision of how race distorted the American dream. Just as his writings on children grew blunter—and increasingly less publishable—so, too, did his writings on race. In *The Tragedy of Pudd'nhead Wilson*, published in book form in 1894, a slave woman ("Only one sixteenth of her was black, and that sixteenth did not show") exchanges her own infant for her master's: "White folks ain't partic'lar" about who is free and who is slave, and she doesn't want her son sold down the river. In *The Mysterious Stranger*, he had a blacked-up skeleton appear in a medieval Austrian castle, good-natured and terrifyingly out of place. In *The Secret History of Eddypus, the World-Empire*, he put himself in the position of an historian from the 2900s, and described how America was discovered by "Columbus and Uncle Remus." "What do you see?" he asked his imaginary reader, gazing back to the 1800s. "Substantially, what you see to-day," he answers: black slaves and "lazy and ignorant" white families who "bear themselves as princes toward the slaves." History had gone around, and that clue about Uncle Remus and the discovery of America—let alone that devilish minstrel in Austria—certainly hinted that the germ had been in the bloodstream for ages.

In private, he railed against racism at home: he wrote "The United States of Lyncherdom," a superbly caustic essay on the lynching of African-Americans, but held it back until after his death. In "The Stupendous Procession," also unpublished until after his death, he satirically reworked the Declaration of Independence: "ALL WHITE MEN ARE BORN FREE AND EQUAL" read a new banner. At the same time, he found new ways to express his anger in public. Most interestingly, his disgust at American imperialism in countries like the Philippines and Cuba gave him a language for his disgust about racial inequality, and an historical vision almost unique to his time. At the height of his fame, he claimed himself "always on the side of the revolutionists," called Theodore Roosevelt "the Tom Sawyer of the political world" (Roosevelt, for his part, once threatened to skin Twain alive), and spent some of his massive cultural capital on dramatically rebellious causes. In "To the Person Sitting in Darkness," published (over friends' objections) in the *North American Review* in 1901, he wrote that "there must be two Americas: one that sets the captive free, and one that takes a once-captive's new freedom away from him . . .": a commentary on the American occupation of Cuba, but also a near-perfect moral for *Huck Finn*. Newspaper writers lined up to respond, publishing piles of editorials of the kind that years before had buoyed and buried Cable. But Twain, older, vastly more famous, vastly more loved, could no longer be touched.

He attacked American generals who committed atrocities during the Spanish-American War, wrote coruscating satires on the use of the "water cure" in the Philippines—what we now call waterboarding. He visited South Africa and wished Cecil Rhodes the kind of goodwill no one seeks: "I admire him, I frankly confess it; and when his time comes I shall buy a piece of the rope for a keepsake." In India, he watched a German hotel manager punch a servant, and it took him back: "I had not seen the like of this for fifty years. It carried me back to my boyhood."

American history was being repeated overseas, and he couldn't believe it. In *King Leopold's Soliloquy*, a slender pamphlet about the colonial genocide in the Belgian Congo printed privately in 1905 when no established publisher would, the ironized critique of American slavery that appears in *Huck* became coarser and more outraged. And once again, it was exactly what someone might write who believed that history was the same thing over and over. King Leopold—Twain's satirical version of him—mocks the "Yankees" for not realizing that, in recognizing his sovereignty in the middle of Africa, they were sanctioning what they had spent generations fighting. "I certainly was a shade too clever for the Yankees," he croons. "It hurts; it gravels them. They can't get over it! . . . [H]aving put down African slavery in [their] own country at great cost of blood and money, [they were] *establishing a worse form of slavery right in Africa.*"

To our modern sensibilities, these concatenations make no sense: the politics seem far left (imagine Twain's words on Cuba applied to Afghanistan or Iraq), the blackface seems reactionarily nostalgic. In Twain's time, however, one *could* signal the other: the *Minneapolis Journal*, in 1901, ran an editorial cartoon featuring an aboriginal Twain, white hair and mustache over darkened skin, and feathers over his loins, facing down a "missionary" in white skin, suit, umbrella, top hat, and paperwork: "Can The Missionary Reach This

Old Savage?" read the caption. He could not: Twain died in 1910 as
outraged as he had ever been, convinced that the twentieth century
was not going to be an improvement on the nineteenth. "It is not
worth while to try to keep history from repeating itself," he wrote
in his notebooks in 1907, "for man's character will always make the
preventing of the repetitions impossible."

In retrospect, we might have done all this differently: instead of
treating *Huck Finn* as a harmless book about children, we might have
noticed that, on matters of education, child rearing, and youth politics, the novel is a high point in his career. And if we were looking
for principle on democracy and race from Twain, we might have noticed that within twenty years of *Huck*'s publication, he blazed trails
we still haven't fully mapped. As Shelley Fisher Fishkin has noted,
in China, in the Soviet Union, in places where fighting for freedom
was a more recent concern than here, they knew this Twain better—
the one who tore into Roosevelt, Rhodes, and King Leopold like an
avenging angel enraged at colonialism's great pawprints on the world.
"The most influential anti-imperialist," one newspaper called Twain,
"and the most dreaded critic of the sacrosanct person in the White
House that the country contains." In fact, we might have looked
at all his writings on race together—exploring more closely, for instance, what Hsuan L. Hsu calls Twain's "shadow-archive" on Asian
and Asian-American political history—alongside his work on children, and celebrated him, instead, for an extraordinary comparative
vision, one that recognized and attacked the foundational structures
that unevenly divided power across a vast reach of political, cultural,
and even temporal boundaries.

Instead, however, *Huck Finn* became regarded as Mark Twain's
major contribution to the national conversation about blackness and
whiteness and history. Canonization began slowly, and with mixed
signals. On one side, William Dean Howells praised Twain's morality
in *Huck*: "He was the first, if not the only man of his section," Howells wrote (completely forgetting Cable at this point), "to betray a
consciousness of the grotesque absurdities in the Southern inversion
of the civilized ideals in behalf of slavery." On the other, songs like
the instrumental "Huckleberry Finn Cake Walk" (1900) suggested
how easily Twain's book might become (like the cakewalk itself, a

slave dance stolen by minstrels, then revised by early ragtime composers) an uncertain marker of black culture's role in the American marketplace.

No prominent voice openly suggested that *Huck Finn* was *really* a book about race, however, until twenty-five years after it was published. Writing in the *Nation* on the occasion of Twain's passing, Booker T. Washington told white readers that they were making a mistake about the book: "It is possible the ordinary reader of this story has been so absorbed in the adventures of two white boys that he did not think much about . . . 'Jim.'" But he should, Washington argued, because "in this character Mark Twain has, perhaps unconsciously, exhibited his sympathy and interest in the masses of the negro people."

Washington, of course, was completely right, and characteristically circumspect: Twain did feel genuine "sympathy" for African-Americans broadly defined, and that sympathy had the dreamlike quality of an "unconscious" act. But Washington was also wary to attach a political agenda to Twain's sympathy, or a political outcome. And that was something later generations wouldn't think twice about. In the 1920s and '30s, the idea of cross-racial "sympathy" in *Huck* gathered underground momentum: if you were a white hipster, you might see Huck as your avatar, and every black man you met as your Jim (see Ralph Ellison's *Invisible Man* for a taste of this). And if you were a white hipster's opposite, you took the opposite tack: Senator Joe McCarthy called for the book's banning in 1949, claiming that it did irreparable damage to the reputation of the South.

McCarthy lost, however, and *Huck* won. *Huck*'s rise in the classrooms of America coincided with the civil rights movement. Racism is first learned, *Huck* told American schoolchildren, and then unlearned through contact with the racial other, and then combated through acts of individual courage and contrition. Lionel Trilling, writing the introduction to a crucial 1948 edition of the book, focused on Huck's willingness to "humble himself" after playing a practical joke on Jim—that early moment from Chapter 13 that Twain sketched out back in 1876. For Trilling, that apology represented the instant when "Huck's one last dim vestige of pride of status, his sense of his position as a white man, wholly vanishes." From there, the rest of the book is "moral testing and development," a refinement of Huck's commitment to Jim's equality.

Initially, this interpretation was "hot," controversial: that 1950s televised *Climax!* version of *Huck Finn* sponsored by Chrysler cut out the character of Jim altogether, and in so doing sidestepped even hinting at advocacy for civil rights for African-Americans. Gradually, however, it became canonical, reproduced in textbooks, teacher's guides, and annotated versions of the novel. In newspapers and periodicals, both conservative and liberal commentators on American culture still celebrate Huck's nonconforming choice. An interested reader can easily find an identical opinion of the novel by right-wing columnist George Will, or civil libertarian culture critic Nat Hentoff, or the editors of *Race Traitor* magazine, whose shorthand for "personal accounts of individual and collective breaks with white solidarity" is "Huck Finn moment[s]." The famed historian Arthur Schlesinger was only one of many who pointed at the scene in Chapter 31 where Huck vows to "*go* to hell" to free Jim as iconic: "That, if I may say so," he wrote in 1989, "is what America is all about." And Huck's moral commitment was convention for American politicians in both major parties: "Huck works hard to keep Jim free," Ronald Reagan said in 1985, not reading closely, "and in the end he succeeds." The Kennedys privately called Lyndon Johnson "Huckleberry Capone"—a contemptuous homage to both Huck and LBJ that Twain himself might have enjoyed.

By the 1970s, *Huck Finn* was the most assigned book in American schools and had become, as Forrest G. Robinson has written, "the leading popular expression of America's self-image when it comes to matters of slavery and race." As this interpretation of the book grew in popularity, interestingly, so, too, did criticism of many of its parts. The more *Huck's* commentary about race was examined, the more flaws appeared in its construction. Walter Blair, perhaps the most influential Twain scholar of the postwar era, was only one of many who dismissed "King Sollermun" and "How Come a Frenchman Doan' Talk Like a Man" as low comedy, "minstrel-show stuff." And when Ernest Hemingway told readers in *Green Hills of Africa* that Huck was "the best book we've had" but to stop reading after Chapter 31, because "the rest is just cheating," he expressed a widespread belief that what followed Huck's vow to go to hell to protect Jim's freedom—the "evasion"—was backsliding. Twain faltered at the end, Leo Marx wrote in "Mr. Eliot, Mr. Trilling, and *Huckleberry Finn*," because he didn't have "the moral vision" to "acknowledge the truth his novel contained."

When one looks at Twain's deep and ascending commitment to racial justice and his affection for black culture, it seems inevitable that *Huck Finn* might be read by many as a song of freedom. It seems reasonable, too, to argue, as many have done, that Twain fell short of finishing the song. At the same time, looking from the perspective of the "Twins of Genius," looking through the prism that extraordinary piece of performance art provides us, one can't help but wonder: How did the twentieth century get this turned around? How did *Huck Finn* become "the leading popular expression of America's self-image when it comes to matters of slavery and race" when what Twain said about the subject as he introduced the book to America in 1884-85 was buried underneath what his touring companion had to say—and when what his touring companion had to say clearly better resembles our modern commitment to an integrated society? Similarly, is it unreasonable to ask that a book meant to speak for a biracial consensus could have meant something, anything, to black readers in its day? Standing next to Cable, Twain looks like the better artist by far. But not the one who knew more about what it means for a white man to surrender some of his privilege in the defense of the liberty of others.

Likewise, can we ignore the fact that Twain adored what we trained ourselves to hate, that he called his "child" that condemned burlesque that drags down the end of his book? Hemingway and dozens of other critics have destroyed that ending in order to make what precedes it sing its politics like the Gettysburg Address. Can we ignore the fact that "King Sollermun" and "How Come a Frenchman Doan' Talk Like a Man" are, as Blair says, "minstrel-show stuff"—but were also the first passages from *Huck Finn* Twain wanted American audiences to witness? Was it not possible that the "minstrel-show stuff" and the "evasion" were the places where Twain was making his point, not running from it?

Through the prism of the "Twins of Genius," in fact, we can

see wrenches in the star-making machine everywhere. This was not meant to be a national book. Twain knew before he even published *Huck Finn* that it would make few fans in the white South, and it didn't: Mark Twain, a critic argued in 1954, had been too "out of touch" with "Southern life" to offer a credible portrayal. Similarly, Twain did have black readers, and the "Twins of Genius" did have black audience members: Cable recalls one African-American man sitting alone in a "choir loft" in Oberlin, laughing disruptively in a way Cable was sure was appreciative. But the fact that Twain refused to permit racial slurs in certain contexts tells us much about the contexts when he did, and tells us he was not imagining a *significant* African-American audience. Twain placed that epithet in Huck's mouth for a reason, as a small dagger drawn toward the consciences of whites. What's remarkable, as Sacvan Bercovitch has observed, is that no such person speaking publicly about the book for the following seventy years seemed to notice or acknowledge that it was even there. In fact, many scholars, writers, and critics during those decades—including really respected ones, like Trilling, Hemingway, and Mailer—began calling Jim "Nigger Jim" though Huck doesn't call him that even once.

For these reasons, among others, we can be little surprised at the list of anomalies that attends *Huck*'s celebrity. It is particularly astonishing, for instance, that a book containing such homages to minstrelsy should rise to national prominence as a civil rights icon at the moment that overt minstrel stereotypes disappeared from American public life, as a lawsuit from the NAACP helped persuade CBS to drop *Amos 'n Andy* from their airwaves. Equally striking is the fact that another icon of the civil rights movement, *Brown v. Board of Education*, by integrating American schools, would also create the multiracial audience that would point out that teaching a book that contains the most charged racial slur in the nation's history over two hundred unmediated times might be the wrong thing to do. *Huck* had been banned for most of its existence somewhere, at some time, but 1957, in New York, was the first time it was removed from elementary school curricula for "passages derogatory to negroes."

The consensus of the twentieth century made one simple mistake about *Huck Finn*, but it echoed: they believed that it made a

difference when Huck said he'd go to hell to free Jim. And they figured Twain failed when it didn't—or, like Ronald Reagan or Arthur
Schlesinger, they figured he didn't fail at all. And as they told this
story, they told the bigger story for which they made *Huck Finn*
stand in: that the "final emancipation" of African-Americans, as Elizabeth Hardwick wrote in 1948, was "real and historical." But that
was exactly what *Huck Finn* was *not* saying. And mistaking a dark
comedy about how history goes round for a parable about how it
goes forward is a classic American mistake. Writing in the aftermath
of the Civil War, surveying all that blood and treasure spent to free
slaves, and then Reconstruction collapsing, convict-lease, the rise of
the Klan, Jim Crow, lynchings—Mark Twain eventually dedicated
Huck Finn to the proposition that, contra Lincoln, there was no new
birth of freedom.

Its opening line is "You don't know about me," and promises
something new. At the book's end, though, there's no "new" in sight.
There's another matron who wants to "sivilize" Huck. Tom hungrily
wants more adventures, and he wants company. Jim is free and even
"rich," and that is new, but the bitter taste from a dozen chapters of
humiliation lingers with the reader, as it must, one presumes, for him.
He tells Huck that he saw Pap's dead body floating in an abandoned
house hundreds of miles and many weeks earlier—which means that
both he and Huck were free the whole time and didn't know it. A colossal, existential waste of time, it seems, for all. Huck then laments
that he even tried to write the book, and tells us that he wants to run
away before "the rest" catch up to him. "I been there before" he says,
and stops writing. And no one—no one—ends a book with a line
like that unless he's given up on progress.

In this context, then, the better question might be why *we* haven't:
why, specifically, we treat arguments over race in *Huck Finn* like they
are new, when many of them are old enough to apply for Social Secu-
rity. It's been sixty years since Ralph Ellison wrote about the "minstrel
tradition" in *Huck*—decades, too, since African-American men and
women first described their humiliation in classrooms where *Huck*
was taught. "Two generations of pain," Margot Allen has called it. "I
can still recall the anger and pain I felt as my white classmates read
aloud the word 'nigger,'" Allan B. Ballard wrote, recalling junior high

school in the 1950s. "I can recall nothing of the literary merits of this work you term 'the greatest of all American novels.'"

In the end, it is almost an accident that there is no overt minstrel moment in *Huck Finn*: Huck and Tom blacked up before *Huck Finn* (in *Tom Sawyer*), and they blacked up after *Huck Finn*, in sequels and notebook sketches, but not in the book itself. Yet, the spirit, the strategies, are immanent there, and that is why the book became such a perfect Trojan horse for sneaking the old race politics into the new. Turning Huck and Jim's friendship into a positive metaphor for race in America may have seemed like a good idea at the time (1948, say), but the truth lies in Twain's friendship with Joel Chandler Harris and his recognition of the success of Harris's *Uncle Remus Tales*. Writing about a white boy befriending an older black man was a way to reach the Victorian market—especially, but not exclusively, young people. What the "Twins of Genius" reinforces for us, in fact, is how much *Huck Finn*, both as book and performance art, mass-marketed the moment of first contact with the racial other. What Cable and Twain did onstage heralded what Elvis and the Beats did in the 1950s, what the blues-borrowing stars of rock and roll did in the sixties and seventies, what white rappers and pop stars do now.

That *Huck Finn* rose as the minstrel show faded in the 1950s, in fact, is no anomaly. *Huck* did the exact work in 1954 (or 1974, or last year) it was partly intended to do in 1884: it imported the minstrel show into the mainstream. But fifty years of silence has left us susceptible to so much farce. Without the obvious symbols, the burnt cork most of all, we can't recognize blackface anymore, even when it is all around us. Part of *Huck Finn*'s brilliance is that it is a blur of so many different literary and theatrical forms, everything from slave narratives to Shakespeare and Scheherazade, from circuses to cross-dressing to anthropology lectures. But there is only one of those forms that we have lost the language to talk about, if we ever really had it—yet it was arguably the most popular form of entertainment in this country for a century.

To see "minstrelsy," which has almost completely disappeared from American public life since the 1950s, is not *technically* difficult. You can visit an archive, locate a scholarly collection or reprint, pick up an old song book or two on eBay, buy one out of the glass-paned cabinet in your local antique store, spend fifteen minutes on You-Tube. If you spend those fifteen minutes on YouTube, you will learn a lot in a hurry, about masks and staged representations of "black" and "white" so rote that they amaze. If you graze the comments section for a minstrel clip, however, you will find that roughly one-third of the contributors are disgusted, roughly one-third admit to being entertained, and roughly one-third argue for renovation and education. And when one-third of the people want something banned because it's pernicious, one-third want it banned to suppress the unpleasant fact that something pernicious once happened, and one-third want to keep the materials close in case some good can be made of them, you get what W. T. Lhamon Jr. calls a "lore cycle." Suppress the surface, suppress the conversation, and you guarantee that the strategies—and with the strategies a haunting number of physical markers, like dance steps and white gloves—endure. Suppress the surface, suppress the conversation, *if you want* the pernicious thing to endure. Different motives—the motives themselves half-buried, contradictory—still take a nation to the same place.

Seventy years ago, minstrelsy was regarded by many as a classic form of American humor. During the civil rights era, it was redefined as unequivocally racist. Since the 1990s, however, attitudes have fractured somewhat, as some scholars (as well as some filmmakers, musicians, and writers) now see a complicated amalgam of racism and identification, at least in certain eras, certain performances; "love and theft," Eric Lott of the University of Virginia called it in 1995. That this academic conversation has barely entered public discussion is obvious. In part, this is due to the ongoing value and potency of the civil rights era critique. But in part, this is due to the fact that refigured minstrel practices remain profitable as long as they remain invisible, and they remain invisible as long as historical minstrelsy can be regarded as something intrinsically different from contemporary practices. It is a scholarly cliché to mention the train of Caucasian singers since the 1950s who have performed music with roots in black life, or the hip-hop performers (of any color) who act out personae that might well have been recognizable on a nineteenth-century stage. In the world where money is made, however, it is vitally important that this cultural production seem new and cool.

In the 1830s, however, blackface was what was new and cool, and the white men and women who performed or watched from the crowd were as often as not the same white men and women who might be hauled into a Manhattan court and charged with "making negro slaves their equals." By the end of the nineteenth century, few blackface performers had a problem like that, save African-Americans such as pioneering vaudevillians Bert Williams and George Walker, who believed they could convey "love for the race" from behind the mask—and who were victims of choice, circa 1900, for white rioters who might not have known the names and faces of any other blacks. That coolness waxes and wanes—that the "kids" in the 1830s did what the "kids" did in the 1950s—is actually an oppressive piece of news if you want to be cool or sell cool. And there are many ways *not* to tell it. "Business seems to find whatever it wants in youth culture," Thomas Frank wrote in *The Conquest of Cool*, "Its look and sound must continually vary, but its cultural task does not change."

We can blame Twain for some of this. He never really had an answer to Frederick Douglass's claim that minstrels were "filthy scum." He was Douglass's friend, and friend to the "filthy scum" as well. He "whited up" during the "Twins of Genius," and in so doing helped invent the mechanism through which uncountable twentieth-century cultural workers ranging from fashion designers to novelists could pilfer materials from people of color without leaving fingerprints. It's in the book, too: if nothing else, the "Twins of Genius" reminds us that the politics of *Huck Finn* were built from infatuation with black culture and language. And the coolhunter, then or now, requires one thing that the classic racist also wants: an enduring engine of racial difference, and some property rights over the cultural creativity that grows from that rift. This is why Twain couldn't release Daniel Quarles from service, even if the labors were only in his mind; this is why, today, the coinage "urban pioneers" is used to describe both professional coolhunters and gentrification leaders, as if, after centuries, there remain neighborhoods inside cities like New York that remain frontiers. *Huck Finn* is a book that brilliantly condemns many modes of racism but protects the privileges of the hip white person, the person who empathizes deeply with marginalized black culture, and who—just as Tom Sawyer enjoys freeing Jim so much he wants to bequeath him to his children to free—requires the ongoing existence of a marginalized black community with which to empathize.

At the same time, once we acknowledge the role of minstrelsy in *Huck Finn*, we can start to have a better conversation about the nature of Twain's achievement and the contortions to which we have gone to make it politically clean. The modern critique of blackface and *Huck Finn* revolves around the idea that Twain tried to create a real and sympathetic portrait of an African-American person, and then reverted depressingly and lastingly to stereotype: that "Jim is forever frozen within the convention of the minstrel darky," as Donnarae MacCann and Gloria Woodard argue. The modern defense, one heard over and over, is that Twain's virtues on this matter outweigh his sins, that "Jim is, after all, the hero," as Jocelyn Chadwick-Joshua writes. The outrage of many modern readers toward the parts of *Huck* that express Twain's own complicity in the structural racisms of his time, as well as the optimism from other readers that the good outweighs the bad, are both legitimate, essential positions. But both positions assume that Twain neatly divided serious from funny, literary from theatrical, truth from lie; that he was unable to find positive effects in pervasive popular culture forms, and unable to find harmful ones in his own life experiences. This perspective, central to so much we say about this book, assumes that there is a realist novel that we can pry away from the joke machine riding on its back. And then it assumes that we can use this map of Twain's mind to discern where lies the civic sins in his vision, where lies his sense of justice, and what inspired them both.

But Twain had none of these filters in place—defiantly so. And neither did the country around him, nor around us. There is, ultimately, something unknowable about Twain, buried amid all these winks and pauses and deadpans. He probably didn't know himself, and that measured anarchy, as more than one critic has noted, is what makes him memorable. But his lifelong affinity for racial masquerade ought to be given its due when, and if, we teach this book. For Twain, the minstrel show was the one institution in American life that acknowledged that race was a joke, and a fake, that skin color was negotiable. And, in his construction, it was also the only real vehicle to say that without facing the kinds of ostracism Cable faced.

These distinctions tortured him, and he worried that torment like a loose tooth: his guilt drove him to listen carefully and obsessively, and to create moments of remarkable empathy and humor at the racial crossings that Cable and few other white American writers of his century could even approach.

If we are concerned about the uses of *Huck Finn*, we might fairly ask whether such moments of wit and artistry can be distilled from their murky and tricksterish origins, and turned into polemics, or whether those murky and tricksterish origins are the point. Does the "assault of Laughter" really win the game of history, as he claimed? It makes a difference. We have Cable to tell us what "serious" on race for a white person looks like. *Huck Finn*, on the other hand, tells us less about how to move forward to integration and equality than what it means to want all the things many complicated white Americans want: justice for all, the pleasures of deferring justice for all, and the hard satisfaction of knowing what a fool and malicious spirit you are to want both. The kind of laughter such a realization would produce might very well be revolutionary—but not if we miss the joke.

Further, that we now regard nineteenth-century minstrelsy as witless, unalloyed racism may be politically appropriate for a country trying to rise above the sins of the past. But if it creates a blind spot that allows a book imbued with minstrelsy to be taught without discernment to millions of American high school students, then, one way or the other, it might be a taboo that serves too many purposes. In truth, Americans know almost nothing about the pop culture of their past, how messy and even creepy it really was, or how it lives on. Twain regarded minstrelsy as a heterogeneous pop genre that he could reference and revise, in ways that, to him, were consistent with vigorous if often paternalistic antiracist principles. It wasn't seepage: he picked and chose, the way someone now might sample Bob Dylan but not KISS (both minstrel descendants, obviously, but scarcely identical otherwise). When one looks at the divide between our modern good intentions and our pop forms—especially our humor, where "polyethnic offenders," as John Strausbaugh writes, govern the scene, or our music, a rich, deeply racialized, and hardly politically sensible playground—can one doubt that commentators in a century might shake their heads at us the way we shake ours at our Victorian ancestors? Tina Fey, while accepting the Kennedy Center humor award named after Twain, wonders if, a century from now, people will look at her work and claim that, like his, it was "actually pretty racist"; Louis C. K., in stand-up, utters criticisms of *Huck* that, minus the swearwords, match those of the prim Concord library committee in 1885; they act like they've seen a ghost, and they have. Did Twain deploy minstrelsy with any less wisdom about how to make an unusable past useful as do such modern icons as *Mad Men* (or *Downton Abbey*) as they critique yet adore the inequalities of recent generations? In our time, adjusting across spectra for what is politically palatable and what is not, might what Twain did be regarded as "hip," as cutting-edge revisionist song, comedy, and storied-up history?

In fact, Twain did something larger than that: he conducted a salvage operation grounded in the counterintuitive notion that the popular culture of his past was actually more progressive than the popular culture of his present. In contrast, we assume the Victorian racial mimic practiced unadulterated stereotyping, whereas the modern imitator is more suave and empathetic. We assume that "cool" is new, and originates in minority households and neighborhoods and fruitfully becomes a moneymaker across a range of our needs and desires, from what we wear, what we eat, and what we hear to how we say it. But this is the "same cow," Junot Díaz tells us, that we bought before; the same turning of racial others into a profitable and "magical thing of desire," as Greg Tate writes. Twain, at least, had the sense and vision to be torn by these things, and left us the codes to see his disgust. Generally speaking, we have chosen not to read them. He loved the idea that race could be transcended, and loathed himself over the idea that such a privilege was doled out one-sidedly. We accept racial distinctions with so much placidity, however, that Twain's most subversive ideas still elude us. "We continue to have a Jim Crow view of the world," David L. Smith observes. "We dress it up politely."

In contrast to the minstrel show, the racial slur "nigger" has retained its visibly scabrous energy after all these decades. It is, as Farai Chideya observes, "the nuclear bomb of racial epithets," and has been for a long time: protests against its use can be traced back to the early 1800s. In contemporary debate, *Huck Finn* is possibly the most prominent icon of defense for those who question whether "the realms of art, scholarship, journalism, and history" on many crucial American topics "can be effectively pursued without critically engaging the word," as Jabari Asim writes. The debate cuts across many of the old fault lines: just as Cable scolded Twain for using it in publicity materials, worrying about the effect on "hypercritical matrons," contemporary observers such as Elon James White argue that the only reason for erasing the slur in *Huck* is "to ease the tension that is felt by parents and teachers of students who would read it."

But the unerased slur, as almost everyone knows, also has relevancy in black culture (and has since the nineteenth century), in music, comedy, and across social media, as an expressive tool, a cooptation of an old weapon. Many sneer at the self-conscious construction known as the "n-word," created in the 1990s to make a theoretical multicultural public place where a racial slur can be used and not used at once. Excising "nigger" from most or all conversations between blacks and whites while recognizing uses in what Paul Butler, a George Washington University law professor, calls "a black space," nevertheless constitutes a real shift in linguistic capital from even the civil rights era, one that Twain would probably have admired, even if it cost him what Randall Kennedy calls "cultural ownership rights." And within this larger conversation, the conversation about *Huck Finn* can, in fact, go many ways.

It is tempting to say that the response to *Huck* is divided between whites and blacks. This is certainly partly true: a poll in 1994 asked black parents if they believed that *Huck Finn* should be assigned in schools, and fewer than one-third said yes. But "there is no single 'black' position on *Huckleberry Finn* any more than there is a monolithic white one," James S. Leonard and Thomas A. Tenney remind us; Robert Fikes describes the history of black response to *Huck Finn* as "love-hate," and one might say the same of non-black readers as well. There is an extensive tradition of African-American authors, academics, and artists finding meaning in the book, using it for inspiration one way or the other, or implicitly endorsing it. And there is an ongoing population of white authors, academics, and artists arguing the opposite, often with heat. For those most invested, the book is a Rorschach test that divides those who think progress happens when we forget the ghosts of the past and those who think progress occurs when we remember them. For some, arguments about history mean nothing when weighed against the violence contained in the word. Langston Hughes, in 1940, wrote famously of the slur that "used rightly or wrongly, ironically or seriously, of necessity for the sake of realism, or impishly for the sake of comedy, it doesn't matter." For others, it is not only a word that persists, but forces us to contemplate the persistence of racism itself. "That teachable moment," David Bradley, PEN/Faulkner Award winner, has said of *Huck Finn*, "is when that word hits the table . . ."

But *Huck Finn* doesn't intend to ignite this particular debate. For Twain, there is no debate: history doesn't ask permission to enter your living room. The question is who we invite to see what happens once it does, and why. It is an established fact that many readers feel "freer" after reading this book; there is even survey evidence to suggest that, taught "properly," taught "intelligently," *Huck Finn* tends to teach racial broadmindedness. And it is an established fact that many others feel oppressed, even cheated, by the book, especially as a result of mandatory reading in unevenly biracial classroom settings. If we release *Huck Finn* from its official duties, briefly or permanently, but with clear heads, then every part of the ideological tangle of repressions and liberations created by generations of teaching it to millions of American schoolchildren badly or well could be unknotted, and we could proceed forward more prosaically, even cynically, but with the kind of wisdom that suits a nation moving into its middle age.

We should not whitewash, as much as Tom Sawyer wants us to: part of the reason Twain used racial slurs was because he thought they were part of the fun. He showed Victorian Americans that he wasn't totally reconstructed, that he still loved words and ideas deemed impolite by his respectable Northern neighbors. And Jim Crow enabled this, allowed him many opportunities to tweak that audience with little concern about what black readers or listeners might think. Likewise, he used racial slurs the way other "reconstructed" Southern white Americans have, as a violent expression of ambivalence on the cusp of a courageous move forward: "When I appoint a nigger to the [Supreme Court]," Lyndon Johnson said in private of Thurgood Marshall, "I want everyone to know he's a nigger." If there was one thing Twain understood—and judging from the frequency with which it occurs in his writings, found particularly haunting—it was the give-and-take of the white American conscience at these moments of profound change.

In other ways, though, we should be aware that Twain is carefully managing what he sees as a viable and familiar antiracist strategy. And for Twain, antiracism was supposed to be fun, too. His use of the "nuclear bomb of racial epithets" in *Huck Finn* and elsewhere almost always means something's unreal, something's being staged. And ultimately, it may have been there to goad complacent white Southerners more than anyone. It aligns most closely with a specific figurative use, employed by both blacks and whites across different eras: it marks the place where racism persists even when political or economic changes suggest improvement. It's the answer to Malcolm X's famous joke: "What do you call a black man with a Ph.D.?" It is *the* sign that we are moving backward as we are moving forward. It's a lightning rod now, but were it somehow not, we might look at Twain's use of the word and describe it as mechanical, a subtle revision of a cliché of white liberals of the age, but still a cliché.

His trusted editors, Olivia and Howells, let it pass, even though neither of them would use the word in polite company. Twain himself accepted Cable's advice and excised it from the printed "Twins of Genius" program. Onstage he said "Negro" unless in character. And he derided a child for saying it aloud on an integrated train at the same time he almost certainly used it onstage. It seems likely that, were he alive today, he would have recognized that his novel was, at best, only partly built for a multiracial audience. In fact, he probably already had: in readings in 1889, at Smith College and in private homes in New York, he performed "The Woman with the Golden Arm" and "King Sollermun." However, for an African-American audience at a benefit in Hartford on May 22, he shelved these pieces. There would be no dialect, no racial role-play, no "ironic" epithets. Instead, he featured "On the Decay of the Art of Lying," a wry defense of deceit in the service of others. It went "exceedingly well," Twain wrote later, and reviewers agreed. For Twain, telling the truth and lying at the same time almost always did. And understanding an audience mattered more than who the audience was.

If Langston Hughes's argument that there is no appropriate use for racial slurs (let alone stereotypes) is sound, then *Huck Finn* in our age is simply unteachable unless edited. It might be a great book, even a *good* book, but as a state-sanctioned one assigned in public schools, at least, it might violate the constitutional protections of black students against discrimination, creating "emotional segregation," as Sharon E. Rush of the University of Florida law school writes. But edit out the racial slurs, and you'd still be left with a troubled reflection on race in America—just one you can read aloud to children with less visible tension. If, however, Langston Hughes's argument is not absolute—and Hughes, Arnold Rampersad tells us, was a "lifelong admirer of Mark Twain"—then coming to terms with *Huck*'s catch-all, the highs and the lows, the against-the-grains and with-the-grains, the mix of social justice and retrograde language, and seeing it all as the product of a coherent vision of history and not just that of a conflicted virtuoso, might be what truly opens up Pandora's box.

We'd know better what went wrong; we'd know our patterns. We might better reflect upon the contorted relationship between our playfulness and our seriousness, the breach between entertainment and politics that Twain and Cable exemplified, the bridge that couldn't quite be crossed: that the debut of "Jump Jim Crow" occurred almost in the same year that Nat Turner rebelled, for instance, and the same year that William Lloyd Garrison started the *Liberator*, the newspaper that inspired abolitionism as a national movement. We might assume less often that a symbolic moment of cross-racial outreach—watching a movie, listening to a song, making a private decision, even casting a vote—substitutes for a substantive change. We might even begin to notice that, just as Huck's vow to go to hell becomes the "evasion," the symbolic moment is usually the red sky in the morning, the sign that a storm of backsliding is set for the next chapter. One hundred years from now, we might recognize that the election of an African-American president was the national equivalent of Huck's private vow to go to hell: it was thrilling at the moment, but signified no structural breakthrough in the relationship between blacks and whites, and instead catalyzed shrewd onlookers to wonder what, in fact, would.

In this manner, the geysers refresh themselves faithfully, to blow

again and again, for the benefit of the tourists. To insist that Twain's
portrayal of childhood was fun and games, and his treatment of race
was not, seems like two different mistakes, but they are flip sides of
the same coin: both make it seem like we are moving faster than we
are. We miss the fact that Twain, on each matter, was fighting a technology of segregation locking into place—was fighting a step away
from a pluralistic society—using nostalgia as a weapon. We miss the
special essence of Twain's vision, which was, to use Victor A. Doyno's
word, "echoic."

Seen from the present, reflecting on the present, it seems like an
easy, forgivable mistake. But seen from the present, with the miasma
of the past as one's companion, all *Huck Finn* does is drag you back,
and drag you back some more. And spending time in that miasma,
without the comfort normally afforded by nostalgia, is a truly sick-
ening experience, and a humbling one. You don't think: How much
smarter and more tolerant we are these days. Instead, you think:
In what miasma am I standing now? What will sicken my great-
grandchildren about my politics? Which of my already tiresome debates will they be compelled, unknowingly, to repeat?

Looking at the book with fresh eyes, one might reasonably ask:
Can't we do something new with this material? Set your filter for
America and Islam, which sounds like it belongs to our generation,
not Twain's, and you'll find the shadow of Mideast crises superim-
posed all over the landscape, starting with that scene where Tom
Sawyer attacks a Sunday-school class of six-year-olds, claiming that
they are "A-rabs." If you were writing a novel *right now* and you had
a child create an attack by "A-rabs" out of false evidence, requiring a response that actually took the form of an attack on Christian schoolchildren—that scene would be fairly topical, wouldn't it,
even though it wouldn't exactly fit an agenda? The more one looks,
though, the more oppressive the exercise. Every gesture that produces new relevancy in *Huck Finn* also produces the deflating conviction that history goes round. Cable was right: we ought to be
more impatient. It should change the debate over a military presence
in the Mideast to remind ourselves that this same problem occupied the Victorians. Or a debate over the national debt, and the size
of government, to note the same concerns shaped arguments when

both were far smaller. And it should change a debate over teaching evolution—or immigration, or voting rights, or race and criminal justice, or standardized educational testing, or violent pop culture, or how to be good parents, or how to fulfill the promises of the Declaration of Independence—to see that it has been taking place for over a century. We've done this already, we should be able to tell each other. And, like good Americans who want to live up to our best myths about ourselves, we'll want to do something, anything, rather than repeat the past. In that moment, we'll understand what *Huck Finn* teaches.

ACKNOWLEDGMENTS

Writing a provocative book about *Huck Finn* and Mark Twain is about the least provocative thing one can do. Generally, one doesn't say anything new about *Huck Finn*—a fact that, in itself, is not even a new thing to observe. There are original insights in this book, or, at least, original juxtapositions of older insights. As well, there is an effort to bring arguments known within the academic community to a larger audience. That is less original, but it is important, and not at all easy. And it is a goal that fits the book's theme: that Mark Twain and *Huck Finn* teach us that American history is "echoic," not progressive. A healthy dose of humility for the sojourner in Twain's world, then, for the problems about which he writes become *your* problems.

In writing this book, I was inspired by, and am indebted to, many inspired scholars and writers, especially for the Twain biographies written by Ron Powers, Fred Kaplan, Michael Shelden, Michael Patrick Hearn, Jerome Loving, Laura E. Skandera Trombley, Karen Lystra, Walter Blair, Andrew Hoffman, and Justin Kaplan; for provocative works of research and analysis by Shelley Fisher Fishkin, Forrest G. Robinson, Lawrence Howe, Jonathan Arac, Victor A. Doyno, Victor Fischer, Louis J. Budd, Tom Quirk, Randall Knoper, Roger B. Salomon, Arthur G. Pettit, and Jocelyn Chadwick-Joshua; and for articles and essays by Toni Morrison, David Bradley, Ann M. Ryan, Gregg Camfield, Stacey Margolis, Eric J. Sundquist, Ishmael Reed, Ralph Ellison, and many other writers and academics. I studied the analysis of the minstrel show by Eric Lott, W. T. Lhamon Jr., Robert C. Toll, J. Anthony Berret, Dale Cockrell, Karen Sotiropoulos, Louis Chude-Sokei, Saidiya Hartman, William J. Mahar, Steven Johnson, Yuval Taylor and William Austen, Sharon D. McCoy, and

Henry Wonham, and the re-creations of the "Twins of Genius" by Guy Cardwell, Fred Lorch, Paul Fatout, and Stephen Railton. A deep thanks to those writers and scholars who provided perspective and historical foundation to the discussion of racial epithets, in *Huck* and elsewhere: Jabari Asim, Randall Kennedy, Elon James White, Sharon E. Rush, and, again, many others. I am perhaps most grateful to the authors who have had the serious conversation about children and Twain, especially Steven Mailloux, Michael J. Kiskis, Albert E. Stone, Cynthia Griffin Wolff, Alan Gribben, Peter Messent, Roberta Seelinger Trites, David Nylund, Elizabeth Prioleau, Keith M. Opdahl, Victor Doyno, Forrest G. Robinson, and Beverly Lyon Clark. They deserve special tribute here. And there are many, many others. The literature on Twain and *Huck Finn* is simply extraordinary. The documentation for this book is nearly as long as the book, and even then, it's not long enough.

I am grateful to the editors of the Twain Papers and Project in Berkeley, and particularly grateful for the assistance of Neda Salem at that archive, for providing copies and microfiche of many key documents. I am likewise grateful for assistance provided by the administration of the Clifton Waller Barrett Library at the University of Virginia, and Lyndsi Barnes and the Berg Collection of American Literature at the New York Public Library. I spent much time in the Library of Congress and Howard University, and received much support from librarians in both venues. I conducted interviews with leading scholars in the field, and am thankful for their commitment and thoughtfulness: those names appear in the bibliography. I also want to thank Michael Shelden, Forrest G. Robinson, Karen Lystra, Henry Wonham, Fred Leebron, Brynnar Swenson, Phil Goff, and Hilene Flanzbaum for reading drafts of the manuscript in its entirety and making essential editing suggestions. As always, I thank Susan Berger and the staff of the interlibrary loan office at Irwin Library at Butler University for their indispensable and tireless efforts.

As always, my amazing agent, Lydia Wills, read, consulted, and supported with respect, humor, and generosity. I have several editors to thank: Sarah Hochman for her enthusiasm and initial support for the project; Anjali Singh for her energy and guidance during its middle phases; and Millicent Bennett for closing the deal with exceptional intelligence, good faith, and steadiness. Thanks, too, to the larger group at Simon & Schuster who looked after this book: Ed Winstead, David Chesanow, Jackie Seow, Loretta Denner, Erin Reback, and Dana Trocker. And a special thanks, once again, to Jonathan Karp. I enjoyed working with each and every one.

Special thanks to Howard Baetzhold, as patient as any good guardian angel must be, and his wonderful family. And to Marshall Gregory and his wonderful family. To Lauren Stark for her help in middle phases of the project, and to Madison Chartier for her gracious and timely assistance during the last edits. And to the students of EN390, whose ongoing enthusiasm about Mark Twain and *Huck Finn*, and inventive readings, inform and inspire this book.

Lastly, to family: thanks to Siobhán, as always, for her love, humor, company, and support. And to Aedan, to whom this book is dedicated.

NOTES

EPIGRAPH

ix **Boston, February 24, 1881:** Twain, *Mark Twain's Speeches*, 258. Also in Fatout, *Mark Twain Speaking*, 148. Much writing on Mark Twain observes the difficulty of naming: whether to call him Mark Twain or by his given name, Samuel Langhorne Clemens. It is a tribute to the porousness of the pseudonym—if calling it a pseudonym is even the right term—that it can cause such problems a century later. For the purposes of this book, I will call him Twain once he starts calling himself Twain—around 1863—and Clemens before that. But it is worth noting that this confusion was not, really, a problem for journalists of his period, who almost seemed to enjoy the conjoinment of names: "Samuel Clemens is the Mark Twain of old," wrote the *Cleveland Herald* on December 18, 1884 (quoted in Baker, "Shrewd Ohio Audiences," 22–23). Budd, *Our Mark Twain*, 73: "Trying to separate Mark Twain from Samuel L. Clemens was like distinguishing the tree from the branches, the dancer from the dance." See also Trites, *Twain, Alcott*, xvi. Hearn, *Annotated Huckleberry Finn*, 16–17, notes Albert Paine observing that it is incorrect to call Mark Twain only "Twain"—but, it would seem, next to unavoidable. Cox, *Fate of Humor*, 3–33, is much recommended here. He reminds us that "Mark Twain," in river parlance, means "*barely safe water*" (23)—not comforting, but not discomforting, either. Shelden, *Man In White*, xxii, notes the "convenience" of using "the name by which most readers know him."

PREFACE

xv **"all modern American literature . . . *Huckleberry Finn*":** During the 1980s and 1990s, several surveys measured the recognition of *Huck Finn*, as well as many other icons constituting national cultural literacy. The National Endowment for the Humanities, in 1989, produced a survey that showed that 95 percent of fourth-year college students could match *Huck Finn* to its author; no other book came within twenty points: see Diane Ravitch and Chester E. Finn Jr., *What Do Our 17-Year-Olds Know?* The Modern Languages Association, in 1990–91, surveyed 527 college and university

English departments, and found Twain the most often taught author: "Class Notes," Peter Applebome, *New York Times*, March 1, 1995, p. B8. See also Arthur N. Applebee, "Stability and Change in the High School Canon," *English Journal* 81, no. 5 (September 1992), 27–32. On 28, Applebee presents a chart describing "Most Frequently Required Titles, Grade 9–12": *Huckleberry Finn* is listed as "required" at 76 percent of public and Catholic schools, and 56 percent of independent schools. No American "classic" is more often required.

Lisa A. Hale and Chris Crowe, in " 'I Hate Reading If I Don't Have To': Results from a Longitudinal Study of High School Students' Reading Interest" (*ALAN Review* 28, no. 3 [Spring-Summer 2001], http://scholar.lib.vt.edu/ejournals/ALAN/v28n3/hale.html), use three survey years (1982, 1990, 1997) and found a decline in the use of *Huck Finn* in the context of a broader decentralization of the standard canon. In other words, it remained the most often used book in American high schools, even though it was used much less: "*The Adventures of Huckleberry Finn* is the only title which graces composite required reading lists for all three survey years. Though a mainstay, its popularity does dwindle. For instance, in 1982, it accounts for 28% of all required titles listed by students, but by 1997, this number drops to 5.12%. Despite this drop, *The Adventures of Huckleberry Finn* still remains the most popular required reading title reported in all survey years by all grade levels."

Ernest Hemingway, *Green Hills of Africa* (New York: Scribner's, 1935), 22. David L. Ulin, "Celebrating the Genius of 'Huckleberry Finn,' " *Los Angeles Times*, November 14, 2010, for an example of modern reporters and critics still citing Hemingway: http://articles.latimes.com/2010/nov/14/entertainment/la-ca-mark-twain-20101114. Other celebrated writers oft-quoted in support of the "greatness" of the book include T. S. Eliot, Lionel Trilling, H. L. Mencken; see Budd, "Introduction," *New Essays*, for a good sampling. For examples of lists: "The American Novel," PBS, http://www.pbs.org/wnet/americannovel/topnovel/; Kevin Hartnett, "The Great American Novel? 9 Experts Share Their Opinions," *The Millions*, July 10, 2013, http://www.themillions.com/2013/07/the-greatest-american-novel-9-experts-share-their-opinions.html; "Banned Books That Shaped America," http://www.bannedbooksweek.org/censorship/bannedbooksthatshaped america. There is contrary evidence as well: "The Bible Remains America's Favorite Book," Harris Interactive.com, April 29, 2014, http://www.harrisinteractive.com/NewsRoom/HarrisPolls/tabid/447/mid/1508/arti cleId/1422/ctl/ReadCustom%20Default/Default.aspx, does not list *Huck Finn*, even though classics like *Moby-Dick*, *The Great Gatsby*, and *The Catcher in the Rye* do appear.

xv **an intensity rarely reserved for the classics anymore:** See Tina Jordan, "Over One Hundred Years After His Death, Mark Twain Hits No. 1 on the Best-seller List," *Entertainment Weekly*, October 17, 2010, http://shelf-life.ew.com/2010/10/17/over-100-years-after-his-death-mark-twain-hits-no

-1-on-the-best-seller-list/. See also Mark Memmott, "New Edition of 'Huckleberry Finn' Will Edit Offensive Words," npr.org, January 4, 2011, http://www.npr.org/blogs/thetwo-way/2011/01/04/132652272/new-edition-of-huckleberry-finn-will-eliminate-offensive-words. Educators are suspended or fired for trying to teach it. And educators are suspended or fired for calling it "racist." See "In Chicago Classroom, Teachable Moment or Racism?" *Business Management Daily,* July 22, 2012, http://www.businessmanagementdaily.com/31559/in-chicago-classroom-teachable-moment-or-racism; "School Fired Woman for Calling Book Racist," Upi.com, July 16, 2012. http://www.upi.com/Top_News/US/2012/07/16/School-fired-woman-for-calling-book-racist/UPI-27371342454578/?spt=hs&or=tn; "Teacher Suspended for Discussing Racial Epithet in Class," Reuters.com, February 17, 2012, http://www.reuters.com/article/2012/02/17/us-education-teacher-race-idUSTRE81G28H20120217. Likewise, as the debate over teacher tenure warms, many editorials, blog postings, and other forms of correspondence use "teaching *Huck Finn*" as a model for the kind of worthy but risky endeavor less secure teachers will shy away from: See, for instance, Diane Morris, "Why Teacher Tenure Matters," April 30, 2013, Women Advancenc.org, http://womenadvancenc.org/why-teacher-tenure-matters/. Lastly, it should be noted that *Huck Finn* is not remotely the most often banned or restricted book in American schools and libraries. See, for instance, Henry, "The Struggle for Tolerance," 27.

xv **Morrison . . . as critic Jonathan Arac writes:** Morrison, "Introduction," *Huckleberry Finn*, xli. Arac, *Idol and Target.*

xvi **eight books, plus dozens of scholarly articles:** This count refers to the following, to be found in the bibliography: Mensh, *Black, White*; Chadwick-Joshua, *Jim Dilemma*; Fishkin, *Was Huck Black?*; Arac, *Huckleberry Finn as Idol and Target*; Davis, Leonard, and Tenney, *Satire or Evasion?*; Rush, *Huck Finn's "Hidden" Lessons*; Dempsey, *Searching for Jim*; Leonard, *Making Mark Twain Work in the Classroom.* The list could easily be extended: See Beaver, Wieck, Fulton, Quirk, Pettit, et al.

xvi **"on the riverbank just like he did":** Pollack, *Real Boys,* describes the "myth" of the "young boy as the rascal and the scamp, the mischievous lad who loves to run and be loud, whose pockets are filled with junk that he considers treasure . . ." (xxii). Huck both helps create this myth and is read within its context. Leonard and Tenney, "Introduction," *Satire or Evasion,* 1. Schill, "Aisle View." "Make Your Own Kids Fishing Pole—Huck Finn Style!" JM Cremp's Adventure for Boys Blog, April 1, 2013, http://funadventureforboys.com/2013/04/01/make-your-own-kids-fishing-pole-huck-finn-style/.

Robinson, preface, *Cambridge Companion,* xiii, creates a chronology for when Huck's "image," at least to scholars, became "more uncertain and troubled," crediting Cox, *The Fate of Humor* (1966), as "the first to challenge consensus." He also cites a moment from the Mickey Rooney 1939 movie version to suggest that such "challenges" were already in the air. However, any recent Google search on the key word "Huck Finn" or "Huckleberry Finn" tends to yield up plentiful announcements of blues and bluegrass music, fishing, boating and camping events and services, and other bucolic rituals associated with a vision of a rustic and outdoorsy past.

xvi **in the time Twain wrote the book:** Kiskis, in "Critical Humbug," has made this case as clearly as any scholar I have read, noting that "the question of Clemens' racial politics has become *the* primary point of much that is spoken and written about his contribution to American culture" and that, in fact, "During his prime years," he was "increasingly aware of and sensitive to the plight of the child" (14). In "Social Justice," Kiskis writes that Twain "devoted a major portion of his fiction to exploring the plight of children" (66). Others, most notably Albert Stone and Steven Mailloux, have made variants of this case. See Mailloux, "Eating Books," 135: "I argue, in effect, that the cultural conversation of the mid-1880s demonstrated less anxiety about race relations than it did about juvenile delinquency and that the cultural censors reviewing *Huckleberry Finn* were preoccupied less with racist segregation practices than with the 'Bad-Boy Boom' and the negative effects of reading fiction." Generally, most Twain/*Huck Finn* scholars who read newspapers from the 1880s come away with the conviction that the politics of childhood mattered much more than contemporary readings account for.

xvi **children's alienation . . . public school curricula:** Twain himself wrote: "A boy's life is not all comedy; much of the tragic enters into it" (*Autobiography*, vol. 1, 157). Mintz, *Huck's Raft*, cites "Hannibal" as the place where "many enduring fantasies about childhood come to life," and observes that "when we idealize Mark Twain's Hannibal and its eternally youthful residents, we suppress his novel's more sinister aspects" (1). Robinson, *In Bad Faith* (much recommended), 64, extends the argument to *Tom Sawyer*: "Can we account for more than a century of critical neglect of the broad strand of outrage in the novel's mingled texture?" Wolff, in "*The Adventures of Tom Sawyer*: A Nightmare Vision of American Boyhood," does superb work with *Tom Sawyer* in this regard: "If we place Tom Sawyer in the "simplistic category of 'All-American boyhood'—we will find ourselves led seriously astray" (637).

xvii **sideways, even backward, on matters of race and freedom:** Many scholars have long noted the circularity of *Huck Finn*, and have debated for fifty years the notion that the "backsliding" moments in *Huck Finn* represent Twain's satire on the failures of Reconstruction to fulfill the promises of equality and opportunity made to African-Americans in the wake of the Civil War. "In 1885 it unmistakably read as a commentary on the Southern question," Louis J. Budd has observed, "to believe this was accidental is to be naïve." In newspaper editorials, and on stages and in most classrooms, though, a consensus endures that the book ends happily on these matters, and that was a motivating factor for why I have written this book. Budd, *Mark Twain: Social Philosopher*, 106; Arac, *Huckleberry Finn as Idol* *and Target* more generally. Special notice should be given to Budd, *Social Philosopher*, 86–110; Tony Tanner, *Reign of Wonder: Naivety and Reality in American Literature* (Cambridge, UK: Cambridge University Press, 1965); Fishkin, *Lighting Out for the Territory*, 199; Fishkin, *Was Huck Black?*, 70–75; Morrison, "Introduction," *Huckleberry Finn*, xxxvi. Others: MacLeod, "Telling the Truth." Doyno, *Writing Huck Finn*, 228–39. Sundquist, "Twain and Plessy." Brown, "For Our Time." Barksdale, "History, Slavery," 20. Nilon, "Freeing the Free Negro," 63–66. Howe, *Mark Twain and the Novel*, 98. Wieck, *Refiguring Huckleberry Finn*, 56–69 and elsewhere. Coulombe compiles a list of critics who have discussed this in "Native Americans," 277, footnote 2. There is also significant work discussing the idea of a "consensus" on individualism that shields *Huck* from criticism: Bercovitch, "Funny," calls it "liberal consensus-in-dissent" (25). Others note the overlap between the key years of the failure of Reconstruction, 1876–83, and the composition of *Huck*: See Schmitz, "Twain, 'Huckleberry Finn,' and the Reconstruction," 60, 63. Schmitz writes that history, essentially, "overwhelms" (66) Twain and *Huck Finn*. Kidd, *Making American Boys*, argues almost uniquely that the "failure" at the end of *Huck Finn* on race is characteristic of other boys' books of the era (58–59). Doyno, *Writing Huck Finn*, 231–39, argues that the ending is a specific parody of the convict-lease system. Margolis, "Huckleberry Finn: Or, Consequences," links it to tort reform during the period, and describes *Huck* as "a fantasy of national responsibility for the bottoming out of black civil rights" (337). Cecil, "The Historical Ending of *Adventures of Huckleberry Finn*," describes the book as a commentary on our "national delinquency": "The book was meant to gall us" (283). Certain scholars even make available linkages between the chronology of Reconstruction's recession and Twain's composition of *Huck*: he began writing when optimism about Rutherford B. Hayes's dedication to civil rights was high (the election campaign of 1876), put it aside as Hayes instead constructed the compromise of 1877 that served as Reconstruction's unofficial retreat, etc. (see Budd, *Social Philosopher*, 87–88).

   Henry, "The Struggle for Tolerance," 38, contra notes "the ingenious lengths to which scholars go to feel comfortable with the final chapters of *Huck Finn*."

xvii **"dedicated amnesia"**: Díaz, "*Mil Máscaras*."

xvii **promote the publication of *Huck Finn***: "Without question the most celebrated reading tour of the decade," Fred Lorch writes. Quoted in Budd, *Our Mark Twain*, 93. Some excellent sources on the "Twins of Genius" are available, and they deserve special mention here: Cardwell, *Twins of Genius*; Lorch, *The Trouble Begins at Eight*; and Fatout, *Mark Twain*, are standard. Most biographies of Twain have a few pages on this passage in Twain's life. Among active scholars, Stephen Railton is unquestionably doing the most visible and interesting work on this. Readers are directed especially to the University of Virginia web site written and directed by him: "Mark Twain in His Times," http://twain.lib.virginia.edu/. It provides copious and well-organized assistance. See also Johnston, "'Remarkable Achievement,'" consulted late in this book's composition, but much recommended for its analysis of how contemporary reviewers constructed opposing portraits of Twain and Cable.

xviii **something richer:** Mintz, *Huck's Raft*, 2–3. Kidd notes the persistence of "boyology," with certain changes in the discourse since the nineteenth century (*Making American Boys*, 1–2); his work is greatly helpful for anyone looking for historical understanding of boys' advice books.

xviii **"America's child":** Calling Huck Finn "America's child," or some variation thereof, is very common. See Lauriat Lane, "Why *Huckleberry Finn* is a Great World Novel," *College English* 17 (October 1955), 3. Alfred Kazin called Huck Finn and Tom Sawyer "*the* American boys of legend . . . represent[ing] some fabled, delicious freedom of boyhood," afterword, *Adventures of Tom Sawyer* (New York: Bantam, 1981), 221. Quoted in Mensh, *Black, White*, 13, 25. Lawrence Howe, "Will Huck Now Be Sold Down the Mississippi?", letter to the editor, *New York Times*, July 25, 1992, 20: "For Huck is not only the most representative American boy in our literature, he is also the character with whom American readers—American white readers—have most deeply identified."

xviii **hungry to put a name on it:** Kiskis, "Social Justice," is excellent here: "Student anxieties are often much more tied to Huck's aloneness and to Clemens' poignant descriptions of Huck's isolation" (70).

xviii *Huck Finn* **and ADHD:** See, for instance, Jillian Wanbaugh, "Huckleberry Finn and Tom Sawyer"; Kate Shambrook, "*Huck Finn and the Hunger Games*"; Ginnye Cubel, "Was Huck Finn ADHD?" A list of student papers is available in the bibliography, and student papers are footnoted when appropriate.

xix **controllers of their own narratives:** Graff, "Introduction," *Growing Up In America*, xiii. In general, the links between *Huck Finn* and the comparatively young academic field of childhood studies are salient. Twain saw childhood, as he saw race, as a social construction, and he created a fictional portrait of childhood that blurred the edges in a way consonant with recent scholars' efforts to explore how strict age divisions tend to repress the individuality of children. Recent childhood scholars, similarly, see children as having agency, some control over their own lives, and a fair amount of control over their parents as well: they see children having some ability to shape commercial culture, and they reject simple formulae for human development. They likewise argue often that childhood was the template for how other minorities would be treated: for instance, David Matza, "Position and Behavior Patterns of Youth," in Graff, *Growing Up in America*, 587: "Youth are not only *a* minority group. Symbolically, they are the minority group in that they have provided a paradigm for imputations and policy regarding disliked ethnic fractions." For a general review, for instance, Heywood, *Childhood*, 4–6. I am especially indebted to my wife, Siobhán, for introducing these concepts to me.

xix **interactive growth during childhood:** Chloe Richardson, "*The Adventures of Huckleberry Finn* and Multiple Intelligences Theory." The books in question are by Howard E. Gardner: *Intelligence Reframed: Multiple Intelligences for the 21st Century* (New York: Basic Books, 2000); *Multiple Intelligences: New Horizons in Theory and Practice* (New York: Basic Books, 2006); and *Frames of Mind: Theories of Multiple Intelligences*, 3rd ed. (New York: Basic Books, 2011). Michelle Trainor, "Huckleberry Finn: A Model": "The latter environment, where Huck truly develops, directly aligns with the modern constructivist learning environment as studied by Jean Piaget, Cathy Vatterott, and Ernst von Glasersfeld, opening the door to an educational critique of *The Adventures of Huckleberry Finn*."

xix **"school or the pulpit":** Twain, "Family Sketch," 17.

xx **"eradicationists"** . . . **"regulationists":** Kennedy, *Nigger*, 126. Asim, *The N Word*, 9–116, provides an excellent overview on the use and response to the "n-word" in the centuries preceding the canonization of *Huck Finn*. I absolutely defer to others regarding expertise teaching *Huck Finn* in many venues: in secondary school classrooms, in classrooms with significantly different (and often more challenging) demographics. My effort here was to produce a body of information providing a background for the teaching of *Huck Finn*, but from an agnostic position regarding whether or not, and to whom, it should be taught. I was guided by two opposing poles: one, an offhand comment made to me by a renowned contemporary Twain scholar, that whatever I wrote, it should be something that gave courage to teachers trying to teach the book; the second, a sentiment best presented in a book from twenty-five years ago by Wayne Booth, *The Company We Keep: An Ethics of Fiction* (Berkeley: University of California Press, 1989, reprint), that, essentially, the decision to not teach *Huck Finn* is an ethical one. There is no law that says a book has to be taught: it should be in classrooms, or leave them, for good reasons that are true to our best, keenest analysis about what we want to teach our children, and we should address that question with as few illusions about ourselves as possible.

xx **not teaching it at all:** Caitlin Genord, "Teaching Critical Literacy Skills": Sources include Maureen McLaughlin and Glenn DeVoogd, "Critical Literacy as Comprehension: Expanding Reader Response," *Journal of Adolescent & Adult Literacy* 48 (2004), 52–56; also Maureen McLaughlin and Glenn DeVoogd, *Critical Literacy: Enhancing Students' Comprehension of Text* (New York: Scholastic Teaching Resources, 2004). Using social media to teach it has also been recommended. See, for instance, Kyle Belting, "#Relevant Runaway." Sources include Kathleen West, "Weblogs and Literary Response: Socially Situated Identities and Hybrid Social Languages in English Class Blogs," *Journal of Adolescent and Adult Literacy* 51.7 (2011): 588–98; Elisabeth Haley, "Old Dog/New Tricks: Reteaching 'Huck Finn' and Pop Culture," *The English Journal* 85.7 (Nov. 1996): 121–22. *Huck Finn* on Tumblr is particularly recommended: see, for instance, http://www.tumblr.com/tagged/huckleberry-finn; http://www.tumblr.com/tagged/huck-finn;

http://www.tumblr.com/tagged/the-adventures-of-huck-finn. *Tom Sawyer* also yields good results. "Huck Finn" or "Huckleberry Finn" in *Urban Dictionary*, on the other hand, yields quite profane results: http://www.urban dictionary.com/define.php?term=huckfinn.

 The discussion of when and how to teach *Huck Finn* is so widespread that it must be covered in several notes throughout this book, and even then, will be incomplete. As an illustrative example, see Titania Kumeh, "Black Writers and English Teachers on Huck Finn," *Mother Jones*, January 13, 2011, http://www.motherjones.com/riff/2011/01/mission-high -huck-finn-english. Note that the article recommends replacing the book with ones written by African-Americans, and in the comment section the author notes that the interview subject also recommended teaching it in tandem with *The Autobiography of Malcolm X*.

xxi **inspiration and foil to Twain's novel:** Cable, "Freedman," and Twain, "Jim's Investments." I deal very little—too little—with the "Jim's Investments" material, which Twain performed less frequently. Still, it seems to function satirically much as the other sections do: as a parody of post-Reconstruction politics, most specifically, the failure of banking systems intended to support freed blacks. The magazine in question is the January issue of the *Century*. Kaplan, *Mr. Clemens*, 255.

xxi **a "racial savior" . . . a *racist*:** Kiskis, "Critical Humbug," 18–19.

xxi **"against the assault of Laughter":** Twain, *The Mysterious Stranger*, 166. Like many of the issues raised in this book—and fitting the book's thesis—there is an old fight here. See DeVoto, preface, *Mark Twain's America*: "I may claim a startling originality in that I have nowhere so distrusted humor as to call Mark Twain a buffoon" (xiii). Knoper, *Acting Naturally*, 1, states an important corollary: most twentieth-century criticism of Twain celebrated his realism and his writing, not his theatrical side. Recent critics have also spoken about the need to find a way to seriously talk about humor in Twain. See, for instance, Ryan, "Black Genes," who notes that "critics are troubled by humor" (170). Robinson, *In Bad Faith*, 120: "Readers have no doubt been subliminally attuned to the incompatibility of slavery with a sustained and plausible comedic perspective on America." Cox, *The Fate of Humor*, is seminal here. Camfield, "*Arabian Nights*," is excellent here as well.

 Cardwell, *The Man Who Was Mark Twain*, 199: "Clemens is not a good informant on the sociology of the South or on the ethics of American democracy." The point that Twain represents a subjective and unreliable position on American history and politics is not made often enough. Jonathan Arac, *Idol and Target*, 3, writes that "if Huck is representative, it can't be in the sense of average or typical, or 'it was just like that.'" Lester, "Morality and *Huckleberry Finn*," 204, writes that "unless *Huck Finn*'s racist and anti-racist messages are considered, the book can have racist results." To me, this point seems deeply important.

xxii **the terms we have:** Ellison, quoted in "Change the Joke," 50. Gubar, *Racechanges* (265) discusses the evolution of the scholarly discussion of minstrelsy: "Until the historical and critical work of such thinkers as Robert Toll, Eric Lott, Michael Rogin, and Toni Morrison, white impersonations of blackness have gone largely ignored by American cultural historians because of morally important taboos that censure such spectacles and that also (though less reasonably) discourage analysis of them." To this group, who (with the exception of Toll, whose *Blacking Up* was published in 1974) were active in the 1990s, we might reasonably add W. T. Lhamon, David Roediger, Alexander Saxton, Joseph Boskin, and Gubar herself. Over the last decade, scholars such as Henry Wonham and Sharon McCoy have done fruitful work more focused on Twain and minstrelsy, while Dale Cockrell and Karen Sotiropoulos have sketched more detailed portraits of other aspects of minstrelsy. See also Cockrell, *Demons of Disorder*, xi–xii, who adds works by Sam Dennison and Carl Wittke to the list of earlier-generation treatments. Lhamon, *Raising Cain*, 5, describes nineteenth-century texts on minstrelsy as well. Mahar, *Behind*, does signal work on the role of parody (of European sources such as opera) in early minstrelsy. Lhamon has edited two volumes (with overlapping content) collecting Jim Crow materials (*Jim Crow, American* and *Jump Jim Crow*). Cole, "American Ghetto Parties," and Chude-Sokei, *Last "Darky,"* have done important work regarding minstrelsy's "astonishing transnational reach" (Cole, "American Ghetto Parties," 224), and on "Black-on-black minstrelsy" (from Chude-Sokei's subtitle)— indispensable for those interested in minstrelsy in a global context.

Taken together, these authors have made several important points regarding the minstrel show: first, that blackface was not an aberration in the history of race and popular culture, but the heart of American mass entertainment for the better part of a century, as dominant in its heyday as rock-and-roll since Elvis, and with strong roots in the mixed-race street cultures of Northern ports such as New York and Baltimore. Second, as Lott argues with discretion in *Love and Theft*, and Lhamon more forcefully in *Raising Cain*, the minstrel show, especially in its early incarnations, possessed "anti-racist dimensions," albeit "corrupt" and more tending to "confound political action" than inspire reform (Lhamon, *Raising Cain*, 6, 42). In fact, most authors produce some kind of timetable that argues that the minstrel show changed over time, and became more repressive: "Early Jim Crow is not the late Jim Crow," Lhamon argues (Lhamon, *Raising Cain*, 191). Finally, all these writers, though with different objects, insist upon the resiliency of blackface strategies even after blackface itself disappeared ("Let's admit their old, low, and large ambition is also ours," Lhamon writes on *Raising Cain*, 1, a line that deeply influences here), and specifically upon the resilience with which white adolescents, artists, and entertainers continued to play out the drama of fascination with, appropriation of, and differentiation from black culture. There are differences among these scholars, to be sure. Lhamon, for instance, argues for "open reading," and believes evidence shows "as much connection among slaves and hirelings . . . as [it] document[s] rifts" (Lhamon, *Raising Cain*, 149);

Rogin argues that the form was "fundamentally flawed," and constituted "Race hatred"—"blackface was an alternative to interracial political solidarity, not the failed promise of it" (Rogin, *Blackface*, 37–38). Toll, in turn, noted that "because minstrelsy's antislavery sentiments contained no call to action, audiences could enjoy all of this on the same night without feeling that Negroes were their equals or that they had to reconcile their contradictory feelings about slavery" (Toll, *Blacking Up*, 86). Rogin's position, in turn, is stated in similar ways by Roediger and Saxton; Lott and Lhamon's aligns with recent postcolonial theory regarding colonial ambivalence and indigenous populations (see Bhabha, "Of Mimicry and Man," especially, but also Said). Cockrell, *Demons of Disorder*, xi–xii, endorses open reading, but argues that the form changed more rapidly between 1832 and 1845 than other critics have described. And, using his own childhood singing experiences as example, he disputes the "theft" paradigm: "It felt more like sharing, or loving" (167).

Regarding *Huck Finn*, many different approaches have already been taken. I am most influenced by Lott, in "Twain, Race, and Blackface," 134, as he argues that the relationship between *Huck Finn* and the minstrel show is comprehensive, not merely restricted to the scenes that most overtly duplicate minstrel set pieces: "Writers who have rightly denounced the minstrel show aura of *Huck Finn* miss the extent to which even the best moments possess a blackface cast." But opinions, obviously, differ. "If *Huck Finn* were merely a 19th century minstrel show," Lance Morrow observes, "then no one could object to African-American parents removing the book . . ." (Morrow, "In Praise"). In this context, readings of "King Sollermun," for instance, become vital litmus for whether or not antiracism leaks through the surface. One needs to believe that an "off-screen" *Huck* exists, one Twain does not directly portray—such as scenes where slaves from neighboring farms all flock to hear Jim speak—that reflect Jim's rhetorical and intellectual savvy. One must be able to read into Jim's silences and pauses, to regard him as constantly appraising Huck, and speaking in codes. Given Twain's own revisions and notes to the manuscript (where he sometimes notes Jim "secretly" choosing not to speak—see Lauber, *Inventions*, 112), his love of pauses, this is not remotely implausible. See Robinson, "Silences," or Shelley Fisher Fishkin, "In Praise of 'Spike Lee's *Huckleberry Finn*' by Ralph Wiley," http://faculty.citadel.edu/leonard/od99wiley.htm.

Most authors—Bell, MacCann and Woodward, Lott, Berret, Wonham, and others—cite Twain's description in 1906 of "the real nigger show—the genuine nigger show, the extravagant nigger show—the show which to me had no peer and whose peer has not yet arrived" as disturbing and revealing (see this book's final chapter). Examinations of Twain's relationship to the performance culture of his time—Randall Knoper's *Acting Naturally: Mark Twain in the Culture of Performance* most prominent—have drawn attention away from canonical efforts to celebrate Twain's "realism" and explore instead his theatrical sense. Toni Morrison argues that *Huck Finn* becomes

a "more beautifully complicated work" when readers "linger over the implications of the Africanist presence at its center"—not "what Jim seems,"
as Morrison writes, but what "Mark Twain, Huck and especially Tom need
from him" (Morrison, *Playing*, 54, 57). In Morrison, "Introduction"—a
fantastic essay—she is probably more critical of the "over-the-top min-
strelization" (xxxv) of Jim than any other component of the novel. Phiri,
"Ghost," reiterates this position. Anthony Berret constructed a portrait of
the resemblances between Huck Finn and a minstrel show of the 1840s,
1850s, and 1860s (which Twain viewed in Hannibal, New York, and San
Francisco). It is essential reading. For Berret, the minstrel show possessed a
standard three-part structure that *Huck Finn* seems to replicate: a collection
of "comic dialogues and sentimental songs" that corresponds to the early
comic exchanges between Tom Sawyer and Huck, Huck and Pap, and Jim
and Huck; an "olio of novelty acts," corresponding to the King and Duke
set pieces; and a finale, "a short musical about life on the plantation, or a
one-act burlesque of a classic drama or opera," that corresponds particularly
closely to the final "evasion" sequence in *Huck* (Berret, "Huckleberry," 38,
44; note that Mahar, *Behind*, disputes that this structure was pervasive, or
even influential, 332). He also notes the obvious link between Huck, Jim,
and Tom as two end men and interlocutor, with Huck "endman most of
the time" (41). Strausbaugh discusses these traits generally in *Black Like
You*, 102–4, and Twain specifically on 196–97. Sotiropoulos, *Staging Race*,
does so on 21. Toll, *Blacking Up*, 52–56. Wittke, *Tambo and Bones*, 52.
McCoy, "Trouble Begins," 235. Jim's position in "King Sollermun" was
well within the tradition of the "stump speech," a set piece where an end
man delivered a comic political discourse (Toll, *Blacking Up*, 55). And Jim
and Huck's debate would have been recognizable as the "Negro quarrel" (in
his *Autobiography*, vol. 2, 295, it is the "Negro quarrel" about which Twain
waxes particularly nostalgic). MacCann and Woodward observe that many
of the derogating and alienating aspects of Jim's personality—his superstitions, "swaggering buffoonery," and periodic stupefaction—are all derived
from minstrel stereotypes (MacCann and Woodward, "Minstrels," 145).
But they also note that the positive aspects of Jim's personality were also stereotypes ascribed to certain black men in nineteenth-century mass culture:
"The 'sympathy' that *Huck Finn* evokes for Jim is part of what minstrelsy
was about" (MacCann and Woodward, "Traditions," 79). Lott does this as
well (*Love and Theft*, 33), describing "the gentle, childlike, self-sacrificing,
essentially *aesthetic* slave Mark Twain created in Jim and thought he recognized on the minstrel stage." Likewise, much of the sympathy minstrels displayed for slaves revolved around the separation of families, which meshes
with Jim's celebrated scene lamenting his treatment of his absent daughter
(75, 82).

Even Huck's "Irishness" was consonant with minstrelsy: large portions
of the first white minstrel actors (and their audiences) were working-class
Irish, who incorporated Irish music, instruments, and low comedy types

with what they conceived to be authentic black culture. Lott, *Love and Theft*, describes minstrelsy in part as "an expression of Irishness through the medium of 'blackness'" (96). Toll, *Blacking Up*, 27, reminds us that "'Jim Crow' resembled an Irish folk tune." Lhamon, *Raising Cain*, 42, describes "recast traditional Irish melodies with fantasy images of fieldhand fun shadowed by violence and dislocation." Lastly, there are E. W. Kemble's drawings: scholarly debate over whether these drawings are "counterpoint" to Twain's antiracism, or reinforce stereotypes of Jim, continues to this day. See also Beverly R. David, "The Pictorial Huck Finn: Mark Twain and His Illustrator, E. W. Kemble," *American Quarterly* 26 (October 1974). As Lott notes: "Blackface furnished Twain's very language of race" (Lott, "Twain, Race, and Blackface," 149). He adds, 141: "Ecstatic in blackface, Twain touched on a form that conveyed exactly the brutality, insecurity, omnipotence, envy, condescension, jealousy, and fascination that characterize popular white racial responses to black people."

As for effects: a debate over the role of minstrelsy in the character of Jim and the novel's plot has taken place since the 1950s. Key early texts are Ralph Ellison, "Change the Joke and Slip the Yoke," and Donald Gibson, "Mark Twain's Jim in the Classroom," *English Journal* 57, no. 2 (1968), 196–202. Gerber, "Introduction," 10, writes of Jim that "far from being the minstrel darky, he shows himself to be an extraordinarily shrewd human being." This is typical: Jim's heroism shines through the stereotype, many say. Bell, "Twain's 'Nigger Jim,'" 124, 127–29, notes that Twain emphasized the "delightful accuracy of minstrelsy," a crucial and damning point. Woodard and MacCann, "Minstrel Shackles," is excellent throughout, and critical of Twain: "Twain's use of the minstrel tradition undercuts serious consideration of Jim's humanity beyond those qualities stereotypically attributed to the noble savage" (142). Arac, *Impure Worlds*, makes some interesting remarks: 62–63, 70.

See Strausbaugh, *Black Like You*, 11–12, 317–24, for a discussion of "minstrelsy" in critique of black comedians, actors, and musicians. Strausbaugh also points out that actual performances in blackface remain more resilient than we care to admit, citing, for instance, "Civil War reenactment groups . . . striving for authenticity" (16, 20, and especially 314–15). He cites estimates that "about a third of the cartoons released by MGM alone in the late 1940s included a blackface, coon or mammy figure" (240), and provides an example for Bugs Bunny (241) as well. McCoy, interview, cites examples of blackface in movies such as *Tropic Thunder* and *Bamboozled* in arguing that a kind of resurgence may actually be taking place. Alexander, *The New Jim Crow*, writes that "it seems likely that historians will one day look back on the images of black men in gangsta rap videos with similar curiosity" to that paid to African-American minstrels from the past (174). Minstrel shows were performed in public much later than we now think, often with public sanction. Boskin, *Sambo*, 93, finds them in the 1970s, and sponsored by the Works Progress Administration in the 1930s. Examples from contemporary media invoking minstrelsy in critique of a new television program, music recording or movie are plentiful; see, for instance, Jasmyne A. Cannick, "Fox TV's New Minstrel Show," *New America Media*, September 28, 2009, http://news.new americamedia.org/news/view_article.html?article_id=9ce02d0c4af8f4a09 452f1fb42d6439e; Heaggans, *The 21st Century Hip-Hop Minstrel Show*.

xxiii **the story we tell ourselves:** See Salomon, *Mark Twain and the Image of History*, 5: "We have been ceaselessly engaged, as Carl Becker has noted, in either reviling our ancestors or dressing them up . . ."

xxiii **and access to economic benefits:** Alexander's main argument in *The New Jim Crow* is that "a new racial caste system" (3) currently operates, and the "war on drugs" is its main engine. She points out that "an extraordinary percentage of black men in the United States are legally barred from voting today, just as they have been throughout most of American history" (1), and that "today it is perfectly legal to discriminate against criminals in nearly all the ways that it was once legal to discriminate against African Americans" (2). "Mass incarceration is, metaphorically, the New Jim Crow," she argues (11). Relevant to this book, she argues that "the popular narrative that emphasizes the death of slavery and Jim Crow and celebrates the nation's 'triumph over race' with the election of Barack Obama, is dangerously misguided" (11). The statistics cited here can be found on 6–7 and 189. See also Reed, "Mark Twain's Hairball," 382–83: "Another thing that hasn't changed: blacks as criminal suspects."

xxiii **"déjà vu":** Kutner and Olson, *Grand Theft Childhood*, 29–56, provide an excellent analysis of the continuity in the political debate about children and violent popular culture since the Victorian era. The idea that debates about children have not changed significantly is commonly made, at least casually, throughout literature on children—about as much as the opposite claim is made. See, for instance, Paley, *A Child's Work*: "The children you will meet" in her book, Paley writes, "are little different from those I taught in the same school thirty years ago" (3).

xxiv **our close relation to the past:** Twain, many believe, once said "history doesn't repeat itself, but sometimes it does rhyme." And he may have. Robert Hirst, quoted in Fishkin, *Lighting Out*, 136, argues that Twain "leads Benjamin Franklin and Abraham Lincoln in misattributed quotes." A handful of critics have drawn attention to the specific idea that Twain's work is particularly valuable in the way that it links the Gilded Age past to the present. Much recommended is Reed, "Mark Twain's Hairball." See also Philip McFarland, "Mark Twain and America's 'Worst President'."

xxiv **"prescient" . . . "patterns":** Reed, "Mark Twain's Hairball," 380. Reed specifically refers to patterns in our racial history; I have expanded this slightly.

xxiv **a "great boy" for reading history:** From David E. E. Sloane, *Adventures of Huckleberry Finn: American Comic Vision* (New York: Twayne, 1988), 33. Quoted in Howe, *Mark Twain and the Novel*, 118. Salomon, *Mark Twain and the Image of History*, provides a short, persuasive overview exploring Twain's "abiding" interest in history, 20–25. Cable, "Cable's Reminiscences": "Every one knows that one of his passions was for history."

xxiv **"Story up history"**: Mark Twain, *Notebooks*, vol. 3, 24.

xxiv **"Mark Twain's Memory-Builder"**: One can see Twain working on the game in his *Notebooks*, vol. 3, 19–32, and elsewhere. Webster, *Business Man*, 218: "*Huckleberry Finn* was quite forgotten." See also 219, 227, where Twain tells Howells to never try to make a history game. "Mark Twain's Memory-Builder Game Boards and Accompanying Material" can be found in the Mark Twain Papers in Berkeley, and is cited here. See also Howe, *Mark Twain and the Novel*, 104–5, 110–11, for excellent analysis on the relationship between board and novel: he describes "the game as an extension of the novel rather than a distraction from it" (105), and should be noted here for discussing the "erosion" of Twain's faith in "Whig historiography" (120). Quotes from the game can also be found in Howe, *Mark Twain and the Novel*, 110. See also Jeanie M. Wagner, "Huckleberry Finn and the History Game," *Mark Twain Journal* 20 (Winter 1979–80), 5–10, who makes the fullest case that, because of his interest in the history game, the end of *Huck Finn* is the "work of a diverted artist" (9).

Salomon, *Mark Twain and the Image of History*, does the most detailed work describing the transition in Twain's thinking regarding the "idea of progress" (10). For Salomon, Twain moved from deep faith in "the Whig hypothesis . . . toward a theory of historical cycles" that we can see explored throughout his later work (32). See especially Chapters 2 and 3. Salomon, it should be noted, finds more nuance in Twain's later beliefs than I describe, isolating, at the very least, a tension between "cyclical theor[ies] of history" and the need to "escape imaginatively from the nightmarish implications of his own rational formulations" (168). Books like *Joan of Arc* and *Connecticut Yankee*, with their complicated antimodern elements, test the limits of these tensions. More specifically, Salomon describes *Huck Finn* as having been composed during "the very years in which [Twain] became a vociferous celebrant of historical progress" while simultaneously "his pessimism, always latent, was steadily deepening and more and more finding expression" (136). For Salomon, *Huck Finn* is "literally saturated with the nightmare of history, a nightmare nowhere mitigated by the hope of progress." Salomon also notes that "this point has been documented by modern scholarship time and again," and particularly cites DeVoto's *Mark Twain at Work* and Blair's *Mark Twain and Huck Finn*. See also Lears, *No Place of Grace*, 19, for a fine, quick description of "optimistic liberalism" in the period during which *Huck* was written. On 164–66, Lears discusses Twain directly, focusing on *A Connecticut Yankee in King Arthur's Court*.

The circularity of *Huck Finn* is also a familiar trope in studies of Twain, especially among those who examine his views on history. See Howe, *Mark Twain and the Novel*, 98, for one example. Doyno, *Writing Huck Finn*, 239, observes that the book is "cyclic in structure." Robinson, *In Bad Faith*, 135, is trenchant: "There is blind, unsatisfying repetition: first, the evasion that gives rise to the compulsion to be distracted; then the evasion of the failure to be distracted in the renewal of the search. For Mark Twain's admirers, this circular pattern has expressed itself in generations of telling and re-telling *Huckleberry Finn*." Wieck, *Refiguring*, 104. O'Loughlin, "Whiteness of Bone," 41. Quirk, *Coming to Grips*, 78, distills an excellent quote from *Tom Sawyer Abroad* that speaks to the issue: "The moral lesson is ultimately useless, argues Tom, 'because the thing don't ever happen the same way again—and can't.'"

xxiv **"I been there before"**: Twain, *Huckleberry Finn*, 362.

xxiv **the foreboding speaks to us anyway**: See Robinson, *In Bad Faith*, 1: "The novel's popularity is evidence of a much greater cultural appetite for dark-ness and ambiguity than is generally allowed."

Over the past two decades, there has been much scholarly discussion concerning the role of narrative—certain narratives—in providing national or community allegories. Arac, for instance, argues against the "hypercan-onization" of *Huck Finn* as an "American" book, and argues that it can only be read as a literary allegory of the life of the nation, not an actual repre-sentation of its ideological composition and development. Arac, in fact, is a wonderful tonic: he warns, for instance, that "talking about *Huckle-berry Finn* has made many smart people say foolish things" (77), speaks of "agonizing scenes of interracial good intentions" (21), and insists that "it is possible to link *Huckleberry Finn* to fundamental national historical experiences, but the link can be made only allegorically" (137). He would, I think, also object to the use of "we," as I do here, to imply a consensus, a unitary audience, that of course does not exist (8).

Others have emphasized that novels can represent "nation as narration" (Bhabha, *Location*, 142). See this passage, where Homi Bhabha quotes Fredric Jameson (Bhabha, *Location*, 140): "Fredric Jameson invokes some-thing similar in his notion of 'situational consciousness' or 'national al-legory,' 'where the telling of the individual story and the individual ex-perience cannot but ultimately involve the whole laborious telling of the collectivity itself.'" A different angle might be drawn from the idea that the "child study" movement of the late nineteenth century stressed the idea of "recapitulation," as discussed elsewhere (see, among others, Lears, *No Place of Grace*, 147, and Kidd, *Making American Boys*, 15, 19, 51, 53, 57). In that intellectual milieu, the idea that the development of a child in nar-rative might also function as an allegory of national development is worth conjecture.

There is an excellent case to be made that "international" readings of *Huck Finn* suffer due to emphasis on its national character, especially when one looks at other books and authors that also treat issues of inequality, servitude, race, and youth in a larger colonial context. Jehlen, "Banned in Concord," 96, for instance, notes that *The Merchant of Venice* receives "artistic license" not extended to *Huck Finn*. See Feroza Jussawalla, "Kim, Huck, and Naipaul: Using the Postcolonial Bildungsroman to (Re)define

Postcoloniality," *Links and Letters* 4 (1997), 25–38. Nicolaus C. Mills, "Social and Moral Vision in *Great Expectations* and *Huckleberry Finn*," *Journal of American Studies* 4, no. 1 (1970), 61–72; and many others. Shelley Fisher Fishkin has done excellent recent work establishing a context for *Huck Finn* in world literature: it does not receive enough appreciation. See Fishkin, *Mark Twain Anthology*, or "Mark Twain and World Literature," *OUP Blog*, http://blog.oup.com/2010/04/mark-twain/.

1. A NEW KIND OF ENTERTAINMENT

3 **reading an old newspaper:** Reed, "Mark Twain's Hairball," 380, writes something similar of *Huck Finn*, how it "tells us a good deal about how nineteenth-century Americans lived—as well as what has changed and what hasn't."

3 **national memory that only required tickling:** *Providence Journal*, October 2, 2013, http://www.newseum.org/todaysfrontpages/hr_archive.asp?fpVname=RI_PJ&ref_pge=gal&b_pge=1. "Graphic and Telegraphic," *Providence Daily Journal*, October 2, 1884, 1.

4 **$1.85 billion:** "The Public Debt," *Providence Daily Journal*, October 2, 1884.

4 **"how God originated species":** "The Doctrine of Evolution," *New York Sun*, November 20, 1884, 1.

4 **riots in the "Arab world":** One can't understate the prominence of Middle Eastern and African affairs on American front and editorial pages of the era: it is a striking continuity with the current era. One small example: *Providence Daily Journal*, November 1, 1884, 1, features two such articles, one on "Gen. Gordon's Reporter Capture" and one on a "Bloody Arab Riot."

4 **"study at the same time":** "Brief Comicalities," *Chicago Tribune*, January 17, 1885, 6. For articles about border and immigration matters, see *Philadelphia Inquirer*, November 27, 1884, 8; "Butchered," *Brooklyn Eagle*, November 22, 1884, 4.

4 **"children delight in watching it":** *Providence Daily Journal*, October 2, 1884, 1.

5 **actual horse and actual wife:** *New York Sun*, November 16, 1884, 9.

5 **"instructive, refined, amusing":** *Chicago Tribune*, January 4, 1885, 6.

5 **"like a skye terrier's":** "Jo-Jo, the Great Russian Freak," *Indianapolis Journal*, January 8, 1885, 7. "Jo-Jo" was an international phenomenon: See Nigel Rothfels, "Aztecs, Aborigines, and Ape-People: Science and Freaks in Germany, 1850–1900," in *Freakery: Cultural Spectacles of the Extraordinary Body*, edited by Rosemarie Garland Thomson (New York: New York University Press, 1996), 169. For a description of the context of "freak" shows relating to ethnicity at this time—a crucial context for understanding Twain and Cable's own onstage reproductions of ethnicity—see Thomson, introduction, *Freakery*, 1–19; Robert Bogdan, "The Social Construction of

Freaks," *Freakery*, 23–37; and Bernth Lindfors, "Ethnological Show Business: Footlighting the Dark Continent," *Freakery*, 207–18.

5 **"the center of his forehead"**: *Cincinnati Enquirer*, January 4, 1885, 5.

5 **"pick my teeth and smoke"**: Twain, *Travels with Mr. Brown*, 232. Twain offered the following analysis of American newspapers of the day, with its "graphic" and "telegraphic" qualities, in 1873: "There was absolutely nothing in the morning papers . . . [Y]ou can see for yourself what the telegraphic headings were: BY TELEGRAPH—A Father Killed by His Son, A Bloody Fight in Kentucky, An Eight-Year-Old Murderer, A Town in a State of General Riot, A Court House Fired and Three Negroes Therein Shot While Escaping, A Louisiana Massacre, Two to Three Hundred Men Roasted Alive, A Lively Skirmish in Indiana (and thirty other similar headings) . . . [W]ell, said I to myself, this is getting pretty dull; this is getting pretty dry; there don't appear to be anything going on anywhere; has this progressive nation gone to sleep?" (Quoted in Brooks, *Ordeal of Mark Twain*, 232). Twain's shock at the violence (perceived, actual, narrative) in American culture is rarely acknowledged as straightforwardly as George Saunders does when he writes of *Huck Finn* that "the book still lives" because this question does: "How can anyone be truly free in a country as violent and stupid as ours?" (Quoted in Fishkin, *Mark Twain Anthology*, 6).

5 **one could even bring a cannon**: "Dynamite Works Blown Up," *Providence Daily Journal*, November 7, 1884, 8. "A Bridge Disaster," "Collision of Trains," "Texas Railway Disaster," *Providence Daily Journal*, October 2, 1884, 1. "Politics and Bloodshed," *Providence Daily Journal*, October 2, 1884, 1. "A Premature Explosion," *Providence Daily Journal*, November 8, 1884, 10.

6 **"BOY MURDERER"** . . . **"pulling at each end"**: "The Boy Murderer," *Cincinnati Commercial Gazette*, March 14, 1884, 1. This account of William Berner's trial and the subsequent riot relies on contemporary sources. More recent writing is available on the subject, but as my argument implies, most (though not all) of the work appears in local interest and Ohio and Cincinnati history venues. For examples, see: Mark Painter, "Riot in 1884 Among Bloodiest in History," *Cincinnati Enquirer*, March 27, 2003, http://www.enquirer.com/editions/2003/03/27/editorial_painterguest .html. There are, as well, genealogical and history blogs of value, interesting first-person accounts, and historical encyclopedia entries: Richard Hofstadter and Michael Wallace, "Cincinnati Riot, 1884," in *American Violence: A Documentary History* (Knopf: 1970): 466–469; *Fleshy Bones,* blog, "The Cincinnati Riots: 1884," March 29, 2011, http://fleshybones.blog spot.com/2009/05/first-cincinnati-riots.html; John A. Johnson, *Behind the Guardsman's Rifle: The Cincinnati Riot of 1884* (Covington, KY: Self-published, 1920), http://www.rootsweb.ancestry.com/~ohhamil3/guards man.html; "J.H. Berner Descendant Report," http://www.rootsweb.ancestry .com/~ohhamil3/J_H_Berner.pdf, among others. This last source tells us that Berner was released after being described as a model prisoner, moved

to Indiana, raised a family, and can be found in census information as late as 1930 managing a hotel or rooming house in Indianapolis.

In some accounts, Palmer is described as biracial. For the most part, though, in 1884 and 1885, he was represented as African-American. See this description of him as Berner's "Negro Pal": "Execution of Palmer," *Columbus Dispatch*, July 15, 1885, http://www.genealogybug.net/ohio_alhn /crime/palmer.htm. Also, different accounts provide different statistics for the number of people killed and wounded, though all converge, roughly, around 45–60 fatalities and 150 wounded.

6 **"divided" . . . arrested shortly after:** "Young Berner's Trial," *Cincinnati Enquirer*, March 19, 1884, 8.

7 **on account of his age:** "The Bloody Harvest," *Cincinnati Commercial Gazette*, March 3, 1884. "The Boy Murderer," *Cincinnati Commercial Gazette*, March 14, 1884, 1, describes a group of boys "peer[ing] eagerly in" at the trial through the window.

7 **wounded hundreds of others:** "Indignation Meeting," *Cincinnati Commercial Gazette*, March 29, 1884, 1. "Keeping the Peace," *Cincinnati Commercial Gazette*, April 1, 1884, 1, lists 48 killed and 139 wounded, but counts differ from different sources.

7 **always ready to rush through:** "The Rising Generation/The Half-Grown Element in the Late Mob," *Cincinnati Commercial Gazette*, April 1, 1884, 1. "At Last," *Cincinnati Enquirer*, March 29, 1884, 1. For an example of national press supporting the riot, see *New York Times*, April 2, 1884, 5.

8 **"to be a murderer myself":** Twain, *Huck*, 87.

8 **by the average American reader:** Carey-Webb, "Racism," 22.

9 **thirteen dead bodies . . . in its pages:** Regarding suicidal ideation, see Twain, *Huck*, 4: "I felt so lonesome I most wished I was dead." See also 124, and 276–77 for the best example: "I knowed for certain I wished I was dead." Bercovitch, "What's Funny About 'Huckleberry Finn,'" describes Huck as a "morbid, haunted young boy" (19). Hearn, *Annotated Huckleberry Finn*, xcviii, counts thirteen corpses. Robinson, *In Bad Faith*, 184: "*Huckleberry Finn* is not a very happy book because Huck Finn is not a very happy person." Morrison, "Introduction," *Huckleberry Finn*, xxxiv, xxxix, xli.

9 **"over a dozen times":** "The Genial Mark: Samuel L. Clemens and George W. Cable in Toronto," *Toronto Globe*, December 9, 1884, 2: "every modulation of his voice shows new and unsuspected fun in writings that may have been read over a dozen times." "Amusements," *Indianapolis Journal*, January 8, 1885, 7, describes the performance of the "King Sollermun" dialog: "In cold type it seems to be trivial to the last degree; but as Mr. Clemens gave it last night, it set the audience to a perfect storm of boisterous merriment." "'Mark Twain' and Mr. Cable," *Providence Daily Journal*, November 10, 1884: "His manner and intonation in portraying the situations of his various characters added to the pictures an appreciation which printed pages alone cannot afford." Some did not agree. See "'Twain' and Cable,"

Pittsburg Dispatch, December 30, 1884: "Either's works shine better in books than when read by them."

10 **considered him past his prime:** The description of Twain in performance that follows here is culled from some of the more detailed reviews of his performance. See, especially, "Some of Mark Twain's Fun," *New York Sun*, November 22, 1884, 1. "Fun on the Stage," *Brooklyn Daily Eagle*, November 23, 1884, 12. William Dean Howells said this of Twain's performance technique: "He knew that from the beginning of oratory the orator's spontaneity was for the silence and solitude of the closet where he mused his words to an imagined audience; that this was the use of orators . . . [H]e studied every word and syllable, and memorized them by a system of mnemonics peculiar to himself, consisting of an arbitrary arrangement of things on a table—knives, forks, salt-cellars; inkstands, pens, boxes, or whatever was at hand—which stood for points and clauses and climaxes, and were at once indelible diction and constant suggestion. He studied every tone and gesture . . . he rejoiced in the pleasure he gave and the blows of surprise which he dealt . . ." (Howells, in *Mark Twain's Speeches*, introduction).

Twain himself discusses his technique in several places. See *Mark Twain in Eruption*, "Platform Readings," and especially 225–28, where he talks extensively about pauses. He writes that an audience can detect "infinitesimal fraction[s] of a moment," and even tiny mistakes with an audience can cause an otherwise "satisfactorily startling effect" to fall flat.

Budd, *Our Mark Twain*, 80, collects reviews describing Twain's entrances: "varying from a 'side-long, awkward stride, amusing in itself' to a 'funny little jogtrot, half-sideways, with a comic look of half inquiry and half appeal.' " These descriptions bely the portrait of a dead-on deadpan, but are consonant otherwise.

Baker, "Shrewd Ohio Audiences," finds that references to Twain in Ohio newspapers during this time period outnumber those for any other writer, but trail Horace Greeley, Henry Ward Beecher, and U. S. Grant. Michael Shelden, *Man in White*, prologue, provides a fine description of how Twain and the white suit became national icons.

10 **crest of a cockatoo:** "The Twain-Cable Evening," *Springfield Daily Republican*, November 8, 1884, 5.

10 **"sardonic":** Walter Blair, *Mark Twain and Huck Finn*, 2.

10 **One side of him dragged, limped:** Cable, "Cable's Reminiscences."

10 **"exactly the right length":** Twain, "How To Tell a Story," *Collected Tales, 1891–1910*, 204.

10 **would rise like ghosts:** "Drowsy" quoted in Trautman, "Twins of Genius," 223. There has been excellent recent work on Twain and deadpan. See Knoper, *Acting Naturally*, 6, 57–59; essential. He describes the "doubleness" of deadpan "between cunning and naivete" (57). Bercovitch, "What's Funny About 'Huckleberry Finn,' " and "Deadpan Huck," does excellent, complicated analysis. Twain himself described it this way: "The teller does his best

to conceal the fact that he even dimly suspects that there is anything funny"; describing Artemus Ward, Twain wrote "when the belated audience presently caught the joke he would look up with innocent surprise, as if wondering what they had found to laugh at" ("How To Tell a Story," *Collected Tales, 1891–1910*, 201, 202). Cox, *The Fate of Humor*, 59: "The reader is at last brought to ask the fatally absurd question of the humorist: '*Is—is he humorous?*' To ask that helpless and hopeless question is to be reduced to . . . transcendent stupidity . . . yet to be so reduced, so taken in, is not a loss but a gain of pleasure."

An excellent description of Twain in performance can be found in Tarnoff, *Bohemians*, 130.

10 **he would never laugh . . . wouldn't smile, either:** Cardwell, *Twins*, 21, 23. Cable claimed he only saw Twain smile once in 104 performances: Kaplan, *Mr. Clemens*, 260. Cable, "Cable's Reminiscences," describes Twain as a "grim controller of his emotions at all times."

11 **like a "storm":** Cable, "Cable's Reminiscences." Knoper, *Acting Naturally*, describes Twain's performance style (45): "the practice of avoiding 'the game of information giving' . . . focusing instead on rhetorical structures and strategies, sounds, and the scrambling of sense that puns and homonyms entail."

11 **"Every word . . . was a joke":** "The Genial Mark: Samuel L. Clemens and George W. Cable in Toronto," *Toronto Globe*, December 9, 1884, 2.

11 **the pauses . . . over and over:** Some of the best writing on *Huck Finn* has dealt with the issue of pauses, of silences. Morrison ("Introduction," xxxiii) writes that "much of the novel's genius lies in its quiescence, the silences that pervade it." Robinson's "Silences" has been a great favorite among my students. Ralph Wiley's unfilmed screenplay for *Spike Lee's Huckleberry Finn* uses silences and pauses to remarkable effect, creating a wholly persuasive version of the book foregrounding Jim's intelligent responses to the conditions of his culture (see Fishkin, "Praise"). Elements of that strategy appear in Courtney B. Vance's screen version of Jim in the 1993 Elijah Wood version of *Huck*.

11 **he chose writing over acting:** Quoted in Knoper, *Acting Naturally*, 10.

11 **not to *support* a book:** A map of the tour can be found at Railton, "Touring With Cable and Huck," at the "Mark Twain in His Times" web site at http://twain.lib.virginia.edu/huckfinn/hftourhp.html.

12 **"Happy Family" . . . a single cage:** "Mark Twain and George W. Cable," *New York Sun*, November 18, 1884, 3. James Cook, e-mail, February 12, 2000. Cardwell, *Twins*, 5. Twain, *Travels with Mr. Brown*, 117: "The Happy Family remains, but robbed of its ancient glory. A poor, spiritless old bear—sixteen monkeys—half a dozen sorrowful raccoons—two mangy puppies—two unhappy rabbits—and two meek Tom cats . . ."

12 **one "genius," one "versatility":** See, for instance, "Genius and Versatility," *New York Times*, November 19, 1884, 5. A frequent slogan was "A Combination of Genius and Versatility That Appeals Freshly to the Intelligent

Public." See *Louisville Courier-Journal*, January 5, 1885, 3. *Providence Daily Journal*, November 4, 1884, 4. And many others.

12 **"the best advertised book"**: *Alta California*, March 24, 1885. Quoted in Fischer, *Huck Finn Reviewed*, 15.

12 **"a walking sign"**: *Boston Globe*, April 2, 1885. Quoted in Fischer, *Huck Finn Reviewed*, 27.

12 **"a new kind of entertainment"**: "News Notes in New York," *Washington Post*, May 3, 1885, 5, quoted in Twain, *Autobiography*, vol. 1, 601, footnote.

12 **usually lecturers lectured**: "Mark Twain and Mr. Cable," *Providence Daily Journal*," November 10, 1884, describes a "select and cultured audience" in attendance. References to "intelligent" audiences were embedded in the publicity. "'Twain' and Cable," *Pittsburg Dispatch*, December 30, 1884. The *Philadelphia Inquirer*, November 22, 1884, 3, describes "the most cultivated and intelligent people of this city" turning out for Twain and Cable, "a very select audience." Many reviews called attention to the hybridity of the performance, its mix of the literary and the theatrical. See, for instance, "Stage and Rostrum/Twain-Cable," *Wisconsin State Journal*, January 28, 1885, 4.

Knoper, *Acting Naturally*, 5, 11, 63: Twain believed that his presence in the theater was a kind of low-culture invasion.

12 **a boy . . . Mark Twain at the same time**: "The Genial Mark: Samuel L. Clemens and George W. Cable in Toronto," *Toronto Globe*, December 9, 1884, 2. See Cardwell, *Twins*, 28, where he quotes the following: "It is always a Huck Finn or a negro who talks like Mark Twain." Cable to Louise S. Cable, March 10, 1886, in Bikle, *Cable*, 149: "The hearing an author read his pages is no longer a novelty, & not being that, there's an end of it."

12 **"cause was just"**: Cable, *Dr. Sevier*, 377.

13 **"from the ground up"**: H. C. Bunner to Walter Learned, January 1884, quoted in Turner, *Cable*, 184, Cardwell, *Twins*, 27.

13 **"their day has come again"**: *Providence Daily Journal*, November 10, 1884, 4.

13 **"signal of their re-enslavement"**: "Blaine's Comments," *Philadelphia Inquirer*, November 19, 1884, 1.

13 **"$1000 apiece"**: "Scaring Timid Negroes," *New York Sun*, November 19, 1884, 1. Under the section entitled "Misrepresentations in Georgia."

14 **"the bloody chasm"**: "The City/An Interesting Chat with Clemens and Cable Upon Their Work," *Minneapolis Tribune*, January 25, 1885, 3: "Cable and I started on this raid the day after the presidential election . . ." *Twain-Howells Letters*, vol. 2, 520 (February 27, 1885): "my four-months platform campaign . . ." See also Cardwell, *Twins*, 9. Budd, *Our Mark Twain*, claims that Twain's "activity in national elections peaked in 1884, when he gave three speeches and made his passionate stand known otherwise" (84). See also 185–86. Budd, *Social Philosopher*, 104, but also 34, 43–44, 80, 107–10, 112, 157, 198, 204, describes Twain's lifelong engagement with the Mugwumps. See also Cardwell, *Twins*, 12. "Literary

bridging of the bloody chasm" can be found in the *Boston Daily Advertiser*, quoted in Lorch, *Trouble*, 164. Twain was conscious of the election day start of the tour: See *Autobiography*, vol. 1, 86. He also called the tour a "pilgrimage" (86), and described he and Cable "robbing the public" (391). The creation of "reconciliation" between white North and white South was an ongoing project in these years. See Cecelia O'Leary, *To Die For: The Paradox of American Patriotism* (Princeton: Princeton University Press, 1999): 119–20. Also Silber, *Romance*, 1. Also Fishkin, "Race and the Politics of Memory," 284–85.

14 **so did Frederick Douglass:** Cardwell, *Twins*, 22.

14 **running the country:** "How Mark Alarmed the Clerks," *Detroit Evening News*, December 15, 1884, 3. Twain loved this story. See *Autobiography*, vol. 1, 391–92, and 607.

14 **crashed against newspaper headlines:** See, for instance, *Mark Twain's Speeches*, 36. Budd, *Our Mark Twain*, 99, notes that Twain's "lecture manager in Australia decided Twain was 'addicted' to newspapers 'almost as much as to smoking bad cigars.'"

15 **a different kind of laughter:** "Negroes' Foolish Fears," *New York Times*, November 19, 1884, 1. An editorial, "The Scare Among the Negroes," can be found on page 4 of the same edition: "This does not argue well for the political intelligence of the Southern negro nor for the character of the influences with which he is surrounded." "Some of Mark Twain's Fun, Scaring Timid Negroes," *New York Sun*, November 19, 1884, 1. The trope of "frightened" or "foolish" African-Americans was general. See, for instance, "Cleveland and Slavery/The Foolish Fears of Many Ignorant Negroes in Detroit," *Detroit Evening News*, December 1, 1884, 2. The *New York Sun* ran reports from all over the country in its front-page reporting: "Misrepresentations in Georgia"; "Alarm in Virginia"; "Uneasiness in Tennessee," etc.

2. SHIFTLESS, LAZY, AND DADBLASTED TIRED

17 **As Mark Twain told it . . . data:** Generally, Twain's account of events can go either way: Louis J. Budd refers to "incorrigible yarning" (quoted in Fishkin, *Was Huck Black?*, 55); Robinson, personal interview, October 8, 2012, observes that later works like "Villagers of 1840–3" display an accurate and detailed memory of the past.

18 ***The Golden Bough* was a best-seller:** Bronner, *American Folklore*, 2, 26, 55. Lang quoted on 23. That these explorations of the past and primitive cultures could reinforce troubling social differentiations in the present is much discussed: See, for instance, Torgovnick on Freud, *Gone Primitive*, chapter 10.

18 **not really expected to survive:** Powers, *Dangerous Water*, 39, *Mark Twain*, 8. Hoffman, *Inventing*, 1.

18 **a good place to start:** Wecter, *Hannibal*, 44.

18 **all of which he hated:** Hoffman, *Inventing*, 15.

18 **"Shiftless" . . . "No study in him":** John A. Fry, quoted in Abbott, "Tom Sawyer's Town," 17.

19 **"I can't do that":** Qtd. in Powers, *Mark Twain*, 43. Paine, *Mark Twain*, vol. 1, 75, offers a variant.

19 **the principles of truancy:** "Perhaps no other child in Hannibal hated school more than Sam Clemens did," wrote Thomas W. Handford, *Pleasant Hours with Illustrious Men and Women*, 306, quoted in Hearn, *Annotated Huckleberry Finn*, 47.

19 **"in no wise dishonorable":** In this paragraph, Laura Hawkins Frazier, quoted in Abbott, "Tom Sawyer's Town," 16. *Mark Twain in Eruption*, 226. John A. Fry, quoted in Abbott, "Tom Sawyer's Town," 17. Wecter, *Hannibal*, 124. Paine, *Mark Twain*, vol. 1, 52. Twain, *Travels with Mr. Brown*, 244. Hoffman, *Inventing*, 5, 15.

19 **Benjamin in 1842:** Robinson, *Author-Cat*, 2. Kaplan, *Singular*, 13, 17.

19 **seriousness of death:** Kaplan, *Singular*, 17.

19 **no economic or social injustice:** Twain, *Autobiography*, vol. 1, 158–59. The definitive article here is Martin, "Genie on the Bottle." Quoted in Kaplan, *Singular Mark Twain*, 28. See also Cardwell, *The Man Who Was Mark Twain*, 158–59, for more discussion of Twain and guilt. It is a common theme. Robinson, *Author-Cat*, 1, describes Twain' "image of what he took to be himself" as "a hopelessly flawed and profoundly guilty man. Remorse harried him relentlessly . . ." Powers wrote that "guilt hung like a fog around Mark Twain's memories of his boyhood" (*Mark Twain*, 43). Quoted in Robinson, *Author-Cat*, 6; see also 10, 31–33.

20 **biography of him—at age seven:** Twain, *Is Shakespeare Dead?*, 20–26: "I wrote the biography," he closes, "and have never been in a respectable house since."

20 **a young slave named "Black John":** Twain talks about Blankenship in *Autobiography*, vol. 1, 397. Fishkin, *Was Huck Black?*, 28–29, 80.

20 **imprinted themselves upon Sam:** See his idyllic description of his Uncle John's Farm, *Autobiography*, vol. 1, 210–11, or "Villagers of 1840–3," 93-108, in Twain, *Huck and Tom among the Indians*.

20 **saved the best roles for himself:** Kaplan, *Singular*, 27. Powers, *Mark Twain*, 23, 28, 32. Paine, *Mark Twain*, vol. 1, 60.

20 **"enjoyed dying" . . . he wrote decades later:** Powers, *Mark Twain*, 34. Kaplan, *Singular*, 19–20. Twain mentions it in his letter to Will Bowen, February 6, 1870, *Huck and Tom among the Indians*, 20. Robinson, *Author-Cat*, 40–44, provides a subtle reading of the account.

20 **his body to the surface:** Wecter, *Hannibal*, 166–67.

20 **"safe in water":** Paine, *Mark Twain*, vol. 1, 35.

20 **He was a sleepwalker:** Hoffman, *Inventing*, 7.

20 **sneak off on a riverboat:** Hoffman, *Inventing*, 17.

21 **"nor wanting to, either":** Twain, *Autobiography*, vol. 1, 155–57. Wecter, *Hannibal*, 171.

21 **It wasn't quite what Tom Sawyer would do:** John A. Fry, quoted in Abbott, "Tom Sawyer's Town," 17.

21 **"spiritually," for decades:** Twain, *Autobiography*, vol. 1, 211. The Huck Finn Freedom Center, in Hannibal, Missouri, pays homage to Quarles and his role in *Huck Finn* as an inspiration for Jim: See http://www.jimsjourney.org/.

21 **make Sam and the other children jump:** Twain to Joel Chandler Harris, *Twain to Uncle Remus*, 11–12 (August 10, 1881). See Twain, *Autobiography*, vol. 1, 533, footnote. Arthur G. Pettit, *Mark Twain and the South*, 19. Powers, *Mark Twain*, 11–13.

22 **disappeared into their quarters:** Kaplan, *Singular*, 23–24. Dempsey, *Searching for Jim*, uses advertisements from Hannibal-area newspapers to demonstrate that the lives of these child slaves were not remotely idyllic— an ellipsis in Twain's account.

22 **"yet not comrades":** Twain, *Autobiography*, vol. 1, 211. Explanatory Notes, *Huck*, 385–86. See Fulton, *Ethical Realism*, 58. Fulton worries that recent attempts to celebrate Twain's oft-stated "preference" for African-American company have overlooked even Twain's own recognition that there were obvious limitations and inequalities in those relationships.

22 **twelve years hard labor:** Quoted in Pettit, *Mark Twain and the South*, 17–18. Blair, *Mark Twain and Huck Finn*, 110. See Dempsey, *Searching for Jim*, 33–48, for an excellent account of this trial and the events surrounding.

22 **"greatest orator":** Twain, "Corn-pone Opinions," *Collected Tales, 1891– 1910*, 507. See Fishkin's canonical work on this piece, in *Was Huck Black?*, 53–67.

22 **"An anvil" . . . years later:** Twain, *Autobiography*, vol. 1, 158. See also 514. Twain to Will Bowen, February 6, 1870, in *Huck and Tom among the Indians*, 21. See Hearn, *Annotated Huckleberry Finn*, 251–52.

23 **"red hell glowing behind him":** Twain, *Autobiography*, vol. 1, 157–58. See also Twain, *Life*, 339–40. Kaplan, *Singular*, 33. Twain mentions it in his letter to Will Bowen, February 6, 1870, in *Huck and Tom among the Indians*, 21, using "we." Martin, "Genie in the Bottle," 68, wonders if it ever happened.

23 **Twain carried for decades:** Quoted in Kaplan, *Singular Mark Twain*, 31.

23 **father's autopsy:** See Brooks, *Ordeal of Mark Twain*, 40. Powers, *Dangerous Water*, 28. Robinson, *Author-Cat*, 3. Kaplan, *Singular*, 5–6. Hoffman, *Inventing*, 20.

23 **confirmed the worst:** Twain, *Life*, 329–32.

23 **"Religious mania":** Twain, "Villagers of 1840—3," 103.

23 **"dead in an hour":** Twain, *Following the Equator*, quoted in Wecter, *Hannibal*, 99, and Dempsey, *Searching for Jim*, 88.

23 **"red life gush":** Twain, *Autobiography*, vol. 1, 158.

23 **"I happened along just then":** Twain, *Autobiography*, vol. 1, 158.

23 **children could find him, and they did:** Paine, *Mark Twain*, vol. 1, 63–64. Wecter, *Hannibal*, 148. Dempsey, *Searching for Jim*, 167. Pettit, *Mark Twain and the South*, 15–16. Bence is mentioned in Twain, "Villagers of

1840–3," in *Huck and Tom among the Indians*, 97. "Played out and disappeared," Twain writes of both brothers. Arac, *Idol and Target*, 47–48.

24 **the woman with the golden arm:** *Mark Twain in Eruption*, 110–11. See Twain, *Autobiography*, vol. 2, 294, and 588, footnote. Fred Kaplan places the year as 1842 (*Singular Mark Twain*, 39); Powers says Twain was ten when it arrived (*Mark Twain*, 35). Bowen, *Rural Entertainments*, "places the J.A. North Company in Bower's City Hotel" in Hannibal in 1849, and the "Sable Melodists" in St. Joseph in 1850 (41). Twain's comments on the minstrel show have appeared in several different venues, in essentially the same form: *Mark Twain in Eruption*, "The Minstrel Show," 110–15, is mostly used here. Many details of the description that follows, in particular, of the "negro quarrel," the old jokes, the costuming, the openness of the stage, can all be found there.

24 **"Sable Genus of Humanity":** Quoted in Bean et al., preface, *Inside the Minstrel Mask*, 1. This dating refers to the debut of the Virginia Minstrels in New York. The Virginia Minstrels, led by Dan Emmet, promised a more "refined" and "authentic" version of the earlier minstrel shows, and focused on music, performing as a quartet. Strausbaugh, *Black Like You*, 102–3. It is not entirely clear whether Twain, as a child, saw this permutation of the minstrel show, or the earlier, supposedly rowdier version. His account, like many of his accounts, feels authentic, but very possibly represents an amalgam of other shows he saw at later times (McCoy, interview). In any case, my account, as presented here, certainly represents an amalgam of descriptions of minstrel shows from the period.

24 **old men who married young women:** Lhamon, "Ebery Time," 275. Many are familiar with the "John Canoe or Junkanoo" traditions, which involve racial inversion. Cockrell, *Demons of Disorder*, provides an excellent overall summary of these traditions, 32–61, especially 32–33 and 37–41. Cockrell claims that "there were adequate numbers of Americans who knew enough about the ritual family" (46). See also Strausbaugh, *Black Like You*, 67, and 37–38: "In the related Pinkster celebrations up North, slaves whitened their faces with flour, dressed in outrageous costumes and wigs that mimicked their masters' and mistresses' finest outfits, and marched around in open parody of Whites' stiffest, most formal behavior."

24 **scared them out of their minds:** Cockrell, *Demons of Disorder*, 36–37, 52–53. For this reason, it cannot surprise that Santa Claus might be cited as a writer of blackface music.

24 **African-American churches and Christmas celebrants:** Roediger, *Wages of Whiteness*, 106–7. Lott, "Blackface and Blackness," 17.

25 **truthfully, still hasn't subsided:** There are several different accounts of this moment: it is iconic. What all variations share is that it was cultural theft. Strausbaugh, *Black Like You*, 58: "Rice claims to have been inspired by watching an old Black slave mucking out some stables in Louisville." Sotiropoulos, *Staging Race*, 20–21, calls it "the apocryphal foundation myth," citing stories that Rice "developed the minstrel character . . . after

he happened upon either a black stable hand or an elderly African American man suffering from rheumatism . . . [I]n reality, Rice likely drew from a variety of performances by both black and white budding entertainers in the New York City neighborhood where he lived . . ." Cockrell, *Demons of Disorder*, writes that "blackface minstrelsy began in myth, and the myth must be treated with great courtesy" (xi). See also 63–91. Cockrell disputes that "'Jim Crow' swept all before it" (64). Lhamon, *Raising Cain*, 153, describes other variants, including "a source in an individual named Cuff, who it is supposed wrestled luggage along the Pittsburgh levee."

25 **an alliance of the low that might rock the nation:** The issue of black audiences for minstrel shows remains controversial. Taylor and Austen, *Darkest America*, 46, note ticket pricing for "colored persons" as early as 1832.

25 **"misfortune" . . . "my broder":** Quoted in Lhamon, *Jump Jim Crow*, 115, 111.

25 **the melody was distinctly Irish:** Toll, *Blacking Up*, 27.

25 **The lyricist . . . was Santa Claus:** Cockrell, *Demons of Disorder*, 72–91, describes the political uses of Jim Crow. For anti-slavery inversions, see 88–89. Cockrell presents the use of Jim Crow at an anti-Catholic riot on 73–74. Much recommended. Jim Crow has been performed many, many times, in many different ways: these accounts also bear the aura of myth, a myth that transforms Jim Crow into a trickster that can go anywhere, be performed by anyone in any way, and that represents America. See Strausbaugh, *Black Like You*, 61: "According to one account, the U.S. ambassador to Ecuador, on arriving in the Mexican city of Mérida, is greeted by a brass band playing the song, who think it's our national anthem. One traveler claims to hear Hindu street performers singing it in Delhi."

25 **a thousand other cues lost to time:** Cockrell, *Demons of Disorder*, 146, writes that "my research shows a surprisingly rapid containment of the social noise of minstrelsy beginning about" 1840.

25 **nationalized . . . by being blacked up:** See Mahar, *Behind*, 145.

25 **as was its appropriation:** Recent scholarly work describing minstrelsy as a global, not American, phenomenon, makes this point particularly clearly. See, for instance, Chude-Sokei, *Last "Darky,"* 150, describing African and Caribbean blackface performances: "'America' becomes reduced to two things: its racism, but also its promise of freedom by way of the iconic presence of African Americans whose journey to claim the space behind the mask is metaphorized as a journey toward freedom . . ."

26 **Walt Whitman loved it:** Lott, *Love and Theft*, 78.

26 **put on a minstrel act:** Toll, "Social Commentary," 93.

26 **"confined to the African race":** Margaret Fuller, "Entertainments of the Past Winter," *Dial* (July 1842), 52. Quoted in Lott, *Love and Theft*, 16. Fuller notes that she has only seen the dance performed by "children of an ebon hue"; she also notes the men and women of African descent produce such "beautiful" music because, "like the German literati," they are "relieved by their position from the cares of government."

26 **"the corrupt taste of their fellow white citizens"**: Frederick Douglass, *North Star*, October 27, 1848. Quoted in Lott, "Blackface and Blackness," 3.

26 **it washed off easily**: Wheeler, *Up-To-Date*, 66.

26 **Champagne corks**: Newcomb, *Tambo*, 8.

26 **a parody of "high and citified society"**: *Mark Twain in Eruption*, 112. See, among others, Strausbaugh, *Black Like You*, 104–6. Nathan, "Virginia Minstrels," 38, observes that the "fixed interlocutor" was not a part of early minstrel shows.

26 **fanfare of horns and drums**: Bowen, *Rural Entertainments*, 38. Dailey Paskman, *"Gentlemen, Be Seated!": A Parade of the American Minstrels* (New York: Clarkson N. Potter, 1976). Lhamon, *Raising Cain*, 45.

26 **"delightful jangle"**: *Mark Twain in Eruption*, 113.

27 **"The *cat-nip*"**: *Christy's New Songster*, 17.

27 **they invented them, in fact**: Taylor and Austen, *Darkest America*, 5. Mahar, *Behind*, 40, notes the preponderance of "nonracial" jokes in early-middle minstrelsy.

27 **the uproarious reveal**: Mahar, *Behind*, 312–16. Men dressing as women, of course, was/is a staple of American comedy not restricted to minstrelsy.

27 **"a sheep in my life"**: From *The Hope of Fashion*, quoted in Mahar, *Behind*, 167. See also Browne, "Shakespeare," and Explanatory Notes, *Huck*, 438–39, for a specific discussion of muddied Shakespeare in the context of *Huck Finn*. Carlyon, "Circus," 5, and elsewhere, for muddied Shakespeare and circus clowns.

27 **"Ain't I right, eh?"**: *Christy's New Songster*, "Stump Speech," 33. Toll, *Blacking Up*, 55. Roediger, *Wages of Whiteness*, 126–27. Bowen, *Rural Entertainments*, 38, also notes the role of the oration in the "olio." Lott, *Love and Theft*, 73. See footnote from introduction on minstrelsy scholarship. Mahar, *Behind*, 65, notes that the stump speech was already common in minstrel shows by 1843.

27 **a minstrel show leftover**: The link between minstrel shows and early circuses and clown performances is well-established. See Bowen, *Rural Entertainments*, 39; Strausbaugh, *Black Like You*, 68; Lott, "Blackface and Blackness," 12–13, for a brief comment about a "certain terror" in minstrelsy. For Mickey Mouse et al., see Emerson, *Doo-Dah*, 60, and especially Sammond. The white gloves on many popular cartoon characters is an example of Lhamon's "lore cycle" (*Raising Cain*, 56–115): Mickey Mouse and Bugs Bunny wore those white gloves in their early cartoons, which were produced when minstrel shows were popular and respectable, and continued to wear them when other aspects of blackface became unacceptable. Mario et al. inherited them in turn, excised of their link to minstrelsy, but still providing evidence of disturbing cultural continuity.

28 **a furtive, desperate life of its own**: *Mark Twain, in Eruption*, 112, likens the makeup around the mouth to "slices cut in a ripe watermelon." Lhamon, "Turning Around," 23: "Do not think black gloss or grotesque white lips, not yet; others apply those signs later."

28 **"blacking box"**: *Mark Twain in Eruption*, 111.

28 **the restless dances of teenagers**: Nathan, "Virginia Minstrels," 35.

28 **wheezed and rang, craftily underplaying**: Dan Emmett, quoted in Emerson, *Doo-Dah*, 91. Emerson's description of the minstrel band here is recommended. See also Johnson, introduction, *Burnt Cork*, 8.

28 **countless other modern performers**: Quoted in Lhamon, *Jump Jim Crow*, 102. Lhamon, *Raising Cain*, 222–23.

28 **"authenticity" like researchers**: Lhamon, *Raising Cain*, 31. Nathan, "Virginia Minstrels," 38. Emerson, *Doo-Dah*, 96. Ralph Ellison, in an interview with Fishkin, *Was Huck Black?*, 90: "These fellows had to go and listen, they had to open their ears to [black] speech even if their purpose was to make it comic." Lott, "Twain, Race, and Blackface," 131, works with this quote. Lott, *Love and Theft*, 41, stresses the importance of this, describing "critics who wrongly hew to the line that white minstrels had no investment in black culture, no idea what they were doing." See also Mahar, *Behind*, 260.

28 **"When the fair land of Poland"**: Regardless of political perspective, most scholars argue that early minstrels often demonstrated "a high degree of familiarity with the plantation and black life" (Boskin, *Sambo*, 81). Strausbaugh, *Black Like You*, 72, writes that "it seems that minstrels' presentations were one part 'authentic' to three parts comic caricature and sentimental fantasy." It may be more important, in other words, to wonder what use they made of that familiarity. *Playbill* citation from "Buckley's Serenaders, New York, March 6, 1854," quoted in Mahar, *Behind*, 53.

29 **parades before the audience at the play's close**: Lhamon has done signal work bringing attention to this version of *Othello*, at that time the most often performed play in North America (Lhamon, *Jim Crow, American*, xix). The play (titled *Otello*) can be found in *Jump Jim Crow*, 343–83, with the closing scenes on 383. The scene on 362, where Desdemona instructs Othello to kiss his child where his "image here is seen," on one cheek and not the other, strongly implies the half-black, half-white makeup. See Lhamon, introduction, *Jump Jim Crow*, and *Jim Crow, American*, as well as his excellent footnotes in *Jump Jim Crow* (445, 450), and "Turning Around."

29 **sly, cracked fun**: The best work on this idea can be found in chapter 1 of Hartman, *Scenes of Subjection*.

29 **a way invisible to your masters**: Cockrell deals in depth with this urban figure, *Demons of Disorder*, 54–56, 92–101, and elsewhere. See also Strausbaugh, *Black Like You*, 78–81. Saxton, "Blackface Minstrelsy," 68–71, 82–83.

29 **electrocuted for no particular reason**: Emerson, *Doo-Dah*, 160, 161, 182–83. Cockrell, "Soundscapes," 55 and 66–67. "Camp-Town Races," Fishkin notes in *Was Huck Black?*, 141, "turns out to be a tune sung by Yoruba mothers to their children." Some have noted the "appalling frequency with which black people die in (Stephen) Foster's songs," Emerson, *Doo-Dah*, 108. Lastly, the second verse of "Oh! Susanna," Emerson, *Doo-Dah*, 127–

28: "I jump'd aboard the telegraph / And trabbled down de ribber, / De lectrick fluid magnified, / And killed five hundred Nigga."

29 "white gals don't know how": *Christy's Ram's Horn Nigga Songster*, 46–47. Quoted in Saxton, "Blackface Minstrelsy," 80.

29 "he's none but mine": *Christy's Ram's Horn Nigga Songster*, 76–77. Quoted in Saxton, "Blackface Minstrelsy," 73.

30 "he gibs us our food": *Christy's Panorama Songster*, 79. Quoted in Saxton, "Blackface Minstrelsy," 78.

30 "De debul say he funeral song": *Christy's Ram's Horn Nigga Songster*, 102. Quoted in Saxton, "Blackface Minstrelsy," 79. Most recent scholars on minstrelsy register moments of subversion, what Strausbaugh, in *Black Like You*, calls "seditious little digression[s]" (95). Toll, *Blacking Up*, 83, writes that "before 1850, minstrelsy occasionally included black slaves who openly resisted oppression," and describes "fundamental ambivalence about slavery" (66) in "many minstrel troupes." He also notes instances where "they also gave their audiences a chance to laugh with sly black characters" (73). Cockrell, *Demons of Disorder*, cautions against the idea that "minstrelsy" was "only about inversion" (160).

30 "we'll gib de white folks a concert": *Christy's New Songster*, " 41–42.

30 "Dey'll in de gutter lay": In Sam Dennison, *Scandalize My Name: Black Imagery in American Popular Music* (New York: Garland Publishing, 1982), 56–57. Quoted in Lott, "Blackface and Blackness," 12.

30 "De Bull frog mighty mad dat day": S. Foster Damon, *Series of Old American Songs*, no. 16, quoted in Lott, "Blackface and Blackness," 10.

31 "which to me had no peer": The illustration on *Tom*, 162, shows Tom and his friends in blackface. *Mark Twain in Eruption*, 110.

31 the politics playing out right in front of them: See, among others, Strausbaugh, *Black Like You*, 172.

31 never seen the dancing, either: Nathan, "Virginia Minstrels," 37.

31 a safe way . . . a dangerous way: Hearn, *Annotated Huckleberry Finn*, 113, quotes the memoir of George Thompson, one of the abolitionists, describing a lynch mob with blackened faces waiting to hang him and his codefendants if they were acquitted.

31 the pitch-perfect imitation: *Mark Twain in Eruption*, 113.

31 "the so-called 'negro minstrels'": Mark Twain to Tom Hood, Esq., and Messrs. George Routledge & Sons, London, March 10, 1873, in Pike, *The Singing Campaign*, 14–15, speaking of the Fisk University Jubilee Singers: "It was the first time for twenty-five or thirty years that I had heard such songs, or heard them sung in the genuine old way—and it is a way, I think, that white people cannot imitate—and never can, for that matter, for one must have been a slave himself in order to feel what that life was and so convey the pathos of it in music . . ." See Emerson, *Doo-Dah*, 96.

32 no amount of reality could persuade them otherwise: *Mark Twain in Eruption*, 112. This aspect of the minstrel show was particularly important to Twain: after his description of the minstrel shows of his youth, he adds

a story about tricking his aunt and his mother into mistaking the "Christy Minstrels" for a group of traveling missionaries (116). See also Strausbaugh, *Black Like You*, 213: "Nineteenth-century minstrels claimed that when they toured the boondocks, the local Whites often mistook them for actual Black people." Lhamon, *Raising Cain*, 172–74, provides an example of what he calls the "*yokel effect.*"

32 **he'd want to be someone like that:** Roediger, *Wages of Whiteness*, 116: "Blackface could be everything—rowdy, rebellious and respectable—because it could be denied that it was anything." He also comments that the "form" "implicitly rested on the idea that Black culture and Black people existed only insofar as they were edifying for whites and that claims to 'authentic' blackness could be put on and washed off at will." Toll, *Blacking Up*, 86: "the minstrel show's structure did not require continuity or consistency . . . minstrelsy's antislavery sentiments contained no call to action"; audiences could, on the same night, "respect the bondsman's intense feelings and desire for freedom and the contented slave's love for this master; laugh with black tricksters making fools of white aristocrats and also at foolish black characters." Lhamon, *Raising Cain*, 50, 53, describes "political bite" that can "also be denied . . . unreadable, irresolvable, backing one agenda or ideology only if . . . excerpted in fragments." Strausbaugh, *Black Like You*, 81: "These young men sound hopelessly confused. They're obviously fascinated with Blackness, admire Black music and dance, but they're simultaneously dismissive and insulting. Are they sincerely imitating Blacks, or just poking fun? Are they attracted or repulsed? Do they admire Blacks or despise them? Love them or fear them? In a word: Yes." Cockrell, *Demons of Disorder*, 162: "Blackface minstrelsy . . . must have been many things to many people." Mahar, *Behind*, 100: "the minstrel comedians used virtually everything available to them to entertain their audiences . . ."

3. STRANGE ANIMALS, TO CHANGE THEIR CLOTHES SO OFTEN

33 **mistaken for a drunken stagger:** Shelden, *Man in White*, xxxvi. Powers, *Mark Twain*, 8. "Mark Twain at Stormfield, 1909 (Edison film)," http://www.youtube.com/watch?v=leYj—P4CgQ.

33 **"the syllables came about every half minute":** Quoted in Tarnoff, *Bohemians*, 232.

33 **the original wax was not saved:** Shelden, *Man in White*, 367.

34 **over two years to earn his pilot's license:** Samuel L. Clemens to Jane Lampton Clemens, *Letters*, vol. 1, 3 (August 24, 1853). Twain, *Life*, 45. 41–144 provides a memorable description of his time learning the river. Powers, *Mark Twain*, 62–69, 73–75.

34 **That was enough:** Twain's account is found in "The Private History of a Campaign That Failed," *Tales, 1852–1890*, 863–82. For biographical treatment, see, for instance Kaplan, *Singular Mark Twain*, 85–86.

34 **"Mark Twain" the following year:** Powers, *Mark Twain*, 101–9, 117.

35 **made him a star in 1869:** All details readily available in most Twain biographies. See, for an excellent treatment of this period: Powers, *Mark Twain*, 139–42, 149–54, 159–64, 172–73, 184–85, 210, 224–27.

35 **"for an hour or so":** In this paragraph, William Stewart, quoted in Powers, *Mark Twain*, 225. Also Powers, *Mark Twain*, 185. Kaplan, *Mr. Clemens*, 15. Twain, *Travels with Mr. Brown*, 187.

35 **before he was through:** Trombley, *Mark Twain's Other Woman*, 6. Trombley also notes that Twain "sailed the Atlantic Ocean twenty-nine times" (6).

35 **if he hadn't beaten up the captain days before:** Twain, *Life*, 128–43.

35 **Shakespeare during down time:** Twain, *Is Shakespeare Dead?*, 4–19.

35 **"awe & admiration":** Twain, *Notebooks*, vol. 1, 253.

35 **"sht," for instance:** Twain, *Notebooks*, vol. 1, 50. See Cardwell, *The Man Who Was Mark Twain*, 163–67.

36 **They'd cut . . . words like "hell":** Blair, *Mark Twain and Huck Finn*, 80. Twain, *Notebooks*, vol. 2, 87: "The *very* funniest things that ever happened or were ever said, are unprintable . . . A great pity." Brooks refers to his "verbal Rabelaisianism" (*Ordeal of Mark Twain*, 185). Cox, *Fate of Humor*, 50: "He informed Archibald Henderson that it was his wife's editing which saved him from the overpowering tendency to destroy the beautiful effects he had created."

36 **remained in his "great deep," as he called it:** Twain to Will Bowen, February 6, 1870, in *Huck and Tom among the Indians*, 20.

36 **"the most patient person that ever lived":** Samuel L. Clemens to Jane Lampton Clemens, *Letters*, vol. 1, 4 (August 24, 1853). Samuel L. Clemens to Jane Lampton Clemens, *Letters*, vol. 1, 10 (August 31, 1853). See Pettit, *Mark Twain and the South*, 23–24. Pettit also notes that Clemens's "single literary effort between 1857 and 1862 was a callous burlesque that referred . . . to the hundreds of slaves who were slaughtered up and down the Mississippi valley after an abortive uprising in 1813."

36 **wandered this far to escape his whiteness:** Twain, *Innocents Abroad*, 76, 88.

37 **"he has seen Mardi-Gras":** Samuel L. Clemens to Pamela A. Moffett, *Letters*, vol. 1, 87–88 (March 9 and 11, 1859).

37 **"black as ink":** Samuel L. Clemens to Ann E. Taylor, *Letters*, vol. 1, 73 (June 1, 1857).

37 **"he prefers negro minstrelsy":** See *Early Tales*, vol. 2, 233.

38 **"let the poor have the bread they earn":** *Mark Twain's Travels with Mr. Brown*, 271, 273. Twain, "Enthusiastic Eloquence," *Early Tales*, vol. 2, 235. See Knoper, *Acting Naturally*, 37, 33. Knoper is discerning on this phase of Twain's career, describing Twain's evolution in the "bachelor subcultures of artisans and bohemians" (23), his "fascination with people on the margins" (23), his evolving affinity for mimicry (24), his ambivalent stance toward "racial and ethnic caricatures" (26). Knoper describes Twain at this time wonderfully as more "an unkempt bohemian with populist impulses than a true dandy" (42). For more information on the San Francisco Minstrels, see Toll, *Blacking Up*, 152, and for fuller treatment, McCoy,

"Trouble Begins." The song described here is quoted on page 237, and can be found in Frank Howard and W. S. Mullaly, *Pass Down de Centre: Plantation or End Song* (1879). This quote can be found in "Pass Down de Centre," Lester S. Levy Collection, John Hopkins University, http://levysheetmusic .mse.jhu.edu/catalog/levy:134.052. Professor McCoy's work with the San Francisco Minstrels and Twain is crucial, and I am indebted to it. See Toll, "Social Commentary," 103, for the quote involving the "poor." For more on "glory-beaming banjo," see Roy Morris, Jr., *Lighting Out for the Territory: How Samuel Clemens Headed West and Became Mark Twain* (New York: Simon & Schuster, 2010), 162; Jack B. Hood, *Banjo Method* (AuthorHouse Books, 2010), 19–20. See Twain, *Autobiography*, vol. 2, 588, footnote.

38 **"raised the question, Was there?":** Kaplan, *Singular Mark Twain*, 133.

38 **"a footing of most perfect equality":** Twain, "Mark Twain and the Colored Man," *Early Tales*, vol. 2, 248. Coulombe, "Native Americans," 266, notes that Twain rarely used racial slurs in the "Western sketches."

38 **in private, roasting flesh:** *Mark Twain's Travels with Mr. Brown*, 71: Of Key West, "the negroes seemed to be concentrated in a single corner of the town, to leeward of the whites—so their fragrance is wasted on the desert air, and blows out to sea . . ." Twain, *Notebooks*, vol. 1, 136. Quoted in Cardwell, *The Man Who Was Mark Twain*, 190, and Pettit, *Mark Twain and the South*, 41–42.

39 **hastened his flight to San Francisco:** Tarnoff, *Bohemians*, 69: "Twain had located a sore spot in the collective psyche and hit it as hard as he could."

39 **that, too, pointed at things to come:** The piece was "Disgraceful Persecution of a Boy," in Twain, *Collected Tales, 1852–1890*, 379–83. Cox, *Fate of Humor*, 16. See also Kaplan, *Singular Mark Twain*, 117, 124. Twain, *Autobiography*, vol. 2, 115–17.

40 **the most progressive locution:** Pettit, *Mark Twain and the South*, 42–43, is excellent here. Steinbrink, *Getting to Be Mark Twain*, 5, writes of *Innocents Abroad*, published in this time frame: "An examination of these revisions demonstrates that Clemens consistently pruned indelicacies, slang, and vulgarisms as he transformed his Quaker City correspondence into the text for the book." Steinbrink makes a wonderful generalization about Twain's metamorphosis during this time, writing that "Mark Twain, too," had to "undergo a reformation" or the distance between "Twain" and "Clemens" would become too large (6). See also Guy Cardwell, *The Man Who Was Mark Twain*, 190–91: "He revised *nigger* to *negro* and removed many of the derogatory comments he had made about Jews and Arabs as well as about blacks. In editorials for the *Buffalo Express* in 1869 and 1870 he sometimes went so far as to capitalize *Negro*, a nicety that was not observed by many American newspapers for another half-century or longer."

40 **"a proud and fiery race":** "Only a Nigger," *Buffalo Express*, August 26, 1869. Twain, *Mark Twain at the Buffalo Express*, 22.

40 **the absence of irony, "is correct":** Twain, *Innocents Abroad*, 240–42.

40 "the white people . . . and their peculiarities": See Kaplan, *Singular Mark Twain*, 185.

41 "Sandwich Islands": See Kaplan, *Singular Mark Twain*, 302.

41 "in one place ever since he was born": "The American Vandal Abroad," in Fatout, ed., *Mark Twain Speaking*, 35–36. This view held for the rest of his life. See quote in Budd, *Social Philosopher*, 169: "I have traveled more than anyone else, and I have noticed that even the angels speak English with an accent."

41 "an almost pathetic unconsciousness": To "Mr. Burrough," November 1, 1876, in *Mark Twain's Letters*, arranged by A. B. Paine (New York: Harper and Brothers, 1917), 289. Cardwell, *The Man Who Was Mark Twain*, 188, observes pithily that "until he was thirty-two years old, Clemens was by almost any standards blatantly racist."

41 Frederick Douglass in their home: Fishkin, *Lighting Out*, 79–80. Kaplan, *Singular Mark Twain*, 231. See Wieck, *Refiguring*, 20.

42 "the freest corner": To "Mr. Burrough," November 1, 1876, in *Mark Twain's Letters*, arranged by A. B. Paine (New York: Harper and Brothers, 1917), 289.

42 "desouthernized Southerner": Howells, *My Mark Twain*, 35.

42 "the mists of the past": Twain to Will Bowen, February 6, 1870, in *Huck and Tom among the Indians*, 20. Cox, *Fate of Humor*, 79: "But the letter also marks the recovery of a past. For what is new four days after the marriage is the presence and particularity of a vast memory of boyhood, which like a generative matrix, releases a compelling sequence of memories."

42 "Uncle Dan'l" . . . *The Gilded Age*: Twain and Warner, *Gilded Age*, 35–40. See Powers, *Mark Twain*, 330.

42 eavesdropped on African-American servants: Pettit, *Mark Twain and the South*, 47. Hearn, *Annotated Huckleberry Finn*, 138, lists Mary Ann Cord and John T. Lewis as the two Twain loved to hear argue.

42 something akin to Jim Crow: Justin Kaplan, *Mr. Clemens*, 174.

42 "a lad of eleven again": Twain to Olivia Clemens, *Letters*, vol. 4, 527 (December 31, 1871).

42 published three years later in the *New York Times*: Fishkin, *Was Huck Black?*, 154, footnote.

43 "white people cannot imitate": Mark Twain to Tom Hood, Esq., and Messrs. George Routledge & Sons, London, March 10, 1873, in Pike, *The Singing Campaign*, 14–15.

43 vocabulary, dance, and story: Bronner, *American Folklore*, 46, 52, 62, 70. For a good, short overview of dialect study, see http://public.oed.com /aspects-of-english/english-in-use/english-dialect-study-an-overview/.

43 "descend upon me & into me": Twain "Sociable Jimmy," *New York Times*, November 29, 1874, 7. Reprinted in appendix, Fishkin, *Was Huck Black?*, 249–52, and quoted here from that source. Twain to Olivia Clemens, *Letters*, vol. 5, 18 (January 10–11, 1872).

44 **"An' no joy!"**: Twain, "A True Story, Repeated Word for Word as I Heard It," *Collected Tales, 1852–1890*, 578, 582.

44 **"this negro talk"**: *Twain-Howells Letters*, vol. 1, 26 (September 20, 1874).

44 **running plenty of dialect and folklore pieces**: Bronner, *American Folklore*, 56–57.

44 **the "colored one," he said**: *Twain-Howells Letters*, vol. 1, 32 (September 30, 1874).

44 **he acknowledged they didn't**: "Not above two or three notices out of hundreds," Howells wrote, "recognized 'A True Story' for what it was . . ." Howells, *My Mark Twain*, 123. Fishkin, *Was Huck Black?*, 30–32, 99. Nagawara, "Image," does precise work showing the actual amendments Twain composed. Coulombe, "Native Americans," 276–77. See Gates, "Trope," 321–22: "the most important contribution to black literature between 1867 and 1876 was not written by a black person at all but by Mark Twain in his 1874 short story, 'A True Story.'" See also Kaplan, *Mr. Clemens*, 180–81. Fishkin, *Was Huck Black?*, 30–32, 97. Twain described the piece as "rather out of my line," *Twain-Howells Letters*, vol. 1, 22 (September 2, 1874). Bhabha, *Location*, 70: "Despite the 'play' in the colonial system which is crucial to its exercise of power, colonial discourse produces the colonized as a social reality which is at once an 'other' and yet entirely knowable and visible."

44 **"nine tenths of the guilt"**: Twain to Karl and Harriet Josephine Gerhardt, May 1, 1883. Oft-quoted. See, for instance, Pettit, *Mark Twain and the South*, 126. Karl Gerhardt was a sculptor who had done a bust of Twain, a photograph of which appears at the front of many editions of *Huck* (see John Bird, "Mark Twain, Karl Gerhardt, and the *Huckleberry Finn* Frontispiece"). Twain had financed a travel scholarship to Paris for Charles Ethan Porter, an African-American sculptor, and is responding here to a letter where Gerhardt expresses concerns about "Porter's living habits and lack of morals."

45 **philanthropies during this decade**: Howells, *My Mark Twain*, 35, with the key quote: "He held himself responsible for the wrong which the white race had done the black race in slavery, and, he explained . . . he was doing it as part of the reparation due from every white to every black man."

45 **endorsed him during the past campaign**: Douglass sent Twain a cordial note in response. Garfield declined the request, and demoted Douglass to "recorder of deeds." See William S. McFeely, *Frederick Douglass* (New York: Norton, 1991), 305–6.

45 **"dusky audiences"**: *Twain-Howells Letters*, I, 356 (February 27, 1881). Quoted in Pettit, *Mark Twain and the South*, 127. There are many references in the critical literature to Twain paying tuition for these black students. See Brown, "For Our Time," 49.

45 **"till he is proved white"**: Twain, *Notebooks*, vol. 3, 57. *Twain-Howells Letters*, vol. 2, 509–10 (September 17, 1884).

46 **It's not ambivalence . . . and he could**: "Plymouth Rock and the Pilgrims,"

in *Mark Twain's Speeches*, 17–24. See Budd, *Our Mark Twain*, 59. Michelson, *Mark Twain on the Loose*, 20–22.

4. AN APPEAL IN BEHALF OF
EXTENDING THE SUFFRAGE TO BOYS

47 **"trundle-bed trash"**: Samuel L. Clemens to Jane Lampton Clemens, *Letters*, vol. 1, 10 (August 24, 1853).

47 **Johanna Spyri's *Heidi***: The publication of *Huck Finn*, in fact, took place within a three-year span when Victorian Americans, whose opinions on children seemed to shift with the wind, made best sellers out of George W. Peck's *Peck's Bad Boy and His Pa* and Frances Hodgson Burnett's *Little Lord Fauntleroy*.

47 **"heaps of money"**: Twain to Orion Clemens, *Letters*, vol. 4, 362 (March 15, 1871).

48 **"ambassador of the children"**: Quoted in Shelden, *Man in White*, 161.

48 **"other forms of social differentiation"**: Heywood, *Childhood*, 4.

48 **didn't live to the age of five**: Mintz, *Huck's Raft*, 134. The date cited is 1895.

48 **One in six labored**: In 1900. Illick, *American Childhood*, 91.

49 **firearms in the classroom to maintain order**: See West, "Heathens," 372–73.

49 **to do better than their parents**: Mintz, *Huck's Raft*, describes "middle-class children lavished with more maternal attention, freed from early labor, given extended time to play and mature, and offered the opportunity to pursue extended education" (199). See also 135–36, and Illick, *American Childhood*, 91.

49 **a middle place between childhood and adulthood . . . examined**: This paragraph has many sources. See Mintz, *Huck's Raft*, 188, 179, 187, 196. Kidd, *Making American Boys*, 67. Heywood, *Childhood*, 28. Illick, *American Childhood*, 72–73, 76–85. Illick also notes the high rate of infant mortality (65). Hulbert, *Raising America*, notes the advent of German-styled kindergartens (29). Jacobson, *Being a Boy*, stresses that Hall's work describes the "boy between about eight and twelve" as a "savage . . . inclined to outdoor activities . . . not yet capable of developing such higher qualities as creativity, spirituality, and altruism" (13).

49 **recite what they had memorized**: Cuban, *How Teachers Taught*, 24–30.

49 **twenty-seven states would have them**: Urban and Wagoner, *American Education*, 198–99.

50 **"I work on, and never think of it"**: "A Contented Boy," *Sheldon's Modern School Third Reader* (Sheldon and Company, 1885, reprint), 44. The evolution of Sunday schools also figured in this standardization of American childhood, and Twain's boy books can be read accordingly. See Illick, *American Childhood*, 70.

50 **"high pressure" . . . poorer districts**: "High Pressure in the Public Schools," *Providence Daily Journal*, November 7, 1884, 5. "The School District System," *Providence Daily Journal*, November 6, 1884, 4.

50 **think for themselves . . . experience nature:** Kate L. Brown, "The Problem of Work," *American Teacher* 1 (September 1883), 3. For advice on exercise, see 4. Mintz, *Huck's Raft*, writes that "fears that boys were 'overcivilized' and cut off from physical challenges prompted a yearning for a return to the primitive life . . ." (193).

50 **see where fruit came from:** Fanny D. Bergen, "Primary Lessons on Botany," *American Teacher* 2 (October 1884), 308.

50 **"the learner educates himself":** Joseph Payne, "Principles in Teaching," *American Teacher* 2 (October 1884), 194.

50 **"look and listen to the voices of nature":** *American Teacher* 2 (October 1884), 292. "A Chapter on Positive Morals and Practical Pedagogy," trans. Marion Talbott, *American Teacher* 2 (October 1884), 294.

50 **"a passion with some boys":** May L. Clifford, "The Discipline of the Primary School," *American Teacher* 2 (October 1884), 260.

50 **"to appear a man":** "A Chapter on Positive Morals and Practical Pedagogy," trans. Marion Talbott, *American Teacher* 2 (October 1884), 294.

50 **"leprous influences":** Comstock, *Traps for the Young*, 42, 41. See also Mailloux, *Rhetorical Power*, 116. See also 120, where Mailloux quotes Comstock speaking on "The Curses of Our City," citing statistics for youth violence in a manner uncannily similar to those practiced today in similar screeds.

50 **fit inside school textbooks:** Stone, *Innocent Eye*, 102.

50 **"intensely stupid":** "What Our Boys are Reading," *Scribner's Monthly*, March 1878, quoted in Stone, *Innocent Eye*, 103.

51 **"the title of tales and novels":** Noah Porter, *Books and Reading: or, What Books Shall I Read and How Shall I Read Them*, 4th ed. (New York: Scribner, Armstrong, 1877), 231–32; quoted in Catherine Sheldrick Ross, "Metaphors of Reading," *Journal of Library History* 22 (Spring 1987), 149. Quoted in Mailloux, "Eating Books," 156.

51 **they "excited" him to bloodshed:** Quoted in Stone, *Innocent Eye*, 100–101.

51 **drinking, and graphic beatings:** Peck, *Peck's Bad Boy*, 79. The Bad Boy was surreally bad, and treated badly: he fed his father rubber hose pieces as macaroni (14), and the father, a drinker, a "masher" (37), and a religious hypocrite, beat him in return with a bed slat (12), a barrel stave (126), and worse. The Bad Boy would get drunk, but did so by not understanding that his father's 'medicine' was really a secret stash of liquor (80). Given free use of the house by his father when the latter was attempting to flirt with a single woman, he'd buy champagne and blast a cork into a policeman's face. He'd get arrested, but then released on the recommendation of the *grocer* (36–39).

51 **the nation agreed:** Peck, *Peck's Bad Boy*, "A Card From the Author."

51 **banning . . . salacious publications:** Hajdu, *Ten-Cent*, 94–95.

51 **in the middle of a civilization:** This discussion owes much to Mailloux, *Rhetorical Power*, 100–129, although Stone's work with the same material predates it. Mailloux's key research finding, I believe, involves the saturation of interest in juvenile delinquency in American media during the first part of the 1880s in particular. His key thesis, as I see it, is that contemporary

readers of *Huck Finn* during this period would have recognized this: "The literary tradition has never been read within the larger scene of cultural debates and social practices concerned with juvenile delinquency" (117); "A novel's relationship to worries over literary effects and juvenile delinquency functioned as a dominant criterion for judging any 1885 book about boys" (128). As this last quote implies, Mailloux makes clear that the 1880s debate emphasized the idea that reading the books made children more likely to commit criminal activity—an analogy to contemporary debates over violent video games that make the same claim. He compiles excellent evidence from newspaper editorials and reportage: See 100, 121–26. He also observes that the popularity of George W. Peck's *Peck's Bad Boy and His Pa*, published in 1883, brought the debate to a fever pitch shortly before Twain published *Huck Finn*: See 100, 120–21.

51 **"his amusement is violence"**: "The Bad Boy of America," *New England Journal*, reprinted in the *People's Advocate*, February 2, 1884, 1. Clark, *Kiddie Lit*, 100, writes that *Huck* "was implicated in an ongoing cultural conversation about bad boys . . . that focus contrasts in turn with the prominence of race in more recent discussions of *Huckleberry Finn*."

51 **"the fell swoop of its children"**: *New York World*, March 24, 1884, 4, quoted in Mailloux, *Rhetorical Power*, 122.

51 **be taken into custody**: "Murder in Boston," *Providence Journal*, November 3, 1884, 1.

51 **"shoot anything we could hit"**: "Boys Who Were 'On The Shoot,'" *Boston Globe*, February 20, 1885, 4.

52 **"several dime novels"**: "Sad Juvenile Depravity . . . ," *New York World*, March 26, 1884, 2, quoted in Mailloux, *Rhetorical Power*, 122.

52 **"Jesse James Gang"**: "Teaching the Young Idea," *Cincinnati Commercial-Gazette*, March 23, 1884.

52 **paragraph on page 3**: *Philadelphia Inquirer*, November 22, 1884, 3.

52 **"INSULTING LITTLE GIRLS"**: *New York Sun*, November 23, 1884, 5.

52 **improperly cleaned and treated jars**: "Adulterated Milk," *Philadelphia Inquirer*, November 21, 1884, 3.

52 **"in ten minutes he was dead"**: "Accidents," *Philadelphia Inquirer*, November 22, 1884, 1. Note that this article appears alongside the review of Twain-Cable. "Insulting Little Girls," *New York Sun*, November 23, 1884, 5. Note that this article is placed alongside the "Amusements" section. "A Child's Sad Death," *Providence Daily Journal*, November 10, 1884, 3. Note that the review of Twain-Cable appears alongside this report. "A Boy Drinks Naphtha and Dies in Ten Minutes," *Providence Daily Journal*, November 10, 1884, 9. Note that this review appears next to "Minstrel and Dramatic Notes."

53 **"the lazy, and the incompetent"**: In this paragraph, see Fraser, *School*, 272–85. Mann, "Tenth Annual Report to the Massachusetts Board of Education," quoted in Fraser, *School*, 52. *The Nation*, quoted in Upchurch, *Legislating Racism*, 50.

53 **"Who Should Have Charge . . . Children?"**: E. J. James, "Who Should Have Charge of the Education of Our Children?" *American Teacher* 2 (October 1884), 136.

53 **"The Mechanical Boy"**: "The Mechanical Boy," *Boston Globe*, November 14, 1884, 4.

53 **"the education of the child"**: Williamson, *Crucible of Race*, 113. "Southern and Northern Negroes," *Atlanta Constitution*, May 18, 1885, 4. Edwin D. Meade, quoted in Fraser, *School*, 282. Budd, *Social Philosopher*, 95–96. Jacobson, *Being a Boy*, 9, discusses this in some depth, how "the family that adjusted itself for the future benefit of its children lost some of its integrity as the children necessarily turned to schools and social groups to teach them the skills they would need to secure desirable employment and to fill their time as they awaited their delayed entry into the job market." Mailloux, *Rhetorical Power*, 108, suggests that this trend originates earlier in the century. Cuban, *How Teachers Taught*, 3–4, describes "fundamental changes in the conduct of schooling," a "broadening of the school's social role . . . to intervene in the lives of children and their families."

54 **"scalped . . . before now"**: Twain, "Those Blasted Children," *Early Tales*, vol. 1, 351–54.

54 **"pepper, mustard"**: Twain, "Those Blasted Children," *Early Tales*, vol. 1, 355–56.

54 **"lay it on another boy"**: Twain, "Advice for Good Little Boys," *Collected Tales, 1852–1890*, 163.

54 **"scald him a little"**: Twain, "Advice for Good Little Girls," *Collected Tales, 1852–1890*, 164.

55 **"belongs to the Legislature"**: Twain, "Christmas Fireside," *Collected Tales, 1852–1890*, 191, 193, 194.

55 **"a boy scattered so"**: Twain, "The Story of the Good Little Boy Who Did Not Prosper," *Collected Tales, 1852–1890*, 374, 377–78.

56 **"He could not even lie"**: Twain, "A New Biography of Washington," *Collected Tales, 1852–1890*, 205.

56 **"wise on such terms"**: Twain, "Benjamin Franklin," *Collected Tales, 1852–1890*, 425.

56 **"tell his letters"**: Twain, *Travels with Mr. Brown*, 251–54.

56 **"Millerite *paying* subscriber"**: Quoted in Stone, *Innocent Eye*, 33.

56 **claimed privately to disdain it**: Gribben, "Boy-Book Elements," 152–53, 155, 159, makes persuasive arguments for the influence of Aldrich's *Bad Boy* on Twain, as well as that of *Tom Brown's Schooldays* by Thomas Hughes. Also Gribben, interview. Gribben, "Boy Books, Bad Boy Books," 298–99, discusses Twain's seeming disdain as well. Clark, *Kiddie Lit*, 56, briefly discusses the importance of Aldrich's book. Blair, *Mark Twain and Huck Finn*, 64–65, discusses Aldrich's influence on Twain. Trites, *Twain, Alcott*, 19, reminds that Dickens is also an influence here, especially *Great Expectations* and *Oliver Twist*.

57 **"that boy myself"**: Aldrich, *Bad Boy*, 7.

57 **"teaching what it should be"**: Howells, review of *The Story of a Bad Boy* by Thomas Bailey Aldrich, *Atlantic Monthly*, January 1870, 124. Quoted in Jacobson, *Being a Boy*, 1, Mailloux, *Rhetorical Power*, 111–12. Ziff, *All-American*, 31.

57 **instead called him "Youth"**: See *Love Letters*, 143, 165, 196, 209, 216, etc.

57 **"the place of calculation"**: Quoted in Shelden, *Man in White*, 215.

58 **"Life seems a serious thing"**: Twain to Joseph H. and Harmony C. Twichell, *Letters,* vol. 4, 237 (November 12, 1870).

58 **"unlocked something expressive:** Powers, *Mark Twain*, 297, 304, 309. Biographers also note that Shakespeare was detached from his son Hamnet, who died in 1595 in Stratford while his father was working in London. Yet it's easy to make the circumstantial case that the complicated teenager with the almost identical name at the heart of Shakespeare's greatest tragedy—first performed four years later—was inspired by the playwright's desire to revive what he had lost. That Twain began to write *Tom Sawyer* weeks after his first son died—and didn't stop writing about children for two decades—suggests a similar drive, a creativity driven by wild, repressed grief. Within six years, Olivia Clemens would bear three more children, all daughters, and Twain would love them with no such repression. But the boys were different, and always would be. See Stephen Greenblatt, "The Death of Hamnet and the Making of *Hamlet*."

58 **in public a child's voice:** Fishkin, *Was Huck Black?*, 26.

58 **"boys out in the street"**: Reproduced in many sources. DeVoto, *Mark Twain at Work*, 25–44. Quote is found on 27. "Boy's Manuscript," in *Tom Sawyer*, 241. See also Twain, *Huck and Tom among the Indians*, 1–19. Blair, *Mark Twain and Huck Finn*, 69, and elsewhere.

58 **"the poor little male juvenile"**: Twain to David Gray, *Letters,* vol. 4, 402 (June 10, 1871). Powers, *Mark Twain*, 300. Kaplan, *Singular Mark Twain*, 271. It would be, as well, a not-friendly parody of lectures on the women's suffrage question during this time, and that might be one reason he never brought it forward.

58 **mourned little in public:** Robinson, *Author-Cat*, 11, quotes Twain to Howells: "Yes, *I* killed him." Twain was referring to "a morning coach ride" and "his failure to keep the child warm." Powers, *Mark Twain*, 319–20.

58 **Twain began to write . . . *Tom Sawyer***: Powers, *Mark Twain*, 321.

58 **"a thing as a boy"**: Twain, *Tom Sawyer*, 3. See also Robinson, *In Bad Faith*, 19.

59 **"composite" . . . troublemaking children:** Twain, *Tom Sawyer*, preface. Loving, *Mark Twain*, 24. Explanatory Notes, *Huck*, 381.

59 **Aunt Polly, Tom's caregiver:** Twain, *Autobiography,* vol. 1, 654, footnote. Brooks, *Ordeal of Mark Twain*, 32.

59 **Tom's sidekick, Huck Finn:** Twain, *Autobiography,* vol. 1, 397, 608–10.

59 **a young slave named Jim:** Twain, *Autobiography,* vol. 1, 212.

59 **the judge's daughter:** Paine, *Mark Twain*, vol. 1, 68.

59   **is not immolated:** Twain, *Tom*, 166–68.

59   **Tom has Sid . . . "better boy":** Twain, quoted in Explanatory Notes, *Huck*, 395.

59   **lure cach other outdoors:** Twain, *Tom*, 93, 162–63, 12–18. See Hoffman, *Inventing*, 243. Wecter, *Hannibal*, 92. Twain, *Tom*, 52. A stylish essay could be written on cats in *Tom Sawyer*, and the many ways they are identified with children. See, for instance, 79: "That Injun devil wouldn't make any more of drownding us than a couple of cats." Or 96: "What was cruelty to a cat *might* be cruelty to a boy . . ." That Huck is carrying a dead cat when he first appears only makes this point more emphatic. He is even called "cat-like" (204).

59   **the revolution in *Tom Sawyer*:** A key distinction made by Gribben, interview.

60   **reform was the villain:** Gribben, "Boy-Book Elements," 166, writes that Twain did not "invent . . . the bad boy in literature—he just invented the bad boy as *hero*." Cox, *Fate of Humor*, 140, emphasizes that "Tom's play defines the world as play, and his reality lies in his commitment to play, not in the involuntary tendencies which are often attributed to him." This is "subtler psychology," Cox believes, than the rule-breaking and "practical jokes" of Aldrich's narrator or *Peck's Bad Boy*. 146: "the real audacity of *Tom Sawyer* is its commitment to the pleasure principle."

60   **"Injun Joe":** Twain, *Tom*, 114.

60   **"lashings" . . . "vigorous[ly]":** Twain, *Tom*, 150, 152.

60   **"knocked . . . sprawling":** Twain, *Tom*, 148–49, 96, 115. Joe Harper is the one "knocked sprawling," though Tom is hit "sprawling" elsewhere.

60   **"skinned alive":** Twain, *Tom*, 143: Aunt Polly says, "Tom, I've a notion to skin you alive." See Messent, "Discipline," 219–21.

60   **"marks of conspicuous originality":** Twain, *Tom*, 250.

60   **"capitivity and fetters":** Twain, *Tom*, 46.

60   **the book's worst beating:** Twain, *Tom*, 150.

60   **subverters of their civilization:** At times, Twain is thick with his similes, all serving to comically narrow the distance between child play and serious adult conduct. *Tom*, 10, for instance: "Tom chased the traitor home, and thus found out where he lived. He then held a position at the gate for some time, daring the enemy to come outside, but the enemy only made faces at him through the window and declined . . ." Wolff, "Nightmare," 646, wonderfully refers to Tom's "carefully constructed rituals of devastation."

60   **Ned Buntline's . . . *Merry Foresters*:** Notes, *Tom*, 261.

60   **"die *temporarily*":** Twain, *Tom*, 65.

60   **rats out those who do:** Robinson, *In Bad Faith*, 34, 58.

61   **"varying moods":** Twain, *Tom*, 114, 132. Messent, "Discipline," 226–27.

61   **"sprawling on the floor":** Twain, *Tom*, 23.

61   **"What's a licking":** Twain, *Tom*, 148.

61   **"the name they lick me by":** Twain, *Tom*, 56. Messent, "Discipline," 225, writes that the beatings "metaphorically" seem to "bounce off" Tom.

61 **molar-wrenching alacrity:** Twain, *Tom*, 48.

61 **to maintain his advantage:** Twain, *Tom*, 115, 23. Robinson, *In Bad Faith*, is excellent on this "gamesmanship" (44). See also 34–36. As is Wolff, "Nightmare," on this "warfare": 642–43. And Messent, "Discipline," 231–233.

61 **"how is a body to know":** Twain, *Tom*, 4–5. Aunt Polly says, "Old fools is the biggest fools there is."

61 **"so to say":** Twain, *Tom*, 115.

62 **who he was addressing:** Clark, *Kiddie Lit*, 80, talks about this confusion. So does Steinbrink, "Who Wrote *Huckleberry Finn*?," 88–89, who stresses Twain describing *Tom* and *Huck* as a "new line of writing for me," an "experiment."

62 **"don't waste it on a *boy*":** *Twain-Howells Letters*, vol. 1, 90 (July 3, 1875).

62 **"take the chap beyond childhood":** *Twain-Howells Letters*, vol. 1, 91 (July 5, 1875).

62 **"history of a *man*":** Twain, *Tom*, 257.

62 **"only written for adults":** *Twain-Howells Letters*, vol. 1, 91 (July 5, 1875).

62 **"explicitly as a boy's story":** *Twain-Howells Letters*, vol. 1, 110 (Nov. 21, 1875).

62 **"pure & simple":** *Twain-Howells Letters*, vol. 1, 112 (Nov. 23, 1875).

63 **"no extra promptings":** Anonymous, review of *The Adventures of Tom Sawyer*, *New York Times*, January 13, 1877, in Gary Scharnhorst, ed., *Critical Essays on The Adventures of Tom Sawyer* (New York: G. K. Hall, 1993), 55, 57.

63 **wherever that might lead:** Stone, *Innocent Eye*, 60, uses the word "pendulum" to describe Twain's movement between writing for adults and for children.

5. BOY NO. 2

64 **in-laws in Elmira:** *Twain-Howells Letters*, vol. 1, 94 (July 6, 1875). "More to be at work than anything else," he said. *Twain-Howells Letters*, vol. 1, 144 (August 9, 1876). This letter would place Twain's composition starting point for *Huck Finn* in early July.

64 **the extent of their service to him:** Twain, *Tom*, 12–14, 7. Mensh, *Black, White*, 26.

64 **disrespecting both Huck and his source:** Twain, *Tom*, 49–51. Tom says, specifically, "I never see a nigger that *wouldn't* lie." On 83, Tom derides Huck about the authority of a "nigger," inverting their previous roles.

65 **"as if I was above him":** Twain, *Tom*, 198–99.

65 **dialect that jumped off the page:** Twain, *Tom*, 199, 253.

65 **"comb me all to thunder":** Twain, *Tom*, 252–53.

65 **wasn't written in first-person:** *Twain-Howells Letters*, vol. 1, 91 (July 5, 1875): "I perhaps made a mistake in not writing it in the first person." Doyno, *Writing Huck Finn*, 19–21, has a fine description of this.

65 **"mainly he told the truth":** Twain, *Huck*, 1. Fishkin, in *Was Huck Black?*, 4, asked readers and scholars to consider "the ways in which African-American

voices shaped Twain's creative imagination at its core." She did her most detailed and recognized work linking the voice of "Sociable Jimmy" to the voice of Huck Finn, but also devoted chapters to Twain's account of "Negro Jerry," to the characterization of Jim, and to Twain's interests and interactions with African-American individuals and traditions.

Also worth noting: there are many examples of critics, especially music critics, who regard the idea of white theft of black cultural production as simplistic. John Leland, in *Hip*, writes of the "myth" of the white boy "stealing" blues music to make rock and roll; Strausbaugh notes similarly that the many myths of T. D. Rice stealing "Jim Crow" tell us that it is a symbolic moment more than an historical one, invoking the idea that white musical culture is "stolen," not multiracial. Fishkin often parses this problem with great care. She quotes, for instance, Dick Gregory, in Fishkin, *Lighting Out*, 109: "We always said Mark Twain got his stuff from things black folks told him. My *grandmother* said that . . ." Gregory's statement can speak to a wide valence of moral judgments on what it means that Mark Twain "got his stuff" from "black folks," and Fishkin leaves a lot of room for the reader to form his or her own judgment.

66 **"You don't know about me":** As Doyno points out, *Writing Huck Finn*, 42, these words were not first-draft. The original version read: "You will not know about me." Quirk, *Coming to Grips*, 6, points out that there was a second version: "You do not know me." He also notes that the original title page read: "Huckleberry Finn/Reported by Mark Twain," and that Twain had called the book "Huck Finn's Autobiography" to Howells in a letter (*Twain-Howells Letters*, vol. 1, 144, August 9, 1876).

66 **first person made the difference:** For instance, Blair, *Mark Twain and Huck Finn*, 75.

66 **Huck's tormentor-educator:** Explanatory Notes, *Huck*, 383.

66 **Pap Finn, Huck's father:** Loving, *Mark Twain*, 24. Twain, *Autobiography*, vol. 1, 397, footnote, 531–32, notes this, and notes that another town drunk, " 'General' Gaines," was partial basis for Pap. Blair, *Mark Twain and Huck Finn*, 10–12, 107, discusses how Twain changed details of his life story to produce greater comic and tragic effects, and how he incorporated parts of Jimmy Finn's life into *Huck*.

67 **not exactly happy—outcome:** See Blair, *Mark Twain and Huck Finn*, 109. Blair does detailed work on the Hannibal links in *Huck*: see, for instance, 106–10.

67 **subterranean memoir:** Blair, *Mark Twain and Huck Finn*, 89–93, well describes the scene as Twain composed. Kiskis, "A Room of His Own," is also excellent here.

67 **"warn't ever sorry for it":** Twain, *Huck*, 105. We don't hear the apology, of course, as a handful of critics have noted. Or Jim's response to it.

68 **George Griffin . . . Hartford:** Pettit, *Mark Twain and the South*, 95. Chadwick-Joshua, *Jim Dilemma*, 18. Fishkin, *Was Huck Black?*, 87–88, cites another source individual: "Patrick McAleer, a white man who was,

in Twain's view, the epitome of a 'gentleman,'" and omits Griffin. See also Explanatory Notes, *Huck*, 386.

68 **stays loyally by his . . . side:** Twain, *Huck*, 51. Steinbrink, "Who Wrote *Huckleberry Finn*?," 98, notes that Jim's entrance on Jackson's Island, where he mistakes Huck for a ghost and says "Doan' hurt me—don't! I haint ever done no harm to a ghos'. I awluz liked dead people" is "minstrel-hall repertoire."

68 **the abolitionist cause:** There has been excellent scholarly work on the link between slave narratives and *Huck Finn*. See Andrews, "Mark Twain and James W. C. Pennington"; MacKethan, "Huck Finn and the Slave Narratives"; Beaver, "Run, Nigger, Run." Mensh, *Black, White*, 35–39, contrasts Twain's interest in these narratives with his interest in minstrelsy. Explanatory Notes, *Huck*, 414.

68 **Twain seems to know them, too:** Twain, *Huck*, 7, 55. Fry, *Night Riders*, 70–72. Fishkin, *Was Huck Black?*, 83–84, directs us to Fry. Godden and McCay, "Say It Again," 667, argue for the "trope of the witch ride as an analogy for whipping." See also DeVoto, *Mark Twain's America*, 65–73. Mensh, *Black, White*, 29–31. Lott, "Twain, Race, and Blackface," 136. Hearn, *Annotated Huckleberry Finn*, 32. See Reed, "Mark Twain's Hairball," 382: "The book is a festival of what linguists call code switching . . ."

69 **directly from African-Americans:** Twain, *Huck*, 111–12.

69 **"it'll be the truth":** Twain, *Huck*, 151. This example is presented slightly out of sequence, as it would not have been in the section Twain wrote in 1876. Robinson, "Characterization," does definitive work on this aspect of the relationship between Huck and Jim, the uneasy way they both seem to savor a good "dodge" (372, 378). See also 382–83.

69 **we've been trained to do:** Twain, *Huck*, 75. The scene runs from 68–75. The definitive case for this reading is made in Jehlen, "Reading Gender." See also Paul Kockelman, "Huckleberry Finn Takes the Turing Test: The Transformation of Ontologies and the Virtuality of Kinds," *Language & Communication* 33 (2013), 150–54.

70 **"a youth like Huckleberry Finn":** *New York Sun*, February 15, 1885. Quoted in Fischer, *Huck Finn Reviewed*, 7.

70 **"the most important persons in this world":** *American Teacher* 2 (October 1884), 282. E. E. Hale, *North American Review*, quoted in *American Teacher* 2 (September 1884), 121.

70 **"write just a little":** Twain, *Huck*, 10, 18.

70 **"robber books":** Twain, *Huck*, 7, 10.

71 **a common school "education":** Quoted in Fraser, *School*, 280.

71 **a long tirade . . . government:** Twain, *Huck*, 33. See Blakemore, "Written World," 25.

71 **"fresh and breezy":** Twain, *Huck*, 3. "Moral Instruction in Schools," *American Teacher* 2 (October 1884), 168.

71 **"scold a child into learning a lesson":** Joseph Payne, "Principles in Teaching," *American Teacher* 2 (October 1884), 219.

71 **"all the marks of a Sunday school"**: Twain, *Huck*, 17.

71 **"work farms"**: "The only hope is in removing them to a good truant's home, school, workshop, and farm," May L. Clifford, "The Discipline of the Primary School," *American Teacher* 2 (October 1884), 260. Illick, *American Childhood*, 87–88, describes the harshness of such institutions.

71 **smoked, and defended the practice**: Note Twain, *Huck*, 3, where Huck protests Miss Watson's hypocrisy for forbidding him tobacco when she "took snuff." See also 47, 106, 268. There is really quite a lot of bonding and meditation that takes place over tobacco in *Huck*.

71 **superstitions . . . Huck believes wholeheartedly**: Hearn, *Annotated Huckleberry Finn*, 24–25. Phiri, "Ghost," 94, writes that "Huck's recourse to superstition . . . reveals the porous nature of the boundaries separating white and black culture."

72 **"made her ease up"**: Twain, *Huck*, 3.

72 **"good and cheered me up"**: Twain, *Huck*, 18.

72 **"all but the cowhide part"**: Twain, *Huck*, 30. This point deserves further emphasis. Many of today's boy's advice books deal extensively with the mismatch between school culture and the "real" emotional and intellectual life of boys. Twain was similarly moved. See Pollack, *Real Boys*, 230–71. Sax, *Boys Adrift*, 15–51. Kindlon and Thompson, *Raising Cain*, 21–50. Likewise, Twain's book could be active in contemporary discussions that examine the invention of "boredom" among children, the reduction of recess and free time, and the importance of fantasy play, even violent fantasy play. See Paley, *A Child's Work*, 33, 45, 102.

72 **a "primer-class"**: Twain, *Huck*, 9–12, 14–15.

72 **superimposing one over the other**: Wolff applies this idea in *Tom Sawyer*, noting that Tom's status as "victim or perpetrator" remains ambiguous ("Nightmare," 645).

73 **"Books, home, the school and the pulpit"**: Twain, "Family Sketch," 17.

73 **"burn the MS"**: *Twain-Howells Letters*, vol. 1, 144 (August 9, 1876).

73 **that was no coincidence either**: See Twain, *Autobiography*, vol. 2, 557, footnote.

74 **the boy's name her younger sister gave her**: Twain, "Record," 93. Literature linking Twain's real children to his fictive ones with any detail is sparse, as is literature isolating women as inspiration for Twain in general. Recommended sources here include Trombley, *Mark Twain in the Company of Women*, chapter 2; Stoneley, *Mark Twain and the Feminine Aesthetic*; Doyno, "Family Man." Kiskis is also strong in isolating links between Twain's family life and his writing.

74 **a "magazine" . . . a mile**: Twain, "Family Sketch," 1–2. Some of the details in this section are taken not from "Record," but from this source.

74 **"tempests" . . . they stop**: Twain, "Record," 2.

74 **"Spartan fidelity to the bitter task"**: Twain, "Record," 49–53. See especially 51.

75 **"enterprising, business-like"**: Twain, "Family Sketch," 2.

75 "reckless inventors of . . . adventures": Twain, "Family Sketch," 23.

75 pulled out of a fire: Clara Clemens, *My Father*, 6. Twain, "Family Sketch," 23–26.

75 "make you say <u>pease</u>": Twain, "Record," 99.

75 "fraternized with the enemy": Twain, *Autobiography* vol. 2, 223.

75 the hogshead barrel Huck favors: The hogshead appears in Twain, *Huck*, 1, and is a carry-over from *Tom Sawyer*.

75 wherever the Clemenses resided: Twain, "Family Sketch," 32.

75 "I'm an angel": Twain, "Record," 24–27.

76 staying out past dark: Clara Clemens, *My Father*, 56, 78, 8.

76 hunted tiger or lion: Twain, "Family Sketch," 3–4. The case for George Griffin as portrayed in "Family Sketch" as a leading influence on the character of Jim is very strong, if circumstantial. Like Jim, for instance, he was involved in ad hoc banking (11); like Jim, he had a daughter upon whom he focused much attention (12).

76 "what does the world go on, for?": Twain, "Record," 75, 79.

76 "approve of the way I pray now": Twain, "Record," 89.

76 <u>without help</u> . . . <u>from any body</u>": Twain, "Record," 84. The same story is also written on the manuscript book's front section, unnumbered. See Doyno, *Writing Huck Finn*, xii, 22, 41. Doyno points out that *Huck Finn* was "created in a supportive, loving familial context" (23).

76 unembroidered + ungilded": Twain, "Record," 83.

76 "<u>my villains must not lie</u>": Twain, "Record," 63, 61. It is a fair question what "boy" is being discussed here.

76 "Her mother had to confess": Twain, "Record," 28.

76 "hypercritical exactness": Twain, "Record," 79.

76 "a weary, lonesome cry": Twain, "Record," 38.

77 after his second daughter was born: Twain, "Record," 4.

77 "nor reverent, either": Twain, "Record," 5.

77 "Papa loves cats": Twain, *Autobiography*, vol. 2, 223–24.

77 "a proclivity for large words": Twain, "Record," 73, 62.

77 "innocent" and "free": Twain, *Autobiography*, vol. 2, 273.

78 "if I left it alone": Twain, "Record," 39. Twain, *Huck*, 277.

78 "lonesomest sound in the world": Twain, *Huck*, 277.

78 "all aqua-fortis the next": Twain, "Record," 45.

78 "fogive po' ole Jim": Twain, *Huck*, 202. There are many discussions of this scene. Morrison is excellent here. Much recommended is Jarrett, "'This Expression Shall Not Be Changed,'" especially 1–2. Jarrett notes that there are also anecdotes from outside Twain's family in his notebooks being used as source material for this scene.

78 "inward colonization": Brodhead, "Spare the Rod," 73. Quoted in Messent, "Discipline," 228. Brodhead describes pre–, not post–Civil War practices and attitudes, but the distinction between "inward colonization" and "outward coercion" seems completely salient here.

79 "make him most distinctively human": Hall, *Adolescence*, 39.

79 **such smart and powerful things:** Lear, *No Place of Grace*, 147. Heywood, *Childhood*, 28.

80 **He saw a world rife with generational conflict:** The best extended discussion of the *Christian Union* letter can be found in Doyno, "Family Man," 40–45, who reprints the entire exchange. Susy Clemens, *Papa*, 194–200, esp. 199.

6. THE TROUBLE BEGINS

83 **"a yarn for youth":** Quoted in Stone, *Innocent*, 93, 97–98.

83 **"Fathers be alike, mayhap":** Twain, *Prince*, 15.

84 **a book Twain knew his children loved:** Stone, *Innocent*, 114–15.

84 **the chair in which he sat:** Stone, *Innocent*, 94, 96, 97, 104. Hoffman, *Inventing*, 241, describes a "Saturday Morning Club" of teenage girls Twain began in 1876.

84 **it didn't sell well:** Budd, *Our Mark Twain*, 86. Cox, *Fate of Humor*, 149, writes that its "failure is universally acknowledged."

84 **family theatrical productions . . . neighbors:** Twain, *Autobiography*, vol. 1, 348, gives an example of this approbation. Susy Clemens, *Papa*, 106, 139–40, 174–82.

84 **bled into the stilted Olde English:** Robinson, interview, observes that the more sedate reputation for *Prince* obscures the fact that it portrays childhood as difficult and even dangerous, like *Tom Sawyer* or *Huck Finn*.

84 **"When he came home empty-handed":** Twain, *Prince*, 8.

85 **"dull work":** Twain, *Prince*, 83.

85 **could be dreamt into happening:** Twain, *Prince*, 49, 9.

85 **The Shepherdsons, a rival clan:** Twain, *Huck*, 146. Explanatory Notes, *Huck*, 492.

85 **the boy to whom he asked the question:** See Explanatory Notes, *Huck*, 502. Fishkin, *Lighting Out*, 94, places this in July–October 1880.

86 **Sam Smarr's chest:** Twain, *Autobiography*, vol. 1, 514, footnote.

86 **"*let them lynch him*":** Buffalo Huck Finn, MS0661.

86 **Then Twain stopped again:** See Explanatory Notes, *Huck*, 506, for the chronology of composition. See DeVoto, *Mark Twain At Work*, 3, 53. An excellent if dated description of the chronology of Twain's composition of Huck is found on 45–104. Same with Blair, *Mark Twain and Huck Finn*, 199–205, and 300–301, etc. See also Kaplan, *Mr. Clemens*, 197; Bell, "Twain's 'Nigger Jim,'"132; Cox, *Fate of Humor*, 158. Loving, *Mark Twain*, 261, has an excellent short summary. Doyno, "Growth from Manuscript," 106, provides a good quick summary of early work on the chronology of authorship. Doyno, *Writing Huck Finn*, xv-xvi, deals quickly and well with the signal event that has altered perceptions of Twain's writing process: the discovery in 1991 of a large lost section of the manuscript. Quirk, *Coming to Grips*, 4–7, 13–14, well describes how this discovery affected timelines for Twain's composition of the book. Hearn, *Annotated Huckle-*

berry Finn, 191–92, xvi, as well. These timelines from different sources do not agree.

86 **the bright bit of chaos . . . about:** See Kaplan, *Mr. Clemens*, 248, for background for this paragraph. He describes the "symbiotic" relationship between *Life on the Mississippi* and *Huck Finn*. Loving, *Mark Twain*, describes this as a moment where "Twain was also revisiting the questions of race and slavery—indeed, perhaps confronting these issues for the first time since writing 'A True Story' in 1874" (256).

87 **"the nation's most famous broken promise":** Margolis, "Consequences," 338. See also Williamson, *Crucible of Race*, 45.

87 **to suppress the African-American vote:** See Chadwick-Joshua, *Jim Dilemma*, 103–4.

87 **Rutherford B. Hayes, whom Twain had endorsed:** Budd, *Social Philosopher*, 65.

87 **appointed more African-Americans . . . predecessors:** Williamson, *Crucible of Race*, 112.

88 **"tokens" of acceptance:** Williamson, *Crucible of Race*, 66. Woodward, *Strange Career of Jim Crow*, 16–25.

88 **fending off starvation:** Ayers, *Vengeance*, 212, 169–72.

88 **"we get another":** Ayers, *Vengeance*, 197. Williamson, *Crucible of Race*, 57–58. Quoted in Christianson, *With Liberty*, 182. Alexander, *The New Jim Crow*, draws an analogy between this "prison boom" and the current one (32). She also provides a good summary of the Jim Crow–era convict-lease system (28–32).

88 **mortality rates double or triple:** "Negro Mortality," *Atlanta Journal*, January 8, 1885, 1. See also Williamson, *Crucible of Race*, 122. Silber, *Romance*, 134.

88 **"predestination" . . . "cheap labor":** Paul B. Barringer and Carl Schurz, quoted in Woodward, *Strange Career of Jim Crow*, 80.

88 **"an inferior race":** Quoted in Ayers, *Vengeance*, 220.

88 **pre-slavery primal state:** Williamson, *Crucible of Race*, 121, discusses similar claims of "regression."

89 **"all dark-skinned races":** Note *Indianapolis News*, February 9, 1885. On page 1, an account of a lynching entitled "Only a 'Nigger' Anyhow." On page 2, under "Gordon in Khartoum": "Since the failure of their Egyptian expedition the English are breathing threatenings and slaughter against the 'niggers,' as they stigmatize all dark-skinned races, not exempting the ancient and high-caste Hindoos."

89 **the resilient appeal of "voodooism":** " 'Uncle Primus' at the Artesian Well," *Atlanta Journal*, January 5, 1885, 4. "Voodooism in Sumter," *Atlanta Constitution*, May 26, 1885, 2.

90 **"The Inevitable Knife to the Rescue":** "Chicken and Cane Stealing in the West Indies," *Nashville Daily American*, March 26, 1885, 6. "A Deadly Rencontre . . . ," *New Orleans Picayune*, September 6, 1875, 1. "A Negro Falls Dead," *Atlanta Constitution*, May 17, 1885, 2. "His Murderers Un-

known," *Nashville Daily American*, March 8, 1885, 2. "Badly Knifed," *Atlanta Journal*, January 8, 1885, 1. "A Fight Among Negro Gamblers," *Nashville Daily American*, February 14, 1885, 4. "Negro Burglar Arrested," *Nashville Daily American*, February 26, 1885, 4. "Waylaid by Negroes," *Nashville Daily American*, February 24, 1885. "Tempting Bait . . . ," *Nashville Daily American*, February 11, 1885, 5. "A Row in Negrodom," *New Orleans Picayune*, October 8, 1875.

90 **"White slaves"**: See, for instance, "Northford Mystified," *Boston Globe*, November 14, 1884, 2, about "the negro, 'Little Deer,' as he calls himself, and his beautiful white victim . . ."

90 **"Africanize[d]"**: See, for instance, also "How They Africanize People in Rapides," *New Orleans Picayune*, September 29, 1875.

90 **"you wah my master yesterday"**: *Cincinnati Enquirer*, January 14, 1885, 8.

90 **"The others received ten lashes"**: "Whipping Post and Pillory," *Nashville Daily American*, February 7, 1885, 2.

90 **"Briscoe died game"**: "Lynched, No Doubt," *Raleigh News and Observer*, December 25, 1884, p. 4. "Lynching of Briscoe," *Baltimore Sun*, published in *Pittsburg Dispatch*, December 30, 1884, 2.

91 **"Officer Norman . . . is working up the matter"**: "Assaulted By Footpads," *Atlanta Journal*, January 7, 1885, 1.

91 **A later report . . . one**: "The Mississippi Troubles, "*New Orleans Picayune*, September 11, 1875, 2. "Lively Times in Mississippi," *New Orleans Picayune*, September 7, 1875, 1. "The Troubles in Yazoo City," *New Orleans Picayune*, September 7, 1875, 4.

91 **"all scared to death"**: "Lively Times in Mississippi," *New Orleans Picayune*, September 7, 1875, 1. "The Troubles in Yazoo City," *New Orleans Picayune*, September 7, 1875, 4. "The Yazoo City Trouble," *New Orleans Picayune*, September 8, 1875, 2.

92 **"it is believed that the negroes"**: "War Between the Races," *Atlanta Journal*, January 3, 1885, 2.

92 **"South Carolina and Mississippi"**: *Boston Morning Journal*, November 7, 1884, 1.

92 **"Urged to Defeat A Free Vote"**: *Providence Journal*, November 1, 1884, 10.

92 **"crooks run us"**: *Detroit Free Press*, January 11, 1885, 5.

92 **"a hypocrite or a Voodooist"**: "Murder and Assassination," *Washington Bee*, November 8, 1884, 2. "Facts for Colored Men," *New York Globe*, November 8, 1884, 2.

92 **"successful" black individuals**: See, for instance, "The Progress of the Race," *New York Freeman*, May 16, 1885.

93 **"Our town is like the embryo seedling"**: *Nicodemus Western Cyclone*, June 17, 1886. White Republican newspapers also presented portraits of successful African-Americans. See, for instance, "Colored Capitalists: Advances from Poverty to Ample Wealth and Power," *Detroit Evening News*, February 15, 1885, 7.

93 **"All went to fooling"**: "Lively Times in Mississippi," *New Orleans Picayune*,

September 7, 1875, 1. "That Peaceful Election," *St. Louis Post-Dispatch*, January 9, 1885, 8.

93   **"staying in the woods until after dark"**: "The Colored People," *New York Sun*, November 18, 1884, 2. *Providence Daily Journal*, November 6, 1884, 4. Carl Wieck, *Refiguring*, 69, describes briefly the "feeling of relief that came with the liberation of whites from the legal constraints of Reconstruction." Ann M. Ryan, "Black Genes," is especially insightful here, describing "white racial politics" as a "comic closure to the tragic losses of the Civil War," and observing that W. E. B. Du Bois associated "white laughter and black pain as a primary illustration of the forces that organize race" (179–80). Budd, *Social Philosopher*, 106, describes "the surprising calm that followed the election of Grover Cleveland," but notes that "tremors from the Southern question went on, as anyone can see by glancing at the newspapers and magazines of the later 1880s."

94   **American Folklore Society**: See the American Folklore Society website: http://www.afsnet.org/?page=AboutAFS.

95   **Jim, of course, and the witches**: Twain, *Huck*, explanatory, 4, 19. See Bronner, *American Folklore*, 22.

95   **resigned his membership**: Bronner, *American Folklore*, 16, among others.

96   **the extended Darwinian past**: See Bronner, *American Folklore*, especially 26.

96   **booked a riverboat passage**: See Silber, *Romance*, 75–76, for a description of the vogue of the Southern trip at this time. Budd, *Social Philosopher*, 93, notes that the first excerpt from *Huck* chosen for publication was the Shepherdson-Grangerford feud, which would have appealed to readers "interested" in the South. Schmitz, "Mark Twain's Civil War," 76–77, cites Harris, Cable, Twain, and Thomas Nelson Page as part of a movement of Southern writers "interested in forgiveness, accept[ing] the humiliation and subjection of the Confederate South, undertak[ing] a therapy of disclosure . . . do[ing] the work of humor."

97   **"au unusually long dream"**: Twain, *Life*, 146, 323.

97   **"the mournful mud and the pensive puddles"**: Twain, *Life*, 332, 203. Silber, *Romance*, 78–80, discusses the idea of the "picturesque" black person in the genre of the "southern trip." She notes, on 80, that Twain "pounced on this racist use," but he also participates.

97   **"weep wid me"**: Twain, *Notebooks*, vol. 2, 552, 562–63.

97   **"nobody but one of her race"**: Twain, *Notebooks*, vol. 2, 546–47. Leonard and Tenney, "Introduction," *Satire or Evasion*, 8, cite this exchange as an example of how Twain employs "ironic, or sarcastic, or simply 'language-realistic' uses for the word 'nigger' . . . invariably sympathetic to the individuals so labeled."

98   **a museum curator . . . a live subject**: Silber, *Romance*, 78, 125, 131–32, comments on the efforts of white Northerners to receive an experience of "authentic" southern blackness, using, in particular, the example of tours by "jubilee singers" from Southern black colleges like Fisk and Hampton.

Twain, as seen elsewhere, wrote glowingly of an appearance by the singers from Fisk. Silber also notes the "aura of national inclusiveness" (127) created by such efforts. Fishkin, *Was Huck Black?*, 41, discusses scholarly interest in African-American speech during this period.

98 **the two white men in America:** Woodward, *Strange Career of Jim Crow*, 77, singles out Harris and Cable specifically in a way that would likely have resonated for Twain: "The literary treatment that the Negro received in the fiction of Joel Chandler Harris and George Washington Cable was no doubt often patronizing, sentimentalized, and paternalistic, but there was never anything venomous or bitter about the Negro in their pages. Rather the total picture that emerges is one that inspires a kind of respect, certainly sympathy . . ." Hale, *Making Whiteness*, 57. Loving, *Mark Twain*, quotes Eric Sundquist saying that the Uncle Remus tales "do not entirely whitewash the Old South but maintain a taut balance between minstrel humor and a subversive critique of slavery and racism" (257).

98 **"the weakest and most harmless of all animals":** Harris, *Remus*, xxi, xxv. See also Bickley, *Joel Chandler Harris*, 44.

98 **rabbits and foxes . . . ever after:** Harris, *Remus*, 13–16, 107.

98 **"pleasant memories . . . slavery":** Harris, *Remus*, xxvii.

98 **he grabbed a rifle:** The Union soldier subsequently stays and marries into the family of Uncle Remus's masters. See "A Story of the War," Joel Chandler Harris, *Uncle Remus, His Songs and Sayings* (New York: D. Appleton and Company, 1928; Michigan Historical Reprint Series, 2005), 201–12.

99 **"Brer Osgood" and "Brer Whitmo'":** Twain, *Notebooks*, vol. 2, 362, footnote. Twain to Joel Chandler Harris, *Twain to Uncle Remus*, 18 (September 5, 1882). Turner, *Cable*, 122. Silber, *Romance*, 139–40, discusses the rise of "dialect" stories during this time, and the prominence of Harris in creating a case for "southern white interpretation" of black experience. Strausbaugh, *Black Like You*, 165, describes a "national craze for Negro-dialect literature"; on 151, he calls it "a kind of blackface literature." See also DeVoto, *Mark Twain's America*, 34.

99 **"ought to be able to read":** Twain, *Life*, 287.

99 **"We had to read . . . ourselves":** Twain, *Life*, 287. See also Twain to Olivia L. Clemens, *Love Letters*, 212 (May 2, 1882). Quoted also in Bikle, *Cable*, 75–76. Alice Walker, "The Dummy in the Window," argues that Harris did not "do" Uncle Remus aloud due to recognition of the culture theft he had committed. Fishkin, *Was Huck Black?*, 117, offers a slightly different accounting of Harris's authorial modesty. Howells, *My Mark Twain*, 99, says of Twain that "no one could read *Uncle Remus* like him; his voice echoed the voices of the negro nurses who told his childhood the wonderful tales."

99 **"the charm and the grace of the women":** Twain, *Life*, 287–88. *Hartford Courant*, quoted in Turner, *Cable*, 140.

99 **"Minstrel Boy":** Turner, *Cable*, 33.

99 **"I shall never forget it":** Bikle, *Cable*, xi.

99 **His best material:** Bikle, *Cable*, x, 59.

99 **Cable was a match:** The portrait of Cable provided in this book is somewhat iconic, if obscure, and relies upon several major sources. Williamson,
Crucible of Race, 93–97, provides a fine short biography on Cable pre-1885.
Twain's visit to Harris and Cable in New Orleans appears in every major
biography. See, for instance, Kaplan, *Mr. Clemens*, 244–45.

99 **Born in a large house:** Bikle, *Cable*, 7. Turner, *Cable*, 3–16, especially 13–
14. "Place Congo" is now part of Louis Armstrong Park, in the neighborhood famously known as "Tremé." Cable wrote a fairly amazing account,
including musical notations, in "Dance in Place Congo," *Century*, February
1886, 517–32. See 528: "Times have changed, and there is nothing to be
regretted in the change that has come over Congo Square. Still a glamour
hangs over its dark past. There is the pathos of slavery, the poetry of the
weak oppressed by the strong . . ."

100 **"the apostles were mere policemen":** *Twain-Howells Letters*, vol. 1, 419
(November 4, 1882). For the biographical information on Cable, see
Turner, *Cable*, 4–5, 16. Rubin, *Heretic*, 20–23, 25.

100 **"black sheep":** Quoted in Turner, *Cable*, 80. Ekstrom, *Cable*, 46, footnote.

100 **"We *are* robbing the cradle":** Quoted in Turner, *Cable*, 28. See also 25–32.
Bikle, *Cable*, vii, 17, 19–20. Ekstrom, *Cable*, a variant, 26. Rubin, *Heretic*,
28–29.

100 **the long lulls between skirmishes:** Turner, *Cable*, 32. Ekstrom, *Cable*, 28.
Rubin, *Heretic*, 30. Rubin, *Heretic*, 29, quotes from a wartime letter from
Cable to his brother Jim: "Be a good soldier, study army regulations, *read
your bible, say your prayers without fear of comment.*"

100 **he thought secession was wrong:** Rubin, *Heretic*, 31, describes one of these
exchanges. Cable, "My Politics," in *Negro Question*, 4.

100 **no clothes at all:** Bikle, *Cable*, 24. Turner, *Cable*, 35. Rubin, *Heretic*, 33.

100 **clerking back in New Orleans:** Bikle, *Cable,* 36–37, 41–42. Turner,
Cable, 37. Rubin, *Heretic*, 32.

100 **a large family, mostly daughters:** Rubin, *Heretic*, 33. Like Twain, Cable
also lost a firstborn son, to yellow fever (73).

100 **the secret history of New Orleans:** Turner, *Cable*, 39, 51. Ekstrom,
Cable, 39–40. Rubin, *Heretic*, 34.

100 **cuttingly satirized . . . racial hypocrisy:** Bikle, *Cable*, 45. Ekstrom, *Cable*,
101.

100 **"unmitigatedly distressful effect":** George Parsons Lathrop, quoted in
Bikle, *Cable*, 48.

100 **while he was still clerking:** Turner, *Cable*, 51.

101 **Bras Coupé, an African prince:** One striking comparison between Twain
and Cable's portrayals of slavery during this period, at least, is that Cable
portrayed cruelty. See, for instance, the torture and punishment of "Bras
Coupé" in *The Grandissimes*: 140, 165, 204, 237–39, and especially 240–
88. Prior to Cable's telling, Bras Coupé was a legendary figure in New
Orleans history: an accomplished musician turned rebel leader after his
arm was amputated as punishment. Cable took substantial and interest-

ing liberties with the story. See Bryan Wagner, "Disarmed and Dangerous: The Strange Career of Bras Coupé," *Representations*, 92, no. 1 (Fall 2005), 117–51.

101 **gray felt hat:** Bikle, *Cable*, vii.

101 **"O, Mr. Cable":** Quoted in Rubin, *Heretic*, 125.

101 **"Your broken French is capital":** Quoted in Turner, *Cable*, 149, 68.

101 **to the greatest writers of the day:** *New Orleans Times*, June 1, 1879, is typical: "The writings of Mr. Cable may be ranked with those of any American prose writer, not excepting those of Nathaniel Hawthorne." Quoted in Turner, *Cable*, 85. See also 86, 100, 107, 144, 168.

101 **Cable's star . . . hotter:** Budd, *Our Mark Twain*, 95, cites a poll in the *Critic*, April 12, 1884, ranking Twain fourteenth on a list of "Forty Immortals," just behind Cable. Oliver Wendell Holmes topped the list.

101 **"nothing else now but that dialect":** Quoted in Turner, *Cable*, 99. See Howells to Cable, March 7, 1882, in Turner, *Cable*, 122. Before meeting Cable, Twain already loved reading aloud his "Jean-ah Poquelin," especially "the Creole-English of the title character," a slave trader (Turner, *Cable*, 61). And the Scribner's editors had begun jotting notes in Creole to each other (Turner, *Cable*, 66).

101 **voodoo dance:** Bikle, *Cable*, 78–79. Turner, *Cable*, 123–24.

101 **walked the Brooklyn Bridge:** Cable to Louise S. Cable, October 28, 30, 1883, January 13, 1884, in Bikle, *Cable*, 103–4, 115.

101 **"the clock struck twelve":** Cable to Louise S. Cable, October 8, 1882, October 21, 1882, in Bikle, *Cable*, 83, 85–86. Turner, *Cable*, 136–37. Ekstrom, *Cable*, 80.

102 **"nothing funny is intended":** G. W. Cable to Mark Twain, March 20, 1883, in Cardwell, *Twins*, 91–92.

102 **"rapidly passing away":** Franklin B. Dexter, July 2, 1883, quoted in Ekstrom, *Cable*, 161.

102 **"every way charming":** Quoted in Bikle, *Cable*, 72.

102 **"as I saw thy first productions":** Cable to Louise S. Cable, November 26, 1883, in Bikle, *Cable*, 111. Turner, *Cable*, 147.

102 **"Howells and James":** *The Critic*, quoted in Turner, *Cable*, 168.

102 **"the Shakespearian era":** *Boston Evening Transcript*, December 5, 1883. Quoted in Turner, *Cable*, 147.

102 **"utterly blemishless piety":** Quoted in Turner, *Cable*, 137.

102 **"more smoothly or orderly":** *Twain-Howells Letters*, vol. 1, 419 (November 4, 1882).

102 **"My Dear Uncle":** See, for instance, G. W. Cable to Twain, January 9, 1883, in Cardwell, *Twins*, 89; Twain to G. W. Cable, January 15, 1883, in Cardwell, *Twins*, 89.

103 **"make you *perfectly* lovely":** G. W. Cable to "Mark & dear Mrs. Clemens," February 16, 1884 (postscript in letter to Twain from J. B. Pond), in Cardwell, *Twins*, 100–101.

103 **"room to swear":** Cable to Louise S. Cable, April 3, 1883, in Bikle, *Cable*,

96. "You see how mild my abuse is compared to what it would be if you were not here," Twain also says.

103 **"viewed from his standpoint"**: *Twain-Howells Letters*, vol. 1, 419–20 (November 4, 1882). See also Cable to Louise S. Cable, April 5, 1883, in Bikle, *Cable*, 97–98, where Cable describes a similar situation.

103 **"menagerie"**: Fatout, *Lecture Circuit*, 204.

103 **Howells and Aldrich**: "Mark Twain and George W. Cable," *New York Sun*, November 18, 1884, 3.

103 **"some empty Boston hall"**: Twain to G. W. Cable, June 20, 1882, in Cardwell, *Twins*, 81.

103 **"no engagement until I see him"**: Bikle, *Cable*, 132.

103 **"utterly free person"**: *Twain-Howells Letters*, vol. 1, 427 (March 1, 1883).

104 **leaving the audience "almost breathless"**: Quoted in Turner, *Cable*, 140. Twain to G. W. Cable, March 7, 1883, in Cardwell, *Twins*, 90–91.

104 **"health & spirits to *waste*"**: *Twain-Howells Letters*, vol. 1, 435–36 (July 20, 1883).

104 **elephants on the Mississippi were too much**: DeVoto, *Mark Twain at Work*, 66, 75. Pages 63–80 reproduce many of Twain's notes from this middle period. Walter Blair, *Mark Twain and Huck Finn*, also does detailed work here: see 220–21, 244, 253, 323, 326, etc.

105 **do the right thing**: See Berret, " 'Hamlet.' "

105 **"Royal Nonesuch"**: Twain, *Huck*, 195–97. The piece is actually called "THE KING'S CAMELOPARD or THE ROYAL NONESUCH," but becomes shortened in later mentions (for instance, 204, 241). There are several sources here. Blair, *Mark Twain and Huck Finn*, 253, 319. DeVoto, *Mark Twain at Work*, 67–68, 84, demurely describes Twain toning down the scene. Kokernot, " 'Burning Shame,' " 33, quotes Twain from a "1907 autobiographical dictation" where he describes doing "great damage" to the original anecdote "to make it proper for print." See also Twain, *Notebooks*, vol. 1, 70. Hearn, *Annotated Huckleberry Finn*, 264–67, does the best work here. See also Explanatory Notes, *Huck*, 438–39, and Ellis, "Bawdy," also recommended.

105 **testing his daughters**: *Twain-Howells Letters*, vol. 1, 435–36 (July 20, 1883).

105 **up near his study**: See note on the history game in the preface. Justin Kaplan describes this scene wonderfully in *Mr. Clemens*, 252. See also Clara Clemens, *My Father*, 79–80.

105 **playing with time sped things up**: Budd, *Social Philosopher*, 103, offers a wonderful line discussing Twain's artistic development, "commanding the subtlety of talking about the past and the present at the same time."

105 **"darkness back again"**: Twain, *Notebooks*, vol. 3, 43, 45. These gazes into futurity were common in Twain's later years as well, and catalyzed his decision to withhold certain works until after his death, timing their publication for "every decade or so" (Shelden, *Man in White*, xxiii–xxiv). This explains, for instance, why his *Autobiography* might be released in 2010 and

become a best seller. It is a brilliant strategy that protects his "brand" for years after his death while also providing an outlet for work he considered too controversial to be published during his life.

105 **Henry the Eighth:** Twain, *Huck*, 199.

105 **history went round and round:** See introduction, Twain, *Notebooks*, vol. 3, 1.

105 **"*I shall like it . . . or not*":** *Twain-Howells Letters*, vol. 1, 435 (July 20, 1883).

105 **"but revise":** *Twain-Howells Letters*, vol. 1, 438 (August 22, 1883).

106 **testing his own:** Doyno, *Writing Huck Finn*, xi. As David Carkeet notes in "The Dialects in *Huckleberry Finn*," 330–31 (quoted in Wieck, *Refiguring*, 135), there are hundreds of emendations to the dialect in the *Huck Finn* manuscript. There were sensible cuts, a few words here or there that were marginally better than what had preceded them. There was some onerous work with what is called "eye dialect": in early drafts, Jim might say "was"; in later drafts, he more likely said "wuz"—which, of course, sounds exactly like "was." *Buffalo Huck Finn*, MS1210: Twain changes "was" to "wuz" three times. It is hard to argue that Twain did this systematically: he often had to backtrack and turn Jim's dialogue into "dialect." Explanatory Notes, *Huck*, 377.

106 **gave him the "raw hide":** *Buffalo Huck Finn*, MS0005, TS0095, TS0085.

106 **in the scheme of American things:** *Buffalo Huck Finn*, MS0576. Twain also added references to effigies or images of blacks and children, to suggest some confusion over the "real": See MS1229, "Look at that nigger made out'n straw on the bed"; MS0080, "I never see such a son."

106 **the *New Yorker* . . . 1995:** Explanatory Notes, *Huck*, 408–9, 463. Mark Twain, "Jim and the Dead Man," *New Yorker* 71, no. 18 (June 26, 1995), 128–30. The raft scene has been later restored by most editors, so that a recent volume of the work will almost certainly include it.

106 **guilty . . . of manslaughter:** Twain, *Huck*, 87, 91.

106 **"Child with rusty . . . kills":** *Buffalo Huck Finn*, MS0365. See also Explanatory Notes, *Huck*, 501.

107 **"So I quit":** *Buffalo Huck Finn*, MS28360. See Explanatory Notes, *Huck*, 403, for a discussion of the composition and revision chronology.

107 **bug-eyed stereotype:** He didn't immediately accept them. See, for instance, Explanatory Notes, *Huck*, 375. Boskin, *Sambo*, 127, notes that Kemble was already known for sketches of African-Americans that emphasized these traits. It is not clear whether or not Twain knew this. In either event, these sketches can be found in any recent edition that reproduces the early ones, of which there are several (see, for instance, Hearn, or the University of California edition cited throughout). See also Briden, " 'Specialty.' " Wonham, "Minstrel and the Detective," 131–32. Kaplan describes this exchange in *Mr. Clemens*, 263.

107 **distinguishing . . . on that matter :** Twain, *Huck*, "Notice." Brown, "For

Our Time," 45, discusses the fact that Twain used the word "negro" in his "Explanatory" note.

107 **he called the shots:** See, for instance, Twain, *Autobiography,* vol. 1, 372.

107 **some "earnest" subject:** Cable to Louise S. Cable, February 13, 1884, in Bikle, *Cable,* 117. Pettit, *Mark Twain and the South,* 132, suggests "miscegenation" and "the possible overthrow of white supremacy in the South." Cardwell, *Twins,* 75, notes that "it is inevitable that they should have talked much of southern people and the southern ethos."

107 **a "literary scheme":** Cable to Louise S. Cable, February 13, 1884, in Bikle, *Cable,* 117.

107 **he held out for 450:** Turner, *Cable,* 171. Cardwell, *Twins,* 8.

108 **"just like him to do that":** Twain to J. B. Pond, July 15, 1884, in Cardwell, *Twins,* 10.

108 **their eyes without reserve:** Cable, *Sevier,* 404. Cardwell, *Twins,* 65. Cable's program is described in Turner, *Cable,* 176–77, and Cardwell, *Twins,* 12.

108 **Howells, Olivia, and other editors:** See Hearn, *Annotated Huckleberry Finn,* xxvi–xxxiv. *Twain-Howells Letters,* vol. 2, 482 (April 8, 1884).

108 **to the point of torment:** To Charles Webster, May 7, 1884, in *Mark Twain, Business Man,* 253. See also Explanatory Notes, *Huck,* 375. Railton, *Mark Twain,* 67, has a fine discussion of Twain's tolerance for "unpleasant" images in the illustrations.

108 **calling the process "infernal":** *Twain-Howells Letters,* vol. 2, 497 (August 7, 1884).

109 **"sprang at us with a shout":** Twain to Joel Chandler Harris, *Twain to Uncle Remus,* 11, 12, 14 (August 10, 1881; December 12, 1881). See, Twain, *Autobiography,* vol. 1, 533, footnote.

110 **"uncertain thing you ever undertook":** This is the published version. "How to Tell a Story," *Collected Tales, 1891–1910,* 204–6. Newspaper accounts of Twain-Cable report him saying "Nobody" or "You have" instead of "You've got it." See "Some of Mark Twain's Fun," *New York Sun,* November 22, 1884, 1. Cardwell, *Twins,* 49. He was still performing it late in life: Shelden, *Man in White,* 79 (here he shouts "You!" at the conclusion). Ryan, "Black Genes," 176, notes that "Twain's performance values seem to parody sexual intercourse." That certainly seems to be the case here.

110 **"when he needs to feel good":** "Mark Twain as Lecturer," *New York World,* November 20, 1884, 5, in Scharnhorst, *Interviews,* 49.

110 **"the faintest bit gross":** G.W. Cable to Twain, October 25, 1884, in Cardwell, *Twins,* 104–5.

110 **"to immortalize its author":** This exchange is frequently cited. See Lorch, *Trouble,* 167–68.

111 **"dashed & destroyed" . . . atrocious:** Twain's notebooks show him testing a variety of pieces for performance. See Twain, *Notebooks,* vol. 3, 60–61, 69–73, 75, 82–84, 89–92, 119–21. Cardwell provides a program in *Twins,* 106. Reproductions can be found in *Adventures of Huckleberry Finn* (Univer-

sity of California edition), "Mark Twain on Tour" section, or at the "Mark Twain in His Times" web site, at http://twain.lib.virginia.edu/huckfinn /hfprogrm.html. Twain to Olivia L. Clemens, in *Love Letters*, 223 (December 29, 1884).

111 **as little as twenty-five cents:** Fatout, *Lecture Circuit*, 217.

111 **"The Trouble Begins at Eight":** Twain had used this slogan before, in 1866. Budd, "'Talent,'" 79. But so had the San Francisco Minstrels, and they had kept on using it, through eighteen years of sold out shows in New York. In 1883, though, Charlie Backus, most responsible for the group's live and sometimes countercultural politics, died. African-American minstrel troupes sent flowers. Newspaper readers of the time, contemplating whether or not to buy a ticket to Twain and Cable's show, might have noticed Twain's bit of tribute—or possessiveness. In New York, they certainly would have noticed. Maybe Mark Twain wasn't putting on a minstrel show. But he was saying what kind of minstrels he liked. McCoy, "Trouble Begins," 240, 245–46, and interview. See also Toll, *Blacking Up*, 150–54. See also Twain, *Travels with Mr. Brown*, 190, where he discovers the slogan written on a wall in jail: "How well I remember writing the advertisement for my first lecture in San Francisco—"

111 **national ridicule:** Turner, *Cable*, 101–2. He was, in fact, capable of severe criticism of the Creole group in Louisiana, even if only through fictional masks.

111 **"the house where I was born":** Turner, *Cable*, 70. Cable to *Literary World*, May 31, 1875, quoted in Rubin, *Heretic*, 93. See also 99–100. Despite his praise, Twain was already irritated with Cable before they departed on the "Twins of Genius." See Kaplan, *Mr. Clemens*, 254.

111 **ten years after he saw them:** Turner, *Cable*, 77.

112 **"A Southern White Man":** Turner, *Cable*, 75–76. Anonymous letter appears in *New Orleans Bulletin*, September 26, 1875. Rubin, *Heretic*, 67.

112 **"Literature in the Southern States":** Turner, *Cable*, 132–34. The speech can be found in Turner, "George W. Cable's Revolt Against Literary Sectionalism," *Tulane Studies in English* 5 (1955), 5–27. Bikle, *Cable*, 84–85.

112 **"The plantation idea":** Quoted in Turner, *Cable*, 133.

112 **torture and mutilation:** Cable, "Freedman," 416. See Hale, *Making Whiteness*, 44–45.

112 **responsibilities attached to his fame:** Lilian Whiting, "Boston Letter," *New Orleans Times-Democrat*, December 16, 1883, quoted in Turner, *Cable*, 150.

112 **"not a worse one":** Cable to Louise S. Cable, December 8, 1883, quoted in Turner, *Cable*, 149. Williamson, *Crucible of Race*, 97, links Cable's revelation on the train to the overturning of the Civil Rights Act of 1875. Woodward, *Strange Career of Jim Crow*, notes that Southern newspapers often commented favorably on blacks and whites sharing train cars, and that "an excessive squeamishness or fussiness about contact with Negroes was commonly identified as a lower-class white attitude" (31). In many ways,

in other words, Cable was not as out of the mainstream as the response to "Freedman" will suggest, particularly in how he reiterated class-oriented distinctions.

113 **"urged to speak and act"**: Cable, "My Politics," *Negro Question*, 20.

113 **"the State to make money"**: Cable, "Convict-Lease," 584.

113 **"to-day's and to-morrow's history"**: Cable, "Freedman," 416. Cardwell, *Twins*, 6. Bikle, *Cable*, 123–24. Turner, *Cable*, 158.

113 **"bumpkins"**: *New Orleans Picayune*, July 7, 1884. Quoted in Turner, *Cable*, 159.

113 **"Somebody must speak first"**: Quoted in Turner, *Cable*, 159.

113 **"you'd *have* to keep cool"**: Turner, *Cable*, 135.

113 **where he stood**: Turner, *Cable*, 158–59.

114 **"your cause is just"**: Cable, *Sevier*, 377. See Turner, *Cable*, 166. Bikle, *Cable*, 130–32. Lauber, *Inventions*, 187. Loving, *Mark Twain*, 262–63.

114 **now began to doubt**: See Cardwell, *Twins*, 14–15.

114 **"culture in Cambridge"**: Quoted in Turner, *Cable*, 168.

114 **"down upon you"**: Turner, *Cable*, 164–67. Ekstrom, *Cable*, 160, footnote.

114 **"The South makes me sick"**: Cable to Louise S. Cable, April 2, 1884. Quoted in Turner, *Cable*, 152. See also 156. Rubin, *Heretic*, 154. Bikle, *Cable*, 122–24.

115 **"I have often done this before"**: Twain, *Mark Twain's Speeches*, 280. Budd, *Our Mark Twain*, 202. See also Twain to Jane Lampton Clemens, from *Letters*, vol. 2, 58 (June 7, 1867), quoted in Steinbrink, *Getting to Be Mark Twain*, xiv: "I am so worthless . . . that it seems to me I never do anything or accomplish anything that lingers in my mind as a pleasant memory . . . [A]n accusing conscience gives me peace only in excitement & restless moving from place to place." It is not a problem finding quotations demonstrating Twain's almost pathological self-recrimination.

115 **less corrupt than Blaine**: Budd, *Social Philosopher*, 107–9.

115 **suppression of black voters**: Pettit, *Mark Twain and the South*, notes that George Griffin was "disgust[ed]" that Twain supported Cleveland in 1884 (99).

116 **"which were his birthright"**: Twain, *Autobiography*, vol. 1, 211–12.

116 **in the final draft, he cut**: Budd, *Social Philosopher*, 91. Howe, *Mark Twain and the Novel*, argues that the trip south allowed Twain to witness the failure of Reconstruction up close (97).

116 **just over the Ohio**: Fatout, *Lecture Circuit*, 221.

116 **review copies of *Huck* to Southern papers**: He went out of his way to say that Southern audiences "catch a point before you can get it out" and "laugh themselves all to pieces." Cardwell, *Twins*, 32. Twain to Olivia L. Clemens, *Love Letters*, 224 (January 1, 1885). Further, let's take a moment to note Twain's timing. Cable's Alabama speech in June 1884 was sharply criticized in the Southern press; Twain, at the same time, was raising his offer to Cable for the tour. In other words, Twain, as was often the case, saw good in opposites.

116 **mixed free black and slave celebrations:** Cable, "Place Congo," 527, places
the ban on street music in 1843—two years before he was born.

117 **"stone dead for thirty years":** *Mark Twain in Eruption*, 115.

117 **"Old Folks At Home" became ritual:** Toll, "Social Commentary," 104.
This flattening is described in Strausbaugh, *Black Like You*, 107–8, 122–23.
See McCoy, "Trouble Begins," 236–37, 240–44.

117 **five thousand at a time:** Taylor and Austen, *Darkest America*, 57–58. See
Sotiropoulos, *Staging Race*, 22: "Black performers often named their troupes
as if they had just walked off the plantation; the Georgia Slave Brothers and
the Georgia Slave Troupe Minstrels were two examples." Sotiropoulos also
notes their popularity during the 1880s, and cites examples of advertising
literature vowing authenticity: "The true Southern darkey is seen just as one
might see him in a journey to the land of cotton through a car window,"
Black America offered (23). Twain's effort to create "authentic" portrayals of
Southern slaves might be seen in this context: he was offering what black
minstrels of his time were offering. Toll, *Blacking Up*, 198.

117 **more slippery . . . ever imagined:** See, particularly, Chude-Sokei, *Last
"Darky,"* chapter 4.

117 *Black Mikado* **. . . 1885 and 1886:** Toll, "Social Commentary," 94.

117 **abolitionist or radical Southerner:** Saxton, "Blackface Minstrelsy," 80–82.
See *Christy's New Songster*, 6–7, "Uncle Sam's Cooks": "Now, boys, I'll tell
you what I think, if you want good Union Chowder, / Don't let yer cooks
fire up too strong, nor put in any powder; / But season well wid Compromise, and when yer dinner's done, / You'll all be glad you didn't go whole
hog or none."

117 **Asians in blackface:** Toll, "Social Commentary," 87; 86–100 is recommended. Toll, *Blacking Up*, 162–80. Roediger, *Wages*, 118. Late nineteenth-century minstrels also made fun of youth (101–2): "Our dandies
now have lots of brass, But very little brains, / Their pants are made to fit
so tight, Their legs are like a crane's."

117 **"children of the get-dough":** *Up-To-Date Minstrel Jokes*, 63.

117 **"true merit and honest worth":** Newcomb, *Tambo*, 18.

118 **disdainful potential . . . new form:** Roger Ebert, "*Birth of a Nation* (1915)."
An excellent short essay on the film. Karen Sotiropoulos, *Staging Race*, notes
that while "white men had blackened their faces in the 1830s . . . the widespread success of popular amusements at the turn of the twentieth-century
seared these images into the American psyche" (3).

118 **"designed to portray his peculiarities":** Newcomb, *Tambo*, 3.

118 **"a way of registering . . . disdain":** Lhamon, *Raising Cain*, 75–76. See
Wonham, *Playing the Races*, 84, where he describes a "transition from active engagement with minstrelsy's unstable representations to self-assured
spectatorship."

119 **the Civil War hadn't solved anything:** Henry Wonham, in *Playing the
Races*, is essential to my thinking here. He notes that "Twain relishes ethnic
burlesque for its power to set in motion an uncertain relationship between

reality and representation" (83). Regarding *Huck Finn* in particular, Wonham writes that "*Huck Finn* can be read as a kind of literary minstrel show. But to embrace this view too closely is to overlook the novel's persistent critique of social pathologies unique to the 'coon' era" (94). He also notes that Twain regards "the death of minstrelsy as a symptom of cultural decline," and that "the novel's minstrel sequences . . . intend to recover through memory and fantasy some of the dialectical force of early blackface within the context of its transformation into a new form of public entertainment. It is a strategy destined to fail" (94, 99). Wonham is particularly adept at illustrating how the character of Jim often seems to be rebelling against the "coon" stereotypes of the later Victorian era when *Huck* was published: that Jim moderates Huck's desire to steal watermelons, among other foods, plays against the stereotype of black men as thieves as well as the conventional racist link between African-Americans and watermelon eating (97). As circumstantial evidence that Twain was using minstrelsy against "coon" stereotypes, this point is crucial. See also Wonham, "Minstrel and the Detective," 123, 125. Camfield, "*Arabian Nights*," is also highly recommended, and discerning on the play between satire and burlesque in Twain's imagination, especially in historical context: "He was attuned to a tradition by which burlesque could convey meaning, but he was writing to an audience that was coming to reject this set of conventions."

Strausbaugh, *Black Like You*, 173, offers a relevant variant about Joel Chandler Harris and *Uncle Remus*: "Launched into popular culture at the very time when Blacks and Whites were being forcefully and legally segregated, the Uncle Remus stories presented an opposite image of Blacks and Whites living together in harmony, mutual respect, and love." Lhamon, "Ebery Time," 275, also addresses this: "What Melville and Twain most beneficially learned from minstrelsy was its structural indeterminacy and improvisation, as well as its insistence on a self that was complexly constituted from a mixed gender, class, and racial sourcepool."

119 **"could be considered a white Negro"**: I am indebted to Rux, "Eminem," 29–32, for this peroration. Young, *Cultural Appropriation*, 6. Sotiropoulos, *Staging Race*, 218; she provides a valuable discussion of the vogue for black music among "white moderns" (9, and chapter 6). Norman Mailer, "The White Negro: Superficial Reflections on the Hipster," *Dissent* 4 (Summer 1957), 279.

119 **"sex, alcohol and drug consumption"**: Rux, "Eminem," 21.

120 **to their corporate employers**: Gladwell, "The Coolhunt."

120 **But it was**: Margolis, "Consequences," citing the different legal debates of the period, suggests that the major paradigm for Cable was "equity"; for Twain, "negligence" (340). Lott, "Blackface and Blackness," 20, notes "the ideological complexity" created by the juxtaposition of Twain's performances of minstrel-like materials, and Cable's "Freedman": "They indicate as well that the contradiction between the book's overt politics and its indebtedness to the minstrel show was much less cumbrous in the nineteenth-century." Mailloux, *Rhetorical Power*, 75, directly compares

Twain's performances of pieces from *Huck* with Cable's "Freedman": "On stage and in print, Jim's two rhetorical performances were potentially just as subversive of racist ideology as Cable's less humorous and more explicit attack." "Potentially" seems key here. See also Ryan, "Black Genes," who notes that "Twain evades political entanglements, yet he intentionally represents this evasion," and that Twain "wants his work to be taken seriously, but he also intends it to be misunderstood" (170, 174). In my interviews with Twain scholars, this point has been stressed: that one cannot prove what Twain "intended" here, as a general principle in literary study, one particularly trenchant in the case of an author who embodies so many seeming contradictions. "Intentionality" in Twain studies is an issue spearheaded by the work of Robinson; see, especially, "An 'Unconscious and Profitable Cerebration.'"

Scholars approach Cable's influence on Twain similarly. Budd, *Social Philosopher*, 93, avers that "Cable's ideas may account for some of *Huckleberry Finn*." Given the intensity of Twain's friendship with Cable at this time, his references to extraordinary conversations, and the overall consonance of many of the shaping ideas displayed in the "Twins of Genius," the claim, and the conditioning use of "may," both seem appropriate.

Some reference ought to be made here of recent scholarship on the relationship of "bohemians" to mainstream cultures and politics. Linchpin texts here are undoubtedly Mikhail Bakhtin, *Rabelais and His World* (Bloomington: Indiana University Press, 2009), and Peter Stallybrass and Allon White, *The Politics and Poetics of Transgression* (Ithaca, NY: Cornell University Press, 1986). Essentially, the scholarly tradition here says that, while "the dominant culture speaks 'to itself in the delirium of its repressed others,' it does not produce 'necessary or automatic political progressiveness.'" (Stallybrass and White, *Politics*, 199–200, quoted in Wonham, *Playing*, 81). See also Knoper, *Acting Naturally*, 53.

7. TWINS

126 **"So I quit"**: Twain, *Huck*, 93–98. The opening preface comes from "The Genial Mark: Samuel L. Clemens and George W. Cable in Toronto," *Toronto Globe*, December 9, 1884, 2. The reviewer then provides a transcription of the section from *Huck* known as "Jim's Investments." The reviewer indicates there was more to the piece, so it is likely that Twain transitions at some subsequent point to "King Sollermun"—and it is also possible, then, that Twain performed both pieces and called them by one name, in which case there is an ellipsis in my reproduction of his performance. Otherwise, though, the reviewer's transcription reads relatively closely to the scene as it appears in *Huck Finn*—not nearly an exact match, but there are no major departures. See also "Laughing at Pure Fun. Mark Twain and Cable Take Turns Entertaining an Audience," *Washington Post*, November 25, 1884, 1, which includes a description of Twain's performance of King Sollermun,

with some transcribed dialogue. It matches closely the version that appears in *Huckleberry Finn*: "It was all on account of his raising . . . He had about five million children. Take a man with two or three. Is he gwine to be wasteful of children like dat?" So I believe that using the scene as written in *Huck Finn* in this context is fairly appropriate, but must come with the clear caveat that no performance notes remain to confirm, and it is very likely that Twain strayed from what appeared here.

Lorch, *Trouble*, 159, shows a page from an edition of *Huck Finn* Twain used during a subsequent tour, nicely marked up. "Remarkable Achievement," at the University of Virginia Mark Twain website, provides reproductions of marked-up pages for the performance of the novel's concluding section: http://twain.lib.virginia.edu/huckfinn/hfending.html.

126 **"boisterous merriment"**: "Amusements," *Indianapolis Journal*, January 8, 1885, 7.

127 **cultivated audience agreed with him**: Mailloux, *Rhetorical Power*, 74, writes that "of course, readers reject the racist slur as a rationalization." A fine line exists, I think, between knowing what readers thought and did and recognizing what was available to them, given the conventions of the time. In my view, the ironic reading was available, but not necessarily ascendant.

127 **prison population, too**: Toll, "Social Commentary," 96–100. And if you read the book, you might notice that Huck and his father are the only white characters "without a recognizable Anglo-Saxon surname" (Hearn, *Annotated Huckleberry Finn*, 52). Roediger, *Wages*, 134, observes that the Irish were regarded as the one group of whites that would consort with blacks. "The two groups often lived side by side . . . both did America's hard work . . . both groups were poor and often vilified . . . [T]hey often celebrated and socialized together . . . [F]or some time there were strong signs that the Irish might not fully embrace white supremacy . . . [L]ove and sex between Black men and Irish women were not uncommon." In *How the Irish Became White*, Noel Ignatiev cites Huck's surname, and the quote about Kemble's drawings being too "Irishy." Ignatiev also suggests that "the facts of Huck's life," including "being the son of the town drunk," are a "very 'Irish' story" (Ignatiev, *How the Irish Became White*, 58). But he also distances himself from an absolute identification that Huck is Irish, suggesting that it might be "pure fancy" (58). Instead, he develops an extended metaphor that juxtaposes Huck's ability to "go the whole hog" in siding with Jim against the Irish-American community's preference for "the privileges and burdens of whiteness" (59).

127 **the story was told in Huck's voice, not his**: Arac, *Impure Worlds*, 161: "The word is part of the historical and social distancing between author and character."

128 **you can "get"—barely**: See Mensh, *Black, White*, 65, 87, who note that the penalty for striking a white person could be capital, and that, for that matter, Huck tends not to think very long about the penalties that might face abolitionists. Hearn, *Annotated Huckleberry Finn*, 143, notes that "according to Missouri law, any slave who lifted his hand against any person

not a Negro or a mulatto unless 'wantonly attacked' was liable to receive a maximum sentence of thirty lashes."

128 **Who is the American voice here:** Smith, "Huck, Jim," 111, describes Huck's mistake as a "category error."

129 **began to reach for the tar and feathers:** See Knoper, *Acting Naturally*, 48: "He transformed African-American tactics of resistance (affected by their translation through minstrelsy) into his own." Godden and McCay, "Play It Again," 673–76, are only one of many critics to see subversion in these exchanges. MacLeod, "Telling the Truth," 14. Lauber, *Inventions*, 168. Bercovitch, "What's Funny About 'Huckleberry Finn,'" 13. Leonard, "Huck, Jim," 141. Mailloux, arguing that "the passages Twain chose to read were often those that most directly involved his humorous critique of white supremacist ideology," writes that "Jim responds by initiating his own version of a Socratic dialogue, and . . . beats Huck at his own game" (Mailloux, "Reading," 112, 116–17). Smith claims that "Jim demonstrates impressive reasoning abilities, despite his factual ignorance . . . [T]he humor in Huck's conclusion, 'you can't learn a nigger to argue,' arises precisely from our recognition that Jim's argument is better than Huck's" (Smith, "Huck, Jim," 111). Fishkin writes that "Jim's argument appears more convincing than Huck's, making Huck's comment that 'you can't learn a nigger to argue' sound clearly like his own 'sour grapes'" (Fishkin, *Huck*, 89). She also provides a nice summation of the recent history of this reading in "Race and the Politics of Memory," 295–96: "Jim dons the minstrel mask as a strategic performance," she writes (296). Gerry Brenner, writing in Jim's voice in "More Than a Reader's Response: A Letter to 'De Ole True Huck,'" implies that Jim was "testin'" Huck, "trying to fine out ef'n I could talk open to dat boy" (Brenner, "Letter," 457). Quirk notes that Jim's sympathy to the imprisoned "boy dolphin," as well as his antipathy toward the patriarch Solomon, both arise from "a profound feeling for or sensitivity to family, imprisonment, and employment" (Quirk, *Coming to Terms*, 73). Quirk is excellent on this section (see 33–35, 63–74), noting that it was likely the last thing Twain wrote in the book: "The remark 'So I quit' appears to be an afterthought—the three words are crammed into the lower right-hand corner of the manuscript page, an emblem that represents Twain's own frustrations as much as they do Huck's, albeit in a very different way." Chadwick-Joshua claims that Jim's argument against Solomon reflects his "deep feeling for family, children, and responsibility": "To him—one whose family can be and is sold away from him and from each other—Solomon's apparent wisdom is interpreted only as the concomitant result of a man's having so much of everything, including wives and children, that slaughtering one would matter little" (Chadwick-Joshua, *Jim Dilemma*, 51). McCay and Godden argue that King Sollermun marks the emergence of "Jim's double-voicing" (McCay and Godden, "Say It Again"). Nor are these merely academic arguments: Watch the enactment of the scene in Mickey Rooney's *Adventures of Huckleberry Finn* (1939). Jim clearly wins. See also

Solomon, "Jim and Huck: Magnificent Misfits," 20–21. Quoted in Mensh, *Black, White*, 10; see also Mensh, 48–53.

130 **"by the inflections of his voice":** All sources from the Springfield event are gathered in this note. Advertisements, *Springfield Daily Republican*, November 7, 1884, 1. "The Enthusiasm. Celebrating in This City," *Springfield Daily Republican*, November 8, 1884, 5. "The Twain-Cable Evening," *Springfield Daily Republican*, November 8, 1884, 4. "The Tragic Tale of the Fishwife," which has several different names—"The Tragical Tale of the Fishwife," "The Tale of the Fishwife and Its Sad Fate," etc.—can be found in "The Awful German Language," Appendix D, in Twain, *Tramps Abroad*, 601–19. 607–8 quoted here.

130 **two shows on Saturday:** *Providence Daily Journal*, Nov. 4, 1884, 5.

131 **"mother riding for life":** " 'Mark Twain' and Mr. Cable," *Providence Daily Journal*, November 10, 1884.

131 **"The second verse was much better appreciated":** " 'Mark Twain' and Mr. Cable," *Providence Daily Journal*, November 10, 1884.

131 **Roberts Lyceum Union Course:** *Boston Morning Journal*, November 14, 1884, 3.

131 **"Hail to the Chief":** "Rejoicing," *Boston Globe*, November 14, 1884, 5.

131 **"everyone must feel satisfied":** *Boston Morning Journal*, November 11, 1884, 1. *Boston Morning Journal*, November 14, 5.

131 **"I enjoyed them the most":** Howells, *Twain-Howells Letters*, vol. 2, 513 (November 14, 1884).

132 **little understood or even known":** *Boston Morning Journal*, November 11, 1884, 1.

132 **3,000 in Philadelphia:** Turner, *Cable*, 179.

132 **"until their faces glowed":** "Fun on the Stage," *Brooklyn Daily Eagle*, November 23, 1884, 12.

132 **then up at 6:** Twain to Olivia L. Clemens, *Love Letters*, 219 (November 23, 1884).

132 **"person of consequence yourself":** Quoted in Kaplan, *Mr. Clemens*, 262, and elsewhere.

132 **than did the whole tour, in fact:** Twain wrote an extended essay describing the acquisition and publication of this book. "About General Grant's Memoirs," *Autobiography*, vol. 1, 75–98. See also 334–35.

133 **waiting for them as well:** Cable to Louise S. Cable, November 25, 26, 1884, in Bikle, *Cable*, 134–35. Cardwell, *Twins*, 22.

133 **rung by the seat of his pants:** Twain to Olivia L. Clemens, *Love Letters*, 221 (December 3, 1884).

133 **seven hundred workers:** "Mills Shutting Down," *Philadelphia Inquirer*, November 22, 1884, 1. "Industrial Depression in New England," *Philadelphia Inquirer*, November 27, 1884, 4.

133 **fears of re-enslavement . . . South:** "Scaring Timid Negroes," *New York Sun*, November 19, 1884, 1. Under the section entitled "Misrepresentations in Georgia."

133 **"citizens of a free republic"**: "Blaine's Comments," *Philadelphia Inquirer*, November 19, 1884, 1.

133 **"bloody chasm"**: *Philadelphia Inquirer*, November 21, 1884, 3.

133 **that massive African territory**: "The Congo Conference," *New York Sun*, November 20, 1884, 3.

134 **the banks of the Congo River**: "Fun on the Stage," *Brooklyn Daily Eagle*, November 23, 1884, 12.

134 **"endure it any longer"**: This quote is oft-referred. Brooks, *Ordeal of Mark Twain*, 84. Cardwell, *Twins*, 25, places it early in the tour, in Philadelphia. See also Wecter, *Love Letters*, 231–32. This is Twain, also quoted by Brooks, 265, later in life: "Another dream that I have of that kind is being compelled to go back to the lecture platform. I hate that dream worse than the other. In it I am always getting up before an audience with nothing to say, trying to be funny; trying to make the audience laugh, realizing I am only making silly jokes. Then the audience realizes it, and pretty soon they commence to get up and leave . . ." The other dream to which he refers is one where he is in "reduced circumstances," about to sail into a "black shadow" on the Mississippi River.

134 **"I always shrink from this"**: Cable to Louise S. Cable, December 8, 1884, in Bikle, *Cable*, 135.

134 **"British applause"**: Cable to Louise S. Cable, December 8, 1884, in Bikle, *Cable*, 135.

134 **his arms "unmanageable"**: *Detroit Post*, December 17, 1884, quoted in Fatout, *Lecture Circuit*, 219.

134 **"if the arms are loaded"**: *Oberlin Weekly News*, February 7, 1885.

134 **"7 generations of that boy's family"**: Twain to Olivia L. Clemens, *Love Letters*, 225 (January 8, 1885).

135 **turned a dynamo on it"**: "Cable and Twain. The Author and the Humorist Arrive in the City To-Day," *St. Louis Post-Dispatch*, January 9, 1885, 7. H. C. Bunner to Walter Learned, January 1884, quoted in Turner, *Cable*, 184, Cardwell, *Twins*, 27. Pond, "Diary," reverses the gender role playing, describing "Mr. Clemens . . . as loving as a woman."

135 **audience members . . . could be carried out**: Turner, *Cable*, 183.

135 **"a double climax"**: Quoted in Turner, *Cable*, 180–81.

135 **serenade their road manager**: James Pond, *Eccentricities of Genius*, 228, 231.

135 **complacency in the author**: See, for instance, Explanatory Notes, *Huck*, 445. Also Hoffman, *Inventing*, 318. Kaplan, *Singular Mark Twain*, 264. Loving, *Mark Twain*, 278–79, regards the vandalism as an "act of subversion" directed at Twain's sympathetic portrayal of Jim or his "implicit determinism."

135 **"less ready to fight"**: Quoted in Hoffman, *Inventing*, 319.

136 **"I thought Cable would be a novelty"**: Quoted in Hoffman, *Inventing*, 320.

136 **"Tom & Huck stock Jim's cabin"**: Twain to Olivia L. Clemens, *Love Letters*, 223–24 (December 29, 1884). Lauber, *Inventions*, 179.

136 *"go* to hell": Twain, *Huck*, 271.

136 "not for a salary": Twain, *Huck*, 325, 331.

136 as much as eighty years: Twain, *Huck*, 310.

136 calls it the "evasion": Twain, *Huck*, 333, 340, 360.

137 "trouble and bother": Twain, *Huck*, 358, 360.

137 "and then tell him about his being free": Twain, *Huck*, 360.

137 "Signs is *signs*": Twain, *Huck*, 361.

137 "a prisoner for us so patient": Twain, *Huck*, 360.

137 American Revolution . . . Emancipation Proclamation: Brown, "For Our Time," 43–44, offers this interpretation, as does Howe, *Mark Twain and the Novel*, 96; Wieck, *Refiguring*, 66–67; Cecil, "Historical Ending," 281; Fishkin, *Was Huck Black?*, 75.

137 eighteen times in the book: Personal correspondence, Emma Faesi Hudelson, January 20, 2014: "forty" appears fourteen times on its own, and four times as part of another number. For edits: See, for instance, *Buffalo Huck Finn*, MS1134, MS0581. For examples in the text: See Twain, *Huck*, 16, 127, 268, 341, 346. Several critics have noted the resonance of "forty," the odd way it recurs throughout the book. One can regard it as the broadest possible clue that Twain spoke in codes to his reader, or to his unconscious or semiconscious affinity for key images and icons in the zeitgeist. Wieck, *Refiguring*, 94–96. Margolis, "Consequences," 338–39. He also wrote "De Mule" in the notes of his manuscript for this final section—underlined three times, crossed out—as if contemplating whether or not to turn a sly half-delivered reference to the most famous broken promise of Reconstruction into something unmistakable. Wieck, *Refiguring*, 100–101. DeVoto, *Mark Twain at Work*, 64.

137 "carpet-bags": Twain, *Huck*, 160, 204, 208, 209, 210, for "carpet-bag" references linked to the King and Duke.

137 dogs . . . on Jim: Twain, *Huck*, 339. *Buffalo Huck Finn*, MS1207.

138 "chawed by a dog": *Buffalo Huck Finn*, MS1104.

138 those politics shaping the laugh: Doyno, *Writing Huck Finn*, 228–29, demonstrates many of these revisions.

138 maybe it was there, and maybe not: Railton, *Mark Twain*, 66: "There is . . . not the faintest hint of contextual evidence that any reader in Twain's time took the ending this way."

138 "They all said kiss her": Twain, *Huck*, 287. See Opdahl, " 'You'll Be Sorry.' "

138 "right out of her stockings": Twain, *Huck*, 330.

139 "don't amount to shucks": Twain, *Huck*, 329, 359, 345.

139 aphorisms that admit their defeat: Twain, *Huck*, 356, 348, 349, 333.

139 his creator's is, too: Twain, *Huck*, 356, 348, 349, 332–37. See Prioleau, "Abused Child," on the "servant girl" exchange, and the butter-brain scene.

139 "the child is born": Twain to Olivia L. Clemens, *Love Letters*, 223 (December 29, 1884).

140 "bedecked with feathers": " 'Twain' and Cable," *Pittsburg Dispatch*, December 30, 1884.

140 **"in my whole repertoire"**: Twain to Olivia L. Clemens, *Love Letters*, 223 (December 29, 1884). Railton, *Mark Twain*, 66, notes that "King Soller-mun" recedes as a performance piece from this point forward during the tour. The "evasion" would be called by many names, in both private and public, including "Remarkable Achievement" and "Dazzling Achievement" derivatives. *Milwaukee Sentinel*, January 29, 1885, 4. "Stage and Rostrum /Twain-Cable," *Wisconsin State Journal*, January 28, 1885, 4. "Mark Twain-Cable," *Montreal Gazette*, February 20, 1885. Twain, III, 84. See "A Night at the Opera House" at the University of Virginia web site, http://twain.lib.virginia.edu/huckfinn/hfprogrm.html, for a program where the piece is called "Escape."

140 **prison reform satire stirred in:** Twain to Olivia L. Clemens, *Love Letters*, 223 (December 29, 1884). Railton's effort to reconstruct what this performance might have been like is valuable: "Remarkable Achievement," http://twain.lib.virginia.edu/huckfinn/hfending.html. If Twain performed the piece this way, he was, in fact, focusing on the burlesque of children's matters over race matters, though not completely obscuring the latter from audience view. Twain, *Notebooks*, vol. 3, 84, also lists "Songs" as intermission material for its performance—though the performance program cited in this note indicates that Cable performed literary pieces as intermission material as well.

8. THE FREEDMAN'S CASE

142 **"the patriarchal tie"**: Cable, "Freedman," 412.

142 **to belong to a more rational future:** Williamson, *Crucible of Race*, 98, provides an opposite perspective on Cable's rhetoric: "He was not impatient, he did not expect a miracle, and he anticipated a great deal of sinning after the message and before the conversion."

142 **"nothing could make it seem small"**: Cable, "Freedman," 413.

143 **the passing of time . . . on its own:** Cable, "Freedman," 412.

143 **"pretended to discover"**: Cable, "Freedman," 418.

143 **"assume them without proof "**: Cable, "Freedman," 414, 417.

143 **"the moon . . . not social equality"**: Cable, "Freedman," 417.

143 **"the opportunity now offered"**: "A Grave Responsibility," *Century*, January 1885, 462.

144 **"posterity will discover ours"**: Cable, "Freedman," 410.

144 **"the merit of his novels decried"**: "The Equality of the Negro. Mr. Cable and the Rabid Southerners," *Chicago Tribune*, January 17, 1885, 8.

144 **"creations of his own imagination"**: Turner, *Cable*, 197. Several have written about this overwhelming response. See, for instance, Williamson, *Crucible of Race*, 99–104. *New Orleans Picayune*, January 11, 1885.

144 **"from the pen of . . . Cable"**: *Shreveport Times*, January 11, 1885, printed in *New Orleans Times-Democrat*, February 2, 1885.

145 "the business advertisement": *Cincinnati Enquirer*, February 6, 1885, 2. *Nashville American*, printed in *New Orleans Times-Democrat*, February 2, 1885.

145 "a good mess of crow": *Oxford Eagle*, printed in *New Orleans Times-Democrat*, February 2, 1885.

145 "strife and bloodshed": *Shreveport Times*, January 11, 1885, printed in *New Orleans Times-Democrat*, February 2, 1885.

145 "Northern progressiveness": Fatout, *Lecture*, 223.

145 in support of his position: "The Equality of the Negro. Mr. Cable and the Rabid Southerners," *Chicago Tribune*, January 17, 1885, 8.

145 "how we feel toward you": "Geo. W. Cable and the Colored Race," *Wisconsin State Journal*, January 28, 1885, 4.

145 "executed such a thing as a forgery": *Selma Times*, printed in *New Orleans Times-Democrat*, February 2, 1885.

145 "sensation of the hour": "The Nation's Capitol/Hon. F. Douglass' Recent Letter in the Republic, on the Negro Problem/Mr. Geo. W. Cable's in the Century," *Cleveland Gazette*, February 14, 1885.

146 "malice against his section": *New York Freeman*, January 10, 1885. *Hub*, January 3, 1885.

146 "[E]very good and great cause": James D. Kennedy, "Our Case in Equity," *Southwestern Christian Advocate*, reprinted in *New York Freeman*, February 28, 1885. "The Nation's Capitol/Hon. F. Douglass' Recent Letter in the Republic, on the Negro Problem/Mr. Geo. W. Cable's in the Century," *Cleveland Gazette*, February 14, 1885.

146 now focused offstage as well: Turner, *Cable*, 192.

146 the husband . . . then the wife: Turner, *Cable*, 205–6.

147 "dry eyes": Quoted in Turner, *Cable*, 206.

147 more people were turned away: Turner, *Cable*, 206.

147 so the members could go to the show: Twain to Olivia L. Clemens, *Love Letters*, 230–31 (January 17, 1885). Cardwell, *Twins*, 62.

147 "heavy as lead": Quoted in Turner, *Cable*, 184.

147 "one of the most spoiled men": Twain to Olivia L. Clemens, *Love Letters*, 237 (February 13, 1885).

147 on the tour's dime: Turner, *Cable*, 190.

147 to catch an early train: Turner, *Cable*, 175. Pond, "Diary," describes Twain "knocking it completely out in one round."

147 "not much on science": Quoted in Turner, *Cable*, 172–73.

148 "a thundering sight too much": Twain to Olivia L. Clemens, *Love Letters*, 231 (January 17, 1885). Around this time, Twain began calling Cable "K" in his letters (Cardwell, *Twins*, 33), for reasons Cardwell describes as "cautious and mordant."

148 "a paltry child": Twain to Olivia L. Clemens, 234–35 (February 8, 1885).

148 "insulting & insolent ways": Twain to Olivia L. Clemens, 235 (February 9, 1885). See also Budd, *Social Philosopher*, 193, about Twain's own treatment of servants later in life.

148 **"a little place like Indianapolis"**: Twain to Olivia L. Clemens, *Love Letters*, 234–35 (February 9, 1885); 236 (February 10, 1885).

148 **audiences were tired of him:** A point often made. See, for instance, Kaplan, *Mr. Clemens*, 267; Cardwell, *Twins*, 121: "By pragmatic tests Cable's reputation for effectiveness as speaker and reader is secure."

149 **to "untwin" himself:** See Pettit, *Mark Twain and the South*, 131–32. Pettit notes Twain's public silence on the "Freedman," and the rather "mild abuse" he received compared to Cable, and offers "jealousy" as a partial motive.

149 **"vicious evasions"**: Cable, "Freedman," 410.

149 **"a superb race of masters"**: Cable, "Freedman," 410. Friedman, *White Savage*, offers the argument that Cable's racial politics, despite their seeming clarity, still contained many statements of racial difference and hierarchy; I have added the comparison that notes their relative absence from Twain's lexicon. Cable described whites as "the finer and prouder race" (quoted in Friedman, *White Savage*, 109) and wrote that "the black race is inferior to the white" in the *New Orleans Bulletin* on September 26, 1875 (quoted in Friedman, *White Savage*, 109).

149 **"even keel with the rest"**: Twain to Olivia L. Clemens, *Love Letters*, 234 (February 5, 1885).

150 **"when I crossed it"**: "Cable and Twain. The Author and the Humorist Arrive in the City To-Day," *St. Louis Post-Dispatch*, January 9, 1885, 7. Pond, "Diary," describes this scene, and says that only he and Cable "retain[ed] their self possession"—implying that Twain didn't.

150 **"whites under foot"**: Twain, *Notebooks*, vol. 3, 88. Lauber, *Inventions*, 188. Some critics describe this as a story idea. Budd, *Social Philosopher*, also notes that *A Connecticut Yankee in King Arthur's Court*, written and published shortly after this point in time, contains scenes where "white men suffered the cruelties of being sold" (106). See Twain, *Connecticut Yankee*, 353–54. Wieck, *Refiguring*, 67–68.

150 **"dirt-eating spirit"**: R. L. Dabney, "Mr. Cable, The Negrophilist," in *The Louisiana Book: Selections from the Literature of the State*, edited by Thomas McCaleb (New Orleans, 1894), 203–5. Quoted in Turner, *Cable*, 218.

150 **"never had any to lose"**: "The Silent South," *Washington Post*, July 14, 1885, 2.

151 **"fair criticism among friends"**: G.W. Cable to Twain, May 15, 1885; Cable to Twain, May 16, 1885, in Cardwell, *Twins*, 108. Turner, *Cable*, 210.

151 **"never have occurred to me"**: Twain to G. W. Cable, May 18, 1885, in Cardwell, *Twins*, 109. See also Rubin, *Heretic*, 171–72.

151 **"And I *paid* it"**: Twain to Cable, June 25, 1895, in Cardwell, *Twins*, 111.

151 **an exorbitant amount:** Turner, *Cable*, 222–23.

151 **essay after essay on the color line:** On January 31, 1885, in a letter to his wife (Cable Papers, Tulane University, quoted in Friedman, *White Savage*, 115), Cable said of the South: "I shall not from choice bring up my daughters in that state of society. The more carefully I study it the less I expect of it . . ." On June 8, 1887 (same correspondent, same source, 116), he wrote,

"More than ever before, my home is in New England. This South may be a free country one of these days; it is not so now."

151 **"neither them nor any worthy interest"**: Turner, *Cable*, 263–72. Cable to William M. Baskervill, quoted on 269. See Williamson, *Crucible of Race*, 104–7. Rubin, *Heretic*, 202–3.

152 **the only example of a negative black response**: Turner, *Cable*, 216.

152 **"my record is made"**: Cable to William M. Baskervill, quoted on Turner, *Cable*, 269. There is evidence that Cable, while unapologetic, did alter somewhat in accordance with public criticism. Rubin, *Heretic*, 242–44, 248.

152 **five thousand dollars . . . in his will**: Turner, *Cable*, 310–11, 345, 355. Rubin, *Heretic*, 271.

152 **taught classes at Yale Divinity**: Bikle, *Cable*, 186–202. Turner, *Cable*, 274–75, 329–36.

152 **to Flaubert**: Schmidt, *Sitting in Darkness*, argues that Cable's *Lovers of Louisiana (To-Day)* (1918) represents an undervalued late effort, one that combines "an enjoyable romantic plot with a novel of ideas critically examining the New South, Progressivism, and colonialism" (207).

152 **"strangulation"**: *Patriotic Gore*, 579, quoted in Rubin, *Heretic*, 19.

152 **the crowd could cheer *him***: Budd, "'Talent,'" 85, 86. The match in question is billiards. Budd, *Our Mark Twain*, 113, 148. Kaplan, *Mr. Clemens*, has a wonderful discussion of Twain's fame during the last decade of his life, 358–62. Loving, *Mark Twain*, 262. Shelden, *Man in White*, xxxiv.

152 **"*the* sterilized Christian"**: Twain, "Seventieth Birthday Dinner Speech," *Collected Tales, 1891–1910*, 713, 717. Turner, *Cable*, 187, describes "a sterile moralist" as the key line. See "Mark Twain's 70th Birthday," *Harper's Weekly*, 44 (December 23, 1905), 1884–1914, especially 1886. It is a good document. On 1889, Cable writes, of Twain's performative control, "In all those seventy nights I never saw him betrayed into so much as a smile . . ." with a "single exception."

153 **"sharp tongue & uncertain temper"**: Twain, *Twain-Howells Letters*, vol. 2, 575 (December 12, 1886).

153 **"his greatness . . . be recognized"**: Quoted in Loving, *Mark Twain*, 264. This is the moment where Twain clearly recognizes Cable's contribution on race—but it is countermanded by many other quotes during the time period.

153 **"the human race"**: *Mark Twain in Eruption*, epigram.

153 **"he has no *audience*"**: Twain, *Notebooks*, vol. 2, 497.

9. HUCKLEBERRY CAPONE

154 **"in regard to slavery"**: "Huckleberry Finn," *Hartford Courant*, February 20, 1885. Only one paper saw anything more than that: "Running all through the book," the *San Francisco Chronicle* wrote, "is the sharpest satire on the ante-bellum estimate of the slave." "The *Chronicle* understands the book,"

Twain told his sister. *San Francisco Chronicle*, March 29, 1885. Quoted in Fischer, *Huck Finn Reviewed*, 24.

154 **"We have not read them"**: *Augusta Chronicle and Constitutionalist*, March 22, 1885. Quoted in Fischer, *Huck Finn Reviewed*, 21.

155 **perfunctory references . . . Huck Finn**: See Chadwick-Joshua, *Jim Dilemma*, xiii. I base this conclusion on Chadwick-Joshua's statement here; Fishkin, interview, where she notes the same point; some measure of logical deduction—there have been so many critics combing this same territory, and no one has found a review of *Huck* in the African-American press of the day; lastly, my own work looking for such a review, which did not exhaust every possible source, but covered significant available resources.

155 **Maybe another generation . . . Maybe not**: Arac, *Idol and Target*, 143, points us in an interesting direction, noting that early publicity for the book emphasized the Duke and the King, the two confidence men who take over the middle section of the book. This can be seen in the trailers for the early movies, and the 1950s-era television special. If neither children nor race are the focus of this book, then perhaps craven confidence men are. Mailloux, *Rhetorical Power*, 102–3, compares the relative silence on race to reviews that clearly referenced children's issues.

155 **"the amusement of his fond parents"**: *Hartford Times*, March 9, 1885. *New York Sun*, February 15, 1885. *Life*, February 26, 1885. Quoted in Hearn, *Annotated Huckleberry Finn*, ixix-lxxi.

155 **"by way of incidental diversion"**: *New York World*, March 2, 1885. Quoted in Fischer, *Huck Finn Reviewed*, 7–8.

155 **"without some hesitation"**: *San Francisco Bulletin*, March 14, 1885, 1. Quoted in Fischer, *Huck Finn Reviewed*, 13.

156 **"severe criticism"**: *St. Louis Globe-Democrat*, March 17, 1885, 1. Quoted in Fischer, *Huck Finn Reviewed*, 17.

156 **"anything less than harmful"**: *Springfield Republican*, March 17, 1885. Quoted in Fischer, *Huck Finn Reviewed*, 20.

156 **"Mark Twain's Bad Boy"**: *New York World*, March 2, 1885, 7. Mailloux, *Rhetorical Power*, 124.

156 **"introduce the N.Y. World in its place"**: Twain, *Notebooks*, vol. 3, 128–30. Budd, *Our Mark Twain*, 110. Mailloux, *Rhetorical Power*, 126–27. Fischer, *Huck Finn Reviewed*, 29.

156 **"but when I speak—well"**: Twain, *Notebooks*, vol. 3, 130.

156 **he was already winning**: *Twain-Howells Letters*, vol. 2, 526 (April 20, 1885).

157 **"kept the proceedings profoundly secret"**: *Sacramento Daily Record-Union*, March 26, 1885. Quoted in Fischer, *Huck Finn Reviewed*, 23.

157 **sales of the book increased**: *Concord Freeman*, March 20, 1885. Quoted in Hearn, *Annotated Huckleberry Finn*, lxxviii.

157 **"and Mark knows it"**: *Packard's Short-Hand Reporter and Amanuensis*, April 1885. Quoted in Fischer, *Huck Finn Reviewed*, 32. *Packard's* reprinted the "Royal Nonesuch" episode.

157 **thanking the library for its "generous action":** *Boston Daily Advertiser,* April 2, 1885. Quoted in Fischer, *Huck Finn Reviewed,* 25.

157 **"boastfully declares that he is not":** *Springfield Republican,* April 3, 1885. Quoted in Fischer, *Huck Finn Reviewed,* 27.

157 **"impervious to a joke":** *San Francisco Chronicle,* March 29, 1885. Quoted in Fischer, *Huck Finn Reviewed,* 24. See also 24–26.

157 **"whatever I touch turns to gold":** Webster, *Mark Twain, Business Man,* 301.

157 **"Practical Morality":** *Critic,* May 30, 1885, 264. Quoted in Hearn, *Annotated Huckleberry Finn,* lxxxiii.

157 **"left unread by growing boys":** Franklin B. Sanborn, *Springfield Daily Republican,* April 27, 1885. Quoted in Hearn, *Annotated Huckleberry Finn,* lxxxii.

158 **"Mark Twain's specialty . . . wasted upon him":** *San Francisco Chronicle,* March 15, 1885. Quoted in Fischer, *Huck Finn Reviewed,* 23.

158 **"salve to my soreness":** Twain, *Autobiography,* vol. 2, 33.

158 **the murder the town . . . pins on Jim:** Twain, *Tom Sawyer Abroad,* 9. Huck Finn, Jim, and Tom appear in the following sequels to *Adventures of Huckleberry Finn*: *Huck Finn and Tom Sawyer among the Indians* (unfinished and unpublished during his lifetime; Twain, *Huck and Tom among the Indians,* 33–81); *Tom Sawyer Abroad*; *Tom Sawyer, Detective*; and *Tom Sawyer's Conspiracy* (unfinished and unpublished during his lifetime; Twain, *Huck and Tom among the Indians,* 134–213). He also wrote a small fragment entitled "Huck Finn" from Huck's point of view in 1902 ("Huck Finn," *Huck and Tom among the Indians,* 260–61). See also Wonham, "Minstrel and the Detective," 125, 128, 137, for links between minstrelsy and these latter works, and also McCoy, "Cultural Critique." Fulton, *Ethical Realism,* 73, observes that *Tom Sawyer's Conspiracy* "inverts the 'evasion' at the end of" *Huck Finn.* See also 74, 81: Fulton makes the crucial point that *Tom Sawyer's Conspiracy* reminds us that Tom and Huck have played in blackface both before and after the events of *Huck Finn.* Cardwell, *The Man Who Was Mark Twain,* 208. Pettit, *Mark Twain and the South,* 164.

158 **a daring rescue:** Twain, Notebook 39, September 1896–January 1897: "Elevens snagged, abduction. Adventures there."

159 **and hunt himself:** See, for instance, Notebook 39, September 1896–January 1897: "Have Huck tell how one white brother shaved his head, put on a wool wig + was blackened + sold as a negro. Escaped that night, washed himself, + helped hunt for himself under pay." Same notebook: "Tom is disguised as a negro + sold in Ark for $10, then he + Huck help hunt for him after the disguise is removed" (Twain originally has Huck for Tom here). Notebook 32A: "Tom sells Huck for a slave." Similar race disguise is also central to *Tom Sawyer's Conspiracy.*

159 **climbing trees in a meadow:** See Stone, *Innocent,* 250–51.

159 **"a solid wall of the dead":** Twain, *Connecticut Yankee,* 402, 427, 446.

160 **"a thousand times more *needs* it":** Twain, *Joan of Arc,* 429, 23, 20.

160 *"the age of seventeen"*: Louis Kossuth, quoted in Twain, *Joan of Arc*, v.

160 **awe children in particular:** Gibson, introduction, *Mysterious Stranger*, 4–11, describes the chronology.

160 "Is it agreed": Twain, *Mysterious Stranger*, 235, 319, 434. The visit to Hell can be found in Twain, *Notebook 43*, June 1897–March 1900.

160 "He looks it, and all that": Twain, *Mysterious Stranger*, 95.

161 **when that same imagination belonged to a child:** Twain, *Mysterious Stranger*, 459, 400, 179–80, 330.

161 "delicate shades of meaning": See Shelden, *Man in White*, 312–16.

161 "live through each part": "The Educational Theatre," *Mark Twain's Speeches*, 76. See also Shelden, *Man in White*, 155–58. See also Budd, *Our Mark Twain*, 169, for other examples of child-centric philanthropy: sending an inscribed copy of a book to a child injured by a train, for instance; Budd, *Social Philosopher*, 202, describes Twain's work with the "Anti Child Slavery League."

162 **social convention by 1894:** Described in Neider, introduction, *Papa*, 14–29. See, especially, 15, 28. On 131, Susy describes being scared by her father's ghost story as a child.

162 **"Yes my black Princess":** Quoted in Neider, introduction, *Papa*, 44.

162 **"heart of hearts I wish it":** Quoted in Neider, introduction, *Papa*, 14. Clara Clemens, *My Father*, 173.

162 **"she always made the plans":** Quoted in Hoffman, *Inventing*, 456.

162 **"the day Livy died":** Quoted in Helen Keller, "Our Mark Twain," in Fishkin, *Mark Twain Anthology*, 161.

163 "a thousand times": Twain, "Death of Jean," 111–12, 115.

163 **"cautious, watchful, wary":** The major source here is the correspondence reproduced in Cooley, *Aquarium*: See 102, xx, 33, 138, 180, 9, xvii, 35, 272, 273, 278, 279, 237. Hill, *God's Fool*, notes that Twain had written "Young girls innocent & natural—*I* love 'em same as others love infants" in 1866, forty years earlier (*Notebooks*, vol. 1, 120), but that the Angelfish represent a transition to something "more than avuncular," "even latently sexual," catalyzed by "symptoms of senility" (xxvii). Lystra, *Dangerous Intimacy*, on the other hand, notes "little erotic content" in the letters, and "avuncular relationship[s]" implied in the photographs, but also notes that "treating children as collectibles is neither charming nor benign" (131–32). Lystra also argues the potential "compensatory function" of the Angelfish, given the loss of one daughter ("Susy, his favorite") and his complicated "late-life relationships" with the others, Clara and Jean: "Clemens appears to have tried to fill a deep emotional hole with fictive kin," she writes (132). Cardwell, *The Man Who Was Mark Twain*, 141–57, argues that Twain's "unusual attention to prepubescent girls" (141) began much earlier, and that "he and his protective circle transformed his pedophilia into a culture-approved, circumspect affection for children" (157). Martin, "Genie in the Bottle," 80–81. See also Dorothy Quick, *Enchantment: A Little Girl's Friendship with Mark Twain* (Norman: University of Oklahoma Press, 1961); also

Dorothy Quick, *Mark Twain & Me* (Norman: University of Oklahoma Press, 1999), made into a movie by Disney. Kaplan, *Mr. Clemens*, 381–82, adds a passage. Trites, *Twain, Alcott*, 19, is also relevant.

T. S. Eliot: "It would seem that Mark Twain was a man who—perhaps like most of us—never became in all respects mature. We might even say that the adult side of him was boyish, and that only the boy in him, that was Huck Finn, was adult." In Fishkin, *Mark Twain Anthology*, 236.

164 **newspaper or a church:** There is a fair amount of evidence that *Tom* and *Huck* had "bad reputations" at this point, part of a complicated (and very gendered) debate about libraries and decency. See Pearson, "The Children's Librarian versus Huckleberry Finn," 313: "The word has gone forth that these two books are to be condemned."

164 **"delights me and doesn't anger me":** Quoted in Hearn, *Annotated Huckleberry Finn*, cxxiii. Hearn collects other excellent examples: See cxxii–cxxvi.

164 **"for his parent's sake":** Quoted in Hearn, *Annotated Huckleberry Finn*, xiii. A nice summary of various *Huck*-related bannings and withdrawals during the first part of the twentieth century can be found in Blair, *Mark Twain and Huck Finn*, 3.

164 **"help believing in him":** Twain to Joel Chandler Harris, *Twain to Uncle Remus*, 20 (November 29, 1885).

164 **"privation, humiliation":** Blair and Fischer, *Huckleberry Finn* (Berkeley and Los Angeles: University of California Press, 1988), 806. Quoted in Hearn, *Annotated Huckleberry Finn*, xcvii.

164 **"more than one family":** Twain, "Eddypus," 191.

164 **Or grow up:** Lear, "Tom and Huck on Shelves," notes that many libraries, roughly four in ten, during this period still kept *Huck Finn* on their shelves—slightly less than those that stocked other Twain classics, like *The Prince and the Pauper* (see 190, 210–12). She also notes comparatively "low holding rates" in the South (215), and that *Huck* (and *Tom Sawyer*) are not really treated as "kids' books" until the turn of the century. By 1910, however, two-thirds of all libraries with children's sections stocked *Huck* on their shelves (203, 219).

164 **"not read to his daughter":** Quoted in Budd, *Our Mark Twain*, 6.

165 **"a kindred soul":** Quoted in Hearn, *Annotated Huckleberry Finn*, cxxx–cxxxi.

165 **"I'd be a kid again":** Quoted in Fishkin, *Lighting Out*, 139. Sheet music can be found at Barbara Wheeler, "The Soundtrack of Mark Twain," http://twain.lib.virginia.edu/projects/wheeler/wheeler.html.

165 **"riverboat scamps":** Hearn, *Annotated Huckleberry Finn*, cxxxii. Inge, "Mark Twain and the Comics," 30.

165 **"an epoch that will never return":** Halleck, *History*, 258.

165 **"chronicles of buoyant boyhood":** Quoted in Hearn, *Annotated Huckleberry Finn*, cxxxviii.

165 **Marlboro man for the preteen set:** See Andrew Erlandson, "Twain and Tobacco."

165 **barefoot, naturally:** Mark Twain, *Adventures of Huckleberry Finn*, illustrated by Richard M. Powers (New York: Doubleday, 1954).

166 **"fun watching them watching":** *Adventures of Huckleberry Finn*, director, Richard Thorpe (DVD, 1939, 2009). *Adventures of Huckleberry Finn*, director, Herbert B. Swope, Jr. (DVD, 1955, 2009).

166 **"all over welts":** *Adventures of Huckleberry Finn*, director, Peter H. Hunt (DVD, 1985, 2007). Twain, *Huck*, 30.

166 **a soporific for modern kids:** See, for instance, "Disney's 'Huck Finn': Whitewashed Twain," Hal Hinson, *Washington Post*, April 2, 1993, p. D1: "a bland, action-adventure film . . . Twain's Huck Finn has more in common with Bart Simpson than he does with this movie's tepid hero." *The Adventures of Huckleberry Finn*, directed by Stephen Sommers (DVD, 2002).

166 **as an "adventure story":** Peaches Henry, "The Struggle for Tolerance," 39. Quirk, "Flawed Greatness," is much recommended for his catalog of *Huck Finn*'s implausible plot points and character details.

167 **"than any that has gone before":** Again, Kutner and Olson are much recommended here. Comstock, *Traps*, 25. "A Crime Against American Children," *Ladies' Home Journal*, January 1909, quoted in Hajdu, *Ten-Cent*, 12. J. Hall, review of *Our Movie Made Children*, in *American Journal of Public Health* 23, no. 12 (December 1933), 1333–1334, quoted in Kutner and Olson, *Grand Theft Childhood*, 47. "Special Regulations on Crime in Motion Pictures," in Prince, *Classical Film Violence*, 302–3. *Comic Books and Juvenile Delinquency*, U.S. Senate Judiciary Committee subcommittee on juvenile delinquency, quoted in Kutner and Olson, *Grand Theft Childhood*, 50. Hoover, quoted in Hajdu, *Ten-Cent*, 84.

The debate about violent video games, and violent fantasy, is a complicated one. Jones, *Killing Monsters*, 23–36, disputes evidence making a link between violent fantasy and violent actions: "It's easy to fall into the trap of thinking that young people emulate literally what they see in entertainment" (11). He also references debates about television and comic books from the 1950s and '60s as analogues to contemporary debates, using the same historical perspective seen in much writing on children and culture (14). Strausbaugh cites a similar historical context to the same point, *Black Like You*, 324–27. Sax, *Boys Adrift*, argues that no evidence exists that "prohibiting violent play or imaginary violence . . . will decrease actual violence" (51). Tom's play fantasy in *Tom Sawyer* does not necessarily lead to actual violence, in other words; how interesting, then, that in *Huck Finn* it does.

168 **talking about the same book:** Clark, *Kiddie Lit*, chapter 4, especially 90–91, discusses the notion that *Tom Sawyer* and *Huck Finn* were canonized separately during the latter parts of the twentieth century: *Huck Finn* was allowed to become a "serious" book, and *Tom Sawyer* became known as a book for children, especially boys. Clark sees this happen as Twain's juvenile tendencies become canonized as the major point of attack on his work. She also includes early twentieth-century sales and library data to illustrate the relative popularity and cultural placement of both books, information

that can also be found in Lear, "Were Tom and Huck On-Shelf?" Clark, *Kiddie Lit*, also provides many examples of authors who make distinctions between the two books based on relatively arbitrary generic boundaries, citing, as example, T. S. Eliot calling *Tom Sawyer* a "boys' book" and *Huck Finn* "a book that boys enjoy," but not "juvenile fiction" (77). *Huck's* "greatness was constructed—and was constructed at the expense of a fundamental respect for childhood and children's literature" (101).

There is also another, more contemporary angle here to consider: what Leonard Sax calls "zero tolerance for violence" in "creative writing and language arts." Sax describes himself writing a short story influenced by the film *The Great Escape* for class "thirty-some years ago" and notes that "I've seen boys who write similar stories today referred for psychiatric evaluation" (*Boys Adrift*, 43). In this context, a reading of *Huckleberry Finn* that emphasized the violence in it, and its protagonist's capacity for violence, is potentially unworkable in school settings.

168 **serious reviews of books for children:** Clark, *Kiddie Lit*, 48–49, 55. See also Mintz, *Huck's Raft*, 186. Marcus, *Minders of Make-Believe*, 43. It is worth noting that the market for juvenile fiction around the time of the publication of both *Tom* and *Huck* was particularly "hot" in magazines, but Twain published early chapters from *Huck* in the *Century*, not a youth magazine by any stretch. (See Marcus, *Minders of Make-Believe*, 60.)

168 **professionalized the act of parenting:** Clark, *Kiddie Lit*, 16.

168 **career suicide:** Clark, *Kiddie Lit*, 71.

168 **the "sanctity" of which must be guarded:** Horace Scudder, *Childhood in Literature and Art*, 241, 245. Discussed in Clark, *Kiddie Lit*, 52–55.

168 **"savagery" before they became good adults:** Hall, *Adolescence*, x, 310, 311, 314, 315.

169 **"impulses of the African":** Warner, *Being a Boy*, 60.

169 **"shall invent a violent *game*":** Twain to Orion Clemens, July 21, 1883. Quoted in Wagner, *History Game*, 7. Jones, *Killing Monsters*, argues that "childhood gun play is universal" (48), and that "young people us(e) fantasies of combat . . . to fight their way through emotional challenges" (6). He quotes a seven-year-old saying to his psychiatrist father, "You know, Dad, you're always trying to turn me into someone who doesn't like violence. But the problem is . . . I do like violence" (62).

169 **designed to lie outside the system:** Trites, *Twain, Alcott*, 71, focuses on "the educational ideologies at work in Twain's and Alcott's novels that specifically employ adolescence to convey the ideology of education as a panacea." Obviously, I believe Twain was not entirely sold on such ideology. See also 78.

170 **powerful or authentic:** Clark, "Preface," *Tom Sawyer*, vii, alludes to this idea: "As the *Harry Potter* phenomenon once more erodes the boundaries between child and adult reading publics, and as children's literature is finding a place within the academy, *Tom Sawyer* is yet again repositioning itself." Chambers quoted in Clark, *Kiddie Lit*, 96. Morrison, "Introduction,"

xxxii, notes that Huck closes the "divide" between "books that academic critics find consistently rewarding" and the "minds of young readers." She also praises the book for its "convincing commentary on adult behavior."

171 *"children stood a chance"*: Twain, *Huck*, 186. See Sax, *Boys Adrift*, 5–6: "Haven't boys always been that way? . . . There's a long tradition of iconic American boys who disdain school, from Tom Sawyer to Ferris Bueller."

Trites, *Twain, Alcott*, 144–45, 160, makes important contributions here, arguing that Twain and Alcott helped shape the idea of "adolescents as metaphors for social change," a figure that is prominent in *Harry Potter*, *The Hunger Games*, and many other conspicuously successful young adult books—"Huck Finn's progeny." She also stresses "the protagonist's isolation as he or she faces exploitation at the hands of corrupt adults or confronts the hostility of an intolerant society," "vernacular style," and "narrator who was also an adolescent."

Ferris Bueller's Day Off, directed by John Hughes (DVD, 2006). *Home Alone*, directed by Chris Columbus (DVD, 1990, 1999). *Spy Kids*, directed by Robert Rodriguez (DVD, 2001). *Harry Potter and the Order of the Phoenix*, directed by David Yates (DVD, 2007). Jeff Kinney, *Diary of a Wimpy Kid* (New York: Amulet Books, 2007). There are others, of course. M. T. Anderson and Kurt Cyrus (illustrator), *Zombie Mommy: A Pals in Peril Tale* (New York: Beach Lane Books, 2012, reprint). Suzanne Collins, *Hunger Games Trilogy* (New York: Scholastic Books, 2013). J. K. Rowling, *Special Edition Harry Potter Box Set* (New York: Scholastic Books, 2013).

171 **the contours of Twain's moral vision:** The best statements of this sentiment can be found in Clark, *Kiddie Lit*, who suggests that appreciating Twain's work in this way can help us "rethink" his "achievements." "Huck's defenders," she notes, "are rarely willing to accept the claim that the book might be a boys' book" (76, 99). Trites, *Twain, Alcott*, xii: "I have not yet found anyone who has investigated the factors that led both Twain and Alcott to write about adolescence in ways that are informed by their reform impulses." See Margolis, "Consequences," 329–31. Margolis focuses on the idea of "effects," and summarizes leading recent efforts to explore the value, both positive and negative, of canonizing *Huck Finn*.

171 *Lost Boys*: A common trope in "boys' advice" books around the turn of the twenty-first century. See Mary Pipher, foreword, in Pollack, *Real Boys*, xvii: "I do believe our culture is doing a bad job raising boys. The evidence is in the shocking violence of Paducah, Jonesboro, Cheyenne, and Edinboro. It's in our overcrowded prisons and domestic violence shelters . . ." Kindlon and Thompson, *Raising Cain*, vii. Garbarino, *Lost Boys*, ix, 2, describes "1997–1998" as "the turning point" in recognition of this problem. Kutner and Olson, *Grand Theft Childhood*, examine this trope somewhat critically (5–8).

171 **a "daring" one for girls:** See Kidd, *Making American Boys*, 167–90, for analysis of recent books on boys. Such concerns also fill magazine pages with ease: see, for instance, Tom Chiarella, "The Trouble With Boys/The

Trouble With Men," *Esquire* 161, nos. 6 & 7 (June-July 2014): 108–17, 140. "8 years later," the cover warns us, "the boy crisis in America is only accelerating."

172 **looking forward and going backward:** Hulbert, *Raising America*, 7, writes that "ambivalence, in fact, has been the secret of their appeal," and notes the "unexpected continuity in the child-rearing confusions that have accompanied industrial America's surge into secular, urbanized maturity . . ."

172 **like they "used to":** See Tulley and Spiegler, *50 Dangerous Things*, for instance: "dangerous" things include "Stick[ing] Your Hand Out the Window" (10–11), "Driv[ing] a Nail" (14–15), "Throw[ing] Rocks" (22–23), "Mak[ing] a Slingshot" (54–55), "Climb[ing] a Tree" (56–57).

172 **That essential formula . . . about to change:** Pollack, *Real Boys*, 6, 52–64. Pollack recommends "talk[ing] openly" about the "boy code" as an essential development (106–8). He also notes the danger in its entrenchment in the school system (232).

172 **a ghostly icon:** Kidd, *Making American Boys*, 168, 175, 177, 183, 185. Mintz, *Huck's Raft*, 1, 5. Garbarino, *Lost Boys*, 4. See also Sax, *Boys Adrift*, 5–6. Kidd in fact observes that "debate about Twain's place in the culture and the canon, alongside a residual faith in boyology, helped establish *Huck Finn* as a masterwork" (19). See also 50–51, 81–83. Kidd notes that negative accounts of Twain's failings allude to his juvenility as much as positive appraisals speak of his ability to understand children. See, for instance, Brooks, *Ordeal of Mark Twain*, 14, where he refers to Twain's "arrested development." On 176–77, Brooks also notes that "Twain . . . instinctively wrote for children," and delivered "happiness . . . the green, luxuriant shoots clustering on the stump of some gigantic tree which has been felled close to the ground." Kaplan, *Mr. Clemens*, 18: "He remained, in many ways, a child demanding attention in a nursery which was as large as the world . . ."

172 **"student-centered" school:** Hulbert, *Raising America*, 23–27, briefly discusses the history of "child-centered" thinking predating the Victorian era. See also Cuban, *How Teachers Taught*, 7.

172 **re-naturing and re-dangering books:** Which those authors know. See Louv, *Last Child in the Woods*: "Can you remember the wonder you felt when first reading *The Jungle Book* or *Tom Sawyer* or *Huckleberry Finn*? Kipling's world within a world; Twain's slow river, the feel of freedom and sand on the secret island, and in the depths of the cave? Environmental educators and activists repeatedly mention nature books as important childhood influences" (166). See also Christy M. Moroye and Benjamin C. Ingman, "Ecological Mindedness Across the Curriculum," *Curriculum Inquiry* 43, no. 5 (2013), 598–99, for a concrete example of a curricular approach.

172 **systems divided by race, by class:** See Garbarino, *Lost Boys*, 5, for a brief discussion illustrating the resilience of this two-tiered image of American childhood divided by both race and class. Sax, *Boys Adrift*, sees a movement where boys' problems are beginning to transcend race and class (7).

172 **the pixilated slaughters they instigate:** Jones, *Killing Monsters*, discusses several studies measuring the level of exposure of children to images of violence (54–55).

173 **students connected with nature:** See Louv, *Last Child in the Woods*.

173 **one-ninth its previous size:** Louv, *Last Child in the Woods*, writes that, in the last "two to three decades," "the shift in our relationship to the natural world is startling"(2). See also Sax, *Boys Adrift*, 30. Doig, "Unleash Our Kids," and Asthana and Revill, "Is It Time?," are typical of the public debate. See also Hillman, *One False Move*, for what appears to be the seminal study on this issue, and which also has much to say about nostalgia for a lost, freer childhood.

173 **copying others when he did so:** William Dean Howells, writing about Thomas Bailey Aldrich's *The Story of a Bad Boy* in 1870, celebrated the "realism" of its portrait of childhood as an antidote to excessive mythologizing (Howells, revised edition of *The Story of A Bad Boy* by Thomas Bailey Aldrich, *Atlantic Monthly*, January 1870, 124. Quoted in Jacobson, *Being a Boy*, 1, Mailloux, *Rhetorical Power*, 111–12). In May 1876, he wrote similarly about *Tom Sawyer* for the *Atlantic*: "The story is a wonderful study of the boy-mind . . ." (Quoted in Jacobson, *Being a Boy*, 44). Clark, *Kiddie Lit*, quotes several critics making similar comments, such as H. W. Boynton in the *Atlantic* in 1903 (89): "A boy . . . will devour tales like *Tom Sawyer* or *Huckleberry Finn*, though he cannot understand their real merit as studies of boy-character." Such formulations, as Clark states, imply that adults are the true audience.

   Mintz, *Huck's Raft*, describes among the "goals of [his] book . . . to strip away the myths, misconceptions, and nostalgia that contribute to this pessimism about the young" (vii). It is a common aspiration in contemporary writing about children. Pollack, *Real Boys*, author's note, similarly references his "ongoing 'Listening to Boys' Voices' research project at Harvard Medical School"—a project the existence of which implies we are listening to myths more than reality when we regard our children. Garbarino, *Lost Boys*, describing his interviews: "Virtually every boy said that he had never before told his *whole* story to anyone" (x). He makes references to "real-life boys" as well (26). Paley, in *A Child's Work*, tells us that "we must begin, again, to watch and to listen to the children" (3).

174 **they need to be "sivilize[d]":** Twain, *Huck*, 1, 31, 362. On 2–3, very early in the book, Huck is consistently chastised for being unable to sit still or focus on his studies.

174 **the chance for expression:** Erin White, "Diagnosis of ADHD on the Rise," Northwestern.edu, March 19, 2012, http://www.northwestern.edu /newscenter/stories/2012/03/adhd-diagnosis-pediatrics.html. Nylund, *Treating Huckleberry Finn*, is undoubtedly the most detailed work on the link, at least symbolic, between *Huck Finn* and ADHD. See foreword by Gene Combs, ix–xi; preface, xiii–xvi, 3–12, 27–28, 43, 44, 69, 89, 107, 129, 135, 154–57, 185–86, 209–19. Nylund argues that, were he alive

today, Huck would almost certainly be diagnosed with ADHD. *Treating Huckleberry Finn*, however, recommends "narrative approach[es]" to treatment, even presenting imaginary interviews with Huck and his caregivers, and using Huck's famous nonconformity as sanction: "Join me on Huck's Mississippi River raft for the next part of the journey: challenging the idea that ADHD is a biological disorder" (12). Much recommended. See also Lawrence Diller, *Running on Ritalin* (New York: Bantam, 1998): he also acknowledges that Huck would be diagnosed. Richters and Cicchetti, "Mark Twain Meets DSM-III-R." Applebaum, "ADHD-ventures," and "Tom Sawyer and Today's Children: Same Behavior, Different Treatment," *Washington Post*, August 2, 2010, http://www.washingtonpost.com/wp-dyn /content/article/2010/08/09/AR2010080904868.html. See also Monica G. Young, "Would Tom Sawyer and Huck Finn Have Been Diagnosed Mentally Ill and Drugged?" *Natural News*, September 1, 2011, http://www .cchrint.org/2011/09/01/would-tom-sawyer-and-huck-finn-be-diagnosed -mentally-ill-and-drugged/. Vonnegut, *Just Like Someone Without Mental Illness Only More So: A Memoir* (New York: Bantam, 2011), 201. Also Natalie Angier, "Debilitating Malady."

175 *classification* as the catch-all cure: Nylund, *Treating*, 13. Mintz, *Huck's Raft*, 5. Concerns that children are overdiagnosed and overmedicated for ADD/ADHD are commonplace. See Pollack, *Real Boys*, 253–62, Sax, *Boys Adrift*, 79–97, among others. Students are particularly trenchant on this point: for instance, Cassidy Olson, "Huckleberry Cured."

175 in a bank or a courthouse: Political biographies of the era, critic Larzer Ziff reminds us, provided their protagonists a bad-boy childhood as if it were a prerequisite for office. Ziff, *All-American*, 38. Peck, *Peck's Bad Boy*, "A Card From the Author." Jacobson, in *Being a Boy*, makes this crucial point: "In presenting a text that could be used as a blueprint for educators, the boy book explicitly served the needs of a developing capitalistic society" (16). *Huck Finn*, I am arguing, only flirts with that kind of service.

175 access to firearms: Child psychologist Robert Zagar provides four markers that double the risk that a child will sometime commit murder: Huck, from a family with a criminal legacy, abused by his father, a "gang" member and drug user (if we substitute smoking for drug use, a reasonable Victorian-for-Postmodern substitution), shows all four. Zagar also provides four markers that *triple* the risk that a child will commit murder: Huck, who uses a weapon, who has been brought before the law, who misses school regularly, shows three of four, at minimum (more if we diagnose him, and let's not, with a "neurological problem"). Zagar and his colleagues' work is cited in Garbarino, *Lost Boys*, 10. Garbarino also cites work by Michael Rutter that shows that "for a boy to be separated from his mother in infancy and early childhood is a very significant risk factor for future development" (47). Huck's mother is clearly absent, and we have few clues dating that absence. Contrarily, as Garbarino notes, most abused children do not become violent. Huck does show some of the more troubling markers of an

abused child: he does, for instance, "draw the conclusion that aggression is a successful way" of getting what one wants (81). But rather than practicing it himself, he merely notes that it works for others. Rather, Huck is an example of the "resilience" of abused children, a resilience often "linked to a compensatory relationship"—in his case, his friendship with Jim (82–83). Kindlon and Thompson, *Raising Cain*, also note the role of a mentor, even citing Twain on the subject (97). Garbarino also notes "spiritual anchors," "intelligence," and "androgyny" as factors contributing to resiliency (154–57, 165–67, 169–70). These also factor in Huck's personality. Lastly, Garbarino notes that "maltreatment" of a child will lead to "survival strategies" that are "antisocial and/or self-destructive" (217). Kindlon and Thompson, *Raising Cain*, note the prevalence of "harsh, inconsistent discipline" in youth among adult criminals (69). All applicable to Huck.

175 **"so lonesome"**: Twain, *Huck*, 4. At-risk children with suicidal ideation, sociologists note, sometimes choose conflict with the law as a manifestation of that self-destructive impulse—what is called "suicide by cop." Huck's decision to help free Jim—to make himself an abolitionist in a time and place where abolitionists faced jail time and tar and feathering—has many motives. But one of them could certainly be that it speaks to his desire to die—that it is "suicide by lynch mob." See Kindlon and Thompson, *Raising Cain*, 174. Prioleau, "Abused Child." See also Jose Barchilon, M.D., and Joel S. Kovel, M.D., "*Huckleberry Finn*: A Psychoanalytic Study," *Journal of the American Psychoanalytic Association* 14 (1966), 775–814. Timothy M. Rivinus and Brian W. Ford, "Children of Alcoholics in Literature: Portraits of the Struggle," *Dionysos: The Literature and Intoxication Triquarterly* 1 (1990): 15–18. Timmen L. Cermak, M.D., "Huck and I," in *A Time to Heal: The Road to Recovery for Adult Children of Alcoholics* (New York: Avon, 1988), 1–8. Sources found in Prioleau's documentation. Also strongly recommended is Donohue-Smith, "Failed Families," and Kiskis, "Family Values," who both talk about the use of *Huck Finn* in social science classes as "case study."

176 **refused to choose**: Twain had a split in his mind about Huck, but it wasn't this split. On the one hand, he saw a particular child. There were kids like him all across the frontier, independent and unschooled, and the fact that they knew violence and innocence at once was a fact of life, and nothing more: "At two o'clock in the morning a highway Robber was hung on a large pine tree. After breakfast we went to see him. At ten o'clock preaching . . . at two o'clock Sunday school. At three o'clock a foot race . . . ," wrote one twelve-year-old girl from Helena, Montana, in her diary in 1865. Quoted in West, "Heathens," 379. On the other, he was thinking something anthemic about children in general—and part of the beauty of the portrait is the way he balanced the general and the particular.

176 **intriguing in-betweens**: Twain, *Autobiography*, vol. 1, 315–16, quotes favorably a letter where a man describes "instructing . . . persuading . . . preparing" his son to "vote against me when he comes of age." "It seemed to me

that this unlettered man was at least a wise one." Opdahl, "You'll Be Sorry," discusses the chain of scholars (Robert Regan, Eric Solomon, Ray B. Browne) who have discussed the role of antagonism toward father figures in *Huck*.

176 **a big part of the reason why:** Garbarino, *Lost Boys*, 1–2, makes a point especially crucial here: that, in the modern era, and until the late 1990s, boys associated with violence as perpetrators or victims were minorities. The spate of high-profile mass murders committed by white, suburban or rural children altered this perception. Huck Finn scrambles these categories: that familiar freckled figure in a straw hat looks very white and rural, but his Irishness and association with Jim suggests that he is not as "white" as he looks.

176 **song lyrics from earlier decades:** *Mark Twain in Eruption*, 110. Pettit, *Mark Twain and the South*, 138.

176 **troubling retrograde intensity:** *Mark Twain in Eruption*, 110. See Wonham, *Playing*, 95, 99–100, for discussions of Twain's remarks. Lott, "Twain, Race, and Blackface," 129. Pettit, *Mark Twain and the South*, 127, 129, 130, describes Twain's ongoing use of "nigger jokes" even after his "de-Southernization."

176 **"troubles out of my mind":** Quoted in Martin, "Genie in the Bottle," 60. See also Quirk, *Coming to Grips*, 79.

177 **"white folks ain't partic'lar":** Twain, *Pudd'nhead Wilson*, 32, 216.

177 **terrifyingly out of place:** Twain, *Mysterious Stranger*, especially 353–56. See McCoy, "Minstrel Mask," and Wonham, "Mark Twain's Last Cakewalk." Twain's reimagining of minstrelsy in *The Mysterious Stranger* is remarkable, and these two articles are essential reading.

177 **"princes toward the slaves":** Twain, "Eddypus," 182, 203. Twain never let go of the Harris–Uncle Remus connection he had made earlier. In 1906, he described "Uncle Remus" as still alive and "over a thousand years old," and described how he had told Susy and Clara during a visit to Hartford that Harris "was the real Uncle Remus whitewashed so that he could come into people's houses the front way." "The sweetness and benignity of the immortal Remus looked out from his eyes, and the graces and sincerities of his character shone in his face" (*Mark Twain in Eruption*, "Jim Wolf and the Wasps," 136). Either Uncle Remus had taken possession of Harris, or Harris had eaten Uncle Remus.

Cardwell, *The Man Who Was Mark Twain*, 207–12, works extensively with the idea of "inversion topos" (208) in Twain's later works: "Clemens entertained with some seriousness the idea of a frightening social reversal, a white-black reversal being the one at once most solidly based in history and the most dramatic" (207).

See also Pettit, *Mark Twain and the South*, 157, 168–73. See also Subryan, "Black Challenge," 99–100.

177 **until after his death:** "The United States of Lyncherdom," Twain, *Collected Tales, 1891–1910*, 479–86. See, for instance, Kaplan, *Mr. Clemens*, 365, Loving, *Mark Twain*, 286, Mensh, *Black, White*, 76. Cardwell, *The Man*

Who Was Mark Twain, 207. Pettit, *Mark Twain and the South*, 136. Budd, *Social Philosopher*, 201.

177 **"ALL WHITE MEN"**: Twain, "Stupendous Procession," in Zwick, *Weapons*, 56. Quoted in Wieck, *Refiguring*, 17.

177 **"Tom Sawyer of the political world"**: Budd, *Social Philosopher*, 186. Kaplan, *Mr. Clemens*, 363. Fishkin, *Lighting Out*, 66. McFarland, *Mark Twain and the Colonel*, 424. On 423–26, McFarland argues that Twain was somewhat unfair and hypocritical in his criticisms of Roosevelt. He also notes that Roosevelt once threatened to skin Twain alive, for remarks he made about missionaries (424).

178 **"new freedom away from him"**: Twain, "To the Person Sitting in Darkness," in *Collected Tales, 1891–1910*, 467. To be clear, the "person sitting in darkness" thinks this aloud, but it is a thin veil over Twain's own opinion. Schmidt, *Sitting in Darkness*, 141–44, believes this veil complicates Twain's opinion. Budd, *Our Mark Twain*, 173–78, discusses the reception to this essay, which was largely critical, but not particularly damaging to Twain's outsized fame. Budd, *Social Philosopher*, 177, 179, describes the recommendations of Twain's friends. Williamson, *Crucible of Race*, 109, writes: "It is, indeed, one of the great ironies of American history that when the nation freed the slaves, it also freed racism." In my reading, Twain recognized this new wave of racism and its relationship to newly free, politically empowered blacks.

Zwick, "Prodigally Endowed," argues that Twain was "the country's most outspoken opponent of the Philippine-American War" (3, 6), and observes that this part of his profile was "quickly forgotten" in the years after his death (3).

178 **no longer be touched**: Zwick, *Weapons*, xxxvi.

178 **we now call waterboarding**: See Zwick, *Weapons*, xxix–xxv.

178 **"rope for a keepsake"**: Twain, *Following the Equator*, 710.

178 **"back to my boyhood"**: Twain, *Following the Equator*, 351.

178 **he couldn't believe it**: Robinson, *In Bad Faith*, 8: "Mark Twain observes that the chains cast off by Lincoln have been reforged in Cuba and the Philippines."

178 **"*worse form of slavery right in Africa*"**: Twain, *King Leopold*, 10. See also *King Leopold's Soliloquy, Collected Tales, 1891–1910*, 666–67. The first part of the quote is in Leopold's voice; the second, from a " 'Report' by W. M. Morrison, American missionary" that he reads aloud. Andrew Carnegie paid for a reprint: See Budd, *Social Philosopher*, 177. Subryan, "Black Challenge," 101. Robinson, *In Bad Faith*, 8, notes a similar dynamic present in "To the Person Sitting in Darkness." See also 224: "Mark Twain . . . identif[ies] American slavery and the contemporary outbreak of imperial oppression as the premier expressions of the lie of silent assertion." Pettit, *Mark Twain and the South*, 134–35, suggests that Twain was "almost alone among white antiimperialists [*sic*]" in making this link.

179 **"preventing of the repetitions impossible"**: The cartoon can be seen in Budd, *Social Philosopher*, between 178 and 179: See, for instance, Twain, "Eddypus," 189–90. Salomon discusses "Eddypus" extensively in *Mark Twain and the Image of History*. For Salomon, "Eddypus" is only one of several late-in-life works that highlights Twain's interest in cyclical theories of history and his willingness to entertain pessimism about the future. These include *Letters from the Earth*, "History One Hundred Years from Now," and some remarkable pieces of writing contained in Bernard DeVoto's edited *Mark Twain in Eruption*, including the one cited in this paragraph: "It is not worth while to try to keep history from repeating itself, for man's character will always make the preventing of the repetitions impossible. Whenever man makes a large stride in material prosperity and progress he is sure to think that *he* has progressed, whereas he has not advanced an inch; nothing has progressed but his circumstances. *He* stands where he stood before. He knows more than his forebears knew but his intellect is no better . . . [F]rom time to time he makes what looks like a real change in his character but it is not a real change; and it is only transitory anyway . . ." *Mark Twain in Eruption*, "Purchasing Public Virtue," 66–67. See Salomon, *Mark Twain and the Image of History*, 33–50. See also "Theodore Roosevelt," in *Mark Twain in Eruption*, 2: "History repeats itself; whatever has been the rule in history may be depended upon to remain the rule."

Segal, "Life Without Father," makes the point that criticism of the ending of the book has much to do with the fact that the characters seem to unlearn learned experiences. In this regard, Twain's vision of childhood and adulthood, and history, blend in a remarkable way.

179 **"the most dreaded critic"**: Quoted in Zwick, *Weapons*, xix. See Fishkin, *Mark Twain Anthology*, xxi. See also Lao She, from "Mark Twain: Exposer of the 'Dollar Empire,'" in Fishkin, *Mark Twain Anthology*, 283–88.

179 **even temporal boundaries**: Hsu, "Sitting in Darkness," 71.

179 **"the first, if not the only"**: Howells, "Mark Twain: An Inquiry," 311.

179 **"Huckleberry Finn Cake Walk"**: Also called "Huckleberry Finn Cake Walk Two-Step." Sheet music can be found at: http://library.duke.edu/ruben stein/scriptorium/sheetmusic/b/b05/b0542/.

180 **"the masses of the Negro people"**: Booker T. Washington, "Tributes to Mark Twain," *North American Review* 191, no. 655 (June 1910), 828–30. See Fishkin, *Was Huck Black?*, 105–6.

180 *Invisible Man*: Ellison, *Invisible Man*, 187–88. See also Fishkin, *Mark Twain Anthology*, xix, quoting Sterling Brown in 1937 praising Huck Finn for showing "the callousness of the South to the Negro."

180 **reputation of the South**: Charles Neider, *Mark Twain and the Russians: An Exchange of Views* (New York: Hill and Wang, 1960), 19–20.

181 **"moral testing and development"**: Trilling, "Huckleberry Finn," 113. Arac, *Idol and Target*, 118–32.

181 **"Huck Finn moment[s]"**: Jonathan Arac, *Idol and Target*, 6. John Garvey

and Noel Ignatiev, "Toward a New Abolitionism: A Race Traitor Manifesto," in *Whiteness: A Critical Reader,* edited by Mike Hill (New York: New York University Press, 1997), 349.

181 **"what America is all about"**: Arthur Schlesinger, "The Opening of the American Mind," *New York Times Book Review,* July 23, 1989, 1, 26–27. Quoted in Arac, *Idol and Target,* 18. See also 121–22.

181 **"in the end he succeeds"**: Quoted in Arac, *Idol and Target,* 105: Arac refers to "Reagan's inaccurate summary."

181 **"Huckleberry Capone"**: The number of American (and international) political figures that have said something about *Huck Finn* is significant, and revealing. Leonard and Tenney, "Introduction," *Satire or Evasion,* 1, cite a 1989 survey of American governors asked to name their favorite book: twelve respond *Huck,* ten respond *Tom Sawyer,* the top two answers. Dwight Eisenhower called Twain the most influential author he had ever read, Harry Truman claimed to have read all his books "several times over," and Franklin Roosevelt, who named the "New Deal" after the reforms the Connecticut Yankee brought to King Arthur's Court, once wrote that he was "fortunate" to have read Twain. *Mark Twain and Harry S. Truman,* foreword by Louis Johnson, 1950, 9. *Mark Twain and Dwight D. Eisenhower,* foreword by Winston Churchill, 1953, 13. These books are all published as a series by the International Mark Twain Society, Webster Groves, Missouri. "Huckleberry Capone" quoted in Jeff Shesol, *Mutual Contempt: Lyndon Johnson, Robert Kennedy, and the Feud That Defined a Decade* (New York: W. W. Norton and Company), 1997, 363: "IF THIS KEEPS UP YOU JUST MAY HAVE TO DUMP OLD HUCKLEBERRY CAPONE . . . LOVE AND KISSES AND GOOD WORK," wrote Ethel Kennedy to Robert Kennedy, February 1967. John F. Kennedy also called him "Riverboat" (107), and Arthur Schlesinger observed that JFK regarded Johnson as a "Mark Twain character."

  Mention here should be made of Harry Truman. See Arac, *Idol and Target,* 4, 6, 110–11. That the president of the United States during the period of *Huck's* ascension to "great American novel" was from Missouri, spoke with a touch of a drawl, and displayed a commitment to civil rights (as well as the casual use of racial slurs) is striking.

181 **"matters of slavery and race"**: Robinson, *In Bad Faith,* 118. See also 119, which is better: "*Huckleberry Finn* continues to be our favorite story about slavery and race because it gives us no more of this reality than we can bear."

181 **"minstrel-show stuff"**: Blair, *Mark Twain and Huck Finn,* 348–49.

181 **"the rest is just cheating"**: Hemingway, *Green Hills of Africa,* 22. DeVoto, *Mark Twain at Work,* 92, writes: "In the whole reach of the English novel there is no more abrupt or more chilling descent." Marx, "Mr. Trilling," 440, 439. He wonders how much worse it might have been if Twain had included the elephant scenes he had envisioned in his notes. Doyno, *Writing Huck Finn,* 221–26, does a good quick summary of the outlines of this familiar controversy. Chadwick-Joshua, *Jim Dilemma,* 4–8, focuses on

characterizations of Jim. As does Oehlschlaeger, "'Gwyne to Git Hung,'" 117–18.

182 **not running from it:** In the *Buffalo Huck Finn*, MS0953: in the first draft of Huck's famous soliloquy about freeing Jim in chapter 31, he tells the reader that he will miss "talking" and being "glad" in Jim's presence. In the last draft—the one available to readers for over a century—Huck says he will also miss Jim's "singing + laughing." In so doing, Twain exchanges a line where Huck will miss Jim's companionship with one where he will also miss Jim's comic and musical value—or the songs and jokes they can make together. Of course, most of these songs and jokes remain offstage, like much of what Twain does with the minstrel show in his novel.

183 **"out of touch":** Jay B. Hubbell, in *The South in American Literature, 1607–1900*, quoted in Schmitz, "Mark Twain's Civil War," 79.

183 **"choir loft" in Oberlin:** A further issue to examine is the relative heterogeneity of those audiences. As Karen Sotiropoulos notes (*Staging Race*, 6, 46–47, 64–66, 195), theaters during this period had different levels that separated class and race from one another, and "theater critics often identified where, as well as when, laughter and applause erupted . . . and were particularly attentive to moments when black audiences in the balcony laughed but whites remained silent." There is next to no example of such theatrical criticism during the "Twins of Genius"; rather, most reviews described uniformly cultivated audiences, with occasional references to children or teens. But both Twain and Cable were adept at describing applause and laughter in terms that implied it was dynamic, that it moved around the hall in interesting ways.

In the one exception, as Cable describes it (Turner, *Cable*, 181–82), he is onstage, performing a line in black dialect: "I feared you gwine fo'git it, boss." During the "death-like stillness which always reigns in the house just then, a black man, sitting behind me in a sort of choir loft all alone & in sight of every one" simply laughed, and "brought down the house." Cable sees disruption, but he barely hints at derision. He provides his own explanation for why the man laughed: he "recognize[d] the mimicked African enunciation and the old southern title of respect," and "let go a suppressed but loud titter of the purest Ethiopian character." The house was brought down, according to Cable, because of the laugh's "character as well as its irrelevancy." Lastly, he notes, without explanation, that "it rather helped than hindered me."

183 **notice or acknowledge:** Bercovitch, "What's Funny About 'Huckleberry Finn,'" 16.

183 **Huck doesn't call him that even once:** Tally, "Bleeping," 103.

183 ***Amos 'n Andy* from their airwaves:** Strausbaugh, *Black Like You*, 227–28. Kennedy, *Nigger*, 131–33. Taylor and Austen, *Darkest America*, 160, suggest that mediocre ratings had much to do with the cancellation, and point out that the show appeared in syndication as late as 1966.

183 **the wrong thing to do:** Henry, "The Struggle for Tolerance," 25–29, dis-

cusses *Brown v. Board of Education* and many of the 1960s–1980s controversies over the book. Different sources provide different figures for the number of times the n-word appears in the novel. Some say 213; some say 215; some say other numbers. For instance, Carey-Webb, "Racism and *Huckleberry Finn*," 23–24, says 213. Kennedy, *Nigger* (109), says 215. Fulton, *Ethical Realism*, 56, says 213. Arac, *Idol and Target*, 20, says 213. And so on.

183 **"passages derogatory to negroes"**: Boskin, *Sambo*, 202–4, describes successful NAACP protests in the 1950s. Mensh, *Black, White*, 3–4, 7, places the New York City ban in historical context. As does Arac, *Idol and Target*, 63–67.

184 **"real and historical"**: Ryan, "Black Genes," 188, describes the tendency to "imagine the possibilities for white heroism by condensing racial politics into a single, decisive gesture." Arac is vital here, pouncing on the idea that the period of *Huck*'s canonization, the late 1940s and early 1950s, overlapped with a period where much white opinion focused on the idea that racism had been defeated. He quotes Trilling: "Americans have spiritually solved any problems involved in blacks and whites living together as free human beings, and we had done so already by the 1880s; all that remains is to work out the details." He also quotes (12) Elizabeth Hardwick, in the *Partisan Review* in 1948. See Elizabeth Hardwick, "Faulkner and the South Today," in *Faulkner: A Collection of Critical Essays*, edited by Robert Penn Warren (Englewood Cliffs, NJ: Prentice-Hall, 1966), 229: it is fairly amazing.

184 **"I been there before"**: Twain, *Huck*, 362. Fishkin distills a wonderful quote from David Bradley on this point, in *Lighting Out*, 202–3: "A lot of snooty academics have spent a lot of time and wasted a lot of journal ink criticizing the end of *Huckleberry Finn* . . . but I notice none of them has been able to suggest, much less write, a better ending. Twain actually tried—and failed. They all failed for the same reason that Twain wrote the ending he did. America has never been able to write a better ending. America has never been able to write any ending at all."

185 **"the greatest of all American novels"**: Ellison, "Change the Joke," 50. Allen, "Two Generations of Pain." Ballard, in *Interracial Books for Children Bulletin* 15, nos. 1–2 (1984), 11. Also "What *Huck Finn* Says to a Black Child," letter to the editor, *New York Times*, May 9, 1982. Quoted in Mensh, *Black, White*, 108; Henry, "Struggle for Tolerance," 29.

Ellison and the issue of minstrelsy in *Huck Finn* deserve further review. In *Shadow and Act*'s second essay, "Twentieth-Century Fiction and the Black Mask of Humanity," he describes *Huck Finn* as a "great classic," and particularly praises Twain for his portrayal of Jim, the escaping slave, as "a symbol of humanity," "ambiguous, limited in circumstance but not in possibility" (Ellison, "Twentieth-Century," 30–32). In the book's third essay, however, "Change the Joke and Slip the Yoke," Ellison's evaluation of Twain's portrayal of Jim shifts: "Twain fitted Jim into the outlines of the minstrel tradition," Ellison writes. While observing that "Jim's dignity and human capacity—and Twain's complexity—emerge" from "behind this stereotype mask," Ellison still concludes that "certainly it upsets a Negro reader" (Ellison, "Change the Joke," 50).

Interestingly, the first essay was written in 1946, and the second in 1958. Ellison's preface to the first essay suggests that he wants this difference acknowledged: "I've left in much of the bias and shortsightedness . . . I'd like to see an editorial note stating that this is an unpublished piece written not long after the Second World War . . ." (Ellison, "Twentieth-Century," 24). What happened between 1946 and 1958 might help explain Ellison's recognition: *Brown v. Board of Education* was 1954; the first banning of *Huck Finn* on account of race took place in 1957; the "minstrel show," as Joseph Boskin has described, was "lowered into [its] cultural grave" around "1955" (Boskin, *Sambo*, 3) by successful NAACP lawsuits and other political actions. By the time Ellison published "Change the Joke and Slip the Yoke" in the *Partisan Review*, in other words, the split narrative of *Huck Finn*'s race sensibility was already under way, and Ellison's ambivalence was a fierce, brilliant straddle, one that said as much about the 1950s as the 1880s.

In a later section of "Change the Joke," he continues to speak about minstrel performers, but his voice switches to the present tense, as if to place the impulse and achievement of that first generation of minstrels in a continuum with their late twentieth-century descendents: "When the white man steps behind the mask," Ellison writes," his freedom is circumscribed by the fear that he is not simply miming a personification of his disorder and chaos but that he will become in fact that which he intends only to symbolize; that he will be trapped somewhere in the mystery of hell . . . and thus lose that freedom which, in the fluid, 'traditionless,' 'classless' and rapidly changing society, he would recognize as the white man's alone" (Ellison, "Change the Joke," 53).

Ostensibly, Ellison wrote "Change the Joke" in response to Stanley Hyman's essay in the same issue of the *Partisan Review*, in which Hyman argued that the "darky entertainer" was a positive African-American folkloric character, one descended from the subversive "trickster" of Africa and antebellum America. But the essay's publication occurred within one year of the publication of Jack Kerouac's *On the Road*, which was merely the best-selling Beat text to contain outright "black envy," in Susan Gubar's words, as well as the appearance of Norman Mailer's "The White Negro" in *Dissent* (Gubar, *Racechanges*, 184). Noting also Ellison's vituperative commentary on American popular music of the Elvis and post-Elvis eras (he referred to "commercial rock-and-roll music" as "a brutalization of one stream of contemporary Negro church music" [Ellison, "Some Questions," 269]), it becomes clear that Ellison saw the intense fascination of white intellectuals and artists of his time with black culture as continuous with the work of nineteenth-century minstrels. Responding to being called insufficiently "ferocious" by Irving Howe, Ellison wrote that Howe came "in blackface" (Ellison, "The World," 110–11), attempting to dictate the terms of what constituted genuine African-American literary expression: "One of the most insidious crimes occurring in this democracy," Ellison argued, solidly in present tense at this point, "is that of designating another, politically weaker, less socially acceptable, people as the receptacle for one's own self-disgust, for one's own infantile rebellion, for one's own fears of, and retreats from, reality" (Ellison, "The World," 124).

185 **white rappers and pop stars do now:** Ross, *No Respect*, chapter 3, recommended here.

185 **cross-dressing to anthropology lectures:** Budd, *Our Mark Twain*, 88, has a great line about the book: "Despite close study of *Adventures of Huckleberry Finn* we know little about how Twain hoped it would strike the hodgepodge of publics he was acquiring." Twain's intent is always very hard to find, in part, precisely because he had audiences, not an audience. Knoper, *Acting Naturally*, 1, reminds us that a variety of performance forms are present in *Huck Finn*: "Yankee monologuists . . . Shakespearian actors, from P. T. Barnum to lecturing mesmerists and mediums." See also Scharnhorst and Trombley, " 'Who Killed Mark Twain,' " 225, citing Ron Powers and *Dangerous Water* on "pastiche."

185 **the most popular form of entertainment . . . century:** Lott, *Love and Theft*, 4.

186 **fifteen minutes on YouTube:** See Bean et al., *Inside the Minstrel Mask*, or Rice and Lhamon, *Jim Crow, American*, and *Jumpin Jim Crow*, for examples of scholarly collections.

186 **renovation and education:** See, for instance, "Minstrel Show Blackface Stump Speech," http://www.youtube.com/watch?v=ezyQdqBETVs.

186 **"lore cycle":** Lhamon, *Raising Cain*, 56–115. Strausbaugh, *Black Like You*, 25–26, discusses Lhamon.

186 **"love and theft":** Straubaugh, *Black Like You*, 70–71, discusses this "third wave." Bob Dylan used *Love and Theft*, the title of Lott's book on minstrelsy, as an album title. For an example of early minstrelsy scholarship, see Constance O'Rourke, *American Humor: A Study of the National Character* (Harcourt Brace and Company, 1931).

187 **"its cultural task does not change":** This paragraph synthesizes several different eras and ideas. "Making negro slaves their equals," quoted in Lhamon, *Raising Cain*, 21. Cockrell, *Demons of Disorder*, 85–86. Sean Wilentz, *Chants Democratic: New York City and the Rise of the American Working Class, 1788–1850* (New York: Oxford University Press, 1984), 258–59, notes early minstrels "mocking the arrogance, imitativeness, and dim-wittedness of the upper class." Nick Tosches, *Country: The Twisted Roots of Rock and Roll* (New York: DaCapo, 1996), describes "the Rolling Stones" as a "new sort of minstrelsy" (163). Strausbaugh, *Black Like You*, 73, also cites the Rolling Stones, and describes the early phase of minstrelsy, the 1830s and early 1840s, as "its rock & roll decade" (99). Lhamon, *Raising Cain*, 160, is more interested in Bob Dylan, calling him "the contemporary heir to blackface history." See also 215.

George Walker, quoted in Sotiropoulos, *Staging Race*, 42. Riots are described on 42–44. Bert Williams also said that minstrelsy was "a thing of the past . . . to cork your face and talk politics is not minstrelsy" (Sotiropoulos, *Staging Race*, 4). This, of course, is a fabulously complex statement to make, given the many meanings of "talk politics," and the likelihood that early minstrels talked politics quite frequently on some level. Clearly, Williams is differentiating between the use of blackface as a means through which to offer dissenting politics, and as a mask that represents racist politics. Twain might have understood this, but he offered no sign. There is evidence that he saw Williams perform (McCoy, interview) in the same rough time period that he lamented in print, in 1906, the passing of the minstrel show. Perhaps, in this case, both Williams and Twain were simply making a distinction between one kind of theatrical genre and another, an older one (minstrelsy) and a newer one (vaudeville, or the variety act). Contemporary reviews suggested that Williams and Walker were more "natural," providing "representations that were closer to actual daily life" (Sotiropoulos, *Staging Race*, 106), and were dismissive of the "colored man making himself ridiculous in order to portray himself." But black critics of the time differed on this issue, many believing the black vaudeville performers were setting back civil rights discourse (Sotiropoulos, *Staging Race*, 106, 167–68).

W. E. B. Du Bois, in an article on "The Humor of Negroes" in the *Mark Twain Quarterly* in 1943, celebrates "Williams and Walker" for a style of humor that he associates with the use of the word "nigger" ("which no one white might use," he stresses) to parody "the striver, the nouveau riche, the partially educated man" (12). It is possible to read this in many ways: as a rebuke of Twain's use of racial slur, or, given its venue, as a tacit endorsement of an exception for Twain. Sotiropoulos, *Staging Race*, 61–80, provides evidence that African-American performers around the turn of the century did convey politically challenging messages through, or despite, stereotypes.

Frank, *Conquest of Cool*, 234.

188 **marginalized black community with which to empathize:** Brown, "For Our Time," 45: "Is Huck another kind of liberal, who wants to play on both sides?" Margolis, "Consequences," 330. Arac, *Idol and Target*, 65, speaks of "Northern liberal smugness," and, on 13, speaks of the identification between Huck and "liberal white American opinion." Cheryl Harris, "Whiteness as Property," in *Black on White: Black Writers on What It Means to Be White*, edited by David Roediger (New York: Schocken, 1998) discusses extensively the "actual property interest in whiteness" (103). Ross, *No Respect*, 23, offers "blackface" as a challenge to the "dominant liberal approach" that creates one perspective on "racial oppression" and another on "ethnicity." Edward W. Said, *Culture and Imperialism* (New York: Vintage, 1994), reads Conrad's *Heart of Darkness* analogously: "It is no paradox, therefore, that Conrad was both anti-imperialist and imperialist, progressive when it came to rendering fearlessly and pessimistically the self-confirming, self-deluding

corruption of overseas domination, deeply reactionary when it came to conceding that Africa or South America could ever have had an independent history or culture" (xviii). "There is nothing to look forward to," Said adds of *Heart* on this matter, echoing Twain's closing shrug in *Huck Finn*: "we are stuck within our circle" (27). Said also describes Rudyard Kipling as "not simply . . . an 'imperialist minstrel,'" and applies a reading to him analogous to that offered here for Twain (146).

The appropriation of culture from African-American sources in urban centers remains widespread—the opposite, and the same phenomenon as Cable and Twain's tracking of African-American culture from its rural roots. See, for instance, Jim Giles, "Twitter Shows Language Evolves in Cities," Newscientist.com, November 17, 2012, http://www.newscientist .com/article/mg21628916.300-twitter-shows-language-evolves-in-cities .html. The home page of the L Report, http://www.Lreport.com/, describes "urban pioneers" as a trademarked term. It is used frequently in describing new trends in gentrification and urban redevelopment, and not without friction: see, for instance, "The Term 'Urban Pioneer' and Media Portrayals of the City," Rustwire.com, May 4, 2011, http://rustwire.com/2011/05/04 /the-term-urban-poineer-and-media-portrayals-of-the-city/; Karin Beuerlein, "Blazing a Trail: Urban Pioneer Neighborhoods," http://www.front door.com/real-estate/blazing-a-trail-urban-pioneer-neighborhoods.

Michael Shelden *(Man in White,* 117) recounts an incident from Twain's later life: in Oxford to receive an honorary degree, Twain is introduced to the maharajah of Bikanir, "dressed in traditional finery." The maharajah asks Twain jokingly if he has "bought Windsor Castle yet?" Twain responds, "No . . . but I'd like to buy your clothes." The desire to dress as the other, the assumption that such a privilege can be bought easily, the mix of empathy and appropriation—it is a perfect metaphor for so much of what Twain did and thought.

188 **"convention of the minstrel darky"**: MacCann and Woodard, "Minstrel Shackles," 142.

188 **"Jim, after all, is the hero"**: Chadwick-Joshua, *Jim Dilemma*, 12.

188 **what makes him memorable**: Michelson, *Mark Twain on the Loose*, writes (5) that "the special experience of reading Mark Twain" is "those instants of anarchic delight, shock, recognition, détournement that vanish in what a poet calls our tapestries of afterthought. . . ." Quirk, "Flawed Greatness," 46: "Critics and readers alike will be sorely disappointed if they search for the greatness of *Huckleberry Finn* in some kind of formal coherence or patterned architecture or veiled cultural critique or semiotic cleverness. My advice is don't go down that road; the bridge is out."

188 **given its due . . . this book**: See Wonham, *Playing*, 74: "To treat Mark Twain's relation to racial caricature as a blind spot in his thinking about race is to dismiss one of his most compelling literary resources." Ryan, "Black Genes," 190, argues that it might be "time to bring this humor into the classroom and to figure out what it all signifies"; it is intriguing advice.

189 **tricksterish origins are the point:** See Bercovitch, "What's Funny About 'Huckleberry Finn,'" 8. The idea of Twain as "trickster" is well established. Henry Nash Smith, "'Funniest,'" 64–65.

189 **our Victorian ancestors:** Strausbaugh, *Black Like You*, 19.

190 **a ghost, and they have:** Fey, "Acceptance." Louis C. K., "Tom Sawyer." He describes Tom Sawyer as a "nice kid," and Huck as "a dirty little homeless little white trash creep . . . the main problem is that he won't stop saying 'nigger.'" Later, he asks "How do you try to feel like a good country when you've done shitty things?" The level of irony is hard to read. See also http://www.youtube.com/watch?v=6o-X1nYmvRI, where Louis C. K. defends Twain and *Huck* against censorship, mistakenly insisting that the phrase "Nigger Jim" appears throughout the novel.

190 **"magical thing of desire":** Díaz, "*Mil Máscaras*." Tate, "Introduction," *Everything but the Burden*, 4.

190 **"We dress it up politely":** Smith, "Humor, Sentimentality," 157. A great quote that presents one major defense of Twain: "Mark Twain is a radical writer because he treats blacks and whites as morally equal . . ." See Greg Tate: "Our obsession with race is surpassed only by our seemingly polite and progressive neutrality regarding race." Quoted in Strausbaugh, *Black Like You*, 30.

190 **"nuclear bomb of racial epithets":** Quoted in Kennedy, *Nigger*, 22. Smith, "Huck, Jim," 107, discusses early protests.

191 **"critically engaging the word":** Asim, *N-Word*, 233. On 106–11, Asim offers an excellent reading of the novel, noting both strengths and shortcomings.

191 **"students who would read it":** White, "The N-Word."

191 **"cultural ownership rights":** Butler, "Why Read That Book?" Kennedy, *Nigger*, 103. Tally, "Bleeping," 106, discusses the origin of the "N-word."

191 **one-third said yes:** Fikes, "Love-Hate," 240, 243.

191 **non-black readers as well:** Fikes, "Love-Hate." Leonard and Tenney, "Introduction," *Satire or Evasion*, 10. Smith, "Black Critics and Mark Twain," 116, asks, "What justifies the racial categorization of critical opinion?" and suggests that "the troubling implications of segregation remain" in this conversation.

191 **implicitly endorsing it:** Morrison, "Introduction," *Huckleberry Finn*. Reed, "Mark Twain's Hairball." See also references throughout footnotes to Du Bois, Ellison, Washington, Douglass, Bradley. There are many others.

191 **often with heat:** See Smiley, "Say." Lorrie Moore suggests sending "Huck Finn to College." Russell Baker also, and better, *New York Times*, "Observer," June 14, 1982: "'Huckleberry Finn' can be partly enjoyed after the age of 25, but for fullest benefit it probably shouldn't be read before the age of 35, and even then only if the reader has had a broad experience of American society." See Leonard and Tenney, *Satire or Evasion*, 18. It goes without saying that no one has ever explored criticism of the ending of *Huck* by such authors as Hemingway in this regard, which is to say that any response by an African-American to the book is regarded as represen-

tative, while white response is not. Holland, in "A Raft of Trouble," 81, provides a rather remarkable coda that implies that the distinction between imagining an act of liberty and actually acting, as well as between racial masquerading and inversion of a subtle kind, is what drives the compulsion to interpret *Huck Finn*: "And so Huckleberry Finn got banned by fish-belly whites in Concord, Massachusetts, where there are or were people skinned in white who do not want their children to know about young Huck Finn, his forged integrity, his charged language and grammatical errors, and the vision burgeoning in his ripe adolescence. And the book more recently has been forced off the required reading lists in New York City, at the University of Massachusetts, and in Deland, Florida, at the insistence of collegians skinned in black who do not see, created in the antics of the Negro Jim, the aspirations of a people and the stature of a man. And we, with our fool imaginations, carry the burden of this lying fiction still as we translate it in our rereadings of it, moved in imaginings if not in undoubted deeds, to set these freedoms free." Toni Morrison, "Introduction," provides a nuanced description of reading *Huck* in several different decades: as a child, finding it "deeply disturbing" (xxxi); as a junior high school student, experiencing "muffled rage, as though appreciation of the work required my complicity in and sanction of something shaming" (xxxi); "Reading 'nigger' hundreds of times embarrassed, bored, annoyed—but did not faze me" (xxxii). Lastly, in the mid-1980s, in response to "demands" to remove the book from curricula: she writes of a "purist yet elementary kind of censorship designed to appease adults rather than educate children" (xxxii).

192 **"it doesn't matter"**: Langston Hughes, *The Collected Works of Langston Hughes, Volume 13: The Big Sea,* edited by Joseph McLaren (Columbia: University of Missouri Press, 2002), 205.

192 **"when that word hits the table"**: Quoted in "Huckleberry Finn and the N-Word," http://www.youtube.com/watch?v=nW9-qee1m9o.

192 **tends to teach racial broadmindedness**: See Henry, "The Struggle for Tolerance," 42–43.

192 **a nation moving into its middle-age**: See Mensh, *Black, White,* 111–12. Kennedy, *Nigger,* makes the most detailed plea for context in dealing with the word: See, among other places, 41, 75, 135.

192 **"I want everyone to know"**: Quoted in Kennedy, *Nigger,* 42. See also 10, 57. Fishkin, *Lighting Out,* 106, notes that Marshall was "no fan" of Twain's. Fulton, *Ethical Realism,* 87, states this in a more thoughtful variant: "The novel serves as a grand 'switch' that subjects the reader to an ethno-linguistic 'traumatic event,' causing him or her to enter into the lives of those on the other side of the race and class line. The constant iteration of the word 'nigger' is part of that trauma."

193 **moments of profound change**: See Barrish, *White Liberal Identity,* 42: "Its activation releases a rush of indistinguishable 'horror or delight' at what seems a loss of control and breaking of bounds."

193 **something's being staged**: See Sundquist, "Plessy," 105.

193 **"a black man with a Ph.D"**: Variant has the answer "Dr. Nigger." Kennedy, *Nigger*, 28–29.

193 **only partly built for a multiracial audience**: Mensh, *Black, White*, 115.

193 **"exceedingly well"**: Twain, *Notebooks*, vol. 3, 444, 462, 468, 473, 486–87, 489. Pettit, *Mark Twain and the South*, 127, is excellent in attempting to parse whether Twain performed different pieces for black audiences and white audiences. Fishkin is less certain: See *Was Huck Black?*, 188.

194 **"emotional segregation"**: Rush, *Hidden Lessons*, 35; she compares *Huck Finn* to *Plessy v. Ferguson*. Wallace, "Case Against Huck Finn," 19, argues that "the use of the word 'nigger' in the classroom does not provide black students with equal protection and is in violation of their constitutional rights."

194 **"lifelong admirer"**: See Arnold Rampersad, *The Life of Langston Hughes*, vol. 1 (New York: Oxford University Press, 1986): 19. Discussed in Quirk, *Coming to Grips*, 134–35. Hughes also described *Huck* as "a conscious (re) visioning of the South and the Southern slave." Quoted in Chadwick-Joshua, *Jim Dilemma*, xi, and elsewhere.

194 **abolitionism as a national movement**: Emerson, *Doo-Dah*, 62–63. Constance O'Rourke, *American Humor*, 98, quoted in Lott, "Blackface and Blackness," 9. Boskin, *Sambo*, 77. See Fields, "Ideology," 152, for discussion of "the simultaneous appearance of antislavery sentiment and racialist ideology."

195 **nostalgia as a weapon**: Mintz, *Huck's Raft*, notes that "two hundred years ago there was far less age segregation than there is today" (viii). Clark, *Kiddie Lit*, 99, brilliantly links the two, writing that "Twain turned to projection onto a nonwhite adult male to broker the widening gap between childhood and adulthood." One might reverse this, and it would still be true.

V. S. Pritchett, "Books in General," *New Statesman and Nation* 22 (August 3, 1941), 113, writing about Twain and Poe: "The peculiar power of American nostalgia . . . is that it is not only harking back to something lost in the past, but also suggests the tragedy of a lost future." Quoted in Hill, "*Huck Finn's* Humor Today," 304.

195 **"echoic"**: Doyno, *Writing Huck Finn*, 239: See DeVoto, *Mark Twain's America*, 278: "His imaginative ferment demanded gigantic expression. The effects must by [*sic*] cyclonic—they must escape the finite altogether." "Cyclonic" is another excellent word to describe Twain's vision.

195 **claiming that they are "A-rabs"**: See Twain, *Huck*, 17, 203–4, 259: The Sunday school is actually attacked by "Spaniards and A-rabs" (15). See Hearn, *Annotated Huckleberry Finn*, 273–75, for a brief discussion. Also Jarrett, "'This Expression,'" 21. Twain, of course, is likely parodying the Crusades here as well, which only makes his historical reach even more intimidating.

ACKNOWLEDGMENTS

197 **not even a new thing to observe:** Cox, *Fate of Humor*, v: "Yet all will not have been lost if my ambition has saved the reader from being subjected to one more laborious study of Mark Twain." He said this in 1966. Albert Stone, quoted in Trites, *Twain, Alcott*, xiv: on Twain, "few writers today can hope to say anything original." He wrote this in 1961. Scharnhorst and Trombley, "Who Killed Mark Twain?" 221–22, note that "the latest MLA bibliography includes no less than thirty-three column inches of citations to Twain scholarship. . . ." Gerber, "Collecting," 7, notes that a leading reference lists 16,750 sources available for Twain as of 1977. On the other hand, there are many studies that self-consciously try to say something new anyway: for example, Michelson, *Mark Twain on the Loose*, 6. Powers, *Dangerous Water*, 21–23. As another example, Quirk, "Flawed Greatness," 40: "But the real point I wish to make is that critics and readers have willingly served as apologists for and accusers of the novel and its creator but seem not to have entertained the notion that there might be other reasons for the book's greatness, no matter how many warts one might discover in it."

197 **the problems . . . become *your* problems:** Doyno, *Writing Huck Finn*, 239. In part, I am referring to the metafact that a book about *Huck Finn* and the controversy surrounding it must partake in the controversy, and contain or at least echo the same traits that create dispute. This refers to many issues, in fact, but most concretely, to the use of the "n-word" in direct quotations or immediate relevant contexts. This book would have been written whether or not Twain employed racial slurs in *Huck Finn*—if anything, it is written as a corrective to the way discussions of the "n-word" have shaped discussions of *Huck Finn*, masking both its real strengths and weaknesses. At the same time, engagement, and the difficult questions it raises, are unavoidable, and truly, shouldn't be evaded. Arguments exist in American public discourse that this word should never be used, or never used in certain contexts, or by certain speakers; other arguments sanction specific uses in specific situations as appropriate, even necessary (both viewpoints are cited in the text). I am implicitly endorsing only narrow and steadfastly germane uses for someone such as myself and for the demographic and professional groups I theoretically represent. Nevertheless, this is a book about the persistence of pernicious patterns in history, and making them persist less, and I regard what I have done here as essential to that goal. Stylistically, I have chosen to model a direct but sparing relationship with the scabrous language of the past (and the complex and often dark history which it represents), also keeping with my book's goals.

198 **it's not long enough:** The word count on this book is roughly 70,000; the word count on its documentation is roughly 50,000. This is largely a tribute not just to the amount already written on Mark Twain and *Huck Finn,* but the quality. I have tried to reflect that fact in these endnotes, where multiple sources might be given credit for the same thought, or for slight variations

of the same thought, and where certain notes also function as annotations of specific ideas from the library of modern criticism of *Huck Finn*. This, too, fits the book's theme. In homage, I have also tried to emphasize the authors and critics who were particularly influential in the composition of this book.

BIBLIOGRAPHY

Abbott, Keene. "Tom Sawyer's Town." *Harper's Weekly* 57 (August 9, 1913), 16–17.

Alberti, John. "The Nigger Huck: Race, Identity, and the Teaching of *Huckleberry Finn*." *College English* 57, no. 8 (December 1995), 919–37.

Aldrich, Thomas Bailey. *The Story of a Bad Boy* (Boston: Fields, Osgood, and Company, 1870; reprint, London: Forgotten Books, 2012).

Alexander, Michelle. *The New Jim Crow: Mass Incarceration in the Age of Colorblindness*, rev. ed. (New York: New Press, 2012).

Allen, Margot. "Huck Finn: Two Generations of Pain." *Interracial Books for Children Bulletin* 15, no. 5 (1984), 9–12.

Allen, Theodore W. *The Invention of the White Race*. Vol. 2, *The Origin of Racial Oppression in Anglo-America* (New York: Verso, 1997).

Altschuler, Mark. "Motherless Child: Huck Finn and a Theory of Moral Development." *American Literary Realism, 1870–1910* 22, no. 1 (Fall 1989), 31–42.

Anderson, Craig A., Katherine E. Buckley, and Douglas A. Gentile. *Violent Video Game Effects on Children and Adolescents: Theory, Research, and Public Policy* (New York: Oxford University Press, 2007).

Andrews, William L. "Mark Twain and James W. C. Pennington: Huckleberry Finn's Smallpox Lie." *Studies in American Fiction* 9, no. 1 (Spring 1981), 103–12.

Angier, Natalie. "The Nation; The Debilitating Malady Called Boyhood." *New York Times*, July 24, 1994. http://www.nytimes.com/1994/07/24/weekin review/the-nation-the-debilitating-malady-called-boyhood.html.

Applebaum, Anne. "The ADHD-ventures of *Tom Sawyer*." *Slate*, August 9, 2010. http://www.slate.com/articles/news_and_politics/foreigners/2010/08 /the_adhdventures_of_tom_sawyer.html.

Arac, Jonathan. *Huckleberry Finn as Idol and Target: The Functions of Criticism in Our Time* (Madison: University of Wisconsin Press, 1997).

———. *Impure Worlds: The Institution of Literature in the Age of the Novel* (New York: Fordham University Press, 2011).

————. "Putting the River on New Maps: Nation, Race, and Beyond in Reading *Huckleberry Finn*." *American Literary History* 8, no. 1 (Spring 1996), 110–29.

Aronson, Marc, and H. P. Newquist. *For Boys Only: The Biggest, Baddest Book Ever* (New York: Feiwel and Friends, 2007).

Asim, Jabari. *The N Word: Who Can Say It, Who Shouldn't, and Why* (New York: Houghton Mifflin, 2008).

Asthana, Anushka, and Jo Revill. "Is It Time to Let Children Play Outdoors Once More?" *Guardian*, March 29, 2008. http://www.guardian.co.uk/society /2008/mar/30/children.health.

Ayers, Edward L. *Vengeance and Justice: Crime and Punishment in the 19th-Century American South* (New York: Oxford University Press, 1984).

Baker, William. "Mark Twain and the Shrewd Ohio Audiences." *American Literary Realism, 1870–1910* 18, nos. 1–2 (Spring–Autumn 1985), 14–30.

Barksdale, Richard K. "History, Slavery and Thematic Irony in *Huckleberry Finn*." *Mark Twain Journal* 22, no. 2 (Fall 1984), 17–20.

Barrish, Phillip. *White Liberal Identity, Literary Pedagogy, and Classic American Realism* (Columbus: Ohio State University Press, 2005).

Bassett, John Earl. "*Huckleberry Finn*: The End Lies in the Beginning." *American Literary Realism, 1870–1910* 17, no. 1 (Spring 1984), 89–98.

Bean, Annemarie, James V. Hatch, and Brooks McNamara, eds. *Inside the Minstrel Mask: Readings in Nineteenth-Century Blackface Minstrelsy* (Middletown, CT: Wesleyan University Press, 1996).

Beaver, Harold. *Huckleberry Finn* (London: Unwin Hyman, 1987).

————. "Run, Nigger, Run: *Adventures of Huckleberry Finn* as a Fugitive Slave Narrative." *Journal of American Studies* 8, no. 3 (December 1974), 339–61.

Beidler, Philip D., and Sara deSaussure Davis, eds. *The Mythologizing of Mark Twain* (Tuscaloosa: University of Alabama Press, 1984).

Bell, Bernard. "Twain's 'Nigger' Jim: The Tragic Face Behind the Minstrel Mask." In Davis, Thadious M., James S. Leonard, and Thomas A. Tenney, eds., *Satire or Evasion? Black Perspectives on Huckleberry Finn*, 124–40 (Durham, NC: Duke University Press, 1992).

Bercovitch, Sacvan. "Deadpan Huck, or, What's Funny About Interpretation." *Kenyon Review* 24 (Spring–Autumn 2002), 90–134.

————. "What's Funny About *Huckleberry Finn*." *New England Review* 20, no. 1 (Winter 1999), 8–28.

Berkove, Lawrence I. "The Free Man of Color in *The Grandissimes* and Works by Harris and Mark Twain." *Southern Quarterly* 18, no. 4 (Summer 1980), 60–73.

Berret, Anthony J. "*Huckleberry Finn* and the Minstrel Show." *American Studies* 27, no. 2 (Fall 1986), 37–49.

———. "The Influence of *Hamlet* on *Huckleberry Finn*." *American Literary Realism, 1870–1910* 18, nos. 1–2 (Spring–Autumn 1985), 196–207.

Besley, Adrian. *The Outdoor Book for Adventurous Boys: Essential Skills and Activities for Boys of All Ages* (Guilford, CT: Lyons Press, 2008).

Bhabha, Homi K. *The Location of Culture* (London: Routledge, 1994).

———. "Of Mimicry and Man: The Ambivalence of Colonial Discourse." *October* 28 (Spring 1984), 125–33.

Bickley, R. Bruce. *Joel Chandler Harris: A Biography and Critical Study* (Athens: University of Georgia Press, 1987).

———. "White No Longer." *Mississippi Quarterly* 51, no. 2 (Spring 1998), 333–37.

Bikle, Lucy Leffingwell Cable. *George W. Cable, His Life and Letters* (New York: Charles Scribner's Sons, 1928).

Bird, John. "Mark Twain, Karl Gerhardt, and the *Huckleberry Finn* Frontispiece." *American Literary Realism* 45, no. 1 (Fall 2012), 28–37.

———. "Mind the Gap: A Reader Reading *Adventures of Huckleberry Finn*." In Martin, Gretchen, ed., *Twain's Omissions: Exploring the Gaps as Textual Context*, 9–20 (Newcastle upon Tyne: Cambridge Scholars Publishing, 2013).

Blair, Walter. *Mark Twain and Huck Finn* (Berkeley: University of California Press, 1960).

Blair, Walter, and Hamlin Hill, eds. *The Art of Huckleberry Finn* (San Francisco: Chandler Publishing Company, 1962).

Blakemore, Steven. "Huck Finn's Written World." *American Literary Realism, 1870–1910* 20, no. 2 (Winter 1988), 21–29.

Boskin, Joseph. *Sambo: The Rise and Demise of an American Jester* (New York: Oxford University Press, 1986).

Bowen, Elbert R. *Theatrical Entertainments in Rural Missouri Before the Civil War* (Columbia: University of Missouri Press, 1959).

Brenner, Gerry. "More Than a Reader's Response: A Letter to 'De Ole True Huck.'" In Graff, Gerald, and James Phelan, eds., *Adventures of Huckleberry Finn: A Case Study in Critical Controversy*, 450–68 (Boston: Bedford Books, 1995). Originally published in *Journal of Narrative Technique* 20, no. 2 (Spring 1990), 221–34.

Briden, Earl F. "Kemble's 'Specialty' and the Pictorial Countertext of *Huckleberry Finn*." In Graff, Gerald, and James Phelan, eds., *Adventures of Huckleberry Finn: A Case Study in Critical Controversy*, 383–406 (Boston: Bedford Books, 1995). Originally published in *Mark Twain Journal* 26, no. 2 (Fall 1988), 2–14.

Brodhead, Richard H. "Spare the Rod: Discipline and Fiction in Antebellum America." *Representations* 21 (Winter 1988), 67–96.

Bronner, Simon J. *American Folklore Studies: An Intellectual History* (Lawrence: University Press of Kansas, 1986).

Brooks, Van Wyck. *The Ordeal of Mark Twain* (London: William Heinemann, 1922).

Brown, Spencer. "*Huckleberry Finn* for Our Time." *Michigan Quarterly Review* 6, no. 1 (Winter 1967), 41–46.

Browne, Ray B. "Shakespeare in American Vaudeville and Negro Minstrelsy." *American Quarterly* 12 (Fall 1960), 374–91.

Brundage, W. Fitzhugh, ed. *Beyond Blackface: African Americans and the Creation of American Popular Culture, 1890–1930* (Chapel Hill: University of North Carolina Press, 2011).

Buchanan, Andrea J., and Miriam Peskowitz. *The Daring Book for Girls* (New York: William Morrow, 2012).

Budd, Louis J. "Mark Twain as an American Icon." In Robinson, Forrest G., ed., *The Cambridge Companion to Mark Twain*, 1–26 (Cambridge, UK: Cambridge University Press, 1995).

———. *Mark Twain: Social Philosopher* (Bloomington: Indiana University Press, 1962).

———. *Our Mark Twain: The Making of His Public Personality* (Philadelphia: University of Pennsylvania Press, 1983).

———. "The Recomposition of *Adventures of Huckleberry Finn*." *Missouri Review* 10, no. 1 (1987), 113–28.

———. "A 'Talent For Posturing': The Achievement of Mark Twain's Public Personality." In Beidler, Philip D., and Sara deSaussure Davis, eds., *The Mythologizing of Mark Twain*, 77–98 (Tuscaloosa: University of Alabama Press, 1984).

———, ed. *Mark Twain: The Contemporary Reviews* (New York: Cambridge University Press, 1999).

———, ed. *New Essays on Adventures of Huckleberry Finn* (New York: Cambridge University Press, 1985).

Budd, Louis J., and Edwin H. Cady. *On Mark Twain: The Best from American Literature* (Durham, NC: Duke University Press, 1987).

Bush, Robert. "Grace King and Mark Twain." *American Literature* 44, no. 1 (March 1972), 31–51.

Butcher, Philip. *George W. Cable* (New York: Twayne, 1962).

———. "Mark Twain's Installment on the National Debt." *Southern Literary Journal* 1, no. 2 (Spring 1969), 48–55.

Butler, Paul. "Why Bother Reading *Huckleberry Finn?*" *New York Times*, January 6, 2011. http://www.nytimes.com/roomfordebate/2011/01/05/does-one -word-change-huckleberry-finn/why-bother-reading-huckleberry-finn.

Cable, George W. "Cable's Reminiscences." http://twain.lib.virginia.edu/huck finn/cablemem.html.

———. "The Convict Lease System in the Southern States." *Century* 27 (February 1884), 582–99.

———. "The Dance in Place Congo." *Century* 31, no. 4 (February 1886), 517–32.

———. *Dr. Sevier* (Boston: James R. Osgood and Company, 1885).

———. "The Freedman's Case in Equity." *Century* 29, no. 3 (January 1885), 409–18.

———. *The Grandissimes*. Foreword by W. Kenneth Holditch (Gretna: Pelican Publishing Company, 2001).

———. *The Negro Question*. Edited by Arlin Turner (Garden City: Doubleday Anchor, 1958).

Camfield, Gregg. "*Huck* and the *Arabian Nights*: The Fine Art of Moral Burlesque." In *Huck Finn: The Complete Buffalo & Erie County Public Library Manuscript—Teaching and Research Digital Edition* (Buffalo, NY: Buffalo & Erie County Public Library, 2002).

Campbell, Guy. *The Boys' Book of Survival: How to Survive Anything, Anywhere* (New York: Scholastic, 2009).

Cardwell, Guy. *The Man Who Was Mark Twain: Images and Ideologies* (New Haven, CT: Yale University Press, 1991).

———. *Twins of Genius* (London: Neville Spearman, 1962).

Carey-Webb, Allen. "Racism and *Huckleberry Finn*: Censorship, Dialogue, and Change." *English Journal* 82, no. 7 (November 1993), 22–34.

Carkeet, David. "The Dialects in *Huckleberry Finn*." *American Literature* 51, no. 3 (November 1979), 315–32.

Carlyon, David. "Twain's 'Stretcher': The Circus Shapes *Huckleberry Finn*." *South Atlantic Review* 72, no. 4 (Fall 2007), 1–36.

Carrington, George C. "Farce and *Huckleberry Finn*." In Crowley, J. Donald, and Robert Sattelmeyer, eds., *One Hundred Years of Huckleberry Finn: The Boy, His Book, and American Culture*, 216–30 (Columbia: University of Missouri Press, 1985).

Cecil, L. Moffitt. "The Historical Ending of *Adventures of Huckleberry Finn*: How Nigger Jim Was Set Free." *American Literary Realism, 1870–1910* 13, no. 2 (Autumn 1980), 280–83.

Chadwick-Joshua, Jocelyn. *The Jim Dilemma: Reading Race in Huckleberry Finn* (Jackson: University Press of Mississippi, 1998).

Chambers, J. K., and Peter Trudgill. *Dialectology* (New York: Cambridge University Press, 1980).

Christianson, Scott. *With Liberty for Some: 500 Years of Imprisonment in America* (Boston: Northeastern University Press, 1998).

Christy, E. Byron, and William E. Christy. *Christy's New Songster and Black Joker* (New York: Dick and Fitzgerald, 1868; reprint, Ann Arbor: University of Michigan Library).

Chude-Sokei, Louis. *The Last 'Darky': Bert Williams, Black-on-Black Minstrelsy, and the African Diaspora* (Durham, NC: Duke University Press, 2006).

Clark, Beverly Lyon. *Kiddie Lit: The Cultural Construction of Children's Literature in America* (Baltimore: Johns Hopkins University Press, 2003).

———, ed. Preface to *The Adventures of Tom Sawyer* (New York: W. W. Norton and Company, 2007), vii–viii.

Clemens, Clara. *My Father, Mark Twain* (New York: Harper and Brothers, 1931).

Clemens, Susy. *Papa: An Intimate Biography of Mark Twain.* Foreword and comments by Mark Twain. Edited and with an introduction by Charles Neider (Garden City, NY: Doubleday & Company, 1985).

Cochran, Robert. "Black Father: The Subversive Achievement of Joel Chandler Harris." *African American Review* 38, no. 1 (Spring 2004), 21–34.

Cockrell, Dale. *Demons of Disorder: Early Blackface Minstrels and Their World* (New York: Cambridge University Press, 1997).

———. "Of Soundscapes and Blackface: From Fools to Foster." In Johnson, Stephen, ed. *Burnt Cork: Traditions and Legacies of Blackface Minstrelsy*, 51–72 (Amherst: University of Massachusetts Press, 2012).

Cole, Catherine M. "American Ghetto Parties and Ghanaian Concert Parties: A Transnational Perspective on Blackface." In Johnson, Stephen, ed. *Burnt Cork: Traditions and Legacies of Blackface Minstrelsy*, 223–58 (Amherst: University of Massachusetts Press, 2012).

Comstock, Anthony. *Traps for the Young.* With an introduction by James Monroe Buckley (New York: Funk & Wagnalls, 1883; reprint, London: Forgotten Books, 2013).

Cooley, John, ed. *Mark Twain's Aquarium: The Samuel Clemens–Angelfish Correspondence, 1905–1910* (Athens: University of Georgia Press, 2009).

Corsaro, William A. *The Sociology of Childhood*, 3rd ed. (Thousand Oaks, CA: Pine Forge Press, 2011).

Coulombe, Joseph L. "Mark Twain's Native Americans and the Repeated Racial Pattern in 'Adventures of Huckleberry Finn.'" *American Literary Realism* 33, no. 3 (Spring 2001), 261–79.

Cox, James M. "A Hard Book to Take." In Crowley, J. Donald, and Robert Sattelmeyer, eds., *One Hundred Years of Huckleberry Finn: The Boy, His Book, and American Culture*, 386–403 (Columbia: University of Missouri Press, 1985).

———. *Mark Twain: The Fate of Humor* (Princeton, NJ: Princeton University Press, 1966).

Crofts, Daniel W. "The Black Response to the Blair Education Bill." *The Journal of Southern History* 37, no. 1 (Feb. 1971), 41–65.

Crowley, J. Donald, and Robert Sattelmeyer, eds. *One Hundred Years of Huckleberry Finn: The Boy, His Book, and American Culture* (Columbia: University of Missouri Press, 1985).

Csicsila, Joseph, and Chad Rohman, eds. *Centenary Reflections on Mark Twain's No. 44, The Mysterious Stranger* (Columbia: University of Missouri Press, 2009).

Cuban, Larry. *How Teachers Taught: Constancy and Change in American Classrooms, 1890–1900*, 2nd ed. (New York: Teachers College Press, 1993).

D'Ascoli, Patricia F. "Coming up Empty: Exploring Narrative Omissions in *Adventures of Huckleberry Finn*," in Martin, Gretchen, ed., *Twain's Omissions: Exploring the Gaps as Textual Context,* 57–74 (Newcastle upon Tyne: Cambridge Scholars Publishing, 2013).

Davis, Thadious M., James S. Leonard, and Thomas A. Tenney, eds. *Satire or Evasion? Black Perspectives on Huckleberry Finn* (Durham, NC: Duke University Press, 1992).

Dawson, Hugh J. "The Ethnicity of Huck Finn—and the Difference It Makes." *American Literary Realism, 1870–1910* 30, no. 2 (Winter 1998), 1–16.

DeLoria, Philip J. *Playing Indian* (New Haven: Yale University Press, 1998).

Dempsey, Terrell. *Searching for Jim: Slavery in Sam Clemens's World* (Columbia: University of Missouri Press, 2003).

Densmore, Chris. "Sam Clemens' First Visit to Buffalo: Stories of Fugitive Slaves." In *Huck Finn: The Complete Buffalo & Erie County Public Library Manuscript—Teaching and Research Digital Edition* (Buffalo, NY: Buffalo & Erie County Public Library, 2002).

Derbyshire, David. "How Children Lost the Right to Roam in Four Generations." *Daily Mail,* June 15, 2007. http://www.dailymail.co.uk/news/article -462091/How-children-lost-right-roam-generations.html.

Devere, William. *Devere's Negro Recitations and End-men's Gags* (Chicago: Charles T. Powner and Company, 1946).

Díaz, Junot. "*Mil Máscaras*: An Interview with Pulitzer-Winner Junot Díaz (*The Brief Wondrous Life of Oscar Wao*)." Interviewed by Matt Okie. *Identity Theory,* September 2, 2008. http://www.identitytheory.com/interview-pulitzer -winner-junot-diaz-wondrous-life-oscar-wao/.

Doig, Will. "Unleash Our Kids." *Salon,* July 21, 2012. http://www.salon.com /2012/07/21/paranoid_parents_kill_cities/.

Donohue-Smith, Maureen. "Failed Families and the Crisis of Connectedness in *Huckleberry Finn*." In *Huck Finn: The Complete Buffalo & Erie County Public Library Manuscript—Teaching and Research Digital Edition* (Buffalo, NY: Buffalo & Erie County Public Library, 2002).

Doyno, Victor A. "*Adventures of Huckleberry Finn*: The Growth from Manuscript to Novel." In *One Hundred Years of Huckleberry Finn: The Boy, His Book, and American Culture,* edited by J. Donald Crowley and Robert Sattelmeyer. Columbia: University of Missouri Press, 1985, 106–16.

————. Afterword to Twain, Mark, *Adventures of Huckleberry Finn* (New York: Oxford University Press, 1996), 1–25.

————. "Samuel Clemens as Family Man and Father." In Kiskis, Michael J., and Laura E. Skandera Trombley, eds., *Constructing Mark Twain: New Directions in Scholarship*, 28–49 (Columbia: University of Missouri Press, 2001).

————. *Writing Huck Finn: Mark Twain's Creative Process* (Philadelphia: University of Pennsylvania Press, 1991).

Du Bois, W. E. B. "The Humor of Negroes." *Mark Twain Quarterly* 5 (Fall–Winter 1942–1943), 12.

Dunson, Stephanie. "Black Misrepresentation in Nineteenth-Century Sheet Music Illustration." In Brundage, W. Fitzhugh, ed., *Beyond Blackface: African Americans and the Creation of American Popular Culture, 1890–1930*, 45–65 (Chapel Hill: University of North Carolina Press, 2011).

Ebert, Roger. "*The Birth of a Nation* (1915)." Film review on Rogerebert.com, March 30, 2003. http://rogerebert.suntimes.com/apps/pbcs.dll/article?AID =/20030330/REVIEWS08/303300301/1023.

Eckstein, Barbara. "Child's Play: Nature-Deficit Disorder and Mark Twain's Mississippi River Youth." *American Literary History* 24, no. 1 (Spring 2012), 16–33.

Ekstrom, Kjell. *George Washington Cable: A Study of His Early Life and Work* (New York: Haskell House, 1966).

Ellis, James. "The Bawdy Humor of THE KING'S CAMELOPARD or THE ROYAL NONESUCH." *American Literature* 63, no. 4 (December 1991), 729–35.

Ellison, Ralph. "Change the Joke and Slip the Yoke." In Ellison, Ralph, *Shadow and Act*, 45–59 (New York: Random House, 1964).

————. *Invisible Man* (New York: Vintage, 1995).

————. "Some Questions and Some Answers." In Ellison, Ralph, *Shadow and Act*, 261–72 (New York: Random House, 1964).

————. "Twentieth-Century Fiction and the Black Mask of Humanity." In Ellison, Ralph, *Shadow and Act*, 24–44 (New York: Random House, 1964).

————. "The World and the Jug." In Ellison, Ralph, *Shadow and Act*, 107–43 (New York: Random House, 1964).

Entin, Esther. "All Work and No Play: Why Your Kids Are More Anxious, Depressed." *Atlantic*, October 12, 2011. http://www.theatlantic.com/health /archive/2011/10/all-work-and-no-play-why-your-kids-are-more-anxious -depressed/246422/.

Fatout, Paul. *Mark Twain on the Lecture Circuit* (Bloomington: Indiana University Press, 1960).

Fears, David H. *Mark Twain Day by Day: An Annotated Chronology of the Life of Samuel L. Clemens, Volume 1 (1835–1885)* (Banks, OR: Horizon Micro Publishers, 2008).

Fetterley, Judith. "The Sanctioned Rebel." In Twain, Mark, *The Adventures of Tom Sawyer*, edited by Beverly Lyon Clark, 279–89 (New York: W. W. Norton and Company, 2007).

Fey, Tina. "Tina Fey's Mark Twain Prize Acceptance Speech." http://www.youtube.com/watch?v=VZlgJyLEB_g.

Fields, Barbara J. "Ideology and Race in American History." In Kousser, J. Morgan, and James M. McPherson, eds., *Region, Race, and Reconstruction*, 143–78 (New York: Oxford University Press, 1982).

Fikes, Robert, Jr. "The Black Love-Hate Affair with *The Adventures of Huckleberry Finn*." *The Western Journal of Black Studies* 35, no. 4 (September 2011), 240–45.

Finkelstein, Barbara. *Governing the Young: Teacher Behavior in Popular Primary Schools in Nineteenth-Century United States* (New York: Falmer Press, 1989).

Fischer, Victor. "Huck Finn Reviewed: The Reception of *Huckleberry Finn* in the United States, 1885–1897." *American Literary Realism, 1870–1910* 16, no. 1 (Spring 1983), 1–57.

Fishkin, Shelley Fisher. "False Starts, Fragments and Fumbles: Mark Twain's Unpublished Writing on Race." *Essays in Arts and Sciences* 20 (October 1991), 17–31.

———. "In Praise of 'Spike Lee's Huckleberry Finn' by Ralph Wiley." http://faculty.citadel.edu/leonard/od99wiley.htm.

———. *Lighting Out for the Territory: Reflections on Mark Twain and American Culture* (New York: Oxford University Press, 1997).

———. "Race and the Politics of Memory: Mark Twain and Paul Laurence Dunbar." *Journal of American Studies* 40, no. 2 (August 2006), 283–309.

———. *Was Huck Black? Mark Twain and African American Voices* (New York: Oxford University Press, 1993).

———, ed. *The Mark Twain Anthology: Great Writers on His Life and Works* (New York: Library of America, 2010).

Foner, Philip S. *Mark Twain: Social Critic* (New York: International Publishers, 1958).

———. *Reconstruction: America's Unfinished Revolution, 1863–1877* (New York: Harper and Row, 1988).

Frank, Thomas. *The Conquest of Cool: Business Culture, Counterculture, and the Rise of Hip Consumerism* (Chicago: University of Chicago Press, 1997).

Fraser, James W., ed. *The School in the United States: A Documentary History*, 2nd ed. (New York: Routledge, 2009).

French, William C. "Character and Cruelty in 'Huckleberry Finn': Why the Ending Works." *Soundings* 81, nos. 1–2 (1998), 157–79.

Friedman, Lawrence Jacob. *The White Savage: Racial Fantasies in the Postbellum South* (Englewood Cliffs, NJ: Prentice-Hall, 1970).

Fulton, Joe B. *Mark Twain's Ethical Realism: The Aesthetics of Race, Class, and Gender* (Columbia: University of Missouri Press, 1997).

Gair, Christopher. "Whitewashed Exteriors: Mark Twain's Imitation Whites." *Journal of American Studies* 39, no. 2 (August 2005), 187–205.

Garbarino, James. *Lost Boys: Why Our Sons Turn Violent and How We Can Save Them* (New York: Free Press, 1999).

Gates, Henry Louis, Jr.. "The Trope of the New Negro and the Reconstruction of the Image of the Black." In Fisher, Philip, ed., *New American Studies*, 319–45 (Berkeley: University of California Press, 1991).

Gerber, John C. "Collecting the Works of Mark Twain." In Beidler, Philip D., and Sara deSaussure Davis, eds., *The Mythologizing of Mark Twain*, 3–14 (Tuscaloosa: University of Alabama Press, 1984).

———. "Introduction: The Continuing Adventures of *Huckleberry Finn*." In Crowley, J. Donald, and Robert Sattelmeyer, eds., *One Hundred Years of Huckleberry Finn: The Boy, His Book, and American Culture*, 1–12 (Columbia: University of Missouri Press, 1985).

Gibson, Donald B. "Mark Twain's Jim in the Classroom." *English Journal* 57 (February 1968), 196–99, 202.

Gladwell, Malcolm. "The Coolhunt." *New Yorker*, March 17, 1997. http://www .gladwell.com/1997/1997_03_17_a_cool.htm.

Gloor, Peter, and Cooper, Scott. *Coolhunting: Chasing Down the Next Big Thing* (New York: American Management Association, 2007).

Godden, Richard, and Mary A. McCay. "Say It Again, Sam(bo): Race and Speech in *Huckleberry Finn* and *Casablanca*." *Mississippi Quarterly* 49, no. 4 (Fall 1996), 657–82.

Going, Allen J. "The South and the Blair Education Bill." *The Mississippi Valley Historical Review* 44, no. 2 (Sep., 1957), 267–90.

Graff, Harvey J. *Conflicting Paths: Growing Up in America* (Cambridge, MA: Harvard University Press, 1995).

———, ed. *Growing Up in America: Historical Experiences* (Detroit: Wayne State University Press, 1987).

Graves, Wallace. "Mark Twain's 'Burning Shame.'" *Nineteenth-Century Fiction* 23 (June 1968), 93–98.

Greenblatt, Stephen. "The Death of Hamnet and the Making of Hamlet." *New York Review of Books*, October 21, 2004. http://www.nybooks.com/articles /archives/2004/oct/21/the-death-of-hamnet-and-the-making-of-hamlet /?page=1.

Gribben, Alan. "Boys Books, Bad Boy Books, and *The Adventures of Tom Sawyer*." In Twain, Mark, *The Adventures of Tom Sawyer*, edited by Beverly Lyon Clark, 290–306 (New York: W. W. Norton and Company, 2007).

————. "'I Did Wish Tom Sawyer Was There': Boy-Book Elements in *Tom Sawyer* and *Huckleberry Finn*." In Crowley, J. Donald, and Robert Sattelmeyer, eds., *One Hundred Years of Huckleberry Finn: The Boy, His Book, and American Culture*, 149–70 (Columbia: University of Missouri Press, 1985).

————. "Manipulating a Genre: 'Huckleberry Finn' as Boy Book." *South Central Review* 5, no. 4 (Winter 1988), 15–21.

————. *Mark Twain's Library: A Reconstruction* (Boston: G. K. Hall, 1980).

————. "'Stolen from Books, Tho' Credit Given': Mark Twain's Use of Literary Sources." *Mosaic* 12, no. 4 (Summer 1979), 149–55.

Gubar, Susan. *Racechanges: White Skin, Black Face in American Culture* (New York: Oxford University Press, 1997).

Gurian, Michael, and Kathy Stevens. *The Minds of Boys: Saving Our Sons from Falling Behind in School and Life* (San Francisco: Jossey-Bass, 2005).

Hajdu, David. *The Ten-Cent Plague: The Great Comic Book Scare and How It Changed America* (New York: Picador, 2008).

Hale, Grace Elizabeth. *Making Whiteness: The Culture of Segregation in the South, 1890–1940* (New York: Vintage, 1999).

Hall, G. Stanley. *Adolescence: Its Psychology and its Relations to Physiology, Anthropology, Sociology, Sex, Crime, Religion and Education*, vol. 1 (New York: D. Appleton and Company, 1907; reprint, London: Forgotten Books, 2011).

Halleck, Reuben Post. *History of American Literature* (New York: American Book Company, 1911; reprint, London: Forgotten Books, 2008).

Harris, Joel Chandler. *The Complete Tales of Uncle Remus*. Compiled by Richard Chase (Boston: Houghton Mifflin, 1955).

Harris, Susan K. *Mark Twain's Escape from Time: A Study of Patterns and Images* (Columbia: University of Missouri Press, 1982).

Hartman, Saidiya V. *Scenes of Subjection: Terror, Slavery, and Self-Making in Nineteenth-Century America* (New York: Oxford University Press, 1997).

Heaggans, Raphael. *The 21st Century Hip-Hop Minstrel Show: Are We Continuing the Blackface Tradition?* (San Diego: University Readers, 2009).

Hemingway, Ernest. *Green Hills of Africa* (New York: Charles Scribner's Sons, 1953).

Henry, Peaches. "The Struggle for Tolerance: Race and Censorship in *Huckleberry Finn*." In Davis, Thadious M., James S. Leonard, and Thomas A. Tenney, eds., *Satire or Evasion? Black Perspectives on Huckleberry Finn*, 25–48 (Durham, NC: Duke University Press, 1992).

Heywood, Colin M. *A History of Childhood: Children and Childhood in the West From Medieval to Modern Times* (Cambridge, UK: Polity Press, 2001).

Hill, Hamlin. "*Huck Finn's* Humor Today." In Crowley, J. Donald, and Robert Sattelmeyer, eds., *One Hundred Years of Huckleberry Finn: The Boy, His Book, and American Culture*, 297–307 (Columbia: University of Missouri Press, 1985).

———. *Mark Twain: God's Fool* (New York: Harper & Row, 1973).

Hill, Richard. "Overreaching: Critical Agenda and the Ending of *Adventures of Huckleberry Finn.*" *Texas Studies in Literature and Language* 33, no. 4 (Winter 1991), 492–513.

Hillman, Mayer, John Adams, and John Whitelegg. *One False Move: A Study of Children's Independent Mobility* (London: PSI Publishing, 1990).

Holland, Laurence. "A 'Raft of Trouble': Word and Deed in *Huckleberry Finn.*" In Sundquist, Eric J., *American Realism: New Essays*, 66–81 (Baltimore: Johns Hopkins University Press, 1982).

Hoppenstand, Gary, ed. *The Dime Novel Detective* (Bowling Green, OH: Bowling Green State University Popular Press, 1982).

Howe, Lawrence. *Mark Twain and the Novel: The Double-Cross of Authority* (New York: Cambridge University Press, 1998).

Howells, William Dean. "Mark Twain: An Inquiry." *North American Review* 172, no. 531 (February 1901), 306–21.

———. *My Mark Twain: Reminiscences and Criticisms* (New York: Harper and Brothers, 1910; new ed., edited by Marilyn Austin Baldwin [Baton Rouge: Louisiana State University Press, 1967]).

Hsu, Hsuan L. "Sitting in Darkness: Mark Twain and America's Asia." *American Literary History* 25, no. 1 (Spring 2013), 69–84.

Hulbert, Ann. *Raising America: Experts, Parents, and a Century of Advice About Children* (New York: Knopf, 2003).

Hunter, Jim. "Mark Twain and the Boy-Book in 19th-Century America." *College English* 24, no. 6 (March 1963), 430–38.

Iggulden, Conn, and Hal Iggulden. *The Dangerous Book for Boys* (New York: William Morrow, 2012).

Ignatiev, Noel. *How the Irish Became White* (New York: Routledge, 1995).

Illick, Joseph E. *American Childhoods* (Philadelphia: University of Pennsylvania Press, 2002).

Inge, M. Thomas. "Mark Twain and the Comics." *Mark Twain Journal* 28, no. 2 (Fall 1990), 30–39.

Jacobson, Marcia. *Being a Boy Again: Autobiography and the American Boy Book* (Tuscaloosa: University of Alabama Press, 1994).

James, Stephen, and David S. Thomas. *Wild Things: The Art of Nurturing Boys* (Carol Stream, IL: Tyndale House, 2009).

Jarrett, Gene. " 'This Expression Shall Not Be Changed': Irrelevant Episodes, Jim's Humanity Revisited, and Retracing Mark Twain's Evasion in *Adventures of Huckleberry Finn.*" *American Literary Realism* 35, no. 1 (Fall 2002), 1–28.

Jehlen, Myra. "Banned in Concord: *Adventures of Huckleberry Finn* and Classic American Literature." In Robinson, Forrest G., ed., *The Cambridge Companion to Mark Twain*, 93–115 (Cambridge, UK: Cambridge University Press, 1995).

———. "Reading Gender in 'Adventures of Huckleberry Finn.'" In Graff, Gerald, and James Phelan, eds., *The Adventures of Huckleberry Finn: A Case Study in Critical Controversy*, 505–18 (Boston: Bedford St. Martin's, 1995).

Johnson, Stephen, ed. *Burnt Cork: Traditions and Legacies of Blackface Minstrelsy* (Amherst: University of Massachusetts Press, 2012).

———. "Death and the Minstrel: Race, Madness, and Art in the Last (W)Rites of Three Early Blackface Performers." In Johnson, Stephen, ed., *Burnt Cork: Traditions and Legacies of Blackface Minstrelsy*, 73–103 (Amherst: University of Massachusetts Press, 2012).

———. "Introduction: The Persistence of Blackface and the Minstrel Tradition." In Johnson, Stephen, ed. *Burnt Cork: Traditions and Legacies of Blackface Minstrelsy*, 1–17 (Amherst: University of Massachusetts Press, 2012).

Johnston, Carrie. "Mark Twain's 'Remarkable Achievement': Effacing the South for Northern Audiences." *Rocky Mountain Review* 67, no. 1 (Spring 2013), 67–74.

Jones, Gerard. *Killing Monsters: Why Children Need Fantasy, Super Heroes, and Make-Believe Violence* (New York: Basic Books, 2002).

Kaplan, Fred. *The Singular Mark Twain: A Biography* (New York: Anchor, 2003).

Kaplan, Justin. *Mr. Clemens and Mark Twain: A Biography*. (New York: Touchstone, 1983).

Kennedy, Randall. *Nigger: The Strange Career of a Troublesome Word* (New York: Pantheon, 2002).

Kesterson, David B. Review of Richardson, Thomas J., *"The Grandissimes": Centennial Essays*. *South Central Bulletin* 42, nos. 1–2 (Spring–Summer 1982), 28–29.

Kidd, Kenneth B. *Making American Boys: Boyology and the Feral Tale* (Minneapolis: University of Minnesota Press, 2004).

Kindlon, Dan, and Michael Thompson. *Raising Cain: Protecting the Emotional Life of Boys* (New York: Ballantine, 2000).

Kiskis, Michael J. "*Adventures of Huckleberry Finn* (Again!): Teaching for Social Justice or Sam Clemens' Children's Crusade." *Mark Twain Annual* 1 (2003), 63–77.

———. "Critical Humbug: Samuel Clemens' *Adventures of Huckleberry Finn*." *Mark Twain Annual* 3 (September 2005), 13–22.

———. "Hank Morgan's Asylum: *A Connecticut Yankee* and the Emotions of Loss." *Modern Language Studies* 36, no. 2 (Winter 2007), 77–87.

———. "Huckleberry Finn and Family Values." *This Is Just to Say: NCTE Assembly on American Literature* 12, no. 1 (Winter 2000), 1–7.

———. "A Room of His Own: Samuel Clemens, Elmira, and Quarry Farm." In Ryan, Ann M., and Joseph B. McCullough, eds., *Cosmopolitan Twain*, 233–53 (Columbia: University of Missouri Press, 2008).

———, ed. *Mark Twain's Own Autobiography: The Chapters from the North American Review* (Madison: University of Wisconsin Press, 1990).

Kiskis, Michael J., and Laura E. Skandera Trombley, eds. *Constructing Mark Twain: New Directions in Scholarship* (Columbia: University of Missouri Press, 2001).

Kitwana, Bakari. *Why White Kids Love Hip Hop: Wankstas, Wiggers, Wannabes, and the New Reality of Race in America* (New York: Basic Books, 2005).

Knoper, Randall. *Acting Naturally: Mark Twain in the Culture of Performance* (Berkeley: University of California Press, 1995).

Kokernot, Walter. "'The Burning Shame' Broadside." *Mark Twain Journal* 29, no. 2 (Fall 1991), 33–35.

Kozol, Jonathan. *Savage Inequalities: Children in America's Schools* (New York: Harper Perennial, 1992).

Kravitz, Bennett. "Reinventing the World and Reinventing the Self in Huck Finn." *Papers on Language and Literature* 40, no. 1 (Winter 2004), 3–27.

Kutner, Lawrence, and Cheryl K. Olson. *Grand Theft Childhood: The Surprising Truth About Violent Video Games and What Parents Can Do* (New York: Simon & Schuster, 2008).

Lauber, John. *The Inventions of Mark Twain* (New York: Hill and Wang, 1990).

Lear, Bernadette A. "Were Tom and Huck On-Shelf? Public Libraries, Mark Twain, and the Formation of Accessible Canons, 1869–1910." *Nineteenth-Century Literature* 64, no. 2 (September 2009), 189–224.

Lears, T. J. Jackson. *No Place of Grace: Antimodernism and the Transformation of American Culture, 1880–1920* (New York: Pantheon, 1981).

Leland, John. *Hip: The History* (New York: Ecco Press, 2004).

LeMenager, Stephanie. "Floating Capital: The Trouble with Whiteness on Twain's Mississippi." *ELH* 71, no. 2 (Summer 2004), 405–31.

Leonard, James S. "Huck, Jim, and the 'Black-and-White' Fallacy." In Kiskis, Michael J., and Laura E. Skandera Trombley, eds., *Constructing Mark Twain: New Directions in Scholarship*, 139–50 (Columbia: University of Missouri Press, 2001).

———, ed. *Making Mark Twain Work in the Classroom* (Durham, NC: Duke University Press, 1999).

Lester, Julius. "Morality and *Adventures of Huckleberry Finn*." In Davis, Thadious M., James S. Leonard, and Thomas A. Tenney, *Satire or Evasion? Black*

Perspectives on Huckleberry Finn, 199–207 (Durham, NC: Duke University Press, 1992).

Levine, Lawrence W. *Highbrow/Lowbrow: The Emergence of Cultural Hierarchy in America* (Cambridge, MA: Harvard University Press, 1988).

Lhamon, W. T., Jr. "Ebery Time I Wheel About I Jump Jim Crow: Cycles of Minstrel Transgression from Cool White to Vanilla Ice." In Bean, Annemarie, James V. Hatch, and Brooks McNamara, eds., *Inside the Minstrel Mask: Readings in Nineteenth-Century Blackface Minstrelsy*, 275–84 (Middletown, CT: Wesleyan University Press, 1996).

———. *Jump Jim Crow: Lost Plays, Lyrics, Street Prose of the First Atlantic Popular Culture* (Cambridge: Harvard University Press, 2003).

———. *Raising Cain: Blackface Performance from Jim Crow to Hip Hop* (Cambridge: Harvard University Press, 1998).

———. "Turning Around Jim Crow." In Johnson, Stephen, ed., *Burnt Cork: Traditions and Legacies of Blackface Minstrelsy*, 18–50 (Amherst: University of Massachusetts Press, 2012).

Lorch, Fred W. *The Trouble Begins at Eight: Mark Twain's Lecture Tours* (Ames: Iowa State University Press, 1966).

Lott, Eric. "Blackface and Blackness: The Minstrel Show in American Culture." In Bean, Annemarie, James V. Hatch, and Brooks McNamara, eds., *Inside the Minstrel Mask: Readings in Nineteenth-Century Blackface Minstrelsy*, 3–32 (Middletown, CT: Wesleyan University Press, 1996).

———. *Love And Theft: Blackface Minstrelsy and the American Working Class* (New York: Oxford University Press, 1993).

———. "Mr. Clemens and Jim Crow: Twain, Race, and Blackface." In Robinson, Forrest G., ed., *The Cambridge Companion to Mark Twain*, 129–52 (Cambridge, UK: Cambridge University Press, 1995).

Louis C. K. "Tom Sawyer vs. Huck Finn." http://www.youtube.com/watch?v=x4vxSf15aBA.

Louv, Richard. *Last Child in the Woods: Saving Our Children from Nature-Deficit Disorder* (Chapel Hill, NC: Algonquin, 2008).

Loving, Jerome. *Mark Twain: The Adventures of Samuel L. Clemens* (Berkeley: University of California Press, 2010).

Lowenherz, Robert J. "The Beginning of 'Huckleberry Finn.'" *American Speech* 38, no. 3 (October 1963), 196–201.

Lundin, Anne H. "Victorian Horizons: The Reception of Children's Books in England and America, 1880–1900." *Library Quarterly* 64, no. 1 (January 1994), 30–59.

Lynn, Kenneth S. *Mark Twain and Southwestern Humor* (Boston: Little, Brown and Company, 1959).

Lystra, Karen. *Dangerous Intimacy: The Untold Story of Mark Twain's Final Years.* (Berkeley: University of California Press, 2004).

MacCann, Donnarae, and Gloria Woodard, eds. *The Black American in Books for Children: Readings in Racism*, 2nd edition (Metuchen, NJ: Scarecrow Press, 1985).

MacCann, Donnarae, and Fredrick Woodard. "Minstrel Shackles and Nineteenth-Century 'Liberality' in *Huckleberry Finn*." In Davis, Thadious M., James S. Leonard, and Thomas A. Tenney, eds., *Satire or Evasion? Black Perspectives on Huckleberry Finn*, 141–53 (Durham, NC: Duke University Press, 1992).

MacLeod, Christine. "Telling the Truth in a Tight Place: *Huckleberry Finn* and the Reconstruction Era." *Southern Quarterly* 34, no. 1 (Fall 1995), 5–16.

Mahar, William J. *Behind the Burnt Cork Mask: Early Blackface Minstrelsy and Antebellum American Popular Culture* (Urbana: University of Illinois Press, 1999).

Mailloux, Steven. "Reading *Huckleberry Finn*: The Rhetoric of Performed Ideology." In Budd, Louis J., ed., *New Essays on Adventures of Huckleberry Finn*, 107–33 (New York: Cambridge University Press, 1985).

———. *Rhetorical Power* (Ithaca, NY: Cornell University Press, 1989).

———. "The Rhetorical Use and Abuse of Fiction: Eating Books in Late Nineteenth-Century America." *Boundary 2: An International Journal of Literature and Culture* 17, no. 1 (Spring 1990), 133–57.

Marcus, Leonard S. *Minders of Make-Believe: Idealists, Entrepeneurs, and the Shaping of American Children's Literature* (New York: Houghton Mifflin, 2008).

Margolis, Stacey. "*Huckleberry Finn*; or, Consequences." *PMLA* 116, no. 2 (March 2001), 329–43.

"Mark Twain and George Washington Cable: The 'Twins of Genius' Tour." Reader's Almanac: Official Blog of the Library of America, October 12, 2010. http://blog.loa.org/2010/10/mark-twain-and-george-washington-cable.html.

"Mark Twain's 70th Birthday." *Harper's Weekly* 44 (December 23, 1905), 1884–1914.

Martin, Gretchen, ed. *Twain's Omissions: Exploring the Gaps as Textual Context* (Newcastle upon Tyne: Cambridge Scholars Publishing, 2013).

Martin, Jay. "The Genie in the Bottle: Huckleberry Finn in Mark Twain's Life." In Crowley, J. Donald, and Robert Sattelmeyer, eds., *One Hundred Years of Huckleberry Finn: The Boy, His Book, and American Culture*, 56–81 (Columbia, MO: University of Missouri Press, 1985).

Marx, Leo. "Mr. Eliot, Mr. Trilling, and *Huckleberry Finn*." *American Scholar* 22 (Autumn 1953), 423–40.

McCoy, Sharon D. "Cultural Critique in *Tom Sawyer Abroad*: Behind Jim's Minstrel Mask." *Mark Twain Annual* 4 (2006), 71–90.

———. "'I Ain' No Dread Being': The Minstrel Mask as Alter Ego." In Csicsila, Joseph, and Chad Rohman, eds., *Centenary Reflections on Mark Twain's No. 44, The Mysterious Stranger*, 13–40 (Columbia: University of Missouri Press, 2009).

———. "Politics, Mark Twain, and Blackface." Humor in America, blog, October 24, 2011. https://humorinamerica.wordpress.com/2011/10/24/politics -mark-twain-and-blackface/.

———. "'The Trouble Begins At Eight': Mark Twain, the San Francisco Minstrels, and the Unsettling Legacy of Blackface Minstrelsy." *American Literary Realism* 41, no. 3 (Spring 2009), 232–48.

McCullough, Joseph B., and Ann M. Ryan, eds. *Cosmopolitan Twain* (Columbia: University of Missouri Press, 2008).

McFarland, Philip. "Mark Twain and America's Worst President." *Huffington Post*, July 18, 2012. http://www.huffingtonpost.com/philip-mcfarland/mark -twain-and-americas-w_b_1683103.html.

McKethan, Lucinda H. "Huck Finn and the Slave Narratives: Lighting Out As Design." *Southern Review* 20, no. 2 (Spring 1984), 246–64.

McNamara, Maura. "Magic and the Supernatural in the African American Slave Culture and Society." http://www.umich.edu/~historyj/docs/2010-winter /McNamara.pdf.

Mensh, Elaine, and Harry Mensh. *Black, White, & Huckleberry Finn: Re-imagining the American Dream* (Tuscaloosa: University of Alabama Press, 2000).

Messent, Peter. "Discipline and Punishment in *The Adventures of Tom Sawyer*." *Journal of American Studies* 32, no. 2 (August 1998), 219–35.

Michaelsen, Scott. "Tom Sawyer's Capitalisms and the De-structuring of *Huck Finn*." *Prospects* 22 (October 1997), 133–51.

Michelson, Bruce. *Mark Twain on the Loose: A Comic Writer and the American Self* (Amherst: University of Massachusetts Press, 1995).

Miller, Margaret. "The Adventure of Childhood: Reexamining *Huckleberry Finn*." http://serendip.brynmawr.edu/sci_cult/courses/emotion/web5/mmiller .html.

Mintz, Steven. *Huck's Raft: A History of American Childhood* (Cambridge, MA: Belknap Press of Harvard University Press, 2004).

Moore, Lorrie. "Send Huck Finn to College." *New York Times*, January 15, 2011. http://www.nytimes.com/2011/01/16/opinion/16moore.html.

Morrison, Toni. Introduction to Twain, Mark, *Adventures of Huckleberry Finn*, xxxi–xli (New York: Oxford University Press, 1996).

———. *Playing in the Dark: Whiteness and the Literary Imagination* (Cambridge, MA: Harvard University Press, 1992).

Morrow, Lance. "In Praise of Huckleberry Finn." *Civilization* 2, no. 1 (January– February 1995), 25–27.

Mugglestone, Lynda. "Nineteenth-Century English—An Overview." http://pub lic.oed.com/aspects-of-english/english-in-time/nineteenth-century-english -an-overview/.

Nabhan, Gary Paul, and Stephen Trimble. *The Geography of Childhood: Why Children Need Wild Places* (Boston: Beacon Press, 1994).

Nagawara, Makoto. "'A True Story' and Its Manuscript: Mark Twain's Image of the American Black." *Poetica* 29–30 (1989), 143–56.

Nathan, Hans. "The Performance of the Virginia Minstrels." In Bean, Anne-marie, James V. Hatch, and Brooks McNamara, eds. *Inside the Minstrel Mask: Readings in Nineteenth-Century Blackface Minstrelsy*, 35–42 (Middletown, CT: Wesleyan University Press, 1996).

Newcomb, Bobby. *Tambo: His Jokes and Funny Sayings* (New York: Wehman Brothers, 1882).

Nicol, Charles. "One Hundred Years on a Raft: A Dirty Word with the Huck Finn Critics." *Harper's* 272, no. 1628 (January 1986), 65–70.

Nilon, Charles H. "The Ending of *Huckleberry Finn*: 'Freeing the Free Negro.'" In Davis, Thadious M., James S. Leonard, and Thomas A. Tenney, eds., *Satire or Evasion? Black Perspectives on Huckleberry Finn*, 62–76 (Durham, NC: Duke University Press, 1992).

Nylund, David. *Treating Huckleberry Finn: A New Narrative Approach to Working with Kids Diagnosed ADD/ADHD* (San Francisco: Jossey-Bass, 2000).

Oehlschlaeger, Fritz. "'Gwyne to Git Hung': The Conclusion of *Huckleberry Finn*." In Crowley, J. Donald, and Robert Sattelmeyer, eds., *One Hundred Years of Huckleberry Finn: The Boy, His Book, and American Culture*, 117–27 (Columbia: University of Missouri Press, 1985).

O'Loughlin, Jim. "The Whiteness of Bone: Russell Banks' 'Rule of the Bone' and the Contradictory Legacy of 'Huckleberry Finn.'" *Modern Language Studies* 32, no. 1 (Spring 2002), 31–42.

Opdahl, Keith M. "'You'll Be Sorry When I'm Dead': Child-Adult Relations in *Huck Finn*." *Modern Fiction Studies* 25, no. 4 (Winter 1979–1980), 613–24.

Paley, Vivian Gussin. *A Child's Work: The Importance of Fantasy Play* (Chicago: University of Chicago Press, 2004).

Pattee, Fred Lewis. *A History of American Literature Since 1870* (New York: D. Appleton-Century, 1915; reprint, Miami: HardPress, 2014).

Pearson, E. L. "The Children's Librarian versus Huckleberry Finn." *Library Journal* 32 (July 1907), 312–14.

Peck, George W. *Peck's Bad Boy and His Pa.* (Chicago: Belford, Clarke & Co., 1886 [1883]).

Peck, H. Daniel. "Two Boys: Versions of Childhood in *The Adventures of Tom Sawyer* and *Adventures of Huckleberry Finn*." Mark Twain and *Huckleberry Finn,* special exhibit, Vassar College Libraries Archives and Special Collections, January–May 2010. http://specialcollections.vassar.edu/exhibit-high lights/mark-twain/peck.html.

Pettit, Arthur G. *Mark Twain and the South* (Lexington: University of Kentucky Press, 1974).

Pfitzer, Gregory M. "Iron Dudes and White Savages in Camelot: The Influence of Dime-Novel Sensationalism on Twain's *A Connecticut Yankee in King Arthur's Court.*" *American Literary Realism, 1870–1910* 27, no. 1 (Fall 1994), 42–58.

Phiri, Aretha. "Searching for the Ghost in the Machine: The 'Africanist' Presence in Mark Twain's *Adventures of Huckleberry Finn.*" *English Studies in Africa* 54, no. 1 (2011), 88–104.

Pike, Gustavus D. *The Singing Campaign for Ten Thousand Pounds; or, The Jubilee Singers in Great Britain* (New York: American Missionary Association, 1875).

Pipher, Mary. *Reviving Ophelia: Saving the Selves of Adolescent Girls* (New York: Riverhead, 2005).

Pollack, William. *Real Boys: Rescuing Our Sons From the Myths of Boyhood*, revised ed. (New York: Henry Holt, 1999).

Pond, James B. *Eccentricities of Genius.* (New York: G. W. Dillingham Company, 1900).

———. "J. B. Pond, Holograph Cash-Book, November 5 1884–Feb. 28 1885." Berg Collection, New York Public Library, New York.

Pond, Ozias W., "Holograph Diary, with MS. Notes by J. B. Pond." Berg Collection, New York Public Library, New York.

Powers, Ron. *Dangerous Water: A Biography of the Boy Who Became Mark Twain* (New York: Basic Books, 1999).

———. *Mark Twain: A Life* (New York: Free Press, 2005).

———. *Tom and Huck Don't Live Here Anymore: Childhood and Murder in the Heart of America* (New York: St. Martin's Griffin, 2001).

Prince, Stephen. *Classical Film Violence: Designing and Regulating Brutality in Hollywood Cinema, 1930–1968* (New Brunswick, NJ: Rutgers University Press, 2003).

Prioleau, Elizabeth. " 'That Abused Child of Mine': Huck Finn as the Child of an Alcoholic." *Essays in Arts and Sciences* 22 (October 1993), 85–98.

Quirk, Tom. *Coming to Grips with Huckleberry Finn: Essays on a Book, a Boy, and a Man* (Columbia: University of Missouri Press, 1993).

———. "The Flawed Greatness of *Huckleberry Finn.*" *American Literary Realism* 45, no. 1 (Fall 2012), 38–48.

Railton, Stephen. *Mark Twain: A Short Introduction* (Oxford: Wiley-Blackwell, 2003).

———. "Mark Twain in His Times." http://twain.lib.virginia.edu/.

————. "Mark Twain Tries to Get the Last Laugh: Hadleyburg and Other Performances." *Mark Twain Annual* 3 (September 2005), 23–36.

————. "The Twain-Cable Combination." In Messent, Peter, and Louis J. Budd, eds. *A Companion to Mark Twain*, 172–85 (Malden, MA: Blackwell, 2005).

Rampersad, Arnold. "*Adventures of Huckleberry Finn* and Afro-American Literature." In Davis, Thadious M., James S. Leonard, and Thomas A. Tenney, eds., *Satire or Evasion? Black Perspectives on Huckleberry Finn*, 216–27 (Durham, NC: Duke University Press, 1992).

Ravitch, Diane. *The Death and Life of the Great American School System: How Testing and Choice Are Undermining Education* (New York: Basic Books, 2010).

Reed, Ishmael. "Mark Twain's Hairball," in Marcus, Greil, and Werner Sollors, eds., *A New Literary History of America*, 380–84 (Cambridge, MA: Belknap Press, 2009).

Rice, T. D. *Jim Crow, American: Selected Songs and Plays.* Edited by W. T. Lhamon, Jr. (Cambridge, MA: Belknap Press, 2009).

Richters, John E., and Dante Cicchetti. "Mark Twain Meets DSM-III-R: Conduct Disorder, Development, and the Concept of Harmful Dysfunction." *Development and Psychopathology* 5 (1993), 5–29.

Roberts, Taylor. "Mark Twain in Toronto, Ontario, 1884–1885." *Mark Twain Journal* 36, no. 2 (Fall 1998), 18–25.

Robinson, Forrest G. "An 'Unconscious and Profitable Cerebration': Mark Twain and Literary Intentionality." *Nineteenth-Century Literature* 50, no. 3 (December 1995), 357–80.

————. *The Author-Cat: Clemens's Life in Fiction* (New York: Fordham University Press, 2007).

————. "The Characterization of Jim in *Huckleberry Finn*." *Nineteenth-Century Literature* 43, no. 3 (December 1988), 361–91.

————. *In Bad Faith: The Dynamics of Deception in Mark Twain's America* (Cambridge, MA: Harvard University Press, 1986).

————. "The Silences in *Huckleberry Finn*." *Nineteenth-Century Fiction* 37, no. 1 (June 1982), 50–74.

————, ed. *The Cambridge Companion to Mark Twain* (Cambridge: Cambridge University Press, 1995).

Robinson, Holly. "Are We Raising Boys Wrong?" *Home Educator's Family Times.* http://www.homeeducator.com/familytimes/articles/8-3article1.htm.

Roediger, David R. *The Wages of Whiteness: Race and the Making of the American Working Class* (New York: Verso, 1991).

Rogin, Michael. *Blackface, White Noise: Jewish Immigrants in the Hollywood Melting Pot.* (Berkeley: University of California Press, 1996).

Ross, Andrew. *No Respect: Intellectuals and Popular Culture* (New York: Routledge, 1989).

Rotundo, E. Anthony. "Boy Culture." In Twain, Mark, *The Adventures of Tom Sawyer*, edited by Beverly Lyon Clark, 213–20 (New York: W. W. Norton and Company, 2007).

Rubin, Louis, D., Jr. *George W. Cable: The Life and Times of a Southern Heretic* (New York: Pegasus, 1969).

Rush, Sharon E. *Huck Finn's "Hidden" Lessons: Teaching and Learning Across the Color Line* (Lanham, MD: Rowman & Littlefield, 2006).

Rux, Carl Hancock. "Eminem: The New White Negro." In Tate, Greg, ed., *Everything but the Burden: What White People Are Taking from Black Culture*, 15–38 (New York: Harlem Moon, 2003).

Ryan, Ann M. "Black Genes and White Lies: Twain and the Romance of Race." In Kiskis, Michael J. and Laura E. Skandera Trombley, eds., *Constructing Mark Twain: New Directions in Scholarship*, 169–90 (Columbia: University of Missouri Press, 2001).

———. "Introduction: Mark Twain and the Cosmopolitan Ideal." In Ryan, Ann M., and Joseph B. McCullough, eds., *Cosmopolitan Twain*, 1–20 (Columbia: University of Missouri Press, 2008).

———. "Mark Twain and the Mean (and Magical) Streets of New York." In Ryan, Ann M., and Joseph B. McCullough, eds., *Cosmopolitan Twain*, 21–63 (Columbia: University of Missouri Press, 2008).

Salomon, Roger B. *Twain and the Image of History* (New Haven, CT: Yale University Press, 1961).

Salsbury, Edith Colgate, ed. *Susy and Mark Twain: Family Dialogues* (New York: Harper & Row, 1965).

Sammond, Nicholas. " 'Gentlemen, Please Be Seated': Racial Masquerade and Sadomasochism in 1930s Animation." In Johnson, Stephen, ed. *Burnt Cork: Traditions and Legacies of Blackface Minstrelsy*, 164–90 (Amherst: University of Massachusetts Press, 2012).

Sax, Leonard. *Boys Adrift: The Five Factors Driving the Growing Epidemic of Unmotivated Boys and Underachieving Young Men* (New York: Basic Books, 2007).

———. *Girls on the Edge: The Four Factors Driving the New Crisis for Girls* (New York: Basic Books, 2010).

Saxton, Alexander. "Blackface Minstrelsy." In Bean, Annemarie, James V. Hatch, and Brooks McNamara, eds., *Inside the Minstrel Mask: Readings in Nineteenth-Century Blackface Minstrelsy*, 67–85 (Middletown, CT: Wesleyan University Press, 1996).

———. "Blackface Minstrelsy and Jacksonian Ideology." *American Quarterly* 27 (1975), 3–21.

Scharnhorst, Gary, and Laura E. Skandera Trombley. "Who Killed Mark Twain? Long Live Samuel Clemens!" In Kiskis, Michael J. and Laura E. Skandera

Trombley, eds., *Constructing Mark Twain: New Directions in Scholarship*, 218–25 (Columbia: University of Missouri Press, 2001).

Schill, Charlie. "Aisle Views: Crowds Will Cheer for Charming Rascal Huck." HJNews.com, July 6, 2012. http://news.hjnews.com/cache_magazine/article _0e9d7be2-c791-11e1-9918-0019bb2963f4.html.

Schmidt, Peter. *Sitting in Darkness: New South Fiction, Education, and the Rise of Jim Crow Colonialism, 1865–1920* (Jackson: University of Mississippi Press, 2008).

Schmitz, Neil. "Mark Twain's Civil War: Humor's Reconstructive Writing." In Robinson, Forrest G., ed., *The Cambridge Companion to Mark Twain*, 74–92 (Cambridge, UK: Cambridge University Press, 1995).

———. "Twain, *Huckleberry Finn*, and the Reconstruction." *American Studies* 12, no. 1 (Spring 1971), 59–67.

Scott, Donald M. "The Popular Lecture and the Creation of a Public in Mid-Nineteenth-Century America." *Journal of American History* 66, no. 4 (March 1980), 791–809.

Scudder, Horace E. *Childhood in Literature and Art, with Some Observations on Literature for Children* (Cambridge: Riverside Press, 1894; reprint, London: Forgotten Books, 2012).

Segal, Harry G. "Life Without Father: The Role of the Paternal in the Opening Chapters of *Huckleberry Finn*." *Journal of American Studies* 27, no. 1 (April 1993), 19–33.

Sharp, Alex. "Applebaum's Column Suggests Tom and Huck Have Behavior Disorders." Suite101.com, August 10, 2010. http://suite101.com/article/apple baums-column-suggests-tom-and-huck-have-behavior-disorders-a272386.

Shelden, Michael. *Mark Twain: Man in White: The Grand Adventure of His Final Years* (New York: Random House, 2010).

Silber, Nina. *The Romance of Reunion: Northerners and the South, 1865–1900* (Chapel Hill: University of North Carolina Press, 1993).

Simpson, Claude M., ed. *Twentieth Century Interpretations of* Adventures of Huckleberry Finn*: A Collection of Critical Essays*. (Englewood Cliffs, NJ: Prentice-Hall, 1968).

Small, Robert C., Jr. "The Literary Value of the Young Adult Novel." *Journal of Youth Services in Libraries* 6 (1992), 277–85.

Smiley, Jane. "Say It Ain't So, Huck: Second Thoughts on Mark Twain's 'Masterpiece.'" *Harper's* 292, no. 1748 (January 1996), 61–67.

Smiley, Tavis, and Stephen Ivory. "The Minstrel Show." National Public Radio, April 3, 2002. http://www.npr.org/templates/story/story.php?storyId=1141031.

Smith, David L. "Black Critics and Mark Twain." In Robinson, Forrest G., ed., *The Cambridge Companion to Mark Twain*, 116–28 (Cambridge, UK: Cambridge University Press, 1995).

———. "Huck, Jim, and American Racial Discourse." In Davis, Thadious M., James S. Leonard, and Thomas A. Tenney, eds., *Satire or Evasion? Black Perspectives on Huckleberry Finn*, 103–20 (Durham, NC: Duke University Press, 1992).

———. "Humor, Sentimentality, and Mark Twain's Black Characters." In Kiskis, Michael J., and Laura E. Skandera Trombley, eds., *Constructing Mark Twain: New Directions in Scholarship*, 151–68 (Columbia: University of Missouri Press, 2001).

Smith, Henry Nash. *Mark Twain: The Development of a Writer* (Cambridge, MA: Belknap Press, 1962).

———. "Mark Twain, 'Funniest Man in the World.'" In Beidler, Philip D., and Sara deSaussure Davis, eds., *The Mythologizing of Mark Twain*, 56–76 (Tuscaloosa: University of Alabama Press, 1984).

Solomon, Andrew. "Jim and Huck: Magnificent Misfits." *Mark Twain Journal* 16, no. 3 (Winter 1972), 17–24.

Sotiropoulos, Karen. *Staging Race: Black Performers in Turn of the Century America* (Cambridge, MA: Harvard University Press, 2006).

Springer, David W. "Runaway Adolescents: Today's Huckleberry Finn Crisis." *Brief Treatment and Crisis Prevention* 1, no. 2 (Fall 2001), 131–51.

Stahl, J. D. "Satire and the Evolution of Perspective in Children's Literature: Mark Twain, E. B. White, and Louise Fitzhugh." *Children's Literature Association Quarterly* 15, no. 3 (Fall 1990), 119–22.

Steinbrink, Jeffrey. *Getting to Be Mark Twain* (Berkeley: University of California Press, 1991).

———. "Who Shot Tom Sawyer?" *American Literary Realism, 1870–1910* 35, no. 1 (Fall 2002): 29–38.

———. "Who Wrote *Huckleberry Finn*? Mark Twain's Control of the Early Manuscript." In Crowley, J. Donald, and Robert Sattelmeyer, eds., *One Hundred Years of Huckleberry Finn: The Boy, His Book, and American Culture*, 85–105 (Columbia: University of Missouri Press, 1985).

Steyer, James P. *The Other Parent: The Inside Story of the Media's Effect on Our Children* (New York: Atria Books, 2002).

Stone, Albert E. *The Innocent Eye: Childhood in Mark Twain's Imagination* (New Haven, CT: Yale University Press, 1961).

Stone, Michael K. *Smart by Nature: Schooling for Sustainability* (Healdsburg, CA: Watershed Media, 2009).

Stoneley, Peter. *Mark Twain and the Feminine Aesthetic* (Cambridge: Cambridge University Press, 1992).

Strausbaugh, John. *Black Like You: Blackface, Whiteface, Insult & Imitation in American Popular Culture* (New York: Jeremy P. Tarcher/Penguin, 2006).

Subryan, Carmen. "Mark Twain and the Black Challenge." In Davis, Thadious M., James S. Leonard, and Thomas A. Tenney, eds., *Satire or Evasion? Black Perspectives on Huckleberry Finn*, 91–102 (Durham, NC: Duke University Press, 1992).

Sundquist, Eric. "Mark Twain and Homer Plessy." *Representations* 24 (Autumn 1988), 102–28.

Tally, Robert T., Jr. "Bleeping Mark Twain?: Censorship, *Huckleberry Finn*, and the Functions of Literature." *Teaching American Literature: A Journal of Theory and Practice* 6, no. 1 (Spring 2013), 97–108.

Tarnoff, Ben. *The Bohemians: Mark Twain and the San Francisco Writers Who Reinvented American Literature* (New York: Penguin, 2014).

Tate, Greg, ed. *Everything but the Burden: What White People Are Taking from Black Culture* (New York: Harlem Moon, 2003).

———. "Introduction: Nigs R Us, or How Blackfolk Became Fetish Objects." In Tate, Greg, ed., *Everything but the Burden: What White People Are Taking from Black Culture*, 1–14 (New York: Harlem Moon, 2003).

Taylor, Yuval, and Jake Austen. *Darkest America: Black Minstrelsy from Slavery to Hip-Hop* (New York: W. W. Norton and Company, 2012).

Toll, Robert C. *Blacking Up: The Minstrel Show in Nineteenth-Century America* (New York: Oxford University Press, 1974).

———. "Social Commentary in Late-Nineteenth-Century White Minstrelsy." In Bean, Annemarie, James V. Hatch, and Brooks McNamara, eds., *Inside the Minstrel Mask: Readings in Nineteenth-Century Blackface Minstrelsy*, 86–109 (Middletown, CT: Wesleyan University Press, 1996).

Torgovnick, Marianna. *Gone Primitive: Savage Intellects, Modern Lives* (Chicago: University of Chicago Press, 1990).

Trautmann, Frederick. "The Twins of Genius: Public Readings by George Washington Cable and Mark Twain in Pennsylvania." *Pennsylvania History* 43, no. 3 (July 1976), 214–25.

Trilling, Lionel. "Huckleberry Finn." In Trilling, Lionel, *The Liberal Imagination: Essays on Literature and Society*, 107–19 (Garden City, NY: Doubleday & Company, 1953).

Trites, Roberta Seelinger. *Twain, Alcott, and the Birth of the Adolescent Reform Novel* (Iowa City: University of Iowa Press, 2007).

Trombley, Laura E. Skandera. *Mark Twain in the Company of Woman* (Philadelphia: University of Pennsylvania Press, 1994).

———. *Mark Twain's Other Woman: The Hidden Story of His Final Years* (New York: Vintage, 2010).

Tulley, Gever, and Julie Spiegler. *50 Dangerous Things (You Should Let Your Children Do)* (New York: New American Library, 2011).

Turner, Arlin. *George W. Cable: A Biography* (Durham, NC: Duke University Press, 1956).

Twain, Mark. *Adventures of Huckleberry Finn: The Only Authoritative Edition Based on the Complete Original Manuscript with All of the Original Illustrations*. Edited and with notes by Victor Fischer, Lin Salamo, Harriet Elinor Smith, and Walter Blair (Berkeley: University of Califonia Press, 2010). All quotes from this volume.

———. *The Adventures of Tom Sawyer*. Edited by Beverly Lyon Clark (New York: W. W. Norton and Company, 2007).

———. *The Adventures of Tom Sawyer*. Introduction by Frank Conroy (New York: Modern Library, 2001). All quotes from this volume.

———. *Adventures of Tom Sawyer and Huckleberry Finn: The NewSouth Edition*. Edited and introduced by Alan Gribben (Montgomery, AL: NewSouth Books, 2011).

———. *The Annotated Huckleberry Finn*. Edited and introduced with notes by Michael Patrick Hearn (New York: W. W. Norton, 2001).

———. *Autobiography of Mark Twain*, vols. 1 and 2. Edited by Benjamin Griffin and Harriet Elinor Smith and other editors of the Mark Twain Project (Berkeley: University of California Press, 2010, 2013).

———. "Boy's Manuscript." In Twain, Mark, *The Adventures of Tom Sawyer*, edited by Beverly Lyon Clark, 239–52 (New York: W. W. Norton and Company, 2007).

———. *Collected Tales, Sketches, Speeches, & Essays 1852–1890*. Edited by Louis J. Budd (New York: Literary Classics of the United States, 1992).

———. *Collected Tales, Sketches, Speeches, & Essays 1891–1910*. Edited by Louis J. Budd. (New York: Literary Classics of the United States, 1992).

———. *A Connecticut Yankee in King Arthur's Court*. Introduction by Roy Blount, Jr. (New York: Modern Library, 2001).

———. "The Death of Jean." In *What Is Man? and Other Essays* (London: Chatto and Windus, 1919).

———. *Early Tales and Sketches, Volume 1 (1851–1864)*. Edited by Edgar Marquess Branch and Robert H. Hirst, with the assistance of Harriet Elinor Smith (Berkeley: University of California Press, for the Iowa Center for Textual Studies, 1979).

———. *Early Tales and Sketches, Volume 2 (1864–1865)*. Edited by Edgar Marquess Branch and Robert H. Hirst, with the assistance of Harriet Elinor Smith. (Berkeley: University of California Press, for the Iowa Center for Textual Studies, 1981).

———. "A Family Sketch." Mark Twain Papers and Project, University of California, Berkeley.

———. "Following the Equator." In Twain, Mark, *Following the Equator and Anti-imperialist Essays*. Foreword by Shelley Fisher Fishkin; introduction by

Gore Vidal; afterword by Fred Kaplan (New York: Oxford University Press, 1996).

―――. *Huck Finn and Tom Sawyer among the Indians and Other Unfinished Stories*. Foreword and notes by Dahlia Armon and Walter Blair (Berkeley: University of California Press, 1989).

―――. *Huck Finn: The Complete Buffalo & Erie County Public Library Manuscript—Teaching and Research Digital Edition* (Buffalo, NY: Buffalo & Erie County Public Library, 2002).

―――. *The Innocents Abroad*. Foreword by Shelley Fisher Fishkin; introduction by Mordecai Richler (New York: Oxford University Press, 1996).

―――. *Is Shakespeare Dead?* In *1601, and Is Shakespeare Dead?* Foreword by Shelley Fisher Fishkin; introduction by Erica Jong; afterword by Leslie A. Fiedler (New York: Oxford University Press, 1996).

―――. "Jim's Investments and King Sollermun." *Century* 29, no. 3 (January 1885), 456–58.

―――. *King Leopold's Soliloquy: A Defense of His Congo Rule*. In Twain, Mark, *Collected Tales, Sketches, Speeches, & Essays, 1891–1910*, edited by Louis J. Budd, 661–86 (New York: Literary Classics of the United States, 1992).

―――. "The Late Benjamin Franklin," in Twain, Mark, *Collected Tales, Sketches, Speeches, & Essays 1852–1890*, edited by Louis J. Budd, 425–27 (New York: Literary Classics of the United States, 1992).

―――. *Life on the Mississippi*. Introduction by Jonathan Raban; notes by Guy Cardwell (New York: Library of America, 1991).

―――. "Little Bessie." In Twain, Mark, *Collected Tales, Sketches, Speeches, & Essays 1891–1910*, edited by Louis J. Budd, 864–74 (New York: Literary Classics of the United States, 1992).

―――. "Little Nelly Tells a Story Out of Her Head." In *Collected Tales, Sketches, Speeches, & Essays 1891–1910*, edited by Louis J. Budd, 823–25 (New York: Literary Classics of the United States, 1992).

―――. *Love Letters of Mark Twain*. Edited by Dixon Wecter (New York: Harper and Brothers, 1949).

―――. "Marjorie Fleming, the Wonder Child." *Harper's Bazaar* (December 1909), 1182–83, 1229.

―――. *Mark Twain, Business Man*. Edited by Samuel Charles Webster (Boston: Little, Brown, and Company, 1946).

―――. *Mark Twain in Eruption*. Edited and introduced by Bernard DeVoto (New York: Grosset & Dunlap, 1922).

―――. *Mark Twain to Uncle Remus, 1881–1885*. Edited by Thomas H. English (Atlanta: Emory University Press, 1953).

————. *Mark Twain's Letters*, vol. 1: 1853–1866. Edited by Edgar Marquess Branch, Michael B. Frank, and Kenneth M. Sanderson (Berkeley: University of California Press, 1988).

————. *Mark Twain's Letters*, vol. 2: 1867–1868. Edited by Harriet Elinor Smith and Richard Bucci (Berkeley: University of California Press, 1990).

————. *Mark Twain's Letters*, vol. 3: 1869. Edited by Victor Fischer and Michael B. Frank (Berkeley: University of California Press, 1992).

————. *Mark Twain's Letters*, vol. 4: 1870–1871. Edited by Victor Fischer and Michael B. Frank (Berkeley: University of California Press, 1995).

————. *Mark Twain's Letters*, vol. 5: 1872–1873. Edited by Lin Salamo and Harriet Elinor Smith (Berkeley: University of California Press, 1997).

————. *Mark Twain's Letters*, vol. 6: 1874–1875. Edited by Michael B. Frank and Harriet Elinor Smith (Berkeley: University of California Press, 2002).

————. "Mark Twain's Memory-Builder Game Boards and Accompanying Material." Mark Twain Papers and Project, University of California, Berkeley.

————. *Mark Twain's Mysterious Stranger Manuscripts*. Edited and introduced by William M. Gibson (Berkeley: University of California Press, 1969).

————. *Mark Twain's Speeches*. Introduced by William Dean Howells (New York: Harper & Brothers, 1910; reprint, London: Forgotten Books, 2012).

————. *Mark Twain's Travels with Mr. Brown*. Collected, edited, and introduced by Franklin Walker and G. Ezra Dane (New York: Alfred A. Knopf, 1940).

————. "A New Biography of Washington," in Twain, Mark, *Collected Tales, Sketches, Speeches, & Essays 1852–1890*, edited by Louis J. Budd, 205–7 (New York: Literary Classics of the United States, 1992).

————. *Notebooks and Journals*, vol. 1: 1855–1873. Edited by Frederick Anderson, Michael B. Frank, and Kenneth M. Sanderson (Berkeley: University of California Press, 1975).

————. *Notebooks and Journals*, vol. 2: 1877–1883. Edited by Frederick Anderson, Lin Salamo, and Bernard L. Stein (Berkeley: University of California Press, 1975).

————. *Notebooks and Journals*, vol 3: 1883–1891. Edited by Robert Pack Browning, Michael B. Frank, and Lin Salamo (Berkeley: University of California Press, 1979).

————. *Notebooks 32, 33, 34, 35, 36, 37, 38, 39, 40, 43*. Mark Twain Papers and Project, University of California, Berkeley.

————. "On the Decay of the Art of Lying." In Twain, Mark, *Collected Tales, Sketches, Speeches, & Essays 1852–1890*, edited by Louis J. Budd, 824–29 (New York: Literary Classics of the United States, 1992).

———. "Only a Nigger." In Twain, Mark, *Mark Twain at the Buffalo Express: Articles and Sketches by America's Favorite Humorist*, edited by Joseph B. McCullough and Janice McIntire-Strasburg, 22–23 (DeKalb, IL: Northern Illinois University Press, 1999).

———. *Personal Recollections of Joan of Arc*. Foreword by Shelley Fisher Fishkin; introduction by Justin Kaplan; afterword by Susan K. Harris (New York: Oxford University Press, 1996).

———. *The Prince and the Pauper*. Introduction by Christopher Paul Curtis (New York: Modern Library, 2003).

———. *A Record of the Small Foolishnesses of Susie and 'Bay' Clemens (Infants)*. Papers of Mark Twain, Accession #6314, etc., Clifton Waller Barrett Library, Special Collections, University of Virginia, Charlottesville, Va.

———. "The Secret History of Eddypus, the World-Empire." In Twain, Mark, *Tales of Wonder*, edited and introduced by David Ketterer, 176–225 (Lincoln: University of Nebraska Press, 2003).

———. *Tales of Wonder*. Edited and introduced by David Ketterer (Lincoln: University of Nebraska Press, 2003).

———. "To the Person Sitting in Darkness." In *Collected Tales, Sketches, Speeches, & Essays 1891–1910*, edited by Louis J. Budd, 457–73 (New York: Literary Classics of the United States, 1992).

———. *Tom Sawyer Abroad*. Foreword by Shelley Fisher Fishkin; introduction by Nat Hentoff (New York: Oxford University Press, 1996).

———. *The Tragedy of Pudd'nhead Wilson and the Comedy Those Extraordinary Twins*. Edited and foreword by Shelley Fisher Fishkin (New York: Oxford University Press, 1996).

Twain, Mark, and William Dean Howells. *Mark Twain–Howells Letters: The Correspondence of Samuel L. Clemens and William Dean Howells, 1872–1910*. Two volumes, edited by Henry Nash Smith and William M. Gibson (Cambridge, MA: Belknap Press, 1960).

Twain, Mark, and Charles Dudley Warner. *The Gilded Age*. Foreword by Shelley Fisher Fishkin; introduction by Ward Just (New York: Oxford University Press, 1996).

Upchurch, Thomas Adams. *Legislating Racism: The Billion Dollar Congress and the Birth of Jim Crow* (Lexington, KY: University Press of Kentucky, 2004).

Urban, Wayne J., and Jennings L. Wagoner, Jr. *American Education: A History* (New York: Routledge, 2008).

Vogelback, Arthur Lawrence. "The Publication and Reception of *Huckleberry Finn* in America." *American Literature* 11, no. 3 (November 1939), 260–72.

Vonnegut, Mark. *Just Like Someone without Mental Illness Only More So: A Memoir* (New York: Random House, 2010).

Wagenknecht, Edward. *Mark Twain: The Man and His Work*, rev. ed. (Norman: University of Oklahoma Press, 1961).

Walker, Alice. "The Dummy in the Window: Joel Chandler Harris and the Invention of Uncle Remus." In *Living by the Word: Selected Writings, 1973–1987* (New York: Mariner Books, 1989), 25–32.

Wallace, John H. "The Case Against Huck Finn." In Davis, Thadious M., James S. Leonard, and Thomas A. Tenney, eds., *Satire or Evasion? Black Perspectives on Huckleberry Finn*, 16–24. (Durham, NC: Duke University Press, 1992).

Warner, Charles Dudley. *Being a Boy* (Lexington, KY: CreateSpace, 2013).

Wecter, Dixon. *Sam Clemens of Hannibal: The Formative Years of America's Great Indigenous Writer* (Boston: Houghton Mifflin, 1961).

West, Elliott. "Heathens and Angels: Childhood in the Rocky Mountain Mining Towns." In Graff, Harvey J., ed., *Growing Up in America: Historical Experiences*, 369–84 (Detroit: Wayne State University Press, 1987).

Wheeler, H. H. *Up-To-Date Minstrel Jokes* (Boston: Up-To-Date Publishing, 1902).

White, Elon James. "The N-Word Belongs in 'Huckleberry Finn.'" *Salon*, Jan. 4, 2011. http://www.salon.com/2011/01/04/huck_finn_n_word/.

Wieck, Carl F. *Refiguring Huckleberry Finn* (Athens: University of Georgia Press, 2000).

Williamson, Joel. *The Crucible of Race: Black-White Relations in the American South Since Emancipation* (New York: Oxford University Press, 1984).

Wolff, Cynthia Griffin. "*The Adventures of Tom Sawyer*: A Nightmare Vision of American Boyhood." *Massachusetts Review* 21, no. 4 (Winter 1980), 637–52.

Wonham, Henry B. "Mark Twain's Last Cakewalk: Racialized Performance in *No. 44, The Mysterious Stranger*." In Csicsila, Joseph, and Chad Rohman, eds., *Centenary Reflections on Mark Twain's No. 44, The Mysterious Stranger*, 41–50 (Columbia: University of Missouri Press, 2009).

———. "The Minstrel and the Detective: The Functions of Ethnic Caricature in Mark Twain's Writings of the 1890s." In Kiskis, Michael J., and Laura E. Skandera Trombley, eds., *Constructing Mark Twain: New Directions in Scholarship*, 122–38 (Columbia: University of Missouri Press, 2001).

———. *Playing the Races: Ethnic Caricature and American Literary Realism* (New York: Oxford University Press, 2004).

Woodward, C. Vann. *The Strange Career of Jim Crow* (New York: Oxford University Press, 1957).

Young, James O. *Cultural Appropriation and the Arts* (Chichester, UK: Wiley-Blackwell, 2010).

Young, Monica G. "Would Tom Sawyer and Huck Finn Be Diagnosed Mentally Ill and Drugged?" *Naturalnews.com*, September 1, 2011. http://www.natural news.com/033477_Tom_Sawyer_psychiatric_drugs.html.

Ziff, Larzer. *All-American Boy* (Austin: University of Texas Press, 2012).

Zwick, Jim, ed. *Mark Twain's Weapons of Satire: Anti-Imperialist Writings on the Philippine-American War* (Syracuse, NY: Syracuse University Press, 1992).

———. " 'Prodigally Endowed with Sympathy for the Cause': Mark Twain's Involvement with the Anti-Imperialist League." *Mark Twain Journal* 32, no. 3 (Spring 1994), 3–25.

INTERVIEWS

Michael Shelden, e-mail, September 16, 2012.

Alan Gribben, October 1, 2012.

Eric Tribunella, e-mail, October 4, 2012.

Forrest G. Robinson, October 8, 2012.

Shelley Fisher Fishkin, October 13, 2012.

Beverly Lyon Clark, October 16, 2012.

Henry Wonham, October 17, 2012.

Sharon McCoy, October 26, 2012.

Karen Lystra, December 4, 2012.

Steven Railton, e-mail, January 7, 19, 22, 2013.

STUDENT PAPERS CONSULTED/CITED (ALL BUTLER UNIVERSITY)

Belting, Kyle. "#Relevant Runaway: Social Media, Popular Culture, and *Huckleberry Finn*," EN390, Spring 2014.

Cubel, Ginnye. "Was Huck Finn ADHD? How Diagnosing a Major Literary Character Reveals a Contradiction in American Sentiment," EN390, Spring 2012.

Denton, Allison. " 'The Gift & The Curse': Examining the Racial Slur in American History, *The Adventures of Huckleberry Finn*, and Contemporary Times," EN390, Spring 2012.

Erlandson, Andrew. "Twain and Tobacco: The Significance of Smoking in *The Adventures of Huckleberry Finn*," Senior Essay, Spring 2013.

Genord, Caitlin. "Teaching Critical Literacy Skills: Exploring Race in *The Adventures of Huckleberry Finn*," EN390, Spring 2014.

Olson, Cassidy. "Huckleberry Cured: The Side Effects of Diagnosing Fictional Children," EN390, Fall 2014.

Richard, Logan. "Strange Bedfellows: The Compatibility of Twain and Žižek," EN390, Spring 2012.

Richardson, Chloe. "*The Adventures of Huckleberry Finn* and Multiple Intelligences Theory: Inspiring Our Students to Be More Like Huck Finn," EN390, Spring 2013.

Shambrook, Kate. "*Huck Finn* and the *Hunger Games*: Exploring Violence in Young Adult Fiction," EN390, Spring 2012.

Trainor, Michelle. "*Huckleberry Finn*: A Model for Exploring Adolescence and the Classroom Environment," EN390, Spring 2013.

Wanbaugh, Jillian. "Huckleberry Finn and Tom Sawyer: The Difference Between ADHD and Environmentally Influenced Misconduct," EN390, Spring 2013.

Zimmerly, Joel. "Huck's Rite of Passage: A Story of Integration Through Fragmentation," EN390, Spring 2013.

INDEX

ABOUT THE AUTHOR

Andrew Levy is Edna Cooper Chair in English at Butler University. He is author of the critically acclaimed *A Brain Wider Than the Sky* and the award-winning biography *The First Emancipator*.